New Deal Labor Policy
and the Southern Cotton Textile Industry,
1933–1941

NEW·DEAL LABOR·POLICY

and the Southern Cotton Textile Industry

1933–1941

★

BY JAMES A. HODGES

The University of Tennessee Press
Knoxville

Publication of this book has been aided by a grant from
The College of Wooster, Wooster, Ohio 44691.

Frontispiece: TWUA pickets in a strike, Greensboro, Ga., May 1941.
Arthur Franklin Raper Papers. Courtesy, Southern Historical Collection,
Wilson Library, University of North Carolina at Chapel Hill

The paper used in this book meets the minimum requirements of the
American National Standard for Permanence of Paper for Printed Library
Materials, Z39.48-1984. Binding materials have been chosen for durability.

Library of Congress Cataloging-in-Publication Data

Hodges, James A., 1932–
New deal labor policy and the southern cotton
textile industry, 1933–1941.

Bibliography: p.
1. Cotton textile industry—Southern States—
Employees—History. 2. New Deal, 1933–1939—Southern
States—History. 3. United States—Social conditions—
1933–1945. I. Title.
HD8039.T42U652 1986   338.4′767721′0975   85-20368
ISBN 0-87049-496-1

TO

Mary, Barbara, Andrew, Patricia

Contents

Illustrations

Acknowledgments

Some readers will know that this book began in the early 1960s as a dissertation at Vanderbilt University and that it lay abandoned by me for many years. Before many had turned in that direction, the dissertation was an early revisionist effort. Most New Deal studies trumpeted reform and change; I discovered the miserable failure of the cotton textile unionists. Baffled as a young scholar about the basic meaning of my work, I turned to other things that interested me. The recent preparation for a new junior-senior seminar in American labor history made me decide to undertake the new work necessary for a book, and the generous support of the Trustees of the College of Wooster for a year's leave combined with the extra support of the college's Henry R. Luce III Fund for Scholarship made possible the modernization and rewriting of an old dissertation. Everyone who teaches at the College of Wooster appreciates its splendid support for scholarship both in the classroom and outside.

I specifically acknowledge the encouragement of Henry Copeland, president of the College of Wooster; Donald Harward, vice president for academic affairs; and Vivian Holliday, dean of the faculty. My esteemed colleagues in the History Department, although disavowing any responsibility for the finished product, cheered me on, and always through the years their own excellence has made me do my best to stay in the same good company. Dewey Grantham of Vanderbilt University directed the older work, and I have been gratified by his confidence, friendship, and help in completing the new one. Readers for the University of Tennessee Press made excellent suggestions for improvement, and to the extent that I was able to make the improvements, the book was improved in every instance. Cynthia Maude-Gembler and Mavis Bryant were most genial and enthusiastic editors. Marlene Zimmerman first deciphered my scribblings for the word processor, but I owe special gratitude to Helen Moore and her competent crew at the Secretarial Services Center, College of Wooster, who came to my rescue at a busy time. I reserve for my colleague, John Gates, the highest accolade. John meticulously read the manuscript for style and clarity. He is not responsible for what infelicity remains, but the reader's lot is much easier because of his efforts.

Everywhere I received the warmest of welcomes from librarians and archivists. They are far too numerous to mention by name but I am deeply grateful for their help. Early in the new effort on this book, I spent over two months at the Newberry Library in Chicago, where I enjoyed a subsidized housing allotment, a comfortable niche in the library, and a friendly reception. I thank the Newberry. My own library, Andrews Library, efficiently supplied me with excellent service and interlibrary loans.

My wife, Mary Carney Hodges, goes about her own life. She neither types nor proofreads. Although she is a great fan of individual historians she has met over the years, she much prefers her own field's reading material to history books. Still, she not only tolerated the long hours I spent in my study as I struggled with this book, but she encouraged them. Her conviction that I should write this book rather than do some other pleasant things to improve my teaching made it possible for me to complete this work.

New Deal Labor Policy
and the Southern Cotton Textile Industry,
1933–1941

Introduction

A half century after the New Deal, the scholarship surrounding it has moved from a settled position of orthodoxy to revisionism to post-revisionism. For years after Basil Rauch's first scholarly attempt to make sense of the New Deal, historians rushed to explain the how, when, where, and why of the New Deal, and, even more important, to take up the standard of New Deal reform. By the 1960s an orthodox view of the New Deal as the mountaintop of American reform had emerged. Henry Steele Commager and Alan Nevins, well known for their genius for artful generalization, summed up that decade's accumulated orthodox study.

Commager in 1964 saw six "permanent" results for American life because the New Deal had come: government responsibility for the public good, physical restoration of the country, government as the umpire of the economy, a streamlined federal government, substantial advances in conservation of natural resources, and a strengthened American democracy.[1] It was unlikely, Alan Nevins wrote in 1966, that "we shall receive any startling new 'revelation,' any facts that will offer the basis for sweeping revision of judgement." The New Deal, Nevins wrote, solved problems one by one, by a single combination "of numerous practical changes, the main test of which was whether or not they worked." Roosevelt, said Nevins, "kept the heart of the old structure" and carried Americans "to a Moabite peak whence once more they saw the promised lands."[2] In 1963 even William Leuchtenburg, more the careful historian than the popular generalizer, entitled the last chapter of his influential *Franklin D. Roosevelt and the New Deal* "The Roosevelt Reconstruction: Retrospect," and in it the theme of permanent change dominated.[3]

Even as many historians moved to settled generalization about the New Deal, the events and movements of the 1960s — the rediscovery of poverty, the Civil Rights movement, and the Black Revolution, followed by loss of faith in a strong federal government, powerful leader, and liberal programs that came in reaction to the Great Society and the Vietnam War — shattered many of the old arguments about the meaning of the New Deal. In 1967, Paul Conkin, for example, challenged the sense of permanent reform that undergirded the orthodox view. The New Deal had not reconstructed America, he wrote;

it was "a sad story, the ever recurring story of what might have been."[4] A year earlier, Howard Zinn, assembling a group of primary readings about New Deal thought, had come essentially to the same view.[5] Soon, attacks by New Left essayists lumped the New Deal with the "conservative establishment" and argued that the New Deal reform had been a conservative effort to save capitalism.[6]

In the 1970s and 1980s, though, historians have blended orthodoxy and revisionism in a much more mature story of success and failure, opportunity and the limits of change.[7] The New Deal has lost the emotional immediacy that dominated historians' work for so long. The new account accepts in some key respects the orthodox argument that the New Deal *was* new. It *did* challenge the Great Depression. It *did* change the relationships of classes and groups, particularly in the subsequent decades. The New Deal, in particular, transfered power to Washington. The New Deal failed to end the depression, but it transformed America into the society that it has become.

The historians' debate on New Deal change lost its ideological tone and took the form of the old historical argument about the extent of continuity and change. In almost all areas of American life, there were distinct limits to New Deal change. For example, from its beginning the Democratic party coalition was volatile and vulnerable, particularly in the bonding of southern Democrats to other elements of the New Deal coalition; after 1938 the coalition had to struggle to create any change at all. New Deal recovery economics was rescued from partial failure by World War II spending, and the redistribution of American wealth was limited. Blacks and women received scant benefits; the bottom third of American society got the barest minimum of relief. Today, awash with new perceptions gained from the passage of a half century, the frontier in New Deal scholarship is to sort out continuity and change more clearly. The questions center on where the limits of New Deal change were and how and why those limits were reached or avoided.

In the orthodox view, the emergence of a national collective bargaining policy contributed one of the most enduring changes brought about by the New Deal. Selig Perlman wrote in 1945 that "for the first time in our history we had a national government that could intervene authoritatively in industrial relations."[8] Milton Derber and Edwin Young contended in 1957 that "there is hardly an aspect of current economic life which has not been profoundly influenced by the events of the 1930s and none perhaps as profoundly as the labor movement and labor relations."[9] In 1960 Walter Galenson called the emergence of unions' collective bargaining strength "a fundamental, almost revolutionary change in the power relationships of American society."[10]

Nevertheless, twenty years later, David Brody could contend that "the labor history of the New Deal era, long considered a settled matter in its main lines, has come unstuck in recent years."[11] This is particularly true in the history of the southern cotton textile industry, where the story of relations between owners and workers unsettles many established generalizations about New Deal labor policy. By the mid-1940s, steel workers, automobile workers, and workers in other large industries, were using New Deal labor policy effectively in well-known struggles to form great industrial unions. Craft unions bloomed in previously unorganized cities and towns. But in Piedmont cotton textile mills, workers remained unorganized and suffered the consequences—the lowest wages of any major group of industrial workers, rigid owner-controlled work places, and uncertain job tenure. In the South the cotton textile workers in the 1930s failed to create a significant permanent union, and their failure constitutes a dramatic example of the limits of New Deal labor policy.

The textile workers and owners struggled with each other in an industry that sprawled through the countryside and small towns of four southern states: North Carolina, South Carolina, Georgia, and Alabama. The industry, although it had antebellum roots, had a modern history dating from the 1880s. In the late 1920s, after years of steady expansion at the expense of the older New England industry, the southern cotton textile industry faced a sharp crisis—chronic overproduction by its numerous small firms, with flat or nonexistent profits. At the time of the New Deal, the industry's leaders turned to the National Recovery Act (NRA) for help in solving their profitability problems. They sought to use the New Deal to create a structure for recovery and private economic gain. As events unfolded, however, the New Deal had no persuasive or, in the long run, successful notion about how to achieve economic recovery or industrial reform. And certainly, in the beginning, New Deal officials had only the most jumbled and often contradictory attitudes towards unions and collective bargaining.

Major alteration in the style of labor relations—particularly labor-management relations built around the radical ideal of collective bargaining—was far from the minds of the southern cotton textile owners. Throughout the NRA period, even as the owners participated in the heralded government-industry partnership of the Blue Eagle period, they waged a relentless war against unions and workers who would join them. In the post-NRA period, which was dominated by the Wagner Act and the "new unionism" it spawned, the owners, dropping all pretense of cooperation, successfully blended old paternalism and new management tactics with traditional barriers to unionism in the industry, to emerge untouched by significant unionism.

The southern cotton textile workers participated fully in the optimism and hope that the New Deal brought to the country. The workers, overwhelmingly housed in company-owned mill villages huddled near the brick mills, had created a worker culture that, while it was southern white American, was distinctive from the culture of southerners who did not work in the mills. Cycles of union activity had come and gone through the textile communities, proving that the workers were not inherently antiunion. Nevertheless, the conditions of their work and lives did not encourage unionism, particularly when the powerful mill owners and other southern elites held and acted on decidedly antiunion views. The workers accepted the reality of their lives. Their reaction to the good news of the New Deal, the possibility of government-approved unionism under the fragile 1920s union, the United Textile Workers (UTW), was practical and realistic. In large numbers they joined the UTW, in the hope of job protection and wage gains. In particular the workers hoped to stop job assignment changes, the hated "stretch out."

The NRA experience, a story of mind-numbing business-dominated bureaucratic boards and empty hopes, was enervating and bitterly disappointing to the workers. The major event was a general strike in September 1934. The strike, the largest in American history up to that time, never had a chance. A desperate UTW endorsed it, but, despite its nationwide character, the strike fell apart before the unyielding resistance of the owners. The New Deal government proved powerless to bring about a conclusion favorable to the worker, even if it had wanted to do so. All the New Deal gained was another board somewhat better than the one before. The strike's failure shattered the evolving southern unionists and left the owners in uncontested command of the mills.

Against all odds, the promise of the second round of New Deal unionism, created by the Wagner Act, elicited another positive response from the southern workers. This time, between 1937 and 1939, they joined in large numbers the Textile Workers Organizing Committee (TWOC), a CIO project. Although this effort left a thin residue of permanent unionism, it too failed. The actual implementation of collective bargaining under the rules of the National Labor Relations Board (NLRB) placed a premium on union power, on the ability to organize workers into active unionism. The TWOC campaign over two years failed to fashion such power. By 1941, the achievements of the New Deal labor revolution, for more than nine in ten southern cotton textile workers, remained painfully basic — the eight-hour day, the forty-hour week, and the minimum wage, the latter becoming effective at a date when it no longer affected many workers in the industry. The threat of unionism, at best, hastened the change from the older and weaker imperatives of cotton mill paternalisms to modern management techniques, a change which here and there improved the lot of the workers.

The UTW barely clung to existence in the lean years of the 1920s. In the NRA years, its leader only hovered on the fringes of the bargaining between the government and industry. Nevertheless, the UTW used that bargaining process and what little power it could drum up from its increasing strength to establish in the southern mills the most important union presence ever. The inept NRA boards, the lack of any clear bargaining mandates from the emerging New Deal labor policy, and the pressure of rising expectations from its southern locals led it to take the losing gamble of the 1934 strike. Nearly moribund in the South by 1937, the union merged with the TWOC. In 1939, the TWOC formed a new union, the Textile Workers Unions of America (TWUA), which carried the tattered union banner forward into the 1940s and beyond.

The UTW made many mistakes in the 1930s. Its leaders were often unimaginative and lackluster; they divided into petty, debilitating factional quarrels that centered around hope of private gain or status; they were often insensitive to the culture and needs of the southern workers. But the union did face an enormous task in trying to organize southern cotton textile workers. The problems included the economic structure of the union; the worker culture of small and isolated mill villages; the serious overall weakness of unionism in the South; the depth of the depression in the textile belt, which insured long lines waiting at the mill gates for work; and the fact that the union was led mostly by ethnic northerners. The 1934 strike failure, for example, could not have been avoided even by the most astute leadership. A successful strike would have called for a sophistication and organizational power that no union in the early 1930s possessed.

The union viewed New Deal labor policy as the solution to its problems. It would use the NRA's Section 7(a) to bring about collective bargaining. It would fight tenaciously in a bureaucratic struggle to force the southern owners to bargain collectively in exchange for economic recovery. When this failed, the union found another weapon in the harder reality of the NLRB. Under the cover of national law, collective bargaining agreements would secure justice for the workers. But it never worked for the union. It would take real organizational power to maneuver collective bargaining through the inherent roadblocks of the NLRB procedures, so vulnerable were they to management resistance and delay. The union was not able to mobilize that power. New Deal labor policy had limited impact in promoting collective bargaining in the southern cotton textile industry, because it failed to provide effective pressure to bring about the necessary changes among owners and workers alike.

At every turn failure awaited those in the southern cotton textile industry who struggled to use the swiftly changing New Deal labor policy to achieve unionization. History, wrote Richard Hofstadter, "forces us to be aware not only of complexities but of defeat and failure; it tends to deny the high sense of expectations, that hope of ultimate and glorious triumph that sustains good combatants."[12] To understand the losing struggle of some cotton textile workers and their leaders to join their union brothers and sisters elsewhere in labor's famous 1930s march is to gain new insight into the limits of reform that shackled the New Deal and to understand better why the New Deal failed as often as it succeeded.

"Cotton textiles need help"
THE SOUTHERN COTTON TEXTILE INDUSTRY
IN THE 1930s

In the spring of 1934, just before the National Recovery Administration would collapse, the Bureau of Labor Statistics inaugurated a new study of the cotton textile industry, prompted by the textile general strike and renewed economic stress in the industry. Economist Arthur F. Hinrichs informed Frances Perkins, secretary of labor, that the "cotton textile industry has been and is desperately sick," and he listed a catalogue of ills as he saw them—an unorganized and dispersed industry, ruinous overcapacity, and a tortuous system of distributing goods from factory to market. "Cotton textiles," he wrote, "need help."[1] A year earlier, in 1933, Benjamin Gossett, president of the American Cotton Manufacturers Association (ACMA), the trade association of manufacturers, had told his fellow manufacturers that it "must be evident to all that there is something wrong about our present system . . . that is dissipating our energies and bleeding our plants to death."[2] Labor relations, union organizations, and New Deal labor policy all operated within the narrowing economic context of the Southern cotton textile industry and cannot be separated from it.

Glenn Gilman, in a management-biased 1956 study of the industry, claimed that the workers had never grasped the way in which its peculiar economic structure shaped their fortunes. So far as the worker was concerned, he wrote, "the complex economic problems of the industry were summed up in two simple indices: the size of his pay check and the frequency of his pay day."[3] The labor leaders, however, were very much aware of the economic problems. Fundamentally, what they sought was to take labor conditions out of the competitive struggle, to neutralize the economic problems affecting labor relations. To accomplish this, the union desperately wanted an industry organized so that successful competition would not be achieved at the expense of the workers, through increased work loads, low wages, and stringent control of the work floor. The labor people understood how the economic problems of the industry severely affected efforts to organize. In the 1930s they increasingly argued that the workers, through their organization, must have some voice in the decisions leading to the solution of these problems. Collective bargaining was the answer to economic problems; it would be a "stabilizing factor."[4] By the 1930s the hard-pressed state of the industry always loomed large in the wrokers' struggle to make New Deal policy work for them. But the earlier history and structure of the industry dictated that owners would pay close attention to even the most marginal of labor costs and to any organization that purported to bring collective bargaining that might drive up their labor costs.

MILLS LIKE MUSHROOMS

Cotton textiles, the flagship industry in the South by the 1930s, dominated the manufacturing statistics of the region, particularly in the four major textile states of North Carolina, South Carolina, Georgia, and Alabama. In 1937, the South's five leading industries were cotton manufacturing, tobacco manufacturing, lumber, cottonseed products, and petroleum refining, in that order. Only the tobacco industry approached cotton manufacturing in value of product, $854,196,393 to cotton's $911,713,976, but cotton manufacturing employed ten workers for every one in tobacco.[5] The American cotton goods industry in 1939, the last normal production year before World War II, employed more people than either the automobile or the steel industry.[6] In 1933, there were 1,057 mills in the country, employing 379,445 workers and paying out $216,384,000 annually in wages.[7] Of these mills, 634 of them, or 59.9 percent, were located in the four leading cotton textile states, with North Carolina and South Carolina first and second.[8] By 1937, the South had 72 percent the industry's value produced and with 316,777 workers had 73 percent of all the industry's workers.[9] Thomas H. Webb, president of the ACMA, estimated in May 1936 that during 1935–36 the southern division of the cotton textile industry distributed over $243,000,000 in wages; $120,000,000 in taxes; and $140,000,000 in dividends, adding $303,000,000 annually to the South's income. Webb estimated the total investment in cotton textiles in the South at close to one billion dollars. "A great industry," he said, "directed by great men doing a great work."[10]

The cotton textile industry had existed in the South for a long time. In the antebellum era, the industry had been tiny and unimportant. The Piedmont's 193,700 spindles in place in 1860 represented only 3.7 percent of the total national spindles. The industry's expansion ground to a halt after the Civil War. As late as 1880, South Carolina, for example, had only fourteen mills employing approximately two thousand workers.[11] In a few short years in the 1880s, however, the industry established itself solidly in the Piedmont and began to march toward national dominance for the South. For years

Southerners had dreamed of bringing mills to the cotton fields, but the two decades after the war had been a period of agricultural adjustment and not one of explosive industrial expansion. In the booming eighties, however, borne on the tide of the New South movement and with access to capital, entrepreneurs turned to mill building, and the much-romanticized cotton mill campaign was on.

The drive to create mills has been seen as a great community effort tied to New South ideology. It was touted as a community effort; the mills would benefit the entire population. Impoverished farmers could expect steady employment, and cotton farmers would find a ready market. The infusion of money would help local merchants. W.J. Cash, in his influential *The Mind of the South*, described the "cotton mill campaign" as if it were a religious revival. "The impulse," he wrote, "leaps from community to community as an electric current leaps across a series of galvanic poles — sweeping the citizens into mass assembly, stirring up the old local patriotism so characteristic of the South and setting these communities to striving to outdo one another in furthering the cause."[12] In 1923, southern journalist Gerald Johnson also saw the new mills of the 1880s as social enterprises "founded apparently in violation of every basic principle of economics and in defiance of known rules of good business."[13] As late as 1956, Glenn Gilman still believed in the cotton mill campaign as a "true social movement, a phenomenon participated in actively by a whole society that found itself faced with the necessity of action."[14] Throughout the 1930s, the myth of the mills as public servants permeated the rhetoric of owners and served to justify their view of themselves as true stewards of the South and its workers.

This charitable view of the establishment of the modern cotton industry has worn thin. "Ever since Broadus Mitchell first suggested that Southerners built cotton mills for basically humanitarian purposes," David Carlton wrote, "this interpretation has haunted the historiography of the postbellum South."[15] In a careful study of the post-1800s industry in South Carolina, Carlton dismisses the view that the cotton mill campaign was a philanthropic or community enterprise. To explain why the South Carolina businessmen built mills, Carlton quoted textile manufacturer H.P. Hammett: "The main object in building a mill by those who put their money into it, is the prospective profits upon the investments; there may be the laudable desire to give employment to the people and to benefit the community — the latter is always incidental and secondary, if at all."[16] Profits of South Carolina mills in the 1880s, given the advantages of abundant cheap labor, good energy sources, and plentiful supplies of cotton, ranged, according to one report, from 18 to 40 percent, though Carlton suggests lower but still healthy returns.[17]

Other authors also have been impressed more by evidence of a search for profits than by great social vision. Melton McLaurin argued that "although the folk movement interpretation holds a considerable amount of truth, it greatly underestimates the complexity of the economic factor that triggered the development of the South's industry."[18] William Walker Thompson, Jr., following the history of one founding family and their company, the Spartan Mills in South Carolina, wrote that "the impelling force in the mill construction boom of the 1880s was the aggregate profit motives of numerous individual entrepreneurs" and not humanitarian motives.[19] Patrick J. Hearden treated the cotton mill campaign as an editorial and publicity event, but even he argued that the principle goal of the mill cheerleaders was not to create a southern utopia, but rather to continue sectional rivalry as a "continuation of the battle that, in its military phase, had been lost in 1865."[20]

Humanitarianism aside, the sporadic expansion of the cotton textile industry in the South was one of the most fundamental changes in the American textile industry as a whole. In 1880, only 5 percent of the spindles existing in the cotton textile industry were in the South; in 1900, however, the South could claim 24 percent, and by 1910, 39 percent of the national total.[21] The nation increased its cotton spindles by 35 percent between 1880 and 1890. In the same period, North Carolina, South Carolina, Georgia, and Alabama increased their combined spindleage by 182 percent.[22] Southern success rested on solid economic advantages characteristic of the Piedmont region.[23] The availability of cheap raw material at first attracted the new cotton entrepreneur. Supposedly, since cotton grew at the very front doors of the mills, tremendous savings in transportation would be effected. Actually, because of the rapid rate of consumption by a mill, local supplies of cotton meant little even to small mills, and all the mills soon imported cotton from as far west as the Mississippi Delta.

More important to the economics of the new Piedmont mills was the expansion of cotton production in the late 1870s, which caused a drop in price. Throughout the South, the fall in price kept mill profits high and at the same time directed capital resources away from agriculture to the cotton textile industry. The new southern mills had the good fortune to enter the industry when raw material costs were comparably low. The lower cotton prices also made it easier to attract labor from the fields to the mills. The economic distress of Piedmont agriculture combined with the surplus agricultural population to produce an abundant labor supply to handle the easily-learned jobs that the new mills offered. The widespread use of women and children as workers in the 1880s, when the industry's work force was 41 percent women and 24 percent children under sixteen, also made it easier to obtain the necessary workers by creating a family wage system.[24] The seemingly never-ending supply of workers ready to take jobs in the mills would always be a high hurdle for unionism.

The surplus labor supply allowed the southern mill owner to pay his workers or "operatives," as he was wont to call them, less than the same type of worker received in the North. Female ring spinners in New England in 1907, for example, averaged $7.36 a week, compared to $5.71 for their southern counterparts.[25] The lower cost of production that resulted enabled the southern mills to compete in the 1800s and 1890s with the older, more experienced industry in New England. Furthermore, this North-South differential continued through the years. In 1927, the average cost per yard of gray cloth produced in the Piedmont was 12.05 cents; in New England it cost 16.41 cents.[26] This cost differential was the major reason for the success of the Piedmont mills. The southern owners knew it and would fight to keep this advantage.

New capital to bolster the initial investment was also needed to make the mills a success. In the 1880s, the average capitalization necessary for a new mill was about $100,000, and local resources were often strained to meet even the initial cost. Gradually, needed capital was supplied by southern urban centers such as Charleston and Atlanta, but northern capital was often important. Textile machinery manufacturers, interested in new business, advanced capital and credit in the 1880s and 1890s in return for mill securities, and commission houses in New York supplied ample credit in return for exclusive marketing privileges. Nevertheless, control, ownership, and a surprising amount of working capital remained local, in the hands of emerging commercial and professional families. The new owners, through their connections with railroads, banking, or commerce, were not naive about business matters; shrewd, hardheaded business leaders directed the new undertaking.[27]

Because of these advantages, for forty years after 1880 the mills mushroomed in the towns and hamlets of the Piedmont. In the years from 1880 to 1923, the total growth of spindleage for the four southern Piedmont states was a staggering 1,120 percent. By 1923, the Southeast had increased its share of the national industry to 44 percent, from 5 percent in 1880.[28] In 1923, too, New England reached its peak development of approximately 20 million spindles in place, as against slightly more than 16 million in the South.[29] In the 1920s, the southern Piedmont and the old textile centers in New England became locked in deadly combat, and the subsequent southern victory would harden the southern owners' resolve to keep every competitive edge possible in the 1930s.

The national cotton textile industry in the 1920s entered into a long period of hard times that lasted sporadically until World War II brought high profits that rivaled those before the interwar period. Despite this depression, the southern states took the lead in value of products manufactured in 1923, in the number of active spindles in 1925, and in total spindles in place in 1927.[30] In the ten years between 1923 and 1933, the number of cotton mills in Massachusetts declined from 245 to 137, in Rhode Island from 153 to 93, in Connecticut from 69 to 35, and in all of New England from 506 to 301.[31]

By 1927, the South produced 82 percent of the coarse yarn and 71 percent of the medium yarn in the United States. New England, in the same year, maintained a slight lead in fine goods, accounting for 51 percent of the total production, but that lead also melted away in the coming decade.[32] Even during the 1930s, the southern accumulation of the national market continued; by 1939 the region had 72 percent of the spindles in place and operating.[33] The South had won the battle, but at its moment of success it found itself battered by the Great Depression. The competitive struggle not only contributed to the ill-fortunes of the industry, but its centrality increased the industry's resistance to coming demands for a new style of labor relations.

The reasons for the southern victory contributed to the stubbornness of the southern owners in their struggle against unionism and collective bargaining. The favorable wage differential was undoubtedly the largest single reason for the flight of spindles from North to South. Textile wages by the 1930s took up 45 to 65 percent of each sales dollar and were thus a crucial aspect of resourceful competition.[34] The average southern textile wage paid in the period from 1894 to 1927 averaged 40 percent below that in other parts of the U.S. Even by the 1920s, the difference was still about 25 percent.[35] In 1932 a textile economist argued that the "basic reason for southern triumph was cheap labor" and that all southern manufacturers were well aware of the fact, as witnessed by their fight against unionism.[36]

The differential enabled the southern mills to make money when the New England industry barely broke even or ran deficits. Between 1925 and 1929, a selected group of southern firms earned 5.8 percent on their stockholders' investment, while similarly selected northern companies earned only 1.5 percent.[37] The Federal Trade Commission reported in December 1934 that southern cotton mills showed rates of return in 1933–34 far in excess of those for northern mills.[38] From the very beginning, southern mills produced at less cost, and managements made money. Low wages were clearly responsible for the southern owner's happy circumstances.

Four other historical developments also contributed to the plight of New England by the 1920s and to the influx of new machinery to the Piedmont: in the South, favorable labor legislation, lack of conflict in industrial relations, and aggressive community support; and a decided failure of managerial acumen in New England. Southern owners were well aware of these factors that had aided their rise to dominance as they struggled with the New Deal labor policy in the 1930s.

The accumulation of spindles and looms in the South was aided by the absence of protective labor legislation that the Progressive years produced in the North. This was particularly true in the heavy use of female labor by the southern mills, where women made up 25 to 50 percent of the work force in individual mills. In six New England states, in the 1920s restrictions on the hours of labor for women varied from forty-eight hours per week in Massachusetts, a heavy cotton textile state, to fifty-six per week in thinly milled Vermont. In the South, the most severe law, that of South Carolina, limited legal working hours for women to fifty-five per week, while Alabama

had no statutory limit at all. In the southern states in the 1920s, wrote George
Tindall, "Legislation regulating the conditions of labor remained in the rudimentary stages, barely established in principle."[39] No law at all restricted the
daily work hours for men, which averaged from fifty-five to sixty hours per
week. Some child labor still existed in southern mills in the 1920s, and though
all the southern states had minimum ages for employment by 1910, only four
went as high as fourteen. And young workers received the lowest wages.[40] The
northern owners also were forced to bear a share of workmen's compensation expenses and unemployment insurance much earlier than did southern
mill owners.

In the 1920s, at least until the explosive year of 1929, southern mill owners
had a long respite from organized labor problems, while northern owners always faced the threat or reality of organization. The southern brand of mill
paternalism, many said, made for more and cheaper productive labor. In the
South, paternalism supposedly allowed the mill worker much more flexibility
in employment. As one trade journal observed as late as 1934, "There is more
cooperation and understanding between the employer and the employee in
the South" than in New England.[41]

Aggressive community support also gave the South a competitive edge.
Southern communities, in the now-common modern practice of industrial
enticement, sometimes provided free land or cheap buildings and frequently
relieved new firms of taxes for a period of years. Low taxes overall also helped
the mills. In 1927, mills in Alabama and Georgia paid only three-sevenths
of total dollars of taxes paid by Massachusetts' mills.[42] Southern communities
provided water, electricity, and rail facilities at very low cost. One partisan
study, though admitting that much southern growth was attributable to traditional economic reasons, described the southern efforts as a policy of "pry-
ing firms loose" from the North.[43]

Managerial conservatism, dominating New England textile management
during the critical years of competition in the 1920s, helped the southerners,
too. New England firms, while modernizing some in the 1920s, had made
the grievous error of letting their plants become partly obsolescent; by contrast many southern firms in that decade continued to invest in new machinery.
When the Draper automatic loom was perfected in 1895, it was widely adopted
in the new southern mills that popped up at the turn of the century. The
installation of this loom had "profound importance" in creating high profits
for the next four decades.[44] But as late as 1929, only 59 percent of New
England's active plain looms were automatic as against 80 percent in the South;
in fancy looms, only 33 percent were automatic, as against 67 percent in the
South.[45] Although New England made a strong if late push for modernization in the 1930s, the South had a distinct edge in modern technology. This
technological margin combined with the wage advantage to ensure a southern win in the 1920s.[46] Southern owners were determined to protect their
new leadership of the industry.

THE SOUTHERN COTTON TEXTILE INDUSTRY
IN THE 1930s

The mature southern cotton textile industry included all mills performing one or more of the functions involved in the preparation of raw cotton for processing, the spinning of cotton fibers into yarn, and the weaving of yarn into cloth. Thus, the industry comprised mills involved in the stages of production from the opening of raw cotton bales to the placing of cloth in the hands of a finisher. Spinning and weaving of cotton was known as basic textile manufacturing, the first stage of a four-stage process. The other three stages were the finishing, distribution, and cutting trades. The finishing stage of cotton textile production in the 1930s occurred largely in plants in New York, Pennsylvania, and New Jersey, although the trend of migration South was beginning to follow the basic cotton textile industry. Many southern basic cotton mills produced finished goods (particularly the towel mills), but since they were a minority of the mills, the finishing industry, with its separate problems and separate identity in the 1930s, falls outside the scope of this discussion.

The unions never sorted out the various textile industries very well. The United Textile Workers, a northern-born union, had evolved with separate and autonomous federations of finishers and dyers, hosiery, silk, carpet and rug, and synthetic fibers and cotton workers. In the South, the union never got close enough to organization to worry about such neat jurisdictional definitions. In 1931, for example, North Carolina had nearly 700 textile mills, comprised of 348 cotton mills, 11 woolen and worsted mills, 31 rayon mills, 34 silk mills, and 184 knitting mills (mostly hosiery). But the main distinction the union made in the South was to separate hosiery and knit goods workers from cotton textile workers. The union made no distinction between the new and much smaller groups of workers in the synthetic fiber industry and those in cotton textiles, though, of course, they were indeed separate industries in the 1930s.

The distribution phase of the cotton textile industry in the 1930s took place mainly in New York City on famous Worth Street, which played a role comparable to that of Wall Street in the world of stocks and bonds. The fourth division of the cotton textile industry, the cutting trades, took cotton fabric and manufactured apparel, a process located in the garment district of New York City, as well as in many other large and small industrial cities. Indeed, by the 1930s, the apparel industry was almost never associated with the cotton textile industry and had a separate union, the successful Amalgamated Clothing Workers Union.

The manufacturing process of primary textile manufacturing, though refined and improved, had not changed in essentials since the perfection of the power-drive loom in the early nineteenth century. The two fundamental processes were spinning and weaving; all other processes, such as picking, carding, combing, slashing, and beaming (the straightening of fibers and the preparation of yarn), related to these two functions.[48] Spinning and weaving took place on specialized machines attended by easily-trained workers. In 1930 the technology had changed little since the 1890s, though during the 1930s substantial improvements—single-process picking, long-draft spinning, the Barber-Colman automatic spooler and high-speed warper—were introduced by many energetic southern mills.[49] All cotton mills, however, did not both spin and weave; some only spun and produced yarn or thread, and others only wove. In the South, however, the majority of the mills were combined mills, both spinning and weaving, while some like the huge Dan River Mills in Danville, Virginia, became integrated mills that finished as well. In 1935 there were 414 combined mills in the South, 250 spinning mills, and 26 weaving mills.[50] In 1938, the average southern spinning-weaving mill had only 30,000 spindles and 700 looms. Only 11 southern firms had 100,000 or more spindles per plant.[51] In contrast to the manufacturing of iron, steel, automobiles, and chemicals and the refining of oil, in the cotton textile industry no single manufacturing process had to be done on a large scale in the interest of efficiency. So, well into the 1930s, the southern cotton mills stayed small, particularly in comparison with New England mills.[52]

The products of the southern mills varied greatly. A mill exclusively manufacturing yarn channeled its products to thread, twine, mops, and insulated wire manufacturers, and to household consumers who bought hand knitting, crochet, and embroidery goods.[53] Yarn woven into cotton cloth became known as gray goods—the unbleached, uncolored products of the looms. Cotton gray goods could include a number of products: sheetings; print cloth; reps; poplins and broadcloth; napped fabrics; shirtings; twills and sateens; duck; towels; denims; lawns; draperies; drills; blankets; tobacco, cheese, butter, and bandage cloths; voile; and pajama fabrics.[54] Within these various groups there was even further specialization as to the quality of goods produced.

The southern cotton textile industry in the 1930s was a large, well-defined industrial world with long-established markets; in it the small mills had stable market niches. By the 1930s, the South dominated the gray goods manufacturing process and continued to gain in the market during the decade. Of 383,000 workers producing gray goods in 1930, 280,000 of them worked in the South.[55] By 1947, 383,463 primary cotton textile workers in the South worked in 801 mills, and they made approximately 80 percent of the cotton gray goods in the nation.[56]

The industry never migrated out of the Piedmont. The region's maps in the 1930 were dotted with small mill towns as the Piedmont sweeps southwest from lower Virginia, through the Carolinas and into Alabama—"Gold Avenue," as Jonathan Daniels called them when he traveled through North Carolina and South Carolina in 1937.[57] In 1934, 588 of the more than 1,000 cotton textile mills in the country were located in towns of less than 5,000 people. Only 150 mills were in cities of over 75,000, and these were mainly in New England.[58] Atlanta, for example, had only 3 mills in the 1930s. Operating in places like Honea Path, South Carolina; Roanoke Rapids, North Carolina; La Grange, Georgia; and Sylacauga, Alabama, the mills spun and wove far from their buyers. In aggregate they were the South's greatest industry, employing one-half the region's factory workers.

They sent their goods to market in what *Fortune* magazine called a tangled pattern.[59] Over two-thirds of the gray goods moved to a finishing plant through northern-dominated brokerage firms, commission houses, and "converters," special entrepreneurs who moved gray goods into finishing plants for direct use in apparel, home furnishings, and industrial products.[60] The industry's involved marketing structure, with its various channels, crosscurrents, and multiple steps, was described in one authoritative study as "one of the most confused and complicated in America."[61] It certainly contributed to the us-against-them feeling that permeated southern industry leaders' thoughts in the 1930s. Southern mill managers, confronting the intricate maze of distribution and decision, often felt unable to control their own economic destiny. Perhaps the determination to keep control of their own relations with labor reflected their concern that too often they had little control of their small companies' fortunes in the larger world.

HARD TIMES

The economic trouble of the industry began well before the depression decade itself. The textile depression, with mills operating under capacity, declining profits, bankruptcies, shrinking plant and stock values, low wages, and long lines of unemployed men and women, was worldwide. Manufacturers in Great Britain, France, and many other European countries had experiences similar to those in America. Even before World War I there were signs of overproduction, but the war-fueled expansion of demand delayed hard times. In 1923–24, however, the earnings of cotton mills began a sharp downward trend that continued until 1940.[62]

For New England, the following years were a period of heartbreaking devastation. Bankruptcy followed bankruptcy. Mills that had been established for years closed down, their machinery sold and their buildings emptied.[63] The South, more prosperous than the North and with built-in economic advantages, escaped much of the ravage that struck New England. In terms of total net profit or loss to net worth, the southern industry had only three deficit years between 1922 and 1940, while the northern industry experienced six. Throughout the period, southern earnings ran significantly higher than northern ones.[64]

The figures showing total net profits are misleading, however, because many of the more efficient mills always showed a profit, balancing those mills that were barely breaking even or running at a loss. An analysis of income tax returns during the years 1926–32 indicated that the industry as a whole had only three years — 1926, 1928, and 1929 — when it made money. The net deficit for the entire seven-year period was $131,141,551. And in 1930–35, the New England states showed a constant deficit, except in 1933.[65] One study contends that in the fourteen-year period 1926–39, during which the industry produced approximately $15 billion worth of goods, its net earned income was only $10 million before federal taxes. Subtract the federal taxes of $74 million which the industry paid during these years, and the result shows that the industry as a whole went into the red some $64 million dollars.[66] For the first time since their founding, the southern mills had hard times over a period longer than a short cyclical depression. Even the profits for successful southern mills were much lower than normal, and in the period 1926–32, less than one-half of the southern mills paid a regular dividend.[67] It is not that southern cotton textile profits fell more precipitously than, say, those for coal or construction, but rather that the depression hit hard at what in the South had been a consistent money maker. Even in 1931 and 1932, the low point of the depression, the industry as a whole operated at 77 percent and 86 percent of capacity respectively. But in spite of its relatively high volume in those years, Claudius Murchison argued in 1935, "the industry experienced the utmost demoralization of prices, wages and employment; with profits virtually non-existent, except in a few isolated cases, and for short periods."[68]

The depression naturally affected the value of cotton mill securities. From 1922 to autumn 1929, the securities of other industries doubled and tripled in value, while textile securities fell. At the end of 1929 they sold on average at less than half their 1923 price. Few cotton textile securities in South or North could be purchased as a safe income-producing investment.[69]

In the 1920s mill owners tried to respond to the depression in their industry. In 1926 they created one of the strongest trade associations in the country, the Cotton-Textile Institute (CTI). Through the CTI, the industry attempted to influence the Hoover administration to moderate the antitrust laws to enable the CTI to control production and pricing, something the CTI's earlier call for voluntary cooperation had not accomplished. The political effort, however, failed, and the structure of the industry made any cooperation action difficult.

Certain overhead costs always remained constant. Whether or not a mill produced at full capacity, mill owners wanted to keep a workforce together. To help meet their expenses, in the 1920s and 1930s mills produced at break-even points or even at a loss. Because of the inflexible overhead costs, the higher the production output, the lower the production costs per unit. Thus, cotton textile production, isolated from immediate markets, sometimes had very little relation to demand. Excess capacity led to chronic overproduction, which in turn, because of the competition for sales, led to low selling prices.

Low prices meant low wages for the workers and low earnings for investors. The low prices were a matter of great concern to the manufacturer. So delicate was the pricing of cotton textiles that a change of less than one cent a yard in return to the mill could make the difference between no return and a yield of 6 percent on the investment.[70] But there was strong pressure on the mills to sell at low prices. Pressure built up to sell at any price obtainable, in order to dispose of accumulated inventories and to secure a segment of the inadequate demand to prevent others from taking away a part of the mill's accustomed trade. At any suggestion of price improvement, the mills increased production, thereby creating "a constant tendency to build up surpluses with resulting price depression more or less chronic."[71]

Ideally, an individual mill should have determined the cost of its production, sold only at a profit or at least a breakeven point, and produced only for a reasonable share of the market. Most mills, however, did not operate in this fashion, and many even thought they could compete by outproducing the other mills. This brought frequent charges of "cutthroat" competition. One New York textile merchant claimed in 1936 that nothing contributed more to the misfortune of "King Cotton than the unethical, unsocial, and uneconomic distributing practices of selling below cost."[72] Excessive competition had a profound effect on the labor force. The cost savings which the producers believed were necessary meant lower wages and increased workloads for the millhands.

Although everyone united in condemning the illogical and frantic competition, the individual mill had little choice but to join in. However efficient the management was in a particular plant, external forces could defeat its effort to make a profit. If a mill speeded up its production, it sold its goods at a loss in a market already overburdened with surplus inventory. If the mill curtailed operations, its efforts were wasted without the cooperation of its competitors, and the mill lost its market; it also took a continuing loss through its inability to stop the drain of overhead expenses and from the disintegration of its workforce.

The mills in the 1930s were still closely held, and each had only a tiny segment of the market. In 1937, the four largest southern cotton textile manufacturers controlled only 4.9 percent of the spindles and 12.1 percent of the total assets of the industry. The sprawling Dan River Mills in Virginia, employing close to ten thousand workers, had less than 2 percent of the spindles and looms in place.[73] The southern industry exemplified the classic economic definition of competition. Integration and combination occurred in the 1930s, but that pathway to profits has largely been taken only since World War II. Although the trend in the New Deal era was toward integration of function backward, forward, and horizontally, and toward concentration of ownership, the industry in the 1930s remained one of numerous small firms, more controlled by the market than controlling it.[74] The marginal producers tended to shave prices in an attempt to stay in operation, and other isolated producers had to do so to keep their markets. While the industry spun and wove at unwarranted production rates, the demand for cotton goods in the 1920s and 1930s was unstable, adversely affected by a slowed rate of population growth, changing consumer buying patterns, the deep industrial depression of the 1930s, a general instability in the industrial use of cotton goods, foreign competition in markets abroad, and the intense competition of textile and nontextile substitutes for cotton.

Plagued by a variety of problems, then, the cotton textile industry was experiencing a depression of unprecedented depth and duration as the New Deal began. The industry's early interest in the New Deal was singularly rooted in its hope of escaping from that depression. The problem facing the industry was how to restore the average as well as the exceptional mill; all questions ultimately reduced themselves to the problem of excess capacity and overproduction. One southern cotton textile executive in 1930, baffled by the problem, told an inquiring scholar that he had no remedies to offer. "Mergers," he said, "will not help. Unions will not help. Surveys will not help." The mill man resorted to fatalism: "The thing will have to work itself out like an epidemic of influenza or the aftermath of a stock market debate or a tidal wave. Either production will have to come down to consumption or consumption will have to catch up with production."[75]

Most manufacturers, however, were not quite so willing for the painful process of attrition to work its will. They took measures that were to have great bearing on the story of labor relations in the New Deal years. There were three notable trends: toward increased productivity per unit of capital; toward the formation of larger production units through consolidation in order to achieve more effective control over supply and demand; and toward joint action on matters of industrial policy. The first of these trends had an important effect on labor in the industry, for competitive pressures on costs, in the absence of any effective regulation, led to a never-ceasing search for lower costs per unit to meet or surpass the costs of rivals. Far too often, the cost competition was met by cutting already low wages. Savings were also accomplished by stretching out the number of machines each worker tended and by the introduction of newer, more efficient labor-saving machinery. These developments, while natural enough for the individual manufacturer, caused labor dissatisfaction; at the same time they increased the productive capacity of the industry as a whole, reinforcing the cycle of low earnings for both worker and management.

New Deal legislation which affected the cotton textile industry attempted to cope with the longstanding depression in the industry. The manufacturers were thoroughly weary of the competitive spiral and the dog-eat-dog pressures in which the strong as well as the weak suffered. They eagerly welcomed the National Recovery Administration. Donald Comer, an Alabama manufacturer, later explained in hearings on the Wagner bill his reasons for embracing the NRA: "I had reached the point where I did not want to continue spinning cotton under conditions operating back under our previous hours and wages, so unsatisfactory and yet under competition impossible to escape."[76] The industry sought control over production, prices, and profits; it never anticipated having to share power with labor.

"But the Cones is still totin' the keys to the mills"
WORKERS AND OWNERS

In 1936, Thomas H. Webb, president of the ACMA, speaking in his comfortable quarters in Pinehurst, North Carolina, repeated the dramatic story of the coming of the workers to the mills. "Out of the mountains and off the farms of sub-marginal values," he said, "came thousands of splendid but desperately depressed people into a haven of economic security—out of huts and hovels they came to better living conditions, out of uncertain conditions they came to health; out of ignorance and poverty they came to intelligence and economic security; out of isolation and rejection they came to social recognition and acceptance; out of despair they came to hope; out of hell for many they came to a haven of refuge. And the parade has not yet stopped." It was to Webb a "story of civil contribution, of racial betterment, of spiritual evolution," a story of "glory and satisfaction."[1]

Earlier, in the 1920s, Gerald Johnson, a well-known southern journalist, had also noted the new critical mass of southern workers. He thought the agricultural condition they came from "so pitiable that it is altogether beyond description" and reported that they "poured into the mills by thousands and tens of thousands." By national standards wages were low and working conditions abominable, said Johnson, "but anything was better than the terrible fight for a bare existence that they had been waging on their rocky, barren farms."[2]

The reality of cotton mill life fell far short of Webb's triumphant vision and more nearly approximated the practicality of Johnson's account. In the beginning, the workers came reluctantly, from unproductive farms in the surrounding countryside. In the first years of employment, the textile workers returned to their farms at intervals and restlessly moved from mill to mill if possible. David Carlton discovered that in a South Carolina mill in the 1880s, between 30 and 40 percent of the workers dropped off the company's payroll within a year and half. Carlton suggested that the floating population in the early decades was, perhaps, 20 to 25 percent of the total mill worker population.[3] W.J. Cash wrote in the 1930s of what he called this "nostalgia for a seat on a fence and the smell of pinewoods," and he emphasized the "constant and pretty extensive flow backward and forward between the land and the mills."[4] This flow lessened through the years as the advantage of mill work over rural poverty became more accepted. Dale Newman, interviewing cotton mill workers decades later, elicited the following exclamation from a woman about her family's journey from farm to mill: "Why wouldn't we want to come!" Her family saw better housing, more frequent and higher income, and "work for us all."[5]

Adaption to industrial work did not mean falling away from the rural South and its traditions. Douglas DeNatale's longitudinal study of tiny Bynum, North Carolina, and its mill community from its nineteenth century beginnings to its formal ending in 1977, stressed the survival of its workers' rural orientation into the 1930s and beyond. Visits to farm relatives were common; vegetable gardening and keeping hogs, cows, and chickens persisted; rural church traditions lived on. "All the evidence," DeNatale wrote, "suggests that continuity between the mill and farm made through family, commerce, and culture were maintained over time."[6] In Jennings J. Rhyne's study of 500 cotton textile families in four different villages in Gastonia County, North Carolina, he discovered in 1926–27 that 256 heads of families or 51.2 percent had farmed before going to the mills and 62.6 percent reported that their fathers had farmed.[7] As late as the 1930s, Broadus and George Mitchell claimed that "the Southern factory 'hand' has therefore had a rural mind. . . . The operatives thought of themselves, with the old pride that goes with poverty on the farms, as individuals, not as members of a group or class."[8]

Nevertheless, as the Southern cotton textile industry matured, the workers slowly began to abandon their rural habits. The passage of time and the growth of the industry made mill workers' lives different from those of their country cousins and from those of the other populations of the Piedmont. Of Rhyne's 500 family heads, almost 4 in 10 had never worked anywhere except in a cotton mill.[9]

Carlton's examination of cotton mill workers of South Carolina between 1880 and 1920 documented the steady development of a workforce with ideals and values different from the ones dominant in towns and cities of the New South. By the turn of the century, Carlton wrote, a breach "developed between mill people and town people," and "despite all the rhetorical self-assurances about white solidarity the operatives were in fact becoming a separate social class, living in sullen opposition on the outskirts of 'civilized' town society." Carlton traced the workers' concerns over social and political matters and their estrangement and defeat, arguing that the workers "lured by the prospect of a material life" had by 1920 "accepted in fact if not in principle, the industrial discipline imposed by the mill owners." Carlton contended that the workers' weaning from rural independence and self-control, the "town victory," and the grievances left unresolved in the wake of that victory explain the workers' later distrust of unions. In 1982, Carlton concluded that the "mill workers of South Carolina remain today as they have for most of the century, acquiescent but not quite willing participants in a world not of their making."[10]

The view of the cotton mill workers as people apart has been persistent if not consistent. On the one hand, industry apologists and disinterested observers alike have stressed an "Anglo-Saxon" heritage that produced individualists who believed in independence and freedom of opportunity. Their "Americanism" was seen in direct contrast with the "foreign" character of cotton textile workers in the North. In the South, claimed John Edgerton, Tennessee woolen manufacturer and president of the National Association of Manufacturers, "exotic radicalism does not thrive, for the workers of the South have a heritage of sturdy Americanism."[11] On the other hand, although American, the South's textile workers were pictured as somehow "different." The ACMA, in its official creed, stated, "Geographic location, history, environment, tradition, and notably the preponderance of the Anglo-Saxon element among those constituting the South's industrial workers, have forever decreed that the Southern ideals, management and industrial philosophy shall differ from those of other sections."[12] To Glenn Gilman, the workers' common rural traditions and their local origins made them a homogeneous, unified workforce. Gilman maintained that southern workers had many of the characteristics associated with Frederick Jackson Turner's frontiersman and that these characteristics combined with the sectionalism produced by the North-South clash to form a unique mix.[13] Whatever they were, American or indigenous southern, overwhelmingly the cotton mill workers were described as people different from their neighbors.

As the growth of the industry led to the development of a permanent population of mill laborers and rural ties loosened, the cultural gap increased between them and the other segments of southern society. Cash saw a wide gulf by the 1920s. In the Piedmont's larger towns, he wrote, a mill worker might wander the streets all day "without ever receiving a nod or a smile from anybody, or any recognition of his existence other than a scornful glance from a shop girl."[14] Even as southerners praised the industry as the New South's best hope, ironically the workers in the industry lost status. Liston Pope argued that by the 1920s three classes had emerged in Gastonia County, North Carolina—small farmers and tenant farmers; mill workers; and what he called "uptown," the mill owners, managers, professional and commercial groups, skilled artisans, school teachers, and various other white-collar groups. Even a "superficial observer" could see, he said, the demarcation of place of abode, occupation, and, ultimately, class.[15]

Dale Newman, in the 1970s, after extensive interviews in a North Carolina mill town, accepted the idea of a cotton mill class. She wrote that "three generations of employer paternalism had produced an hereditary work force of poorly educated, economically insecure and socially isolated individuals."[16] Even the farmers isolated themselves from the mill workers. In the 1950s

William Polk observed that the "Southern farmer still tends to look on himself as a better and freer man than the mill worker. . . . When poverty drives him off the land into the mill, he considers it a comedown for him to move from Tobacco Road to Mill Village; even the clodhopper looks down on the lint-dodger."[17] Not much had changed since the late nineteenth century, during which time, as McLaurin observed, "mill hands in urban mills were not accepted by the townspeople, who applied to them such epithets as 'linthead,' 'cotton-tails,' 'factory rats,' and 'cotton mill trash,'"[18] "Life in the mill village," according to Newman, "nurtured attitudes of low self-esteem and perpetrated the rigidities of the closed society. Considered and treated an inferior by society, cotton mill workers came to feel inferior."[19]

Southern mill workers were seen as peaceful and tractable. The mill worker of Alabama, wrote one student after visiting the mills in the 1920s, "is docile, well-behaved and co-operative to a large degree," a judgment cultivated by mill owners.[20] The workers were presented by southern manufacturers as echewing class strife and as manipulable and cooperative in every way.[21] Far from being stable and placid, however, they were a volatile workforce. They often had real power on the work floor. Docility, peacefulness, and tractability were not part of their folk tradition. On the work floors well-understood rules of management obtained, particularly in the etiquette of relations between second-hands (foremen) and overseers and the workers themselves.

Up to the 1920s, work discipline was more often traditional than modern and industrial. Jessie Lee Carter, interviewed in 1980, remembered that in the mills of the 1920s, "we just stopped working when we wanted to."[22] In the pre-New Deal decades, unwritten social contracts defined proper treatment of workers in terms of mutual respect, southern rural manners, worker self-identification, and the hoary tradition of owner paternalism. When such contracts were broken, the workers reacted. The history of almost every mill is replete with work stoppages and worker complaints. Mack Duncan, a loom fixer in the 1930s, recalled that though mill workers were always kind of "shy and reserved," they still "grumbled and complained" among themselves.[23] Jonathan Daniels, a sharp observer of the South, scoffed at the idea that the southern cotton mill worker was a willing tool in the hands of the owners. No-one knew the truth better than the mill owners themselves. "They know a secret," Daniels wrote, "which they have steadily and loudly denied: they know there is no dependable docility in their cousins at the looms."[24]

Southern cotton mill workers differed greatly from the official propaganda image of happy, contented workers. As low-paid, lowly-regarded industrial workers in a land of traditionally rural ways, they adhered to the old pattern of the unwritten social contracts. But at the same time, by the 1930s depression and modernization were making some of them aware of the possibilities of change. Harriet Herring believed that the workers had long suffered from a tension between traditional rural individualism and the emergent class consciousness of the mills, but that in the 1930s "certain modifications" became apparent, including a greater receptivity to labor organizations. As early as 1926, Jennings Rhyne discovered in his sample of workers that over four in ten favored unions, while only three in ten opposed them.

Paul J. Smith, chairman of the 1930 AFL organizing committee in the South, also noticed the slow awakening. Smith acknowledged that in the transformation of "an agricultural region to an industrial empire the southern worker has unquestionably accepted the doles proffered by his employer—doles of wage increases, doles of working hours, doles of working conditions." But, Smith went on, the southern worker accepted it "under a slumbering protest."[25] By the advent of the New Deal, the cotton textile workers, despite their distinctive culture and long history of separateness, had become an identifiable industrial workforce, open to unionism.

LIVING IN A PLACE APART

Heightening their sense of separation from other people, almost three of every four cotton textile workers in the early 1930s lived in company-owned housing.[26] Carlton discovered that by 1920 one-sixth of South Carolina's white population lived in mill villages.[27] The village system had its roots in the practical problems of assembling a workforce in small towns and rural places. William D. Anderson, a leading southern cotton textile manager in the 1930s, attested to its importance, declaring that "no textile development could have taken place in the South without the mill village."[28] As the workers in the transportation-poor Piedmont came to the mill, houses had to be erected in its shadow. The process of building them continued from the 1850s to the 1930s.

By the 1930s, however, controversy surrounded the villages and their role in the lives of the workers. Visiting Northern liberals saw miserable conditions. Sinclair Lewis came South in 1929 and wrote caustically of conditions he observed in Marion, North Carolina. The houses were hovels; the food meager and unnourishing; the people lean, anemic-looking, and generally unhealthy; and few community services were provided by the mills. Paul Blanchard and Myra Page produced the same bleak picture in their reports.[29] Others ridiculed the charges that mill village life was harsh and oppressive. The *Manufacturers' Record* in the mid-1920s believed the village system to be a positive good. "It would be hard," wrote the editor, "to find a more satisfied group of workers in the country than exists in the southern textile villages." Political scientist William Hays Simpson in 1941 studied many of South Carolina's mill villages and pronounced them, as he did later in a 1945 followup study of the entire South, progressive communities better off than their surrounding neighbors. If the truth were known, he said, "Life in the mill communities is usually happy, healthy, and carefree, and there are more social and recreational activities than in the non-industrial communities near by, and there is a much more finer community spirit."[30] But more impartial observers, like Jennings J. Rhyne in 1930, stressed a confusing spectrum—some villages had miserable living conditions, with shack-like housing rising crazy-quilt over the terrain, unsanitary conditions and polluted water supplies, inadequate heat, and unkempt, ugly appearances; but other villages were neat and attractive, well laid out and often landscaped, with fine weather-tight cottages provided with modern utilities, albeit depressingly alike in architecture.[31]

George Tindall argued that the "diversity of mill villages" was "above all the product of evolution." Before World War I, the villages did not have running water and plumbing, electric lights, sidewalks, and other improvements. By the 1920s and 1930s, Tindall wrote, modern conveniences had been added and many of the older and most of the new villages "were attractive and substantial indeed." He believed that "many features of the villages were highly exaggerated in the pattern of attack and defense" and subscribed to the view that even at their worst, the villages improved on the shacks in the Piedmont fields or the cabins in the hills.[32] John Van Osdell, Jr., another historian, agreed. The "later the houses were built," he wrote, "the more comfortable, attractive, and sturdy they were likely to be. To the visitor from the North the tiny mill houses, often in need of paint and balancing in typically southern style on shaky looking brick piers, seemed ugly and squalid, but to those who had known crumbling tenant shacks or log cabins whose wide chinks welcomed the wind and the rain, the mill homes seemed snug and comfortable."[33]

Martha Gelhorn, the novelist, serving in 1934 as one of Harry Hopkins' famous field reporters, visited North Carolina and South Carolina mill towns. She was shocked by disease, particularly the high incidence of syphilis, and exclaimed, "The children are growing up in terrible surroundings, dirt, disease, over-crowding, undernourishment." She thought the mill villages were miserable places, but she made it clear that they were better places than the surrounding communities. She wrote to Hopkins, "The houses in some mill villages are pretty good."[34]

The debate over village amenities can obscure the real meaning of mill village culture for the workers and for subsequent attempts at unionization. The villages, grim and monotonous to outsiders, were not alien places to the workers, but home. "For a small child," remembered an older worker, "the village was a warm and friendly place."[35] The villages created a homogeneous culture reinforced over time, a culture which Douglas DeNatale argued gave the workers "a means of dignity and control in their lives."[36] John Bodnar, after interviewing industrial workers in Pennsylvania about life in the 1930s, calls their home and family life the "enclave," the crucible in which worker culture was created.[37] Mill village life in the Piedmont generated an indigenous culture common from village to village. The fate of workers in the villages, over the years, molded a workforce of people poorly educated, economically insecure, and socially isolated. For example, before the worker entered the mills he or she averaged only eight years of education. Under 3 percent, in one study, were high school graduates in the 1920s. Even the overseers in the 1930s came from the ranks and had no higher education. Dale Newman wrote that "of one supervisor, it was joked that all he could write was: 'Hired, Fired, and K.C. [his name].'"[38]

But even living in the closed culture of the village, with its limited horizons, the workers and their families participated in many normal ways in Piedmont society. They developed extensive recreational outlets such as baseball, fishing and hunting, movie-going, and motoring; social organizations (mill village churches, lodges, and women's groups); and, above all, they enjoyed complex networks of kin and extended family activities. While the cotton mill workers were a distinctive group, they were, after all, only a subculture in the larger context of being white southern Americans of a rural tradition.[39]

The village played an important part in labor relations, particularly in times of conflict. Despite complaints about the burdens of being landlords and the lack of return on capital invested, the owners held onto the villages well after the automobile and bus brought greater mobility to their workers. In the unsettling days of 1933, the Cotton-Textile Institute formed a committee to consider the advisability of mills' selling their villages. The committee's report was terse: "It is impracticable at this time to offer any plan looking to home ownership in existing mill villages by employees." Workers, the report claimed, still needed homes close to the mills, and employees "prefer to live in houses owned by the mills."[40] Having the workers so closely concentrated increased the power of paternalistic owner practices, preferences, and cultural direction, such as it was. On the other hand, what looked like a golden target for union organizers—workers concentrated within a few blocks—often proved illusory. Organizers worked publicly when they moved through a village, their every visit known to the inhabitants and, soon enough, to the mill managers. The most potent weapon an owner had was the threat of eviction from the village; eviction meant the loss not only of roof and walls, but of the lifeblood of community as well. On balance, mill villages were a burden rather than a haven for organizers.

WORKING IN THE MILLS

Before the New Deal, work consumed half the southern cotton textile workers' day. At 5:00 A.M. in Gastonia County, North Carolina, and all over the textile belt, the mill whistles blew, and the long blasts from the different mills mingled together. It was time to get up. At 5:30 another blast punctuated the Dixie morning—twenty-five minutes until the worker had to get to the work station. At 5:45 another scream said ten minutes left. Promptly at 5:55 the fourth whistle blast signaled the foremen to start the

machines. The day's work had begun, and from a block away the mill's rum-
bling could be heard. Later, the whistle regime continued. At 12:00 the whistle
sounded, and Gastonia County's twenty five thousand textile workers left to
go to the villages to eat a hot meal. At 12:30 P.M. and again at 12:45 remind-
ers of the mill's waiting presence sounded. At 12:55 it was time to start again,
the whistle said. After an eleven-hour day in the mill, the final whistle blast
came at 6:00. On Saturday, at 11:00 A.M. the final whistle completed the sixty-
hour week. "Next day," said a textile worker in 1938, "starts like the one before and ends about the same."[41]

But work discipline and workloads as late as the 1920s and even the 1930s
were more relaxed than in modern textile plants.[42] Workers took time out
for soft drinks, conversation, and the use of snuff tins. Harry Adams, a retired
textile worker, remembered the long days and thought the work less hard
than when the eight-hour day and production standards came to the mills.
The hot noon meal at home was an attractive respite. After the modernization
drive of the late 1920s, things tightened up. One worker told this story: "In
other words, they got you so geared up so if you bring your dinner in the
morning, a fellow asks you, says, 'What you got in that bag?' You say 'my
lunch.' He says, 'Well, you better eat [it now] because you ain't going to have
time to do it after you start work.'"[43]

In short, although long, hard, and worth complaining about, the work day,
to Piedmont mill hands surrounded by farmers who worked from sunup to
sundown, seemed bearable if not desirable. Betty Davidson of Burlington,
North Carolina, recalled that though you had to "get production" in the 1930s,
you were not pushed "like they are now." Vernon Cooper of Bynum, North
Carolina, recalled years afterward that the move from the sixty-hour week to
the New Deal's eight-hour day "was like you was on a vacation."[44] And the
sixty-hour week itself was not steady. Absenteeism ran high, as much as forty
or fifty days a year per worker. In the summer many of the mills worked on
a four-day schedule.

In the mills, the southern workers were unskilled or semiskilled machine
tenders. One worked on a picker, a card machine, a slubber or stripper, a
spinning frame, or a loom. Many of the jobs were interchangeable; about half
required nothing but picking up and carrying the product from machine to
machine. Spinning, spooling, and doffing could be learned in a few days,
though proficiency in spinning could take longer. Weaving, winding, and
beaming could take weeks to acquire proficiency. Loom-fixing, the aristocratic
job, also required a long learning process, mostly rote learning. The Bureau
of Labor Statistics in the 1930s considered anyone who tended a machine to
be semiskilled, but William D. Anderson of the Bibb Manufacturing Company in Georgia argued passionately to his fellow manufacturer, Robert R.
West of Dan River Mills, that textile workers were menial laborers and not
skilled workers. Anderson wrote: "No education is required. No training course
is necessary. No technical qualifications are demanded. Nothing is required

but reasonable intelligence, good health, and a reasonable complement of physical equipment. You can take a young woman or young man off the milker's stool or away from the hoe or from between the plow handles — and make a good textile worker out of them in a few weeks."[45] Glenn Gilman believed that "better than 84 of every 100 textile workers are aware of the fact that they can be replaced by others with little or no training."[46]

In the late 1940s, some workers described a mill as the "deathhole" or the "sweatshop."[47] Noise drove some workers out after the first day. The noise of a loom room was literally deafening; to be heard one had to shout close to an ear. Some workers reported that to communicate they learned to lip read. The mills, which had to have steam humidifiers to make the cotton work better through the machines, in the 1930s worked with the windows closed and sometimes painted blue (they are bricked over now). The mills were suffocatingly hot in summer and uncomfortably warm in winter. The workers complained of dust in the opening and carding rooms and lint in the spinning and weaving rooms, a lint that filled the air and covered everything so that cleaners and sweepers had to be constantly at work to keep the machines moving. Even today, with modern air intake systems and with air conditioning, which came to the mills in the 1950s and 1960s, many cotton mills have difficulty meeting air pollution standards.[48] The mills, old even by the 1930s, had been surrounded by fences in the 1920s and, with their two or three stories of red bricks, looked like fortresses or prisons. The gates were shut after workers entered, and gatehouses controlled access. Inside, worker facilities such as toilets, lounges, food, and refreshment stands were primitive.

The work itself did not — except in some ending processes of finishing, cutting, and packaging — consist of endless, quick, repetitive motions done at a workbench. The workers in weaving, spinning, carding, and warping controlled the machines they operated. The worker's pace of work was controlled as much by the number of machines he or she had to tend as by the speed of the machines themselves. Weavers, for example, spent at least 50 percent of their time "patroling" or moving over a large space to observe the looms and attend to ones that needed attention. They had time for quick breaks if the machines were working well. The same was true for spinners. Workers did not control the workplace, but every mill reached an accomodation of the pace of work to both worker and owner expectations, or else trouble arose.[49] Worker dissatisfaction in the 1930s centered around disruption of the traditional work standards that the waves of industrial efficiency engineering, inspired by hard times and modernization, brought to the mills.

The workers believed in the worth and dignity of their labor. Betty Donaldson of Burlington, North Carolina, said of her work in the 1930s: "I enjoy weaving. I always enjoyed my job. I always enjoyed working . . . you always enjoy watching a loom run — that's when you're making money." Zelma Montgomery Murray of Burlington, North Carolina, began spinning in 1922 and recalled: "I loved my job over there." Terrie Dyer of Charlotte, North Carolina, who went to work in the Highland Park Mill in 1926, said: "I really did enjoy my working in the draw-in room." Mack Duncan went to work in 1931 and in 1979 still claimed: "I enjoy weaving."[50] Douglas DeNatale discovered that older workers in Bynum, North Carolina, had the same sentiments, and he argued that the satisfaction from working in the mill was part of the cultural process of worker identification of "common interest."[51] Edna Hargett claimed workers in the Highland Park Mill of Charlotte, North Carolina, in the 1930s had "comradeship we don't have now." The most common remembrance of older cotton mill workers is, "We were like one big family."[52]

In 1899 women workers constituted approximately 33 percent of the workforce. This proportion declined until 1914, when it started to rise again; by 1930 approximately 38 percent of the workers in southern cotton mills were women, and 36 percent in 1936.[53] The number of women in the industry began to increase thereafter; by the mid-1970s they constituted 47 percent of the workers.[54] The women worked predominantly in the most unskilled or easily-learned jobs, such as spinning, spool winding, and burling, or cloth inspection. Although women worked as weavers, they tended to fill the jobs that required less lifting and hauling. They almost completely took over repetitive cutting and packaging jobs.[55] Women worked for less pay and at less prestigious jobs than men. In 1925, for example, male mill workers in Alamance County, North Carolina, averaged $3.91 per day while female workers made only $2.48. In 1937, throughout the South, skilled women workers, principally weavers, received 42.49 cents an hour compared to the males' 49.26 cents per hour.[56]

Because of the demands of childcare and home-making, women tended to drop in and out of the mills even more than males, and when they worked they still carried the burden of doing most of the work at home as well. But despite the greater passivity and indifference to unions attributed to women, they acted much in concert with their husbands, children, and other male kin in labor disputes.[57] The male-dominated union organization made little use of female organizers, and in the 1930s throughout the industry a gender-specific policy existed that included protective labor laws and restrictive job assignments. Some mills would hire no women for the third or even second shifts.

The employment of children under the age of sixteen, who in 1899 had made up fully one-quarter of all workers, steadily declined, particularly after 1914. In 1914, child labor accounted for 15 percent of the total workforce, but in 1930 only 3.8 percent of the workers employed in the mills of the South were children, although 20 percent of the workforce was under twenty years old.[58] Many southern cotton manufacturers had fought a proposed child labor amendment to the Constitution, engendering much bitterness, and this past opposition was well remembered by the critics of the industry's labor policy.[59] Eventually the Fair Labor Standards Act would end child labor, but by 1931 all southern states prohibited factory work for children under fourteen, and night labor and more than an eight-hour day for all under sixteen.[60] More importantly, in the industry the profitability of child labor had declined. Claudius Murchison, an industry spokesman, said in 1936, "No cotton-millman wants to employ under sixteen. Every cotton-millman knows that employment of people under sixteen is a losing proposition."[61] Child labor was not a problem that New Deal labor policy had to attack.

Hourly earnings, fulltime weekly earnings, and average yearly earnings in southern cotton mills were at all times before and during the New Deal years much lower than the averages in all manufacturing industries in the U.S., though they exceeded those of farm labor or independent farmers in the Piedmont. In hourly earnings in 1930, cotton manufacturing was at the very bottom of the scale of major industries.[62] Wage rates varied slightly by states. In 1930, Alabama cotton textile workers averaged twenty-six cents per hour, Georgia workers twenty-seven cents, and South Carolina workers twenty-eight cents, while North Carolina workers, at thirty cents, were the best paid.[63] Many workers, of course, received less than these average wages. Only a few workers enjoyed steady employment; the result was low annual earnings. In the 1920s in North Carolina, the highest paying state, a textile worker's annual wage was only about half of the National Industrial Conference Board's "Minimum American Standard" for an adequate living standard.[64] In March 1928, Professor G. Croft Williams of the University of South Carolina prepared a monthly minimum budget for a family of five in Columbia, South Carolina, a budget which he called "hardly more than a barracade to keep out the wolf of starvation." It came to $90.81. But no ordinary textile worker could make that much, and in fact wages in Columbia's sixty-seven manufacturing establishments of all kinds averaged only $75.28 a month.[65] Only by the decades-old family wage system of the cotton textile industry did workers and their families survive.

Cotton mill owners or spokespersons worked intensely to justify these low wages. Claudius Murchison explained in 1936, "A great majority of the southern workers were agricultural workers and they regarded themselves lucky if they got as much as a dollar a day." The people welcomed a wage "that is substantially above what the people in that community have received" in the past. "The justification for that wage," he testified before Congress, "does not lie in its relationship to what is being paid in other parts of the world. It lies in its relationship to what exists in that community."[66] William D. Anderson, the Georgia manufacturer, quite simply attributed the low wages to the unskilled nature of the work. The "uninformed public," he said, should not class cotton textile workers with machinists, carpenters, plumbers, bricklayers, or steel workers, all of whom underwent apprenticeship or technical education. "Those of us in the business," he said, "know that we can take a young man or young woman from the cotton field and make a satisfactory textile worker in six to eight weeks." "They earn," he declared, "an honest living and they have had a good roof over their heads and have not suffered for fuel, food, or clothing."[67] Donald Comer of Alabama's Avondale Mills agreed. A mill worker, he wrote, could make "more money than the farm boy or girl right at his door can make working from sunup to sundown six days a week."[68] The *Textile Bulletin* argued that, on a basis of value added, "the worker in no other industry receives so great a share of the value." The magazine compared the 1929 value-added figure of $1,473 in cotton textiles to $5,000 per worker in the sugar industry, whose workers received only $532 more a year than textile workers.[69]

Though the unions in the 1930s worked hard for wage increases, in truth, the pressure from cotton textile workers themselves was not intense. The workers protested wage cuts more often than organizing for wage increases. They wanted to protect the status quo. A. Steve Nance, the leader of the Deep South textile union movement in 1937, in a frank interview with Jonathan Daniels, acknowledged this embarrassing fact. He agreed that the workers had not rushed to join marches for higher pay. He told Daniels: "But even if the workers get only $5 a week that's almost riches to people whole sole family cash income has been only $200 a year. And what should I say about long hours to people who have worked from 'kin to cain't' from the earliest they see in the fields till the time when they can't see at all."[70]

Even the sixty-hour week represented improvement to workers with memories. In 1900, mill workers had labored from sixty-three to seventy-five hours per week, with an average close to sixty-nine. By the early 1930s, South Carolina had established a law limiting regular hours to ten a day and weekend hours to fifty-five. In the mid-1920s, the mill owners themselves reduced hours in sporadic attempts to cut production, so that in the South the average work week on the immediate eve of the New Deal was around fifty-five hours per week.[71] Even that, of course, pressed workers, and the union appeal in the 1930s for regulated workloads and shorter hours addressed the core of worker discontent more than the call for higher wages.

John Bodnar's observation, after interviewing industrial workers in Pennsylvania's factories in the 1930s, about the relation of their culture to protest, unionization, and change applies as well to southern cotton textile workers.[72] Bodnar argued that the workers he interviewed "sought security and survival through kinship ties, job structures, and community relationships" and created a world "which has largely remained hidden from generations of American labor historians who have been preoccupied with strikes, the rise of trade unionism, and, recently, the struggle for control of the workplace." Hidden from scholars too much taken by economic pragmatism, social idealism, and middle-class aspiration, the Pennsylvania workers' world "was influenced with values and patterns that influenced not only their day-to-day existence," but the "ultimate nature" of their protests. Bodnar believed that "deeply conservative tendencies pervaded the American working classes well before the labor unrest of the 1930s." The workers in the 1930s wanted to "preserve what was familiar."[73]

Many southern cotton mill workers, too, assessed with considerable intelligence the means of survival and adaptation in their world. They had a fundamental sense of realism and pragmatism, and an essential conservatism that came from marginal living.

John Kenneth Moreland, an anthropologist, lived for a year, 1948–49, in a small Piedmont textile town called Kent. The town consisted of four mills served by four villages inhabited by close to fifteen hundred workers. Defining a typical mill worker's personality, Moreland wrote, "He accepts life as he finds it, and is not aggressive in seeking to change his condition." The people of Kent, to Moreland, lacked confidence and were cautious, noncompetitive, anxious, repressed, hostile to strangers, and, in the end, a puzzle in their deep resistance to change.[74] Robert Blauner, in a much later study of textile workers, reported that 84 percent believed that the mills were a good place to work. But textile workers, despite their job satisfaction, Blauner's wrote, felt powerlessness, meaninglessness, and self-estrangement, and had low aspirations for improvement of their lives. Only in the concrete reality of "family" religion, and community" did the textile workers overcome alienation.[75]

Southern mill workers saw problems through the prism of their time and place, and unionism represented a real threat to the village and mill status quo. Hamilton Basso in his 1935 novel *In Their Image*, set in Aiken, South Carolina, included scenes of the 1934 strike. Basso portrayed the cotton mill workers as passive, afraid of change, and fearful of risking what little they had by joining a union.[76] The workers in the 1930s would use unionism more as a lightning rod than as a new refuge. They knew who had power. One cotton textile worker realist, who was fired and blacklisted for heading the union in Greensboro, North Carolina, in 1930, knew that he had made a major decision when he joined the union: "I came to the crossroads when I was eighteen, and I took the road that led me to the mill. I came to the crossroads again when I was fifty-one, and I took the road that caused me to be kicked out of the mill and onto the farm again." A fellow realist, who worked at the Cone mill in Greensboro, made just the opposite decision: "No, sir," she said, "no union for me . . . the Cones is still totin' the keys to the mill."[77]

SUMMER CLOUDS: UNIONISM BEFORE THE NEW DEAL

Despite the culture-imposed barriers, four distinct cyles of union activity had occurred in the southern cotton textile industry before 1933. In the mid-1880s the Knights of Labor organized workers, particularly in South Carolina. The high tide of this surge was a losing 1886 strike against several mills in Augusta, Georgia. By 1888 the Knights' locals were dormant everywhere.[78] In a second cycle of unionism, an AFL union, the National Union of Textile Workers (NUTW) in the late 1890s created over fifty southern locals with as many as 5,000 members (6 percent of the workforce), but it faded away in 1900 when it lost major strikes in North Carolina, Virginia, and, again, at Augusta, Georgia.

Amidst the wreckage of the NUTW, the AFL formed the United Textile Workers (UTW), which quickly foundered in 1902 in yet another strike in Augusta, Georgia.[79] This defeat of unionism, following a decade after the Knights' earlier attempt, had disastrous consequences. "Southern workers," Dennis R. Noland and Donald E. James argued, "learned not to rely on the UTW or, indeed, or any union. Employers became convinced that a firm stand would break a strike, and UTW leaders learned to avoid involvement in Southern disputes."[80] The UTW, even in its northern base, represented less than 3 percent of all textile workers in America.[81]

The UTW again came South in the World War I era, 1914 to 1921. But despite a small victory here and there, the southern push failed to bring permanent unionism, and the recession of 1921 forced the AFL to abandon its crucial financial support. The claimed membership of forty to fifty thousand workers in the southern locals disappeared. John Van Osdell, Jr., wrote that the workers who had gone on strike crept back "not chastened but outraged, bitterness against the union rankling in their breasts."[82]

The most celebrated years, though, were 1929–31, when the South was shaken by a series of strikes. In a few weeks in March and April, 1929, large-scale strikes broke out in four widely separated places: in Tennessee at Elizabethton; in Ware Shoals and Marion, South Carolina; and in Gastonia, North Carolina, one of the leading centers of the cotton manufacturing industry. Many other strikes and disputes followed. Large groups of pickets clashed with strikebreakers, national guardsmen, and special mill police forces. Communities divided, and in some cases hysteria gripped the South.[83] Eight people died in clashes. But the mills soon reopened, and place by place the workers went back to work, although walkouts and strikes continued in the region during 1930. The cycle ended with a dramatic strike at Danville, Virginia, that began in September 1930 and ended with a UTW defeat in January 1931.[84]

Although the UTW claimed that it had signed fifty thousand workers into its locals, the only tangible gains were in South Carolina, where some workers received a 5 percent wage increase and the fifty-five-hour week. Only a few dedicated unionists remained in the southern mills. Most of the mills and workers were untouched by the strikes and never saw a labor organizer.[85]

Irving Bernstein argued that although the 1929–31 upheaval was a "revolt in the Piedmont," the millhands, the mill owners, mill village culture, the textile depression, and union weakness defeated the unexpected revolution.[86] Another historian, John Van Osdell, Jr., also saw it as a failure: "After nearly two years of intermittent struggle the great Piedmont revolt came to an end, its dismal history unenlivened by a single union victory; its only apparent accomplishment a reinforcement of the southern antipathy toward labor organizations; its gains for the union-led strikers at individual mills almost too negligible to be mentioned." But to Van Osdell, the effort was "not that of a desperate attempt by a long-suffering working class to throw off the heavy weight of an oppressive industrial system encrusted with stale tradition, but almost precisely the opposite." The owners had broken faith and trust as they modernized in response to changing conditions in the industry, and "the millhands rose in order to force their employers to return to the old, tradition-sanctioned ways."[87] Ray Marshall concurred: "The spontaneous strikes which swept the South in 1929 were not signs that the southern workers were ready to join unions to improve their conditions; they were acts of desperation to prevent the worsening of conditions which . . . were improvements for workers recently removed from marginal agriculture."[88]

The owners, pressed by hard times, had neglected the work floors. A widening gulf between workers and bosses," George Tindall wrote of the 1920s strikes, "increased the sense of alienation."[89] Scientific management had arrived. Time experts had entered the mills and speeded up the work processes. The stretch out, as the workers called it, had come. Gustav T. Schwenning, an economist living in the North Carolina textile belt, wrote in 1931 that "it seems clear . . . that wage reduction and the introduction of the so-called stretch out system were the fundamental causes of the series of labor disturbances, rather than a concentrated determination on the part of southern textile employees to exercise their right of collective bargaining."[90] Another objective contemporary academic observer, Benjamin U. Ratchford, argued that the "fundamental cause" of the Gastonia strike was the attempt to impose New England efficiencies on southern workers.[91] Just before the strikes, in many places in the South wages were slashed and workers put on "short time." In Bernard Cone's three Greensboro mills, where he regarded unions as "harbingers of evil," in 1930 union members were fired, denounced, and evicted from company houses. Workers could not subscribe to the supposedly prolabor Raleigh *News and Observer.* And the workers worked only a three-day week for six to eleven dollars. A weaver with twenty-eight years of experience in the Cone Mills saw little hope. It seemed to him he said, "that I could look out there in the years and see the awful misery ahead for working people. Thousands throwed out of jobs and the rest drove like machines till they died before their life was half over."[92] Reaction, not advocacy, marked the so-called "revolt in the Piedmont."

After the 1929–31 cycle, the UTW retreated once again to its northern base. The southern workers had conformed to the modern social science contention that people join movements not because they are alienated, deprived, or frustrated, although they might be that, but in terms of what it costs to join and what they can get out of doing so.[93] In the late 1920s most workers had not taken the risk of joining unions. W.J. Cash, describing labor relations in the 1920s, wrote of "a broad calm on all fronts . . . a calm broken now and then, to be sure, but broken only as the surface of a great pool is broken by vagrant raindrops from a distant summer cloud."[94]

Unions were anathema to the owners. Just before the New Deal, Bernard Cone, a veteran cotton textile entrepreneur, expressed the owner attitude characteristic of the staunch antiunionism of most American businessmen. "I am so old-fashioned," Cone told a North Carolina business professor, "that I believe a man who is fortunate enough to have acquired or built a cotton mill, in this free country of ours, has the right to say in the first place, whether he will run it or not; in the second place to invite other free men to come and work in his mill at prices he feels he can afford or is willing to pay." The employee, emphasized Cone, should be free to refuse the job and wage, but "if after accepting it, he becomes dissatisfied with the terms . . . let him quit. Let him go elsewhere and seek another job more to his liking. Do not let him stand at the mill door and seek by violence to keep others from working who want to work and are satisfied with the terms."[95] Robert R. West, president of the Dan River Mills, in 1936 forcefully denounced collective bargaining. He believed that individual bargaining or, as he called it, "rugged individualism" was the American way.[96]

The industry's arguments against unionism can be examined in microcosm and vivid detail in the surviving transcript of a mass meeting of workers and officers of the Bibb Manufacturing Company called for Mill Number One in East Macon, Georgia, on June 20, 1933. The meeting was arranged to address rumors that the UTW might be trying to organize at the Bibb. The first speaker was the factory manager, H.W. Pittman. He reminded the workers of all the "social service activities" that the "Bibb Family," the company, had given to them, as well as of "the fine spirit that prevails throughout our village and community." But, he told the assembled workers, "It has come to our attention and we have noticed in the newspapers that there is a plan on foot to kindly break into our big Bibb family." Pittman told the workers "that a Textile Union here would do nothing for our people that they would not have and what they cannot get without it." The doors to management were always open, he said, and "when a man is born into the Bibb family or becomes connected with the Bibb family they have all the rights and privileges that anyone should want or should ask for." It would "break the hearts of the officers of this company" for the union to "break up that close fellowship" of worker and officers. Pittman was followed by James Porter, vice-president of the Bibb, who reminded the workers that "you do not have to join, you do not have to do anything. All you have to do is ask for employment, we will give it to you and if you have grievances you come up and state it. . . . There is no reason in the world why our people should get into a mess of this kind."[97]

Southern cotton textile management reacted violently and quickly to the unionization of their workers. Many people thought the southern owners unique in their intense "determination to keep out labor unions at all costs."[98] Professor Gustav T. Schwenning of the University of North Carolina found them "to be obsessed with the idea that the economic rehabilitation of the South was accomplished in large measure because the region was unhampered by unionism."[99] Solomon Barkin of the TWUA also described the southern textile employer as a "case unto himself" and maintained that the South was utterly "blind" to the advantages of strong unions.[100] Rep. Kent Keller, a Democrat from Illinois, reporting on hearings for federal regulation of the textile industry, concluded that southern mill owners were more obstinate in their refusal to bargain than their counterparts in the North and East.[101]

The vast majority of southern mill employers had no experience with unionism and collective bargaining. Management was close and personal. As late as 1939, a survey showed that few mills even had a professional personnel manager; only 7.7 percent maintained a specific employment department. The southern cotton textile managers stood staunchly against unions at the beginning of the New Deal, and few in the 1930s changed their basic belief that unions were inimical to the southern mills and the old order of things. They saw the establishment of the union as a fundamental threat to the social structure of the Piedmont and the villages. To embrace unionism was to embrace the whole complexity of industrial society and to destroy the southern "garden of innocence." To accept the union as an agency mediating between owner and worker would have been to admit that communications had broken down; it would have meant that the southern worker was dissatisfied and that charges of exploitation were true.[102]

Southern communities held deeply antiunion ideals and often frustrated the union organizers as much as the owners themselves did. Dr. Witherspoon Dodge, the Textile Workers Organizing Committee's preacher-organizer, in a moment of such frustration in 1939, cried out: "The South, geographically and physically speaking, is a part of the United States of America. Socially speaking, it is separated considerably from the rest of the country by mountains of pride and rivers of prejudice and valleys of ignorance and swamps of reactionary stupidity and every now and then washed out with floods of lawlessness."[103] The industry and the community were tied closely together in the small towns. The belief that the industry in some way "belonged" to the community was a part of the cotton mill campaign myth, vestiges of which remained alive. Public sentiment against the dangers of disrupting the economic life of the community by disrupting the mill was often overpowering. The mills often exerted complete control over the communities. *Fortune* described Kannapolis, North Carolina, a town composed of fifteen thousand inhabitants and completely owned by Cannon Mills, as a "medieval city" standing "aloof and self-controlled in the midst of empty country, suspicious of all strangers, loyal to its feudal lords."[104]

With economic control came the mills' domination of residents' words and ideals. Local merchants and professional people were happy to accept the economic and social philosophies of the companies that operated the mills. The local newspaper, radio station, and civic and fraternal organizations readily agreed with the mills' antiunion policies. Local government officials such as police chiefs, sheriffs, and judges often served as unofficial adjuncts of the textile management. The union's Dr. Dodge, who had been beaten in Augusta, Georgia, called the officers of the law in mill towns "impure, contaminated, totally corrupted, hermetically sealed, contemptible hypocrites and stooges of the corporation."[105] When conflict came, a community could be torn apart, taking sides for or against the union. But more often the community remained either hostile to the workers, neutral or, at best, vaguely supportive of the workers without supporting the unions.[106]

The religious tradition of the mill communities also often acted to reinforce owner opposition to the union. Many of the workers belonged to more fundamentalist congregations, which preached salvation in the world to come and a fatalistic acceptance of the world around them as only a temporary travail.[107] Union men and women claimed that the relationship between owners and churches was diabolical and that mill owners used money and theology to attack unions. James Johnson, a UTW organizer, said that, in several mill towns as late as 1936, if a worker did not go to church on Sunday, he or she did not go to work on Monday.[108] Although Liston Pope, in his book on religion and community in the cotton mill town of Gastonia, North Carolina, understood relationships between church and workplace as a complex intermingling of owners, town, workers, and competing denominations, he agreed that some mill owners controlled mill-town churches and used the churches subtly to expand their powers.[109]

Dale Newman discovered a mill village in which the Baptist church "was an important instrument of social control." The mill superintendent was superintendent of the Sunday school, chairman of the board of deacons, chairman of the pulpit committee, and church treasurer. He advised the minister in the mid-1930s to "save souls and not to deal in problems that were none of his business."[110] Nevertheless, the use of religion was always a two-edged sword. The union often used the churches as refuge and support.

PATERNALISM

Paternalism appeared to the owners as the natural and healthy alternative to unionism. The mill owners had grown up using paternalistic management techniques derived from the mills' early history. They accepted as "perfectly normal and natural" the idea that they had a duty to care for low-income workers.[112] In the 1950s, Gerald Johnson argued that early cotton textile paternalism had been a necessity as the workers came from farms to machinery and village life, and that paternalism often reflected genuine conviction and good will on the part of the owners.[113] Captain Ellison A. Smythe, a noted South Carolina owner, recalled in 1938, when he was ninety, that in the early years paternalism had been necessary because the employees "were largely illiterate and helpless." Smythe, however, believed that modern conditions had made paternalism obsolete and that it had no place in the industry in 1938.[114]

Many of the second and third generations of mill executives in the 1930s disagreed with Smythe. They would not accept the thesis that the relation of management to labor should be only contractual and not paternal. Like their fathers and grandfathers, they announced their firm belief that the mill owners had, by their enterprise and managerial skills, saved thousands of workers from starving, degraded lives. They still, at least in public rhetoric, believed it was their duty to minister to the workers in small individual ways.

Fuller E. Callaway, founder of Callaway Mills, expressed it best when he claimed that his business was making American citizens and running cotton mills was a way to pay the expenses of this process.[115] *Cotton*, a trade journal, captured this spirit in its praise of the Bibb Manufacturing Company of Georgia, a chain of eight plants employing seventy-five hundred workers. The Bibb "family," as the journal reported the company liked to be called, was "famous for its modern practices, its villages, its progressive, sensible program of social service work and religious activities." Bibb's president, William Anderson was, the journal said, called the "Bishop of Georgia" and manifested "a deep, abiding concern for the enrichment of the lives of the thousands dependent upon the concerns which he and his associates direct, for their spiritual, intellectual, and mental development."[116] Donald Comer, the Alabama manufacturer, asserted in a 1960 interview that his greatest pleasure and sense of accomplishment had come from his involvement in what some called paternalism. He was proud that textile workers were no longer called "lint heads" and that the Avondale Mills' aggressive welfare program had helped to destroy that image.[117]

Most paternalistic programs produced much less benefit to the workers than promised and had less impact on the workers' real beliefs than owners hoped for. By the 1930s, although the programs perpetuated themselves and owners vociferously defended them, they were little more than another management tool: a happy work force meant better production and higher profits. Paternalism was not even as widespread as is usually thought. Harriet Herring's study of welfare work in the 1920s revealed that in the mills she gathered evidence from in North Carolina, many owners contributed to village churches, but far fewer employed community workers or had health clinics and group insurance plans. And only a small group still contributed to mill community schools.[118] Profit had long ago replaced philanthropy.

Paternalism differed from place to place, as different accomodations had been arrived at. Harry Boyte, interested in class analysis, argued that the long history of paternalism was no less than the long history of successful class exploitation. Paternalism over the decades had been "an elaborate system of relationships which preserved the illusion of the white workers' independence while in reality it maintained brutal control over all aspects of workers' lives." Paternalism, he contended, truncated workers' "independence and integrity" and gave them no "social terrain" to establish an "autonomous consciousness."[119] "The consequence of paternalism," wrote George Tindall, "was often an atmosphere of despotism."[120]

Such views do not fully take into account the workers' ability to use paternalism for their own benefit. The paternalistic ethos was so ingrained in the industry by the 1930s that it had become commonplace to worker and owner alike. Owners expected to have to do something extra. Workers expected the perquisites of paternalism at whatever level these had been delivered in the past. Workers were not without some power, nor were they always unwitting victims of paternalistic practices. DeNatale wrote that the communal ethos which emerged in the villages "could not strike at the central economic relationship between management and workers, but it did allow workers to define the paternalistic relationship in their own terms. The mill workers' folk culture activity mitigated some of the consequences of their position and constituted a psychological resistance to their situation."[121]

By the New Deal, paternalism faced frequent criticism. Virginius Dabney, a liberal journalist, attacked it and believed that it had outlived its usefulness.[122] Charles Gulick, an economist, wrote in 1930 that fifty years constituted "a sufficiently long period for the social subsidy" and that it was high time that southern workers attained not the paternalistic crumb but a "satisfactory plane of living, adequate educational opportunities, and a reasonable degree of participation in determining the conditions of their employment."[123] In 1937–39, economist Frank DeVyver, visited sixty-six representative mill villages in the Carolinas' textile district. He concluded that the trend was towards "the elimination of what might be called unessential yet expensive phases of welfare programs." but that "considerable" programs such as kindergartens, night schools, health services, bonuses, and Christmas presents, although decreased, remained. The trend, though, was to "leaving welfare or community work to mill officials or individuals and to people themselves." DeVyver wrote: "Paternalism is yet by no means a decadent institution among southern mills. It is, however, declining in vigor and there are indications that it is gradually disappearing in the same manner as seventy-five years ago in New England."[124]

This proved to be only half true. Solomon Barkin, research economist for the Textile Workers Union of America, reflected on the changes in paternalism which had begun to appear in the 1930s and called them only a "humanistic" approach that encouraged loyalty to the company and wove the workers into "the employers' social and economic fabric."[125] To some, the alternative to paternalism was a contractual relationship achieved by collective bargaining; faced with this alternative, mill owners, rather than junking paternalism, kept and modernized it as yet another cudgel in the struggle against the New Deal labor revolution.

"I had no hand in making up this code"
BARGAINING IN WASHINGTON, 1933

On 27 June 1933, in the auditorium of Herbert Hoover's Commerce Building, began the first flight of the Blue Eagle, soon to be the crest of the National Recovery Administration (NRA). NRA administrator Hugh Johnson had assembled a star cast for the New Deal show. William L. Allen, the deputy administrator, ostensibly served as chair, but the ebullient Johnson took center stage at a huge "partnership table." Behind Johnson sat members of three advisory groups—industry, labor, and consumer. Many of them, if not the ignored consumer representatives, were well-known people. Such eminent businessmen as Walter C. Teagle of Standard Oil; Alfred P. Sloan, Jr., of General Motors; and Gerard Swope of General Electric had come to listen and advise. Frances Perkins, secretary of labor, was there, as well as William Green of the AFL and John Lewis of the United Mine Workers.[1] Before the stage "sat hundreds of perspiring industrialists, flanked by the press" in a scene, said a textile journal, as "dramatic as was the event itself."[2] The mood was almost festive, as industrialists and labor leaders smiled "at each other across the rostrum in apparent recognition of a common problem and a common goal."[3] They were there to hammer out the first code to be established by the National Industrial Recovery Act (NIRA), that of the cotton textile industry.

Confusing negotiations and countervailing power had brought this group of odd bedfellows together. In the first weeks of his administration, President Roosevelt had avoided the sticky problem of industrial revitalization. He had, to be sure, talked to various people and vaguely commissioned inquiries into possible schemes of action. He asked Sen. Robert Wagner of New York to look into plans for business self-government under federal regulation, and New York banker James Warburg had been approached to gather ideas. But nothing happened, and by early April 1933 the President was still without any plan in mind. Roosevelt soon would be forced to do something.

On 21 December 1932 Sen. Hugo Black of Alabama introduced a bill to prohibit interstate shipment of goods produced by workers working more than thirty hours a week. Black and his supporters believed the plan would force employers to hire more workers; he predicted that the bill would put six million people back to work, provide a permanent solution to technological unemployment, and by creating new aggregate purchasing power, end the depression.[4] Labor leaders flocked to support the bill, as the AFL made it the centerpiece of its recovery program. Thomas McMahon, president of the UTW, testified on behalf of the bill, arguing that it would bring "stability out of present chaos."[5] On 6 April 1933 the Roosevelt administration faced an unexpected problem when, by a thunderous majority of fifty-three to thirty, the Senate passed the Black bill. As historian William Leuchtenburg put it, FDR, "who believed that the Black bill was unconstitutional, that it was inflexible, and that it would retard recovery, was stung to action."[6] The NIRA would come out of the administration's stepped-up search for an alternative to the Black bill.

The NIRA represented the thoughts of many people, welded together by a fast-working committee. Three groups, of varied business and government background — some of whom had been at work before the pressures of the Black bill moved FDR to action — worked independently. By early May, there were as many ideas as there were advisors; various people supported centralized national planning, business rationalization through self-governing by business groups, economic stimulation by massive public works spending, and acceptance of the Black ideal of wage and hour regulation. On 10 May 1933, impatient himself and pressured by the Black bill, Roosevelt issued his famous order that the drafting committee he had appointed lock itself in a room until it could come out with a single proposal. But the effort took longer than the few more hours Roosevelt had anticipated. Two groups — one led by Hugh Johnson, whose original page-and-a-half draft proposal had grown bulkier; and the other led by Senator Wagner — argued back and forth over the labor provisions, the role of the public works program, and congressional delegation of economic power to the President. Finally, on May 15, the drafting committee produced a bill which historian Bernard Bellush called "a crazy patchwork quilt of confusing ideas."[7] Business leaders got self-regulation and the suspension of antitrust laws through the code system; national planners thought they had achieved their goal through the creation of the National Recovery Administration; and labor, mostly through the efforts of Senator Wagner and the input of some labor economists, got Section 7(a) and minimum wage and maximum hours. The bill also had a public works section which would initially appropriate $3.3 billion.

The pressures on the drafting committee persisted in the congressional debate, and while the bill passed the House easily, 325–76, some Senate members opposed the grant of power to the President as well as the suspension of antitrust laws. After an intense debate, the bill, with a few insignificant changes, passed narrowly, 46–39. Roosevelt signed the bill on June 16, describing it as the "most important and far-reaching legislation ever enacted by the American Congress."[8] *Textile World*, a major journal of the textile industry, shared the President's sense of the importance of the act, telling its readers that "no piece of legislation passed within our memory has been fraught with more significance, or has promised to make more history, than the National Industrial Recovery Act."[9]

Title One of the NIRA propelled the cotton textile industry to Washington. Under Title One's sweeping grant of power, the President established the NRA on 20 June 1933 with Hugh Johnson as administrator. The NRA's purpose was clear — to promote self-rule of industry under federal supervision, to control overproduction, to increase wages and control the hours of labor, and to stabilize and then to raise prices. The NRA was to accomplish these goals through the creation of codes of fair competition which would govern whole industries or trades. The trade practices established by the codes would have the force of law, and infractions could be punished by the federal courts. All the codes had to be approved by the President, and when so approved would set the standards of fair competition for the industry. Any actions taken in compliance with a code were exempt from the antitrust laws. Although the act said almost nothing about what the codes should contain, it did specify that every code had to contain Section 7(a), the NIRA labor provisions, and that every code should set maximum hours and minimum wage provisions. The President could cancel or modify a code at any time.[10] Code-making began when an industry or trade association group which the NRA judged sufficiently representative submitted a proposed code to the NRA. After sufficient preliminary meetings of the NRA staff and industry representatives, and the input of NRA's three advisory boards — the Industrial Advisory Board, the Consumer's Advisory Board, and the Labor Advisory Board — a public hearing was held, after which Hugh Johnson submitted the code, intact or amended by the process, to the President for approval, modification, or rejection. By spring 1935 this system had produced 546 codes of fair competition and 185 supplemental codes, covering some twenty-two million workers and filling thirteen thousand pages in eighteen volumes.[11]

The first step in the emergence of a national collective bargaining policy was Section 7(a) of the NIRA. It provided that each code of fair competition should guarantee that "employees shall have the right to organize and bargain collectively through representatives of their own choosing," that "no employee and no-one seeking employment shall be required as a condition of employment to join any organization or to refrain from joining a labor organization of his own choosing," and that "employers shall comply with the maximum hours labor, minimum rate of pay, and other conditions approved or prescribed by the President." Section 7(a), built on the experiences of the War Labor Board of World War I, had survived the business drafts through the efforts of Senator Wagner. "At one point," wrote his biographer, J. Joseph

Huthmacher, Wagner had to deliver an ultimatum: "No 7(a), no bill." Historian Frank Freidel believed that Section 7(a) went farther than FDR and Perkins had really envisioned and that they had not meant to send such strong signals to organized labor. Roosevelt inclined more toward nineteenth-century paternalism than unionism. William Leuchtenburg argued, "Essentially a 'patron' of labor, Roosevelt had far more interest in developing social legislation to help the workers than in seeing those gains secured through unions"; the details of collective bargaining "vexed him."[12] But despite the howls of protest from the business community against Section 7(a), FDR remained neutral and deflected the attacks on the NIRA in the name of the national emergency.[13]

Labor leaders, virtually frozen out of the hasty and confused process that had produced the NIRA, embraced Section 7(a) as a second-best program when the Black bill lost out to FDR's plan of recovery. Somewhat disingenuously, labor leaders preferred to see in Section 7(a) a grant of power and a clear call for workers to join unions, though in reality the language embodied more of an open-shop provision. Given the legal history of collective bargaining, however, union leaders thought the language a legitimation of collective bargaining, even if the section fell far short of the mandatory bargaining they had tried to obtain in the congressional debate. Irving Bernstein wrote that Section 7(a) was "enabling legislation and nothing more. Its promise would be fulfilled only if the labor movement acted with speed and vigor."[14] It was not "labor's Bill of Rights," nor was it the "Magna Charter" that William Green, president of the AFL, termed it. It was more what New Deal bureaucrat Francis Biddle said, an "innocuous moral shibboleth." A month after the passage of the NIRA, Hugh Johnson observed that labor unions "have intimated or openly stated that it is a purpose of the National Recovery Act" to "unionize labor," but that such union contentions were "incorrect." "Labor," said Johnson, "in any industry has the right to organize and bargain collectively; the law also recognizes the right of individual workers to bargain for their own conditions of employment."[15]

Employers all across the land believed devoutly in the latter part of Johnson's interpretation of 7(a). Although antiunion contracts were banned, employers thought themselves to be within the law if they made efforts, without coercion or direct interference, to keep their workers out of independent unions or to create company unions, which many quickly did. Section 7(a) did not specifically designate what management tactics for persuading workers to keep clear of unions constituted unfair labor practices. Vague and ambiguous, the act was, as Perkins said many years later, a "problem in semantics."[16] Thus, as the public hearings opened and labor leaders approached the textile industry's most talented leaders to bargain for fulfillment of the code's potential, they did so without any real power. And the process of securing real benefits under the code, given no clear commitment in the early New Deal to national collective bargaining, depended upon organizational strength.

BEGINNINGS

The cotton textile industry came to Washington better prepared than either the government or the union. Leaders had a grasp on their problem, the cotton textile depression, since they had fumbled through early attempts at cooperative action in the late 1920s. The depression had hit hard by that decade's end, even in the South. The region's production of cotton textiles fell only approximately 20 percent between 1929 and 1932, a moderate drop compared to other industries, but even this relatively small decline in volume in an industry that operated on such close margins caused widespread demoralization. The price of cotton goods frequently dropped below production cost. Mills operated either in the red or perilously close to it, and profits, except in a few isolated cases, plummeted.[17] George Sloan, president of the Cotton-Textile Institute, declared in 1931 that the long history of excessive production had contributed to a "chronic lack of confidence on the part of buyers and financiers and discouragement to all concerned." At the same meeting, an Alabama manufacturer deplored the practices which prevented the owners from matching production to demand. "Why we do it I don't know," he said, "but if we keep on conducting our business the way we have conducted it in the last two years we are all going into bankruptcy."[18] Two years later the owners were psychologically and emotionally ready for a new "deal."

Earlier they had promoted trade associations as a means of saving themselves. From 1900 to 1925, the industry spawned from its early social organizations what historian Louis Galambos called "service organizations," with a formal organization and a paid staff. Organization members lobbied within and without the industry to bring it greater stability and higher profits. These organizations even experimented with calls for voluntary production controls and industrial information pools, although nothing really worked, so small was the response. The depression shocked the industry into even more serious efforts at stabilization and cooperation. On 20 October 1926, after months of effort, the manufacturers formed the Cotton-Textile Institute (CTI), a joining of the American Cotton Manufacturers Association, the southern group, and the National Association of Cotton Manufacturers (NACM), the New England association. Walker Hines, a corporation lawyer with offices in New York City, served as the first president. In 1929 George Sloan, another New York lawyer, educated at Vanderbilt University Law School, became president. Tall, handsome, young, articulate, bright, and diplomatic, he was an ideal spokesman for the sometimes blunt and truculent cotton men.[19]

The CTI advocated price stabilization agreements, production control, and even emergency curtailments when inventories built up. The CTI was not an overnight success. Three years after its formation, almost a fourth of the yarn industry had not joined; the majority of the nonconformers were smaller southern mills. Louis Galambos concluded that the CTI was "unable to achieve stability" in the economic structure of the industry by 1929. Nevertheless, the CTI itself had become a stable organization supported by the leaders of the industry and had, more importantly, developed a philosophy. Galambos noted, "Framed in terms of the traditional guild objectives of stabilization, cooperation, and control, the associative philosophy stood in sharp contrast to the laissez faire, competitive concepts that had held an unchallenged dominion in the nineteenth century."[20] This philosophical development among its leaders, coupled with the swelling impact of the depression, enabled the industry to move rapidly to implement the New Deal plan for recovery.

The last gasp of voluntary action before the code was an ill-fated CTI plan in 1930 to cut production by limiting each day shift to fifty-five hours a week and the night shift to fifty hours. The "55-50" plan was a complex agreement which depended for success on signed pledges from an overwhelming majority of the producers. The CTI struggled for three years to make the plan work, and George Sloan would later claim that by 1933, 88 percent of the industry observed the "55-50" limit.[21] But Sloan pushed the outer limits of weak statistics. Thomas McMahon of the UTW told a Senate committee in 1933 that in some instances "the ink was scarcely dry when some of those who were signers of this proposition broke it."[22] Throughout the southern Piedmont, many small firms ignored "55-50," and by 1933 southern manufacturers had despaired of such voluntary action and "gentlemen's agreements." Benjamin Gossett, the North Carolina manufacturer, told the southern owners at their annual convention in spring 1933 that "the handwriting is on the wall. The hour has struck. Therefore, in the existing crisis, the textile industry more than ever before faces the positive need of sustained cooperation."[23] The NRA code made that possible.

By 1932, CTI leaders had decided to seek legislation and political help for the troubled industry. In particular they wanted changes in the antitrust laws to create a business authority to regulate the industry. It was natural in 1933, then, for the CTI to turn to the new administration, and its large southern membership responded enthusiastically to FDR and the New Deal. Even Ben Gossett, the ACMA leader who later attacked the New Deal bitterly, in 1933 thought Roosevelt "sound, energetic, encouraging, and inspiring."[24] From December 1932 on, CTI leaders — particularly Sloan, Hines, and Goldthwaite Dorr, CTI's lawyer — met with the New Dealers working on recovery plans. Hines actually met with FDR on 11 April 1933 and found the President receptive to the CTI's evolving plans for self-regulation under the cover of federal law. Shortly after that meeting, the NIRA drafting committee began its work, and the CTI, with doors open to all of the committee's three groups, was busy on all fronts.[25]

Many of the southern manufacturers were probably listening to the radio on 7 May 1933 when the President gave the second of his famous "fireside chats." In this address, he concentrated on economic recovery and talked of a partnership of government and business for the purpose of improving working conditions and regulating competition. Roosevelt used the cotton textile industry as an example of how voluntary agreements had broken down in the past because of the failure of a small percentage of the industry to cooperate. "Government," he declared, "ought to have the right and will have the right, after surveying and planning for an industry, to prevent, with the assistance of an overwhelming majority of that industry, unfair practices and to enforce this agreement by the authority of Government."[26] Within two days, the CTI executive committee telegraphed the President that they supported him and that one-third of the industry had agreed to eight-hour shifts per day for two forty-hour shifts per week, "40–40." The CTI suggested that the federal government enforce these standards by law.[27] Soon the CTI had gathered two-thirds of the industry behind the new "40–40" plan, and events moved swiftly. Even before final action by Congress on the proposed NIRA, the CTI, asked by Hugh Johnson, formed the Cotton Textile Industry Committee (CTIC) with nine members from the southern industry, six from New England, and four from the marketing side of the industry in New York. By 24 May 1933 the CTIC had assembled in Washington to begin drafting a code.

The committee quickly agreed that "40–40" might mitigate "the disastrous social and economic effects of the cut-throat competition," but it had no experience with a mandated minimum wage.[28] In their initial meeting with Johnson, their original proposal of an eight or nine dollar minimum was brusquely rejected as too low. In May and June, the committee and the NRA haggled back and forth. The only suggestion of labor input was an NRA effort by William Allen and Alexander Sachs to consult with Thomas McMahon, president of the UTW. Neither McMahon nor any other unionist was present when the CTIC met with Johnson or his deputies. By June 19, only three days after FDR signed the NIRA, the CTIC and the NRA had a draft code with public hearings set for June 27. Announcing this achievement, Johnson declared "We are going to have to do this job in a goldfish bowl."[29] Nothing so public had happened so far. The crucial initial proposals had been made in hearings, with labor excluded, and except for some quibbling questions by Frances Perkins on job classification, the NRA pattern was set.

The industry proposal struck directly at the owners' perceived problems. The code would set a minimum wage of ten dollars a week in the South and eleven dollars in the North, with apprentices, cleaners, and outside employees excepted. The work week would be shortened to forty hours for production workers, and plants would be limited to two forty-hour shifts per week. Companies would regulate themselves by giving to the CTI weekly and monthly production reports. The proposed code acknowledged Section 7(a), and it asked employers to abandon any requirement that employees join a company union.[30] For the businessmen, the code promised a curb on competition and the excessive production that had driven profits down. For labor, there was the mixed blessing of a minimum wage and maximum hours, all set without collective bargaining. In the flow of messages back and forth in the hectic weeks before the hearing, Donald Comer, writing to fellow manufacturer William D. Anderson, pressed home the importance of getting an agreement on these two points: "I am impressed with the fact that the more nearly we can settle these points in Washington in our conference there, the less need there will be for union labor organization in the plants themselves because if Washington is going to fix the wages and tasks, that is all organized labor could promise to do and thereby industry will be better off as a result."[31]

THE PUBLIC HEARINGS

The proposed code, despite the minimum wage provision and shift hours limitation, was well received by an industry desperate for good news. "Government directly in business is undesirable," said the editor of *Cotton*, "but Government may work *with* businesses to the advantage of the country at large."[32] Even David Clark, the conservative editor of the *Textile Bulletin*, thought well of the venture, though he expressed dissatisfaction with the small proposed North-South wage differential.[33] The industry congratulated itself on leading the way in the upcoming hearings, which were expected to help develop the technical procedures for the whole national recovery process, which so far had been a matter of exploration and ad hoc rule-making. The purpose of the hearings themselves had not been made clear, and to end this confusion Donald Richberg, Johnson's senior aide in the NRA, said that the cotton textile hearings were to be neither judicial nor legislative, but an "administrative inquiry" for the purpose of adequately "advising the administration of facts."[34] Procedures would be developed as the hearings took place. In retrospect, what actually happened was a rudimentary bargaining session with one side, the owners, using its power to bring the NRA and organized labor, the almost forgotten "partner," to agreement.

On the first day, June 27, with over 800 people in the sweltering auditorium, the industry leaders led off. George Sloan presented the proposed code, submitting statistical proof of the need and arguments for the individual provisions, and describing the long cotton textile depression. Sloan predicted that the forty-hour week would immediately result in the employment of 100,000 workers in the cotton textile mills. Robert Amory, speaking for the distressed New England mills, followed Sloan and predicted that the code would bring about full employment in the industry in sixty days. Amory, however, voiced the ritual disapproval of a code-sanctioned wage differential between North and South, although by then New England producers had already decided to accept it.[35]

The southern manufacturers had chosen the energetic, colorful William D. Anderson, president of the mighty Bibb Manufacturing Company, to present the southern case. Anderson agreed that the North-South differential was a problem — it was too small. In a long and impassioned defense of the cost of maintaining southern paternalism and the mill villages, it was folly, he declared, to think that the mill workers in the South could exist without these services. Anderson thought, therefore, that the differential should be greater, in order to help the southern owner pay for them. Woven into Anderson's picture of·heroic southern owners and loyal workers who lived simple and decent lives with few actual cash needs was solid support of the code.

The first effective nitpicker to appear was Senator James F. Byrnes of South Carolina, who testified that he had received numerous complaints about the stretch out in his home state. He expressed fear that if employers radically increased the workloads, the resulting stretch out would nullify the benefits of shorter hours and higher wages which the code might bring. He recommended that a committee representing both labor and management be appointed by the NRA to study the stretch out problem and recommend restrictions that might be included in the code. The NRA and the owners had excluded such labor questions from their proposed code. But with the nation looking closely at the very first code, Johnson quickly agreed with the senator and adopted the suggestion on the spot, without consultation or delay. The first NRA labor board evolved out of Johnson's impulsive decision.

The *New York Times* had predicted that labor would attack the proposed minimum wage and the forty-hour week, and the second day, when labor leaders were to talk, was expected to be lively. But the owners, in a move clearly well thought out ahead of time, asked for the opening slot. Thomas M. Marchant, president of the ACMA, marched to the "partnership table" and announced that a dramatic emergency meeting of the CTIC had taken place the night before. The committee, said Marchant, had decided to recommend an amendment to the code that would abolish child labor in the industry. The move, supposedly a complete surprise to many in the auditorium, was "greeted by ringing cheers from several hundred people."[36] Johnson responded with lavish praise for the humanitarian motives of the owners. In reality, the employers had given nothing away. The depression had already driven the children out.

William Green, president of the AFL, testifying next, had to begin his comments with praise for the very owners who had for decades opposed the abolition of child labor. He carefully expressed labor's desire to cooperate with the recovery program, and, in particular, with the NRA, but Green feared that a forty-hour work week in cotton textiles would set a bad precedent for the other codes to follow. The AFL leader still battled for the thirty-hour week. Green argued that only 69,000 cotton workers would be reemployed, whereas if a thirty-hour week were adopted, the industry would need 210,000 more workers than were currently employed. Green also expressed dismay at the proposed minimum wage and suggested that a minimum wage of fourteen and sixteen dollars was more appropriate than the obscenely low ten and eleven dollars. "We are not here," he declared, "to determine how cheaply

life can be maintained, nor to fix minimum wages on that basis." Sen. Hugo
Black echoed Green's support of the thirty-hour week and expressed his hope
that the NRA would never "adopt a minimum wage of $10.00 per week for
men who work in America." Sidney Hillman, respected president of the
Amalgamated Clothing Workers Union, eloquently backed Green's statement
that forty hours would not provide for all the unemployed workers and called
the ten dollar minimum "absurd." Several consumer groups would join the
attack on the minimum wage level as well.

Thomas McMahon, UTW president, was expected to carry the weight of
labor's argument. McMahon, born in Ireland in 1870 and active as a young
immigrant in the Knights of Labor, had been president of the UTW since
1921. He was, by all accounts, something of a bumbler. Frances Perkins described him as a "plump, jolly, elderly man" who had "years ago resigned
himself to the idea of a small union in a few factories."[37] On this day, however, McMahon aggressively attacked the proposed code. He did not believe
that "common sense" could "accept or condone" a wage of ten dollars a week
for forty hours of labor. He proposed fourteen dollars. The bargaining was
on. At last McMahon relented from the hard-core thirty-hour stance, saying a thirty-five-hour week would be acceptable. He pushed for the inclusion of all menial laborers such as cleaners and outside helpers under the
code's provisions and asked for a code regulation banning women from night
employment.[38]

A small tempest-in-a-teapot occurred after McMahon finished. William L.
Allen, the sometimes forgotten chair of the hearings, blazed back at McMahon
for his attacks on the wage and hour provisions. McMahon, Allen claimed,
had not objected in previous meetings when the proposed code had been
formed, and Allen was now "flabbergasted" by McMahon's stand. Johnson
interrupted Allen's eruption to point out that preliminary discussion of the
code by McMahon implied no commitment to it, and McMahon simply told
Allen, "I had no hand in making up this code." This exchange epitomized
the perfunctory nature of the hearings. Although Irving Bernstein would later argue that the code was a "humiliation for the United Textile Workers
of America" and Louis Galambos would say that McMahon's apparent incon-
sistency fatally weakened labor at the hearing, McMahon's words, although
perhaps not literally true because he had been in consultation with the NRA,
indicated the UTW's lack of power at both the pre-code and public hearing
stages.[39] The owners bargained with Hugh Johnson; the union, representing
less than 3 percent of the workers, was largely a supplicant at the partnership
table, albeit a supplicant to the NRA rather than the owners.

By the end of the second day, the conflicts were in the open and what
Johnson and the NRA had accepted previously was there for all to see. One
result was pressure on the NRA to increase the minimum wage rate, something that had been agreed to already. Another pressure came from Johnson's
intention to establish codes as rapidly as possible for the ten big industries

—textiles, coal, petroleum, steel, automobiles, lumber, garments, wholesale trade, retail trade, and construction. How Johnson bargained on textiles would affect later negotiations involving stronger unions. On the third day of the hearing, the consumer groups expressed strong disapproval of the code but offered no solution to the problems at hand. During the day, William L. Allen, referring to labor's objections, suggested that the manufacturers raise the minimum wages and lower the maximum hours as a compromise, but no direct bargaining took place between the CTIC and the labor men.

The CTIC decided to take the initiative again, and at the beginning of the fourth day of the hearings, Stuart Cramerton, a North Carolina manufacturer, suggested several revisions to the proposed code which he emphatically emphasized were offered voluntarily. Citing its duty in the war against the depression, the CTIC proposed that the minimum wage be raised by two dollars, from ten and eleven to twelve and thirteen. Cramerton explained that "recognition of the fact that the buying power of the country must be increased" prompted the proposal. According to the *New York Times*, this proposal "electrified" the audience, prompting Johnson to praise the textile manufacturers once again. "You men have done a very remarkable thing," he declared, "a patriotic thing."

Drawing less notice than the wage proposal was a very important revision of the proposed code. The CTIC asked to become itself the Code Authority, with the responsibility of enforcing the code and acting as a "planning and fair practice agency."[40] The CTIC also suggested that, as the Code Authority, it should have the power to approve or disapprove the installation of new or additional machinery in the industry. The CTIC had moved directly to control individual mill production. The Code Authority would also be granted the right to recommend to the NRA changes in the code and curtailment of production as needed. This revision was to be of crucial importance in the months ahead, and this extraordinary grant of economic power to an industry committee, not elected yet beyond the reach of government action, set a pattern for management domination of the codes to come. Boldly, the CTIC had grasped at what it had sought so desperately in the Hoover years.

The NRA, elated by the minimum wage bait, rushed to support the revisions. Dr. Alexander Sachs, director of NRA's Research Planning Division, appeared in support of the committee's revisions. He estimated that the code provisions, as revised, would bring about the immediate employment of one hundred thousand workers and would restore to the cotton mill workers their 1929 purchasing power. Thoroughly outgunned and acutely aware of their lack of power, labor leaders voiced no public objections to the amendments. Perhaps they even thought they could go to the workers, claiming victory in the minimum wage struggle. In any case, Johnson's immediate enthusiastic acceptance of the revisions would have convinced them of the futility of further objections. Only June Croll, a representative of the small and radical National Textile Workers Union, rose to criticize vehemently the entire code, calling it "totally inadequate" to the workers' needs. Hugh Johnson, the key broker in the negotiations, announced his great pleasure with the revisions and sent the revised code to the President. The first public NIRA show was over.

Most bargaining sessions produce winners and losers, and in this one the industry had won a great deal. It could control production much better now. From well over a hundred hours of production a week, every mill in the industry was by law reduced to eighty. The Code Authority controlled the expansion and entry of new mills by its ability to prohibit installation of new production machinery. It could even initiate curtailment below eighty hours, subject to the approval of the NRA administration. The minimum wage guaranteed a floor against cutthroat competition, and mandatory periodic reporting of production statistics and prices by small firms would make for a cleaner open-price system. Furthermore, the limit on production hours presumably would reduce warehouse inventories and thus stop destructive dumping at any price obtainable. With the owners in charge, the Code Authority became synonymous with the Cotton-Textile Institute.[41]

Southern workers were at a disadvantage in the hearings. The UTW had only a handful of southern members in June 1933. No one spoke for the men and women who made the yarn and wove the cloth. Johnson and the cotton manufacturers presented the amended code as an accomplished fact. The spirit of cooperation prevailed. Despite their misgivings about the code's wage and hour provisions, labor leaders voiced no violent objections because they had no real alternatives to the code. And in truth, the workers would benefit from its wage and hour provisions. The brutal work week of the past would disappear. The minimum wage, though low, did raise some wages, and it was a powerful philosophical statement of worker dignity and owner responsibility. On the other hand, abolition of child labor was a throwaway gift. No one at the hearing really discussed the lives of cotton mill workers, their shop grievances, or the mechanism by which they could join the new partnership.

Where the union fell short was in losing the opportunity to examine the meaning of Section 7(a), the missing item on the partnership table. The owners had looked askance at this section; it was there by NIRA mandate, and it troubled them. Donald Comer wrote to George Sloan just before the public hearings and during the drafting sessions with NRA, expressing his regret that no headway had been made to "soften" the Section 7(a) language that would be in the code. Perhaps, he said, "some of us have been unnecessarily disturbed about this, but I think that when 7-a has something put in there by Mr. Green, which he says if anybody dares take out, he will bring all the forces of his influence to defeat the whole bill, that should be sufficient warning to us."[42] Comer's fears were not justified. Collective bargaining made no gains in Washington that summer, and Hugh Johnson in no way viewed Section 7(a) as establishing the principle of majority-rule unionization. Nothing in the record indicates that the cotton textile managers believed that they were endorsing free, independent trade unions.

Industry representatives from all parts of the country quickly endorsed the code. Sloan praised his employers for their courage to be first, saying, "Someone had to pioneer."[43] A correspondent of the *Daily News Record*, a textile newspaper, wrote, "No-one who listened could have avoided being favorably impressed with the type of men who spoke for the cotton industry, with their evident willingness and desire to follow out the spirit of the recovery law."[44] The trade journal *Cotton* praised the "sense of sincerity and earnestness" displayed in the hearings.[45] William D. Anderson, proud of his work, declared that "a new day has dawned for all who are in any way concerned with the manufacturer and distribution of cotton textiles."[46] Donald Comer, president of the big Avondale Mills chain in Alabama, expressed confidence that the public approved of the industry's effort to help itself.[47] The *New York Times* reported that both the workers in the South and the owners were "rejoicing" over the code.[48] Francis Gorman, the competent vice-president of the UTW, termed the code the "most progressive step in the industry in many years."[49] Hugh Johnson issued a glowing press release. "Never in economic history," he said, "have labor, industry, government, and consumers' representatives sat together in the presence of the public to work out by mutual agreement a 'law merchant' for an entire industry. There were no harangues. Epithets gave way to agreements—it is the atmosphere of the New Deal."[50]

The President used his prerogative to make some minor changes in the code after it came to him. He strengthened the code's language to give better assurance that the higher wage brackets would be maintained in relation to the minimum wage. The President also stipulated that the reduced hours would in no way reduce weekly salaries in the upper brackets, and he broadened the code to include office workers in the mills. The Code Authority, after considerable anger over this and much huffing and puffing about failed trust and partnerships, accepted Roosevelt's changes. After Roosevelt signed the code, he said, "I know nothing further that could have been done. I can think of no greater achievement of cooperation, mutual understanding, and goodwill."[51] The senior partner who had never appeared at the partnership table was pleased.

THE CODE AND THE INDUSTRY, 1933-34

Excitement and hope spread through the Piedmont. In South Carolina, industry leaders estimated that the new code would mean a total wage increase of around $5 million annually for textile workers in the state.[52] Stuart Cramerton, a North Carolina owner, estimated that an additional fifty thousand southern workers would be hired when the code went into effect.[53]

On the day the code went into operation, long lines of eager jobseekers waited at the gates of the southern mills; even before that day, the adoption of the cotton textile code caused a speculative boom in the industry as manufacturers sought to increase production at a lower cost before the cost increases expected to result from the code were felt. The industry also faced the impact of the Agricultural Adjustment Act (AAA), which authorized, among other things, a processing tax on raw cotton. The tax to help pay the AAA support prices was heavy, amounting to 4.2 cents per pound of raw cotton or about 50 percent of the prevailing price. The tax was to become effective 1 August 1933 and would apply not only to the manufacturing of all cotton after that date, but to all goods in inventory as of August 1. According to George Sloan, "The eagerness of buyers, therefore, to secure goods that carried neither the processing tax nor the higher cost of production under the cotton textile code led to an unprecedented demand in May, June, and July."[54]

Because of this rational economic behavior, July production ran at 122 percent of the average level of production in the six years from 1922 to 1927, and inventories reached the lowest point in eight years. The *New York Times* sent a reporter to Gastonia, North Carolina, where the famous 1929 strike had occurred, and the report came back that Gastonia was booming under the NRA, with workers delighted with the same higher pay for fewer hours worked.[55] The increased production spilled over into August, as the code reduced the work week to forty hours and many of the southern mills went from one single long shift to the "40–40" plan; the natural consequence was a sudden and substantial increase in mill employment. George Sloan estimated that the industry employed some 145,515 new employees from March to September 1933, to reach an all-time high of 465,915 workers.[56]

The boom continued well after the code went into effect. In summer and fall 1933, there was a sharp rise in wholesale prices of gray goods, and the industry increased production to take advantage of the favorable price situation.[57] The Federal Trade Commission later reported that the annual rate of return on stockholders' equity in 230 southern cotton mills rose from 6.8 percent for the first six months of 1933 to 13.82 percent during the period from June to December.[58] The New Deal had brought the most profitable year since 1928 to the southern cotton textile industry.

Reviewing the economic condition of the industry in October 1933, Hugh Johnson called its performance under the code "one of the bright spots" of the NRA. But summer and fall optimism soon faded into winter discontent.[59] Just as quickly as it had boomed in late summer, demand fell off sharply in the late fall. The price rise leveled off and began to fall, while the higher code-induced costs of production stayed firm. Ralph Loper, a well-known textile engineer, surveyed the southern portion of the industry in fall 1933 and reported increases of over 100 percent in the labor costs of many mills. He estimated that the average labor cost per unit of product for the industry as a whole had increased 70 percent. Loper also asserted that the forty-hour week, with an eighty-hour limit on the use of machinery, had increased the cost per unit of product for taxes, insurance, obsolescence, and all other fixed items.[60] The cotton textile manufacturers were soon complaining that the increased costs were not being met by a corresponding increase in prices, and that the mills could not continue to absorb the new costs. A bitter wail went up against the cotton processing tax of the AAA. Herman E. Michl, a textile economist, estimated that this tax alone increased the manufacturing cost of individual mills between 8 and 13 percent.[61]

Southerners began to attack the code with greater dissatisfaction than New Englanders because the South was more adversely affected by the wage and hour provisions. New England mills expanded production as the upsurge of orders flooded the mills in summer and early fall 1933; many southern mills, however, had been on a two-shift, 110-hour week (or a long single shift), and the production curtailment to eighty hours meant that the South bore the brunt of the reduction in capacity that the code mandated. From October 1933 to March 1934, the effect of the code's operation was to reduce the average hours per week worked in the industry by 25 percent, and to increase the average hourly earnings by 67 percent, the largest increase of any major industry. Employment in the industry in the same period increased 39 percent; per capita earnings rose by 21.9 percent.[62] The South bore the burden here, too. The code raised wages in the South high enough to reduce the North-South differential to the smallest amount in history. In 1924, the differential was 65 percent; immediately before the code went into effect, it was 39 percent; by early 1934, the differential had fallen to only 18 percent.[63] None of these results of the code particularly pleased the southern manufacturers in winter 1934, as they watched their profits shrink away.

By October 1933, accumulating inventories and below-cost prices indicated to the Code Authority that the old problems of low demand and overproduction had returned. The Code Authority then used the grant of powers received in June 1933 to recommend in November that during December and for perhaps ninety days, cotton textile mills limit their machine hours to 75 percent of the maximum hours permitted by the code, while excessive inventories were sold off. This recommendation by the Code Authority, quickly approved by Hugh Johnson despite protests within the NRA ranks, reduced production hours from eighty to sixty per week, and reduced the workers' normal week from forty to thirty hours.[64] The effect for workers was that of an immediate pay reduction of 25 percent per week. George Sloan later reported that it "was the unanimous feeling of the Committee [the Code Authority], including its government representatives, that this emergency recommendation would help preserve an equitable sharing of present inadequate business and employment among the mills and the communities dependent upon" them. And in 1935 he reported that the "good results" from the action were undeniable.[65] Inventories, which had been steadily increasing in October and November 1933, stopped rising as the amount of goods sold in December about equaled the amount produced.[66]

But the situation deteriorated again in January 1934, despite the curtailment's continuation. Higher prices weakened demand, and even with a 25 percent curtailment, inventories rose. Other textile industries, undergoing the same cycle, also pressed for a machine curtailment throughout the entire textile industry. Again, in May 1934, the Code Authority placed another curtailment recommendation before Johnson which precipitated a general strike threat by the UTW. Even some manufacturers protested the curtailments. And inside the NRA, a growing group of economists doubted the effectiveness of production cutbacks as temporary weapons and argued that an attempt to create prosperity through scarcity was not a noble public goal for the NRA. They argued for increased demand instead.[67] As the controversy continued, the depression crept back in the industry. In 1934 profits dropped well below the spectacular year of 1933, shrinking in aggregate in the South from $25.3 million to $18.9 million.[68]

By summer 1934 it was clear that the code was not doing what the owners had bargained for in 1933; available capacity had not come into balance with demand. Oddly though, the code, even under attack, had come to seem a raft in the stormy seas, and the owners still clung to what they thought they had gained. Douglas Woolf, editor of the *Textile World*, reported in February 1934 that the bulk of the industry supported the code as an "absolutely indispensable part" of cotton manufacturing.[69] George Sloan, in March, wrote that the code was responsible for what little stabilization had been achieved, claiming, "The industry as a whole is getting back the dollars it has put into production of the goods; in the main, something for depreciation, and, in some branches, something toward interest on investment."[70]

The southern manufacturers were restless, however. Thomas Marchant, in his presidential address at the April 1934 ACMA meeting, delivered a scathing attack on the New Deal, asserting that the New Deal was holding back recovery by the "repeated stirring up of political uncertainties." New capital investment, he said, awaited the return of the "confidence factor." Marchant urged that the government undertake no new action which would affect the cotton textile industry and that the cotton code be allowed to "settle" without any further change.[71] Heeding his advice, the ACMA passed a resolution expressing its support of the cotton code as a partnership plan in government and business, but the resolution asked that the code be allowed sufficient time to prove itself before any further change. After almost a year of operating under the code, the industry's original optimism concerning self-government was waning, but hope persisted.

A clearer perspective today indicates that the cotton textile code's economic history followed rather clearly that of the nation as a whole. The industry would only do as well as the economy at large. The NRA's philosophy consisted of three sets of economic ideals, each in conflict with the other two. First, the antitrusters and, second, the national planners could be seen in a concentration on national goals and national organizations, but these two groups of planners were sharply divided in their analyses of the depression's causes and their suggestions for corrective policy. Third, the cotton code makers came from the "business rationalizers," as historian Ellis Hawley called them, who wanted to control the entire process for the basic goal of industrial profits.[73] In NRA economic policy, as in so many other aspects of its policy, the New Deal did not achieve a unified or successful approach to recovery. And by itself, the cotton code produced neither a sound industry nor peaceful and fair labor relations.

"I don't like so much interpretation"
THE BRUERE BOARD AND LABOR RELATIONS,
1933-34

In the glowing aftermath of the four day hearing in Washington, it appeared that a dream had come true for the cotton textile industry. Even Francis Gorman, the vice-president of the UTW, in a moment of excess in November 1933, declared the cotton code "the greatest accomplishment of the United States in a generation."[1] The Raleigh *News and Observer* in August 1934, when a general strike threatened the entire textile industry, remembered fondly that in summer 1933 the industry had developed "an apparent spirit of cooperation that gave the New Deal a special blessing."[2] The immediate economic effects of the Code — shorter hours, higher hourly earnings, and increased employment — pleased the workers. The owners, thinking they would escape the ruinous and deeply-embedded destructive competition that had tugged at the industry for so long, put aside their skepticism and rejoiced. Unfortunately, the owners did not reap widespread prosperity for any lasting period, and the code became a mixed blessing for the workers. The forty-hour week and the minimum wage took root in the treacherous soil of the industry, but worker hopes of creating an industry governed by collective bargaining and strong unions withered in less than a year.

Initially, the heady experience of even being in the same auditorium with the owners and the plethora of codes, boards, and authorities excited the labor leaders, still bruised from their beating in 1929-30. Thomas McMahon in his official report on the code to the workers wrote euphorically: "I look forward with hope to the better day now dawning for our textile workers, and feel that the 'New Deal' will be so successful in the development of a cooperative spirit between employers and workers that all will hail and bless the day on which President Roosevelt had the courage, vision and ability to present such a program for the rehabilitation of industry in our nation."[3] Textile labor intended to march along with the New Deal.

McMahon was encouraged by union activity elsewhere. Labor leaders such as William Green, David Dubinski, and John L. Lewis quickly developed the theory that Section 7(a) intended workers to join unions and that Section 7(a) was the legal foundation of a new labor movement. Throughout the country, workers in mills, factories, and mines responded by joining trade unions by the thousands. Union membership grew from approximately 2.9 million in 1933 to 8.5 million in 1939. In six years, over 5 million workers had joined a union.[4] The result, wrote labor historian Milton Derber, "was a boom in unionism" in 1933–34, "which was destined to surpass in both scope and strength all previous union booms, including the rise of the Knights of Labor in 1885–86, the first major AFL expansion between 1897 and 1904, and the World War I upsurge in 1916–20."[5] Irving Bernstein saw the passage of Section 7(a) as "the spark that kindled the spirit of unionism within American labor . . . the lean years, it seemed, had come to an end."[6]

Even in the South, the burnt-over region of union hopes, workers moved. The workers, said one contemporary observer in Durham, North Carolina, "were not 'educated for unionism,' they joined unions because the spirit of the Blue Eagle was in the air."[7] H.D. Lisk, UTW organizer in the South, said in 1936 that "when the NRA first came in, conditions improved wonderfully compared to what conditions were before that time." Textile workers, said Lisk, believed that the NRA was something that "God had sent to them."[8] Early in 1933 the UTW had languished in its usual state of ineffectiveness, with only about fifteen thousand dues-paying members and a token organizing and administrative staff. Only when the New Deal was inaugurated in March, wrote Robert R.R. Brooks, did "a ray of sunshine" streak "its dismal skies."

By August 1933, the textile workers were pouring into the UTW in a volume greater than the union had ever experienced.[9] In South Carolina, less than a month after the President signed the code, union locals appeared in about 75 percent of the textile mills.[10] Estimated UTW membership in September 1933 was 40,000. By June 1934 the union claimed 250,000 members, and by August 1934, 270,000.[11] McMahon stated that the demand for organizers to come to mills was so great in the month immediately after the code's signing that "it was impossible to meet it." Between July 1933 and August 1934, he reported that unions had issued over 600 charters to local unions.[12] The NRA research staff in August 1933 reported to Robert Bruere, as he prepared to head the first NRA labor board, that "the evidence is conclusive that the membership of the United Textile Workers of America" is "substantial and growing." The membership was estimated at an incredible 340,000 workers, with 185,000 of them in cotton textiles.[13]

A significant proportion of this growth occurred in the South. Union activity in the industry was a development that the manufacturers had not anticipated when they accepted the NRA. Section 7(a) had meant nothing to them as a statute affecting labor-management relations. Francis Gorman asserted in 1934 that at least 75 percent of the southern cotton textile employers "accepted Section 7(a) with their tongues in cheek" and that they had paid it scant heed at the code hearings.[14] They never believed that collective bargaining would intrude into their industry, and they believed Section 7(a), which was translated into the cotton code as Section 17, to be a vague, noncompulsory sentiment. John Law, president of two South Carolina firms, Saxon Mills and Chesne Mills, believed that he expressed the views of the southern industry in "asserting that there is nothing in the National Recovery Act, and under the Constitution of the United States, nothing that can be legally written into the Act, that will compel the humblest employee in the industry to join this or that union."[15] The *Textile World* denounced the union leaders for taking advantage of the recovery program to promote the UTW drive for members, a drive which the magazine referred to as "membership mania."[16] In the southern cotton textile industry, the cotton code's inclusion of Section 7(a) encouraged the renewed union and alarmed an intractable management. Each side welcomed the cotton code; each sought to use it to further its own interests.

THE BRUERE BOARD

The NRA's emerging labor policy was confusing. There were many boards, much activity, and often little decided in a firm and lasting manner. "The Riddle of 7(a)," wrote Irving Bernstein, "had to be faced in Washington — in the administrative agencies, in Congress, and, ultimately, in the White House."[17] Conflicts quickly arose over the meaning of "the right to organize and bargain collectively," which Section 7(a) guaranteed. The NIRA had not spelled out any provisions to administer or enforce Section 7(a). As the questions mounted, Hugh Johnson had the President, by executive order of 5 August 1933, establish the National Labor Board (NLB), under the direction of the NRA, to settle by mediation, conciliation, or arbitration any controversies between labor and management which might retard the recovery program of the New Deal. The NLB was without statutory authority, and if it was defied by either management or labor, the board's only recourse was to submit the case to the Compliance Division of the NRA or to the U.S. attorney general. This enforcement procedure was so clumsy that during the NLB's short life of less than a year only four Blue Eagles were removed in cases submitted to the NRA, and the one case referred to the attorney general was still before the courts when the NRA collapsed in 1935.[18] Working under these constitutional and legal difficulties, the board often found itself ignored by labor and management.

Nevertheless, despite its lack of enforcement powers, the NLB began in its interpretations of Section 7(a) to lay the foundations for a common law federal policy which would, in theory, protect the right of employees to organize and bargain collectively. A rickety federal labor policy grew out of the board's decisions on discrimination against union employees, the rights and privileges of company unions, the principles of majority rule, and the basic meaning of collective bargaining. But the constant evasion of NLB decisions and a continuing controversy over the principle of majority rule, which neither Hugh Johnson nor F.D.R. would embrace, led Sen. Robert Wagner on 1 March 1934 to introduce his Labor Dispute Act, which embodied much of the later 1935 Wagner Act. The bill faced business opposition, NRA attacks, and, most important, a chilly reception by the White House. Amended to death, the bill was soon replaced, amid the crisis of a series of 1934 strikes, by Public Resolution 44, signed on 19 June 1934.

The resolution authorized the President to appoint a board empowered to conduct elections by secret ballot, to elect representatives for collective bargaining and to investigate and mediate labor controversies arising under Section 7(a) of the NIRA. As J. Joseph Huthmacher wrote in chronicling Wagner's defeat, "Roosevelt continued to view the formulation of a labor policy as a secondary problem, and, unlike Wagner, he failed to recognize the connection between free unions and collective bargaining on the one hand and wages, purchasing power, and recovery on the other."[19]

On 29 June 1934, under the authority of Public Resolution 44, Roosevelt created in the Department of Labor the three-person National Labor Relations Board (NLRB) to supersede the NLB. The new board, often called the "first NLRB," was authorized to appoint its own staff, investigate controversies arising under Section 7(a), and order and conduct elections for employee representatives. The board could enforce its orders by petitioning, through the Justice Department, the federal circuit courts of appeal for enforcement. Remarkably, the board's duties and powers resembled those of the NLB, though it had escaped the dominion of the NRA. Under chairperson Lloyd Garrison, dean of the University of Wisconsin Law School, the NLRB eschewed mediation and attempted to act as a judge creating administrative law.

In the following months, the NLRB made a number of key decisions. Employees had to bargain in good faith; employers had to bargain on wages, hours, and working conditions, as well as grievances; employers had to rehire any worker discharged because of union membership; employees had to negotiate before calling a strike; and a majority of employees constituted the legal bargaining unit. The NLRB, following the path laid out by the NLB, developed a set of labor law principles that would become the guidelines for the Wagner Act. But the NLRB, like its predecessor, lacked power to enforce its decisions swiftly and evenly. It had to rely on a tardy and reluctant Justice Department for enforcement, and Justice feared a court test of Section 7(a). The President also exempted from NLRB jurisdiction all cases arising in industries whose codes provided for labor boards. Before the New Deal had to face up to the constitutional, legal, and political problems of its emerging labor policy, the Supreme Court in May 1935 destroyed the NRA, Section 7(a), and, of course, the first NLRB. But the blow did not come before the structures of a national labor policy had emerged in principle if not in law.

Actually, the first major NRA labor board was not the NLB, but the code-established Cotton Textiles National Industrial Relations Board. Several other major industries such as coal and automobiles would also develop their own boards, exempting themselves from the uncertain jurisdiction of the NLB and its NLRB successor. In their work, the smaller boards mirrored the larger patterns of New Deal labor policy, and their histories illuminate the problems of that policy. The NRA special industry boards worked amid the same confusion as the better-known national boards. NRA historians explain the problem as "one of confusion and of overlapping authorities, functions and purposes, noting that the inter-relationship of these cannot be understood if they are considered as the product of a logical place." Instead one must see them "historically as agencies created in haste, to meet the exigencies of a rapidly shifting set of power relations."[20] This pragmatic quality of federal labor policy was evident at the cotton code hearings, where the NRA policy had been to hear both sides, weigh the facts, and declare a policy which it considered helpful to economic recovery. No NRA masterplan for settling future labor disputes existed. Indeed, throughout the first two years of the New Deal, labor relations were never an important priority for the Roosevelt administration.[21] Johnson set recovery as his goal, and he avoided any obstacle which slowed progress toward that end. In the code negotiations, the NRA and Johnson had worked in classic New Deal fashion as mediator to bring the code to completion.

The focus on recovery and the desire to expedite it dominated New Deal labor policy in the cotton textile industry. The first labor board came into the code haphazardly, with no planning at all, merely to satisfy a U.S. senator and to keep the procedures moving along. On the first day of the hearings, 27 June 1933, the stretch out problem, which had long been a troublesome issue in the industry, came to the attention of the codemakers through the testimony of Sen. James F. Byrnes of South Carolina. Johnson eagerly accepted Byrnes' proposal for a committee to study the problem, and by the end of July, a three-man committee was in place. Chair Robert W. Bruere of New York, an economist, former editor of *Survey* magazine, and an arbitrator in the clothing industry, represented the NRA. Benjamin E. Geer, president of Furman University in South Carolina, president of a small cotton mill, and member of a cotton textile business family, represented the employers. Johnson chose George L. Berry from Tennessee, an old-line unionist and president of the AFL's Printing Pressmen, as labor's representative. Berry had no connection at all with the UTW, and he consistently voted with the other two members.

The stretch out, the study committee's goal, was a longstanding problem. The pressure of the cotton depression of the 1920s had tempted owners to employ the stretch out, increasing the number of machines each worker tended. Part of the problem, however, resulted from the substantial technical progress in the late 1920s and early 1930s which speeded up the machines themselves. The introduction of machines for one-process picking, long-draft spinning, automatic spooling, high-speed warping, and even higher-speed automatic looming meant more machines per worker, although theoretically such change did not cause an increase in work load.[22]

Stretch out was the one issue which most concerned textile workers, much more than wages and other working conditions. Worker complaints were constant throughout the 1930s. A labor newspaper in Winston-Salem, melodramatically called stretch out a "giant monster that has wrecked beyond repair the lives of so many textile workers . . . a monster so cruel and ruthless and yet so subtle that at times it has cursed brothers by blood to become mortal enemies overnight, a creature that through the efforts of so-called efficiency experts . . . has caused such widespread misery and suffering."[23] Bernard Cannon, a sociologist, spent months at a mill he called Clothville, in South Carolina in the late 1940s, studying worker culture. He wrote vividly of the coming of stretch out to the mill in 1929. "At Clothville," he wrote, "nobody knew enough about unionism to call a strike," yet the issue of stretch out brought hundreds of workers swarming into a ballpark darkened to protect their identities. "The meeting was held in pitch dark," wrote Cannon, "yet hundreds of people swarmed the speakers, stimulated by a felt need to get together, to do something collectively to halt the effects of the stretch out which they envisioned as a spector quite beyond their control, though it affected them and their friends directly and personally."[24]

Martha Gelhorn, the novelist on assignment as private reporter to Harry Hopkins, reported to him in fall 1934 that stretch out "is the constant cry of the workers," although one owner told her, "I just don't know what you're talking about; never heard of that word; it just doesn't mean a thing to me." But workers told her of speeded-up machines and brutal workloads, particularly in the hot summer months when the heat in the unairconditioned mills was intense. It was not uncommon, she said, for two or three women workers to faint during each work shift. "When you get out," said one, "you're just trembling all over and you can't hardly get rested for the next day." Gelhorn told Hopkins that when she visited a cotton mill her naked eyes could "tell that the workload is inhuman," with the workers on the move constantly. She asked one worker how he felt. "Tired," he said, "tired and weary—like all the others."[25]

In the late 1930s, a former textile worker, long blacklisted in the industry because of his union activities, remembered when the Cone Mills of North Carolina first began its efficiency readjustments in 1925 and the resulting worker protests, which were partially effective. As the leader of the protesters, he demanded adjustments "made in our work so we'll again feel like free humans living in a free country." He told the general manager that "to work under the stretchout system is the same as committing suicide, and we've made up our minds not to do it. But our jobs is not to be taken from us. We mean to defend them if necessary until our blood runs down the streets of White Oak."[26]

On the eve of the cotton code hearings, the *New York Times* noted widespread reports that textile companies in the South were using the stretch out to cut costs.[27] Thomas McMahon later pointed out that from 1926 to 1934 the number of spindle hours run per worker hour had increased 28.1 percent, but industry leaders consistently denied that a stretch out even existed to any significant degree.[28] An NRA economist in 1934 tackled the problem of deciding a fair workload and found it difficult to solve. The quality of the cotton being worked on any given day, the length of the cotton's staple, the density of the weave, the weight or size of the yarn, its strength and quality, and complexity of the weave, the humidity of the atmosphere, and the condition of the loom could determine how many machines a worker could tend comfortably.[29]

Donald Comer made the same point to George Sloan in 1934. No cotton mill was exactly alike. Said Comer: "To undertake a study of the task load in twelve hundred cotton mills with the working conditions in every one different because of one reason or another makes an impossible job, I think." He compared the task to that of deciding how many acres a farmer should plow each day, a task made impossible because of variation in the ground to be plowed. It would, he said, "just be chasing the end of the rainbow when we start out on a program of trying to standardize cotton mill tasks."[30] In a 1934 CTI pamphlet, Joseph E. Sirrine, a textile engineer from Greenville, South Carolina, made the most formal defense of the industry. He portrayed the stretch out as nothing but technological progress and claimed that the work in cotton mills was no more time-centered than that in other modern industries. Standardization of workloads was impossible because of the many variables involved; Sirrine argued that cotton mill owners knew that the result of overloading was inferior products, making a stretch out self-defeating. "The assignment of machine load," he wrote, "must therefore be reasonable in order to be profitable," and he concluded, "No right-thinking employer has any desire to impose an undue burden on his workers nor can he afford to do so, but he must at least be in a position to work out his problems in his own way."[31] In summer 1933, owners denied the existence of a stretch out and talked instead of the "progressive principle of reassignment of work in the mill, through improved machinery, improved yarn, and increasing the personal efficiency of the operative."[32]

Despite these arguments, the overwhelming volume of worker complaints and other evidence indicate that mill managements were pushing hard to increase productivity per worker. Production quotas became standard by the 1930s. In December 1933, Elliot Dunlap Smith, director of industrial studies at the Institute of Human Relations, Yale University, produced the most objective study of the phenomenon. He admitted the utility of labor-saving technological changes but observed that such changes always caused worker upheaval. More than that, he said, "the introduction of labor-saving mechanisms seriously increases the danger of mismanagement." The changes of the late 1920s and early 1930s found both management and labor "so settled in the old ways that it was hard to learn the new" and with "losses staring them in the face, what the directors demanded . . . was quick economies." Many mills "grasped at the possibilities of expansion of workers' duties, while neglecting the slow, expensive work of improving the conditions and methods by which only could the assignment of increased numbers of looms be prevented from resulting in excessive loads." Smith studied eleven mills and found the stretch out to be a reality in four, while in seven others, carefully planned technological change, well managed and fully explained to the workers, resulted in higher productivity and few worker complaints.[33]

Jonathan Daniels, another knowledgeable observer, admitted the necessity of technological progress but had no doubt that in economic crisis owners pushed the outer limits of the workload. "Men and women angrily shout, 'Stretch out!' and stretch out exists. Avarice hidden behind the pretense of efficiency and exploitation often talks big of progress," said Daniels, but "the most stretch out is that which workers paid upon a piece basis, put upon themselves. No foreman could drive them so fast. No system could spread their work so far."[34] The UTW fought both the stretch out and the piece rate system. To the union, the stretch out was a fact. The union claimed that to the mill workers the stretch out meant "driving, speeded-up machines, running ever faster and farther, with more and more human effort to keep up with them and as energy and strength fail, losing hope of ever catching up with them."[35]

The NRA study committee gave this complex, emotional problem the quickest of brushovers. The owners had resented Johnson's on-the-spot agreement with Senator Byrnes to form such a committee. Bruere saw his committee's investigation as a means of reassuring them that the code would work, as well as demonstrating to workers that someone was taking their grievances seriously. The committee's work consisted essentially of visiting mills in South Carolina and holding public hearings in Spartanburg on 13 July 1933 and in Greenville the next day. Bruere reported that the executives were nervous and suspicious, but that when they saw that the committee did not "attempt to hold closeted interviews with workers," they relaxed. By the time the executives testified, they had departed from the position of "rigid denial" of stretch out to a position of acknowledging a complex problem that should be dealt with by "conference and adjustment machinery which should include workers' representation."[36]

The committee moved so quickly and so superficially that it submitted a report to the NRA on 21 July 1933. The committee concluded that, while "sound in principle," the stretch out system had been abused in some cases by employers "through hasty and ill-considered installations with resultant overload on the employees." The report stated that, despite abuses, it was not feasible to contest the application of the stretch out by a rigid formula. The committee had obviously seen stretch out only in terms of new machinery and efficiency studies and not in another common form, the arbitrary increase of workloads. The brief report suggested that solution might be achieved through further study and the development of a plan for "conference and comment" by both labor and management when new workload assignments were considered.[37]

The study committee recommended that in every factory where alleged stretch out existed, or where new workloads were being considered, a mill committee be established with equal representation from employers and employees. The mill committee would adjust differences of opinion on workloads, and the creation of such a committee would be without prejudice to the freedom of association guaranteed in Section 7(a). In all cases, the decision of the mill committee would be binding on employer and employee. In every cotton textile state the NRA should also establish a state board of three members—one each from management, labor, and the public—to function as an appeal agency and as a general administrative body for establishing mill committees throughout the state.

The study committee suggested the establishment of the Cotton Textile National Industrial Relations Board (CTNIRB) to oversee and appoint the state boards. The board would have the "power of final determination in all questions brought before it on appeal" from the state boards. The report reflected the arbitration experiences of its chairperson, but it did not suggest that the elaborate organization it recommended would consider anything other than the problem of stretch out. The committee clearly saw the procedure recommended as one for dealing with worker complaints, not with labor disputes.

As the study committee went about its task, rumors of violations of the cotton textile code's provision concerning wages and hours were heard, the majority from the southern textile centers.[38] The Labor Advisory Board of the NRA, having received charges of violations from scattered worker sources, in late July requested Hugh Johnson to investigate the charges.[39] Johnson, with the stretch out study committee report on his desk, made the quick decision to use the elaborate administrative structure which the report had recommended as a way of meeting the Labor Advisory Board's complaint. Accordingly, he announced on 2 August 1933 that the study committee had been permanently appointed as the CTNIRB.

As originally proposed, the CTNIRB, or the Bruere Board as it came to be commonly known, was, in Johnson's charge, to "guarantee a peaceful settlement of all disputes" in the cotton textile industry. "It is to serve as a model for such strife-torn industries as coal and steel and to point to a way out of the jungle of industrial warfare to the peaceful valley of mutual cooperation."[40] Almost overnight the board had passed from being a grievance board to being an all-purpose labor relations board. The Johnson order accepted intact the Bruere proposal for setting up local mill committees and state boards. Bruere would become a full-time NRA employee, while the other two members, Geer and Berry, would serve only as public-spirited citizens paid on a per diem basis.

The Bruere Board became a legal entity by an amendment to the cotton textile code. The amendment, quickly proposed by George Sloan, president of the CTI and by August president of the Code Authority, was accepted immediately by Johnson and President Roosevelt. The amendment directed the board to consider stretch out problems and "any other problems of working conditions in the cotton textile industry."[41] The amendment did not change Section 17 of the code, and it in no way implied collective bargaining as an industry standard or goal. Only the management-dominated Code Authority and the NRA validated this new labor board. No public hearings were held. The goldfish bowl was in storage.

Because it was created under the Code Authority, however, the board often worked in considerable confusion. Was it an NRA board or a Code Authority board? Clearly, in a legal sense, it was an NRA board, but Bruere always felt responsible to the Code Authority which, under Section 17 of the code, had responsibility for labor relations. Bruere never clearly understood who he worked for and confused everybody by his ambivalence. In the months ahead, the Bruere Board never did establish its independence from the Code Authority, which was virtually synonymous with the Cotton-Textile Institute and of course never saw itself as an NRA agency.[42]

The amendment to the cotton textile code only vaguely described the duties of the Bruere Board. Over a period of time, however, the board gradually assumed responsibility—in the same common law way that the evolving NLB did—for handling all labor problems in the cotton textile industry, including discrimination for union activities, stretch out complaints, classification and definition of occupations, disputes over wages and hours, procedures for collective bargaining, and any other alleged violations of code provisions affecting relations between employees and employers. Soon after its establishment, the Bruere Board commissioned three-person boards in nine states: North Carolina; South Carolina; Georgia; Mississippi; Alabama; Tennessee; Louisiana; Massachusetts; and, Rhode Island. These boards, following the original recommendations, were in turn responsible for establishing labor-management committees in individual cotton mills. The Bruere Board expected that the individual mill committees would settle labor-management problems at the local level. In case of a failure to arrive at a settlement, recourse should be to the state boards. The national board was to be the "court of last resort."[43] The whole structure still smacked of an elaborate grievance procedure, rather than a procedure to develop lasting labor laws.

The state boards had difficulties. The board members, representing labor, management, and the public, were to work without salary or even per diem. Only expenses were paid. It is not clear that the boards were ever fully formed or continuously appointed. Most were clearly inactive from the very beginning. The UTW quickly decided to bypass the state boards altogether if possible, and to appeal to the national board directly. The beleaguered state chairperson of North Carolina, Theodore Johnson, wrote on 27 May 1934 that he had always confronted a UTW "uniform policy to ignore" his board.[44]

Only in South Carolina was there a genuine effort to make Bruere's system work. There, H.H. Willis, a forty-two-year-old professor of textile engineering at Clemson University, actually reported that thirty-eight mill committees had been formed. In his first report, Willis claimed to have written over one thousand letters, traveled fifty-five hundred miles in South Carolina, and spent fifty-two days on the road. He reported that he had settled some twenty cases about wage disputes and had mediated in five strikes. Willis spent $1,951.14 pursuing labor peace, and he argued forcefully to Bruere that union complaints about code violations "are absolutely without foundation."[45] But his board had formally considered only one case.

In North Carolina, Theodore Johnson was not nearly that active, but by spring 1934, ten formal cases on code violations had been to the state board.[46] Johnson, however, soon earned the deep enmity of UTW organizers, and the Bruere Board had to hold a hearing to clear him of UTW charges of antiunion and illegal code activities. Only in Georgia was there any other state board activity, and both there and in North Carolina no progress toward the mill committee system was reported. The state boards clearly saw themselves only as mediating boards, replicating the federal service already available.[47]

The Bruere Board itself was not a sitting board working daily in labor relations in the cotton industry. Bruere was the only active member of the board, and he told George Sloan in September 1933 that Geer and Berry "left it largely up to me to develop the work of our board."[48] The board held only monthly meetings, and its deliberations seldom took a full day. The crucial meeting of 25 November 1933, for example, which confirmed Bruere's and Sloan's procedures for handling complaints, lasted only three hours in the morning. Although public hearings were held in a few cases, the board itself never devoted any sustained time to the discussion of labor policy. Bruere had a fulltime executive assistant, L.R. Gilbert, who managed the office and correspondence and served as a major liaison officer to the rest of the NRA hierarchy as well as the daily contact person with Sloan's office in New York City. The entire edifice of the New Deal's labor policy agency in cotton textiles confirmed subsequent judgments about the early New Deal. It was ad hoc, superficial, and exceedingly temporary in tone and concept.

Bruere early decided to separate labor difficulties into two categories: labor "disputes" and labor "complaints." With reference to disputes, the board would attempt, it said, to mediate strike disputes and would act as arbitrator, upon invitation. Above all, it encouraged the state boards to make such work unnecessary by forming mill committees. Bruere accepted the argument that under the code the board had no power at all in disputes. George Sloan, president of the Code Authority, had settled the matter in July 1934 when he called the board's activities "a purely cooperative and voluntary method of adjusting disputes."[50]

For all practical purposes, the board opted out of the problem of strikes in the industry, and it never was involved in any of them except in the events leading to the great strike of September 1934. The board always saw Section 7(a) as a neutral statement. It never conducted a representation election, and it ignored entirely the developing sense of collective bargaining being created by the NLB. To the board, Section 7(a), as a mechanism of collective bargaining, did not mean anything in an administrative sense.

Bruere, however, was determined to make the board an effective national grievance agency for the industry. But the rising volume of complaints and the growing sense that the state boards would not do the job forced some new decisions. The Bruere Board had only a tiny budget, no staff, and a chairperson who believed that the Code Authority had ultimate responsibility for labor relations. The UTW quickly mounted a campaign to have workers send complaints directly to the board. To handle this unanticipated turn of events, Bruere, in consultation with his quasi-boss George Sloan, worked out a system by September 1933 whereby the board's Washington office acted as a central clearinghouse to collect individual complaints of whatever nature, including complaints alleging violations of Section 7(a). The complaints, neatly excerpted to a few brief sentences on one of the several boilerplate forms Bruere devised, were sent to Sloan's office, headquarters of the Code Authority, in New York. The Code Authority hired two and sometimes three field examiners to "investigate" the complaints of code violations. Under this arrangement, reports on the field investigations were not even sent back to the Bruere Board, but were routed to NRA's Planning and Supervisory Committee of the Cotton Textile Industry, a nonfunctioning committee chaired by Hugh Johnson.[51]

Presumably, if violations continued, Johnson would use the general compliance machinery of the NRA, itself cumbersome and ill-defined, to effect cooperation. In fact, the industry was left to investigate itself, a procedure quite in line with the NRA theory of self-regulation. Even if the Bruere Board had done its own investigations, something never considered in Bruere's original proposal nor in Johnson's hasty establishment of the board, little would have been accomplished. The Bruere Board, created by amendment to the cotton code and considered to belong half to the NRA and half to the Code Authority, had no coercive power whatsoever at its own disposal. Its only real weapon was persuasion, but the quiescent parttime board neither sought power nor persuaded anyone.

Complaints to the board included every conceivable labor problem.[52] The excerpts sent to the Code Authority omitted the name of the complainant. Only the mill and its location were identified. Numerous complaints charged that workloads had been increased unfairly (stretch out); if true, such action would have violated the code. The largest number of complaints argued that code wages were not being paid, though many of the complainants thought the minimum wage was guaranteed even if forty hours were not worked. George Googe, southern organizer for the AFL, stated on 13 August 1933 that he had collected five hundred individual complaints about cotton code violations to place before the NRA. "No mills that I know of," declared Googe, "are living up to the Code as signed by the President."[53] Discrimination against union membership was another common charge, with workers claiming that they were arbitrarily fired for the most minor step toward union organization. Consider this excerpt from a 3 July 1934 complaint from the Norris Cotton Mills, Cateechee, South Carolina: "They are doing everything they can think about to down the union. Fire union men or women if they just look cross eyed. The superintendent said he was going to fire one that got up the textile organization; *going to fire everyone he could*" [emphasis original]. Many complaints were vague and of a general nature. One from the Thomaston Cotton Mill, Thomaston, Georgia, dated 21 July 1934, said, "We don't make enough to have a decent living. I hope you will do something about our wages soon." The Bruere Board dutifully acknowledged each complaint in a letter to the sender and often enclosed a mimeographed sheet of the code regulations allegedly violated. Often the worker was advised to approach the state board to set up a mill committee.

The Code Authority reported to the Bruere Board on the complaints it investigated. The two agents in the South visited the mills identified, asked to see time books, and asked questions about workloads. They sometimes questioned workers, but they had no specific names of complainants. At best, their reports were only three or four sentences long. Not surprisingly, they reported almost no stretch out, only misunderstandings of new scientific work assignments or substandard workers being dismissed. They concluded that discrimination for union activity was almost nonexistent and that many workers confused production layoffs with being fired. For example, of the complaints received in August 1933, the Code Authority reported that it had made sixty-nine investigations, in which seven minor violations of the code were found and quickly corrected. Twenty-one of the investigations concerned stretch out, and the Code Authority reported that three of the investigations had resulted in work changes.[54] Robert Bruere toured the South himself in late August and early September 1933 and concluded that the Code Authority reports squared with what he had found. By fall 1933, the Bruere Board thought it had a smoothly running procedure in place.

TOWARDS CONFLICT

In the South, the workers expected changes if a truly New Deal was on the way. Restlessly, many signed the UTW cards in anticipation of better things to come. Throughout late summer and fall 1934, a number of short-lived strikes, resembling the strikes of 1929, broke out. They were spontaneous nonunion walkouts of a few days to protest a stretch out or some other shop floor condition. UTW officials often moved in quickly to mediate the strikes, willing to use the Bruere Board and even, if necessary, the mill committee system. But by early fall, though the industry was still in the throes of the post-code prosperity, the union recognized that its momentum had slowed and that nowhere in the South had collective bargaining become a reality. Eventually the union would have to deliver something to its members.

In October 1933, McMahon, breaking the carefully builtup sense of union cooperation, reported that the code was "not functioning properly" and was "not increasing employment and raising wage totals to the extent claimed by the proponents." Left unsaid was the union's disappointment that Section 7(a) had not brought collective bargaining. The union vigorously attacked Robert Bruere's grievance procedure. McMahon claimed that he had personally sent fifteen hundred complaints of code violations to the Bruere Board, but had received no evidence that these complaints had been investigated, much less adjusted.[55] The production cuts of December 1934, with accompanying reduction of weekly earnings, coming as it did without any consultation with the Code Authority or public hearing, shocked the union. The UTW protested vigorously and went so far as to ask the AFL to consider the advisability of a general strike by American labor to force a thirty-hour week at forty-hour wages.[56] The UTW leadership realized that the 25-percent production cut would reduce the minimum wage per week in the South from twelve dollars to nine and that workers already working at about half the national average industrial wage would find survival even more difficult.

By early 1934, the pressure of its new members and the surge of union membership across the country in other industries forced the UTW to become more aggressive as the voice of the nation's textile workers. The new locals were mostly paper affairs, with no firm foundation in collective bargaining to justify their existence. As the boom effect of the code in the industry had subsided and a new recession began, the pressure on the manufacturers to meet competition was passed on to the workers, first in production cuts and then, inevitably, in a push for higher productivity. Relations between managers and workers in the mills once again deteriorated, bringing dangerous levels of tension. The UTW found itself in a difficult situation. Its policy in summer and fall 1934, of organizing vigorously and cooperating with the Bruere Board in settling labor disputes, had not worked. Neither the owners nor the board paid any attention to collective bargaining. Indeed, the board's whole procedure had been designed as if unions did not exist, and it paid no attention to the struggles of the NLB to add meaning to Section 7(a). Increasingly, though, questioning workers demanded more concrete action by the union.[57] The time had come for the textile union to put flesh on the spare bones of Section 7(a).

The obvious target was the Bruere Board, the focal point of federal labor policy for the cotton textile industry. President McMahon sent an open letter to the UTW locals in January 1934 in which he spelled out the union's dissatisfaction. The UTW leader lashed out at the Bruere Board for its failure to enforce Section 7(a). The Bruere Board had refused to recognize the NLB's rule of majority representation and had referred all questions involving Section 7(a) to the Code Authority for investigation. The UTW also argued that the board was ineffective in obtaining reinstatement or redress for workers fired or disciplined for joining the union. McMahon also rapped the board for its failure to halt stretch out, its first assignment. Furthermore, the UTW now openly attacked the mill committee system, seeing it as a form of company union and as a potential device for blocking the progress of independent organization. A functioning mill committee system minimized the need for a union. For the first time McMahon sharply criticized the Bruere Board for using agents of the employers' Cotton-Textile Institute to investigate charges against the members of the institute, emphasizing the inherent conflict of interest. McMahon also cried out against the procedure under which the board made no provision for reporting back to the original complainant the outcome of investigations.[58]

Despite these criticisms, the cautious McMahon was careful to avoid an open break with the Bruere Board. He feared confrontation with the NRA and the powerful mill owners. His policy was to continue to cooperate with the board. Even after the list of complaints in his open letter, he wrote, "To say all this is to make no charges of unfairness against the National Cotton Industrial Relations Board — the members are quite cooperative." He told the members of the union that "clearly our course of action for the immediate future is to cooperate wholeheartedly in the use of the machinery, hoping and believing that it will bring about more peaceful and orderly industrial relations." The union "must give it a full and unprejudiced trial" and judge it by "good works."[59] The only overt action McMahon proposed was that the cotton code be reexamined in public hearings to study the UTW's criticism. He also asked that the hearings consider his charges that the minimum pay scale was frequently being adopted as the maximum. McMahon's open letter garnered no response from the board, the NRA, or the industry.

Cotton textile employers and the Bruere Board held complementary views of what constituted peaceful and progressive labor relations. *Cotton* asserted in September 1933 that UTW claims of code violations developed "from biased or prejudiced sources" and contended that the "mills as a whole have adopted the spirit as well as the letter of the code."[60] This contention still persisted in spring 1934. Thomas M. Marchant, president of the ACMA, told the cotton manufacturers in April 1934 that with but few exceptions he had "found the textile industry of the South diligently seeking to carry out the provisions of the code."[61] The previous month Marchant had written to Hugh Johnson that labor-management relations in the southern cotton textile industry were excellent. "Not in my thirty-odd years of mill experience," declared Marchant, "have I ever seen the textile workers as happy and contented as they are today."[62] George Sloan, Code Authority chairperson, constantly defended the Bruere Board and its procedures. In December 1933, he denied code violations, emphasized peaceful labor-management relations, and argued that field representatives of the Code Authority were "constantly checking" claims of violations.[63]

The Code Authority gave little thought or discussion time to labor relations, but that may have been because they had so little to discuss.[64] They all agreed on the need to oppose unions and collective bargaining. Donald Comer, chairperson of the working conditions subcommittee of the Code Authority, wrote in 1933 to fellow manufacturer William D. Anderson, noting growing NRA acceptance of unions and expressing his fear that the New Deal's acceptance of unions could "be the beginning of the end of the old order of things." Personally, he said he was not opposed to unions if they "can submit to responsible leadership for industrial workers that will insure orderly attention to the job at hand, that will result in 6 percent profit on the invested capital." Nevertheless, he saw no need for them in 1933. The code provided for "handling every question that can arise between owner and employee."[65]

But labor problems would not go away. The first major action of the Code Authority was to accept the Bruere Committee report on stretch out and to accept stretch out, if genuine, as a code violation.[66] Comer's correspondence with other Code Authority members such as Cason Callaway, Charles Cannon, and William D. Anderson concerned itself more with such matters as the cotton processing tax, prices, exemptions, and profits, but he also talked about the labor problems that affected the code. Labor and unions were a messy intrusion. George Sloan wrote to Thomas Marchant of this frustration in September 1933, observing, "What you have to say in regard to the labor agitation in our industry has caused me more concern than almost anything else that has transpired under the Code. There is hardly a day that I do not discuss the matter long distance with some of the Washington officials, and it begins to look, so far as publicity is concerned, that someone has put the quietus on these people."[67]

Like the Bruere Board, the Code Authority saw the code's labor relations provision as nothing more than a grievance procedure. Collective bargaining was not an outcome of the 1933 bargaining in Washington. "Overemphasis of the collective bargaining clauses" wrote Sloan to Hugh Johnson in October 1933, "has been a seriously disrupting force by leading employees to think that they must become affiliated with some particular union to get the benefits of the Recovery Act provisions." Sloan reported to Johnson that the Code Authority thought it was important that "labor and industry should end futile discussions of strikes and remain at work" and that the NRA never "force" unionism "as a preliminary step to collective bargaining."[68] Formally, in response to complaints of code violations, the Code Authority voted not to reopen the code for "labor questions," and Sloan reported that there were few real complaints, evidence of the "smoothness with which the Cotton Textile Code is functioning in respect to its labor provisions."[69]

The NRA continually supported the Code Authority and the Bruere Board, even though the board had paid no attention to the NLB's attempt to put teeth into Section 7(a). The board itself had to force Benjamin Geer, the industry spokesman, to cooperate at all in settling labor problems. In October 1933 he actually contended that the Bruere Board and the state boards had no authority to "adjust controversies" at individual mills over wages, hours, or working conditions, and he consistently balked at accepting the principle of majority rule in determining a bargaining agency for collective bargaining. Bruere, in a telegram to Sloan in late October 1933, asked Sloan to interpret the board's powers![70] The NRA ignored contradictions in labor policy from industry to industry. In April 1934, the NRA issued a press release praising the work of the Bruere Board, saying that it had transformed the cotton textile industry from a "strife-torn" to a "harmonious" group. The NRA reported that the board had settled over 3,200 cases of "misunderstandings" between employer and employees. Oddly enough, the news blurb stated that the board, by perfectly interpreting Section 7(a), "guarantees collective bargaining, guarantees a worker protection if he cares to join a labor union, does not force a worker to join any type of labor organization, but protects his rights to affiliate with any group, does nothing to remove the right to strike, but provides the means for settling all problems of working conditions without the need for strikes and lockouts." But the Bruere Board was not trying to obtain its ends by "bludgeoning"; its goal, said the NRA, was to bring cooperation through "peace and voluntary arguement."[71] Even in spring 1934, the NRA still had great expectations for its showpiece first code, though of course everywhere else the NRA had begun to experience disintegration, failure, and increasing attacks on the concept of the great partnership of government and business.[72]

By the end of winter 1934, the relief and surge of optimism in the cotton industry that had greeted the New Deal's code of fair competition had changed back to apprehension and a growing recognition that not much had changed. The business boom of late 1933 had ended, and index figures computed by the Department of Commerce showed a decline in cotton textile production, measured in percent of operating capacity, from full production in October 1933 to 72.6 percent in June 1934. The decline in business evidently put all too familiar pressure on the individual producers to reduce production costs through stretch out, layoffs, and wage reductions in the higher-paying categories.

Increasingly, protests came from the workers, and the UTW specifically attacked deteriorating working conditions in the South. The union claimed that although minimum wages had been increased in the southern mills, top wages for highly skilled workers had been reduced, thereby decreasing the wage difference between skilled and unskilled workers. The UTW had made the charge since fall 1933, though George Sloan had written to Hugh Johnson claiming that the charge was "nothing short of a colossal falsehood."[73] Furthermore, the union repeatedly argued that in cases where the wages had not been cut, the mill owners had sought to lower production costs by increasing the production of the individual workers through the use of illegal stretch outs, though the Bruere Board had begun to deny that stretch out existed at all.[74] The UTW also charged that the code wages were too low and were responsible for "dire conditions of abject poverty" among southern workers. A letter which the UTW claimed had been received from a southern worker revealed the increasing resentment toward the mill owners. "They claim," wrote the worker, "they are not making money. Well, if they are not making money, I ask you, how can they afford to build these fine mansions to live in? How can every member of the family own his or her own car? How can they spend the hot summers at the seashores? How can they afford to send their children to college and obtain the best education?"[75]

Pressure continued to build on the UTW leaders as the rank and file clamored for relief. Thomas McMahon, the aging president, was not inclined to take any radical steps. Consistently, he stuck to his policy of abiding by the Bruere Board's complaint system, even though it had decided only a few cases. He mounted no more than a rhetorical attack on federal labor policy. Under attack himself in the union, he was suspicious of "radical" elements within the UTW; he possessed a "deep-seated antipathy to socialism and communism."[76] But the active young vice-president, Francis Gorman, although also a business unionist and comfortable with the old traditions of the UTW, was more liberal and practical than McMahon. Increasingly McMahon let Gorman make the decisions and provide the leadership.[77]

On 1 March 1934 the NRA finally held a conference of interested parties to review the various textile codes, part of the famous "field days" of criticism that Johnson had initiated in late February. Gorman, appearing for the UTW, took the opportunity to direct the now familiar flood of criticism at the cotton textile code, the Code Authority, and the Bruere Board. He reminded the NRA that labor had not been given sufficient opportunity to make its views known in the formation of the code, and he objected to the several modifications of the code without consultation with labor. Gorman ripped the Code Authority for its failure to include labor representation; consequently, Gorman said, the UTW had to depend on the public press for information about the operation of the code. He complained that the code contained no guarantee to keep wages high for the more skilled cotton textile workers.

Gorman directed attention to the North-South wage differential and requested a study leading to its disappearance. He proposed a four-point action program for all the textile codes, to be adopted immediately, according to which labor would send representatives to the Code Authority, the NRA would appoint a new industrial relations committee to govern labor-management relations in all the textile industries, the NRA would overhaul and increase the efficiency of the industry's information and reporting system, and, the most forceful demand, the new industrial relations committee would vigorously enforce the collective bargaining provisions of Section 7(a), by which Gorman meant bargaining unit elections and the requirement that management actually bargain.[78]

Gorman's pleas for improvement of the code and support of collective bargaining received almost no attention from the mill owners, who always refused publicly to acknowledge the UTW's existence. Many of them believed that the UTW claims of increased membership were pure fiction, bluff and bluster. They discounted cards signed and the hastily organized locals of 1933 and early 1934. Thomas M. Marchant told the annual ACMA meeting in April 1934, only weeks after Gorman's Washington proposals, that the southern workers were "better satisfied and more economically safe than they have been for a long time." Robert Bruere appeared at the same meeting, making one of his rare public statements in defense of the Bruere Board, to inform the mill owners that the board was "proceeding cautiously" on Section 7(a).[79] Bruere would later tell a group of UTW organizers that the board had worked slowly and unobtrusively because its power was limited "by the law" and that in dealing with labor problems it had to consider what the "whole administration thinks." A southern UTW organizer interrupted him at that point, saying, "I don't like so much interpretation. I like to see a board make a decision and say yes or no."[80]

The Bruere Board with a labor member indifferent to textile workers was paralyzed by its indecision regarding whom it worked for and what labor law really was. Wary of majority rule collective bargaining policy; working with scant resources; and dependent on the NRA, the Code Authority, and the never-guaranteed goodwill of the owners, the board, by spring 1934, had contributed to the improvement of workers' lives in the South only to the extent that its grievance system had worked in a few specific cases. It found itself ill equipped for the great test to come.

Hillside Cotton Mills plant, LaGrange, Ga., 1933. The plant was built around 1915, so was relatively new, but note the rural atmosphere. Courtesy, Georgia Dept. of Archives and History.

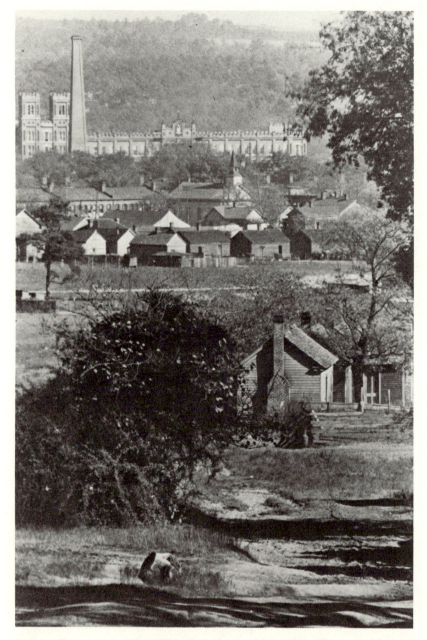

Augusta, Ga., 1912–1915. King Mill in the background. Note the mill's grand appearance and how it looms over the surrounding houses. Courtesy, Georgia Dept. of Archives and History.

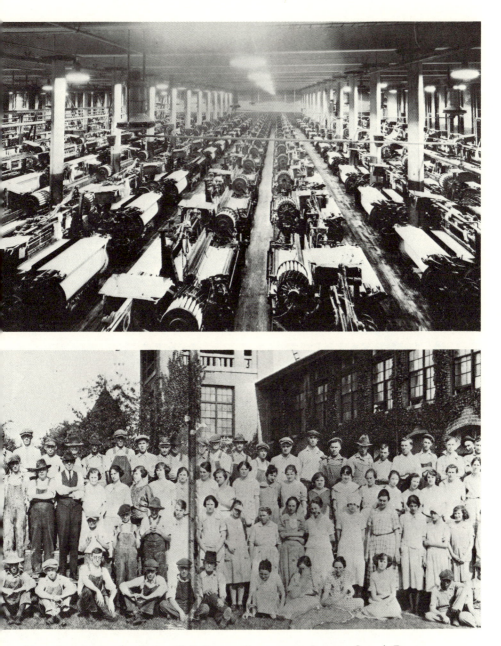

Above: Loom room of a cotton mill, LaGrange, Ga., ca. 1930. Courtesy Georgia Dept. of Archives and History. *Below:* Employees of the Dixie Cotton Mills, LaGrange, Ga., 1923. The mill opened in 1895 and today is part of West Point Pepperell, Inc. Note the younger workers; the depression and the code eliminated workers of this age. Courtesy, Georgia Dept. of Archives and History.

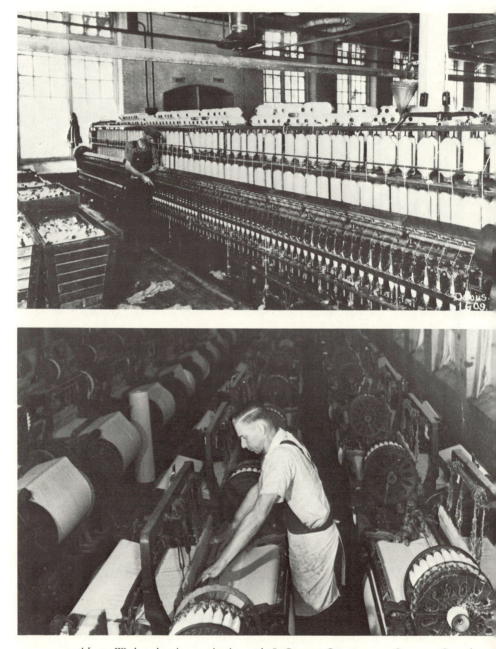

Above: Worker cleaning a spinning rack, LaGrange, Ga., ca. 1930. Courtesy, Georgia Dept. of Archives and History. *Below*: Working at the Mary-Leila Cotton Mill, Greensboro, Ga., Oct. 1941. Arthur Franklin Raper Papers. Courtesy, Southern Historical Collection, Wilson Library, University of North Carolina at Chapel Hill.

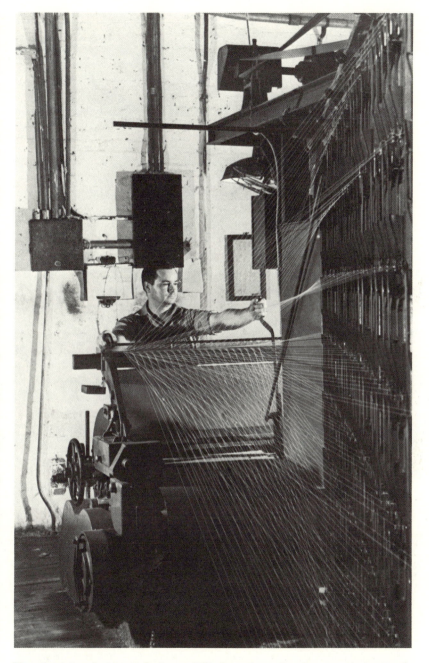

"Drawing-in" at the Mary-Leila Cotton Mill, Greensboro, Ga., Oct. 1941. Arthur Franklin Raper Papers. Courtesy, Southern Historical Collection, Wilson Library, University of North Carolina at Chapel Hill.

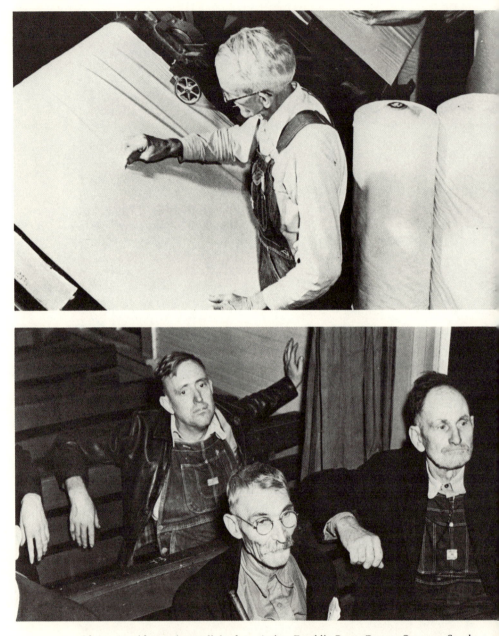

Above: An older worker on light duty. Arthur Franklin Raper Papers. Courtesy, Southern Historical Collection, Wilson Library, University of North Carolina at Chapel Hill. *Below*: Union meeting of textile workers, Greensboro, Ga., Nov. 1941. Arthur Franklin Raper Papers. Courtesy, Southern Historical Collection, Wilson Library, University of North Carolina at Chapel Hill.

TWUA pickets in a strike, Greensboro, Ga., May 1941. Arthur Franklin Raper Papers. Courtesy, Southern Historical Collection, Wilson Library, University of North Carolina at Chapel Hill.

"President Roosevelt is the only man on God's green earth who can stop this strike"

PRELUDE TO THE GENERAL STRIKE, MAY–AUGUST 1934

From spring 1934 to fall 1934, cotton textile industry leaders, the NRA and its labor board, the workers, and the union were caught up in a long struggle which finally culminated in a general strike, the largest strike in American history up to that time. Worker and union discontent boiled into open hostility on 22 May 1934, when Hugh Johnson approved the Code Authority's proposal for a second production cut to last sixty to ninety days. The new production plan called for two daily shifts of thirty hours each, with the hourly wage rates remaining the same. As so often in the past, the owners and the NRA ignored the union as they decided on a course of action.

As early as 25 March the *New York Times* reported calls in the industry for another period of production curtailment similar to that of the previous December and January. By 5 May the UTW, strongly opposed to another curtailment, announced that it had formed an emergency committee to deal with this new threat. McMahon noted the increasing unemployment in the industry and predicted that another curtailment would only make the lot of the workers more miserable. He asked that President Roosevelt intervene to stop any curtailment order.[1] Failure to do so, he declared, would mean disaster to the industry. UTW leaders feared that the proposed curtailment would force a crisis and necessitate a response from the UTW in a crucial test of the union's strength. The growing discontent of the workers could not be dismissed by the union.

The Code Authority ignored the union, as it always did, and on 8 May 1934 announced its intention to continue studying the "feasibility" of a production cut. The Code Authority insisted to the NRA that curtailment was necessary to offset overcapacity in the industry. Sloan reported on 22 May that in the last two weeks of April 1934, cotton textile sales had amounted to only 49 percent of production. Almost every firm, he stated, had large amounts of unsold inventory on hand.[2] But the Code Authority faced a divided NRA.

The economists there had developed strong arguments against the earlier curtailment, and they opposed a second. Hugh Johnson, still a devout believer in self-regulation and stabilization, overruled them after some wavering, and, under intense pressure from Sloan, accepted the Code Authority's new effort to subdue the dragon of overproduction.[3] Johnson acted without consulting with the UTW, and McMahon immediately protested the hasty action, telling Johnson, "I believe this lack of confidence on the part of the employer will bring chaos into the industry." In his letter of protest, the UTW leader requested a conference with the Code Authority. In effect, he was requesting industrywide collective bargaining. He demanded that hourly wage rates be increased to offset the hour reduction, and he urged that wages of skilled and semiskilled workers be standardized. McMahon, attempting to deal with the ubiquitous stretch out once and for all, also requested that machine workloads be reduced.

Johnson's out-of-hand denial of McMahon's demands created a sense of crisis in the union. On 28 May, Francis Gorman threatened a general strike in the cotton textile industry involving 300,000 workers if the NRA curtailment went into effect. "There won't be a cotton mill open in the country in two weeks," Gorman declared, "if this order is carried out."[5] Gorman's bold threat met immediate resistance in the industry. David Clark, editor of the *Textile Bulletin*, scoffed at the threat and ridiculed McMahon and Gorman, writing that southern workers would not follow "these two foreign-born professional agitators at a time when they know that the mills in which they are working can not get enough orders to keep their spindles and looms busy." Even the moderate editor of *Textile World* announced that the action of the UTW was not only "economically unsound but socially inimical." The editor thought such a strike threat in a business depression was "stupidly timed" and "insincerely launched." The Charlotte *Observer* saw the proposed strike as a "biting snap" by labor at the NRA hand from which it had been "liberally feeding."[6]

Hugh Johnson, hoping to avoid trouble in the already tense atmosphere of 1934, with its many strikes, decided that the time had come to consult labor.[7] He arranged a conference between himself and McMahon for 1 June. Johnson also asked Bruere and Sloan to attend. Sloan refused the invitation to attend as chairperson of the Code Authority and as president of the CTI, although in a major concession, he consented to attend as George Sloan, private citizen. On 31 May, the same day that Johnson announced the conference plans, Sloan, on the attack, declared that the threatened strike was "an attempt to overthrow by force the provisions of the Cotton Textile Code." Sloan said that the curtailment order would have little effect on many mills since they were already running only 75 percent of the time.[8]

Sloan and the industry were already disappointed over what the code had accomplished, and particularly with the Code Authority's inability to establish even suggested price lists because of industry resistance and NRA opposition.[9] The industry chafed at what it considered NRA meddling in self-government. Sloan gloomily reported to Code Authority member William D. Anderson, who had similar complaints, "Unhappily we have not reached the point, and I doubt if we ever will, when the Code Authority will be allowed to handle matters of this kind [the curtailment] without the government's approval."[10] Sloan came to Washington in no mood to compromise, although Johnson expressed confidence that no strike would occur and the curtailment order would go through, with some concessions to the UTW. Johnson believed that the cotton textile industry's refusal to recognize the UTW as a national bargaining agency, and not production cuts, was the real reason for the strike threat.[11]

Another conference, less publicized, also took place. On 30 May a group of UTW organizers met with Robert Bruere to voice their dissatisfaction with his board's attitude toward collective bargaining and its handling of worker complaints and the stretch out. Bruere made clear his belief that the board was more responsible to the Code Authority than to the NRA, and he once again asked for cooperation with his grievance system. The UTW, he argued, operated on a "war basis," with workers on one side and management on the other. Time was needed to bring peace.[12]

Johnson had to mediate the crisis. With Sloan in one room and the UTW contingent in another, he shuttled back and forth to produce a document acceptable in both rooms. Johnson put great pressure on the UTW, while Sloan remained noncommittal. Late on the second day, the UTW abandoned its strike threat. The Labor Advisory Board of the NRA would add one more labor representative, and the Bruere Board would add one member representing textile labor and one representing industry. A representative from the UTW would advise the NRA members of the Code Authority but would not be a member of the Code Authority. An investigation of the economic conditions of the cotton textile industry would be undertaken by NRA's Industrial Planning and Research Committee. Specifically, the NRA was to determine if the industry could pay higher wages, if the wage differential for higher skills had been kept, and if production cuts were necessary and at what level the cotton textile industry needed to operate to meet essential demand. Finally, the union agreed that the already-approved production cuts of June, July, and August would go into effect.[13]

McMahon and Gorman, who had by now assumed *de facto* leadership of the UTW, directed their locals to cancel plans for a strike. The union happily proclaimed to the press that settlement was "the beginning of a new day for the cotton textile workers."[14] The hesitant union, uncertain of its strength in a confrontation, had bitten at another razzle-dazzle NRA bait. But that was all it could do, short of the showdown strike which it had threatened. The CIO's Textile Workers Organizing Committee (TWOC) argued later that in this period a considerable discrepancy existed between members on the UTW books and the number functioning in the locals. The TWOC argued that the UTW had not "built to hold."[15]

Reluctant to force the issue, the union merely played for time in the June agreement and hoped, in vain, that the New Deal labor policy would eventually come to its rescue.[16] On the other hand, George Sloan, still on the offensive, claimed the settlement as a victory for the ideals and practices of the Code Authority. The CTI leaders "celebrated when they saw the settlement."[17] William Anderson wrote to congratulate Sloan. "We have won a great victory," he claimed, "and in fact mopped up" McMahon and Gorman. Nevertheless, Donald Comer, although pleased, was not happy in having to deal with the UTW and the NRA, whom he "thought to be determined to turn industry over to the workers."[18] Johnson praised the settlement he had wrought and used the occasion to laud the work of the Bruere Board. In the South, cotton textile industry leaders breathed "a long sigh of relief," although few owners there thought the truce was final. A general feeling existed throughout the industry and the NRA that the union would try to consolidate its gains, rather than push its demands.[19] But the curtailment's effect and the economic distress of the workers and owners continued to feed the festering discontent in the Piedmont.

As the summer began, the NRA speedily announced the results of its hasty investigation into the economic problems of the industry, called for in the June settlement. The report, issued on 15 June by Leon Henderson's Research and Planning Division, concluded that "normal demand" in the industry, the demand if there had been no depression, required a minimum of ninety hours per week of productive machine operation. That was ten hours more than the industry operated under the code. The NRA economists used the report as a weapon in their struggle in the NRA against the economics of scarcity. Ignoring the fact of the depression, the report disagreed with the production cuts, stating that "the real problem is not how to restrict production of the cotton textiles, but how to make available to the entire population an adequate supply of cotton goods of all descriptions."[20] Such a conclusion was singularly unhelpful to the NRA, the Code Authority, and the union, none of which had the luxury of assuming that there was no business slump.

Henderson released a second report on 29 June which found no sound basis under existing conditions for a general increase in cotton textile code wage rates. The report said that hourly wages throughout the industry had already increased 70 percent since summer 1933, and that the weekly pay on an hourly basis was 12 percent over that of 1929 in purchasing power. These figures provided backing for the owners, although in summer 1934 no worker had a full forty-hour work week, because of the mandated production cuts. Late in the summer, on 14 August, the NRA issued its third and last report, which concluded that on the whole the industry had maintained the wage differential between skilled and unskilled labor in accordance with the requirements of the code.[21]

The first report only confused its readers, while the other two appeared to argue that the workers' economic position was stronger in 1934 than before the code was instituted. The reports ignored the destructive impact of the production cuts and the continuing business recession in the industry. The NRA also made no attempt to evaluate the code, collective bargaining, or workers' complaints of stretch out and continued harassment for union activities. The economists at the NRA had ended their work, and the reports wafted away on the summer air. Few people paid any attention to them.

Pursuant to the June agreement, Johnson amended the cotton code on 10 July.[22] One amendment added a new labor representation to the Bruere Board. Accordingly, on 10 August, Johnson appointed Council M. Fox, an inexperienced young southern UTW organizer from North Carolina, chosen from a list of six submitted by Thomas McMahon. An industry representative was also appointed. Shortly afterward, McMahon himself was appointed to the Labor Advisory Board of the NRA, and Abraham Binns, a UTW official from New England, became the union adviser to the government members of the Code Authority. A confusing second amendment of the code spelled out the exclusive powers of the Bruere Board to handle labor complaints. Johnson probably saw it as ending the ambiguity that Bruere had created by his insistence that the Code Authority had ultimate power in matters of labor complaints. The third amendment permitted the employees in a mill to choose their mill committees from whatever sources they desired, even if the chosen members were not workers in the mill. The Code Authority would find this amendment illegal, since it was made without the consent of the industry. In summer 1934, however, the mill committees were little more than a dream in the head of Robert Bruere.

BEFORE THE BATTLE

The NRA effort to achieve a peaceful solution to the labor-management conflict in the cotton textile industry came too late. In some places, rather than just run at the shortened hours, mills would close every fourth week, leaving workers without a weekly paycheck.[23] By mid-summer, the UTW members, reeling under the impact of the production cuts and with wages averaging $11.50 a week for the most unskilled workers, a sum below even the promised minimum, were bent on bettering their condition.

The UTW, spreading the gospel of the New Deal, had awakened many of the textile workers of the South, and now UTW leaders perched precariously on a tiger's back. "When we first received word about the textile code, the Blue Eagle, and our right to organize," said J.P. Holland, secretary-treasurer of the Alabama State Textile Council, "it seemed too good to be true. It was a real New Deal for us."[24] But Hamilton Basso reported that by the middle of 1934, the southern worker's attitude had changed since the optimistic days of the previous summer. "Southern textile workers," he wrote, "feel they have been betrayed. It is impossible to emphasize the faith they had in the Code. They thought they were going to get a break at last. A President in the White House who was 'for them.' When the Code went into effect there were dances and celebrations."[25] A year later, the workers waited with growing frustration for the good times. The editor of *Textile World* reported in July that "not one shred of cooperation, sympathy, or mutual understanding exists between southern manufacturers and textile labor organizers."[26]

Johnson, perhaps having second thoughts after the June settlement about dealing with the UTW, asked Gorman to supply membership documentation so that the NRA could ascertain if it were a bona fide agent for textile workers on a national scale. On 21 June Gorman sent a long letter to Johnson claiming 205,000 dues-paying members and another 65,000 who had signed pledgecards without initiating dues. At least 50,000 more workers could be expected to join shortly. Gorman said that at least 185,000 of the workers were in cotton textiles.[27] Robert Bruere, responding to George Sloan's repeated arguments that the UTW exaggerated its membership rolls, told Johnson that the UTW undoubtedly spoke for a large number of textile workers and that its membership was "substantial and growing." He discounted Gorman's claim that over 200,000 workers in the South were paying dues or that the union had so many signed pledgecards, but he believed the UTW did have the "loyalty" of about half of the nation's cotton textile workers.[28] Harassed days later by Sloan on the nature of UTW membership, Bruere appeared to retreat from the generous estimate he had given to Johnson, indicating that the number of dues-paying members might be well below 165,000, but even to Sloan he still argued that the UTW was "national in scope, and the only organized union in the industry, and [has] a large membership."[29]

The UTW, encouraged by its expanded power in New England and savoring its first gains in cotton textiles in the South, became much more aggressive in its criticism of code conditions, although in nature the complaints were not new. The NRA machinery had not worked to protect the rights of employees under Section 7(a) to join unions. Stretch out, the leading worker complaint, was still a brutal and growing practice. Curtailment had not worked, and weekly earnings had fallen to disastrously low levels.

By June the UTW developed a specific request. The UTW wanted the thirty-hour week with a weekly paycheck equal to that of a forty-hour shift.[30] Significantly, the union never claimed that many employers had ignored the NRA minimum wage regulations. In the widely-dispersed industry, there appeared to be remarkable conformity to the principle of the minimum wage. Clearly, though, stretch out, with its complex problems of definition and interpretation, remained an unresolved issue. Inept or desperately pressured management often did try to squeeze more production from workers, and the code regulations were so vague on stretch out as to make its prevention impossible, since management always had the right to define what was standard work and what was substandard work. The UTW arguments regarding

Section 7(a) had the ring of truth. Everywhere, southern cotton textile owners fought unions and Section 7(a) either by flagrant antiunion activities or by acting as if the union did not exist.

The Bruere Board's attitude toward Section 7(a) especially irritated the UTW. On this point, the board manifested openly its generally pro-owner philosophy. It refused to accept the principle of majority rule in collective bargaining that quickly developed in many other industries. Technically the board was correct in this stance. Thomas I. Emerson, an NRA lawyer, advised the board in March 1934 that the federal courts had not ruled on the NLB's majority-rule philosophy and that the Bruere Board, since it was an independent board operating under the authority of the cotton code itself, was bound only by its own interpretation of Section 7(a). In the absence of a court ruling, the NRA Legal Division said that the Bruere Board could decide collective bargaining rules independently.[31]

Benjamin Geer was adamantly opposed to any collective bargaining, even that conducted at the behest of a majority vote by a bargaining unit. Indeed, Geer went so far as to claim that *every* individual member of a bargaining unit would have to agree before the bargaining unit had any validity. Bruere also refused to support majority-rule bargaining, so wedded was he to his mill committee–state board system, which he still hoped would make collective bargaining by unions redundant. He believed his system fully met the requirements of Section 7(a), and the indifferent labor member of the board, George Berry, never attacked this interpretation. In fact, no collective bargaining at all took place in the South during the Bruere Board's tenure.

By summer 1934, the union men were complaining bitterly that the employer-dominated Code Authority had conducted only sham investigations of worker complaints. Sham or not, only cursory investigations were conducted by the Code Authority. The CTNIB, from 8 August 1933 to 8 August 1934, received and submitted to the Code Authority 3,920 complaints alleging violations of the cotton textile code. Of these complaints, 1,724 concerned the wage and hour provisions of the code, 438 the "labor provisions," and 984 the stretch out, while 774 were classified as miscellaneous.[33] The Code Authority made only 96 investigations of violations of wage-hour provisions and found only one case to be a valid complaint. Some of the "investigations" were no more than letters of inquiry to the mill management involved.

The Bruere Board reported that it had "answered" 1,932 of the complaints (an answer being nothing more than a letter acknowledging receipt of the complaint), and that up to May 1934 it had made 968 separate investigations of complaints.[34] The latter figure is puzzling. The board must have added up complaints received from single mills later visited by a chairperson of the state boards. The Code Authority had sent only two cases to the Compliance Division of the NRA, a point the union complained of bitterly.[35] The UTW charged that the state boards were mostly inactive, failing to investigate complaints fairly and moving very slowly when they moved at all. Most frustrating was the Code Authority's argument that by summer 1934 a little-noticed code amendment made by Johnson and the Code Authority had ended the prohibition of the stretch out as a separate provision and made it a labor question under Section 17 of the code (the code's restatement of Section 7(a) of the NIRA).[36]

On 9 August, the chairman of the NLB, Lloyd Garrison, received a confidential six-page report from one of his agents in the South, Frank Coffee. Coffee had visited 153 mills, selected at random, in four major southern cotton textile states. He reported that "labor officials and employees are unanimous in their condemnation of the National Textile Labor Relations Board [the Bruere Board] and practically unanimous in their condemnation of the various state boards." Labor leaders, he wrote, had given up on the Bruere Board and concluded "that their only recourse is through the use of their economic strength." On the other hand, he reported, "all mills are living up the code in practically every way" and that management believed the code had given labor "all the breaks." Coffee found management most opposed to the collective bargaining section of the code, and he said that "very few mills do not bitterly resent organization of employees." One young UTW organizer, Paul Christopher, became so angry at the Bruere Board, particularly for its inactivity surrounding union claims that southern employers routinely disciplined or dismissed workers for joining the union, that he wrote a two-page letter of complaint directly to Bruere, accusing Bruere of denying textile workers "the rights to which they are justly entitled under the code."[37]

Southerners vigorously defended the cotton textile industry and its code against the UTW charges. The Atlanta *Journal* praised the industry, claiming, "In no other region or industry has the recovery program found more loyal support than in the cotton textile industry of the South," which had "yielded" many "natural privileges" to advance the New Deal.[38] The Raleigh *News and Observer* declared that the threat of labor trouble in the cotton textile industry was particularly "discouraging" in view of the textile industry's long record of cooperation with the NRA. The industry, said the *News and Observer*, "came with an apparent spirit of cooperation that gave the New Deal a special blessing. No more stirring evidence of the commitment of industry to a consideration of labor and higher concept of trade practices was given anywhere than in the textile industry."[39]

Industry spokesmen denied that there had been massive code violations. In April 1934, Thomas M. Marchant, president of the ACMA, argued that not only the letter but the spirit of the code overwhelmingly had been obeyed, and he called for transgressors to be punished. If there should be "any of our Southern people," he said, "who have any idea that they can wink at any of the provisions, or can evade by some process of shrewdness, I hope they will immediately be discovered and whatever teeth there may be in the National Recovery Administration law, will sink into their very vitals."[40] George Sloan, president of the Code Authority, took every opportunity to assure the public that "both in the letter and in the spirit of observance the industry has given the Recovery Administration its full measure of support and cooperation.[41]

At the end of June Sloan summarized in a press conference the benefits labor had received during the first year of the code's operation. He argued that there had been an increase of 40 percent in the number of workers employed in the industry, with the figure standing in June at 460,000; and he observed that payrolls in the industry during the first ten months of the code, compared with the ten months prior to the code, had increased 78 percent, along with an increase of 67 percent in hourly wage rates. Working hours, on the average, had decreased by 26 percent as the mills went from the standard fifty-five-hour week to a forty-hour week. Sloan called upon the workers for faith in and responsibility to the Code Authority. He was opposed to new code provisions unless long experience dictated the need, and he urged "a never-relaxing recognition of the partnership relation between industry and government."[42]

Sloan once again ignored the UTW and rejected any role the union might claim to have in the partnership. He vigorously defended the Bruere Board. Even though he considered the Bruere Board's procedures "purely cooperative and voluntary," he contended that the board had "functioned with marked success." Sloan denied that the board was partial to the industry or that the industry controlled it. Instead, he claimed that the board had shown great "judicial qualities" and an "impartial attitude."[43] *Textile World* also leaped to the defense of the Bruere Board. "Dr. Robert Bruere," the editor said, "has done, in our opinion, a masterful job to date."[44]

In the developing battle of 1934, both management and labor used statistics to demonstrate the accuracy of their positions in the dispute over the code, and the statistics often clashed. Fortunately, early the following year the Bureau of Labor Statistics made public a study on wage rates and earnings in the cotton textile industry which gives a clear, impartial picture. The report argued that there had been overwhelming compliance with minimum wage provisions of the code. The study noted that between July 1933 and July 1934 average hourly earnings had increased 64.5 percent. Its findings substantiated industry claims of increased hourly earnings under the code and indicated that the UTW exaggerated in its charges of wage violations. There were only scattered violations by a few renegade nonconforming mills. But, as the report showed, *real* earnings per week *had* slipped. In no week since the adoption of the code had the industry averaged more than 36.5 hours per person per week, though 40 hours were necessary to obtain the minimum weekly earnings. Workers had earned more money per hour, but they had worked less and so had slimmer pay packets, in an industry that paid less than any other major industry in the country.

The report substantiated UTW claims that some mills worked three weeks and then closed down for the fourth, resulting in payless weeks for workers. In October 1934, the average U.S. industrial wage was 55.4 cents per hour.

In cotton textiles it was 38 cents, and the curtailment orders drastically lowered the takehome pay of the workers. In August 1934, under the June production cuts, weekly earnings were 9 percent less than in August 1933 in the North and 18 percent less in the South. In many cases the workers had lower real earnings during the curtailment than they had before the code became effective in July 1933, and the drop occurred when the general cost of living was on the rise again. Real earnings declined 25 percent from August 1933 to August 1934. Furthermore, the report made clear that, contrary to the earlier NRA study, the code had operated to narrow the differential between the weekly earnings of the most skilled and less skilled workers.[45] The frustration of the southern workers in summer 1934 lay in the fact of actual pay cuts, and pay cuts had usually spelled labor trouble in the industry.

Despite the heroic production cuts of the summer, profits in the industry remained anemic, probably making the wage situation in cotton textiles unavoidable. The industry did not have the demand to employ everybody for forty hours a week, but the increasingly heated atmosphere overrode hard economic reality. The workers knew only that they were suffering and that the owners were determined to make sure that no real union established itself in the industry in the midst of a continued business slump. Almost to a company, the owners denied the right of the UTW to serve the collective bargaining agent for the workers.

The lack of an aggressive federal policy to assist workers in establishing unions helped the owners enormously in their successful fight. The employers obviously continued to harass workers who belonged to the UTW. Workers, fearful of losing their jobs and their places in the mill village, only tentatively considered the UTW as a possible means of improving their lives. After a year of the code, mill owners and mill management still ruled supreme on the mill floors. For the cotton textile workers Section 7(a) had been only an invitation to a fancy dress ball they were too poor to attend, and their resentment at their exclusion had grown.

THE BATTLE COMES

The UTW had buckled under the pressure in Washington, in the NRA mediation of their threatened strike, and the settlement had proven unproductive. There was no collective bargaining with the Code Authority. The NRA studies were in-house and informal, with no discernible impact. The Bruere Board stayed firmly on its course. Indeed, the union leaders were enraged during the summer by one of the board's most irritating decisions.

The case before the board was an alleged violation of the code's wage provisions by the Eagle and Phoenix Manufacturing Company of Columbus, Georgia. Dealing with the wages of slasher tenders, the case was complex. It had been started as early as 19 October 1933, when the first complaint arrived at the board, only to be sent on to the Code Authority for investigation. Nothing happened, and on 11 March 1934, the board received notice that the slasher tenders had walked off the job, shutting the plant down. The Bruere Board ordered its state board to "adjust" the dispute. Work began again, but the company refused to cooperate. The workers had to strike in late May 1934 to get the company even to agree to recognize the mill committee formed by the state board. The state board upheld the workers' contention that their wages should be eighteen dollars for a forty-hour week, compared to the company's sixteen. The company appealed to the Bruere Board but refused to come to the first scheduled June hearing. Much to the disgust of the UTW, the board rescheduled another for August 1.

Meanwhile, the strikers and the company settled their differences by agreeing to abide by the Bruere Board's decision, and the strike ended on 25 June 1934. But the Bruere Board on 28 August reversed the state board's decision and found for the company, a decision that enraged the UTW leaders. At the public hearing it was clear that George Berry, the labor member, knew little about the case, and he voted with Bruere and Geer; Fox had not yet joined the board.

Something of the gap between Bruere and the union can be seen in letters about the case that he sent to Berry, in which he castigated the UTW for not taking responsibility for "the irresponsible action of local workers." Bruere actually proposed that the CTNIRB work only through George Googe, the AFL's chief southern organizer, as the "only labor leader throughout the South who has made a conscientious attempt to cooperate with us in building up candid and decent cooperative relationships."[46] For the UTW, the Eagle and Phoenix case was the major breaking point with the code.

Recognizing that they had lost their gamble in accepting NRA-brokered settlement of their complaints in early June and responding to the swelling protest from cotton textile workers, particularly in the South, the UTW officers decided on 18 July 1934 to call a special convention to meet in August to consider labor's response to the crisis in the industry. Pressure from Alabama workers had finally forced the UTW to play its weak hand. As in 1929, short, unorganized, and spontaneous walkouts had popped up in the South in late spring and throughout the summer. Eight occurred in May, five in June, and nine in July, but a wave of strikes that rolled across North Alabama's cotton mill towns beginning on 16 July caused the union to enter the fray again. Huntsville's five thousand workers led the way, and soon, in such towns as Florence, Anniston, Gadsden, Cordova, Jasper, Guntersville, Albertville, and even in the proud Avondale Mills in Birmingham, some seventeen to twenty-three thousand of an estimated forty thousand workers in North Alabama decided, against the advice of Thomas McMahon, to walk out. McMahon "killed the other strikes," one worker said referring to the aborted strike threat in May, but "we're not going to let him kill this one."[47] All but two of the forty-two UTW Alabama locals voted to strike. John Dean, the area UTW organizer, had to join the parade and become the strike leader. Worker protest had brought the UTW to the picket lines.

The UTW did not know how to handle the Alabama strikes that had occurred without its sanction. McMahon and Gorman, fearing a demoralizing defeat, kept low profiles and let Dean, whose vigorous efforts earlier may have incited the workers, lead. They supported the AFL's efforts to settle the strikes through the services of the well-known and respected AFL organizer, George Googe. The Bruere Board offered to help as well, but it made clear that it considered the strikes a violation of the June agreement. Hugh Johnson, in August, reported to the White House that the situation in Alabama "is very obscure" and that it would have been settled except for a call for a general strike by Norman Thomas which "takes the strikes out of the economic field and into the political field of socialist or communist agitation."[48]

Dean was neither socialist nor communist, but he was suddenly a deeply troubled union leader. He quickly turned to the Federal Mediation and Conciliation Service and drew up a list of union demands. The strikers called for a minimum wage of twelve dollars for a thirty-hour week, abolition of the stretch out, reinstatement of workers discharged for union activity or because of alleged substandard work because of stretch out, and recognition of the UTW as the workers' bargaining agent.[49] The Alabama strikers, though they had created a dilemma for the UTW, had at least summed up the major issues of the summer.

The strikes in Alabama, because of their widespread nature, took everyone by surprise, for less than a quarter of the workers in North Alabama were union members. Although one reporter said they were ill-led and surrounded with a "haze of uncertainty,"[50] most of the strikes were orderly, although a few unruly conflicts around the picket lines occurred.[50] On 5 August John Dean was abducted from his hotel room, probably by vigilante members of the American Legion. Taken to Fayetteville, Tennessee, he quickly returned. The Alabama mill owners hired special guards to patrol the mill fences. In South Alabama, the workers, with no active UTW locals, never struck, and at the Avondale Mills' Sylacauga plants, the mills were guarded by the workers themselves against possible outside pickets.

With full warehouses, the Alabama owners showed no disposition to meet with the workers. With support for their stand pouring in, the Alabama owners took the high ground by declaring that since the mills had observed all NRA rules and regulations, the strikes were really against the government and a problem for federal authorities. David Clark, editor of the *Textile Bulletin*, urged the owners to stand fast. Sooner or later, he declared, "the status of the racketeers must be settled, and this is probably a good time."[51]

The union made little progress in Alabama with its demands. Many of the struck mills operated with nonstriking personnel, although with reduced production. Most of the mills could have broken the strikes with a determined effort, but instead an unannounced lockout developed. The owners, with full inventory and low prices, decided to let the strikes run their course. The Alabama strikes may have encouraged a false sense of strength in the union. The UTW leaders in New York were cheered by what they considered worker unity and the example of the courageous Alabama workers excited workers in Georgia and the Carolinas. But in Alabama, even in North Alabama, many workers opposed the strikes. Probably well less than half of Alabama's cotton textile workers struck or were in sympathy with the strikers. As early as 18 July 1934, Hugh Kerwin of the Federal Mediation and Conciliation Service reported to Frances Perkins that one of his field men had reported "considerable opposition to the stoppage of work; that textile businesses had slowed up just now and that there is a danger of the union losing members."[52] Nevertheless, the strikes dragged on throughout July and August, and just as they were about to fall apart, they merged with the nationwide general strike.

The special convention of the UTW met in New York City on Monday, 13 August, with over five hundred delegates present. The stirred-up southern locals were well represented. During the first day alone, southern locals presented over fifty resolutions calling for a general strike in the cotton textile industry.

The southern delegates even talked of turning to the ambitious and more militant Emil Rieve of the hosiery workers if the convention did not develop a plan of action. In the first two days of the meeting, the UTW officers — president McMahon, vice-president Gorman, vice-president William F. Kelly, and secretary-treasurer James Starr — spoke to the convention. Their speeches reviewed the familiar complaints that the union had presented time and again to the employers, the Bruere Board, and the NRA. McMahon, the lead speaker on the first day, did not mention a general strike, though he vaguely threatened large strikes to come if the stretch out was not ended. He urged adoption of the thirty-hour week and a return to the machine load conditions of 1921. "Unless we arouse ourselves from the lethargy now prevailing," McMahon told the workers, "the NRA, if allowed to function in the future, will become a plaything for the manufacturers."[53] All of the officers argued that the time had come to challenge labor conditions under the code, for the mood of the convention left them no alternative except to get out in front and lead. They accepted the same goals the Alabama strikers had set, demonstrating that McMahon and Gorman had been forced to the wall by the rank and file. Francis Gorman correctly summed up the workers' attitude when he told the convention that he was convinced "that there is a grim determination not to continue under the present conditions in spite of the consequences."[54]

On the third day a unanimously passed resolution from the delegates to discuss a general strike began the landslide. The southerners led the way. Oliver Carson later reported that "back in the mill towns, particularly those in the southern states, the bitterness and resentment of the workers knew no bounds." One delegate shouted from the floor that the mills had to be closed

from Alabama to Maine, as "the only language the employers will understand."[55] On the fourth day of the convention, 16 August, in a turbulent hour-
long debate, more than a dozen workers from the South spoke of the terrible
conditions there. The *New York Times* reported that some of them had hitch-
hiked to the convention. W.N. Adcock, a Huntsville, Alabama, striker, spoke
to the convention with bandages on his head. He said: "I have been wounded
in the head and shot in the leg, but I am ready to die for the union." The
delegates roared in response. When Gorman argued that a general strike was
the only course of action for the union, he was, according to the *New York
Times*, met "with wild applause." McMahon was also swept along: "Maybe
we've procrastinated too long," he said, "but the day has arrived—the hour
is here."[56] With only ten dissenting votes, the convention instructed the officers of the union to call a general strike in the cotton textile industry on or
about 1 September 1934. Strikes in the silk, woolen, and rayon branches of
the industry were also authorized, but the dates of those strikes were left up
to the newly created emergency strike committee.

McMahon, mindful of the June settlement, promised the convention that
mediation by the NRA would not prevent the strike. "We will tell General
Hugh S. Johnson that we appreciate his efforts but that he is not big enough
and has not enough authority to help us."[57] Organization and direct negotiation with the mill owners, McMahon said, was the only way for the UTW
to reach its goals. But even while trembling on the edge of the strike preci-
pice, the UTW leaders still hoped for magic intervention from the New Deal.
Although Hugh Johnson and his NRA were thoroughly discredited in the
workers' eyes, there was still the President. Ominously for UTW hopes for
New Deal salvation, the prevailing pattern of dealing with strikes had been
one of White House concern but conspicuous nonintervention, except for
murky efforts at conciliation and settlement under the auspices of the Labor
Department.[58] McMahon, however, still hoped for and publicly called for
presidential interference. "President Roosevelt," he declared, "is the only man
on God's green earth who can stop the strike."[59]

A general belief existed among NRA officials, textile employers, and the
general public, particularly in the South, that a successful strike could not
be organized by the UTW.[60] Many people were convinced that even if the
UTW leaders did carry out their plan to strike, the mass of workers would
not support them; it would be a failure. The Charlotte *Observer* argued that
the UTW might "be vocalizing the opinions of the organizers and the agitators within their organization rather than the masses of the members who
will doubtless think twice before they obey instructions from official circles
to step out of a condition in their employment, the likes of which they have
not enjoyed in their lifetime."[61] The Columbia *State* also doubted that South
Carolina workers would join the strike in any large numbers. The workers were
happy, and the UTW did not speak for them.[62] The *Textile Bulletin*, which
often accurately reflected southern owners' thinking, predicted that the strikes

would "probably flourish for a while" with disorder and bloodshed, but would gradually "disintegrate with not a thing to show as an advantage."[63]

Secretary of Labor Frances Perkins, taking note of McMahon's plan to ask Roosevelt for intervention, advised the White House that the President should not meet with any UTW delegation. The grievances, she said, "are very complicated," and she strongly recommended that the President send the grievances, without the UTW delegation, to the newly created National Labor Relations Board (NLRB), the replacement under Public Resolution 44 for the NRA's National Labor Board. She believed the NLRB, soon to be commonly known as the Garrison Board, could settle the issues and avert the strike.[64]

The executive council of the UTW named the popular Francis Gorman as chairman of the strike committee, rather than McMahon, and Gorman dramatically announced that he would lead the strike personally, from Washington rather than from the New York City headquarters. The AFL belatedly expressed its approval of the strike and extended an offer of cooperation through the services of its organizers and state federation officials, but privately the AFL turned down the UTW's request for money before the strike began. AFL president William Green told the UTW "there was no chance" of financial help, but as the strike gained a foothold, Green helped the UTW raise five thousand dollars from the hatters' union, ten thousand from the International Ladies Garment Workers Union, and five thousand from the United Mine Workers. At the same time, however, Green pressured the UTW to settle the strike.[65]

Gorman started the strike with no war chest, no broad-based labor coalition support, bristling hostility from the industry, and growing animosity from Hugh Johnson, who by this time, in the throes of his own problems, felt the NRA slipping from his grasp. But Gorman, following the trail of accumulated grievances and Alabama workers' demands, requested that the industry immediately establish a thirty-hour week with forty-hour paychecks and that the minimum wage scales be graduated upward according to skill. He attacked the stretch out problem by demanding that employers agree to an industrywide standard for a maximum workload. He also called for the reinstatement of all UTW members dismissed for union membership and for the recognition of the UTW by the Code Authority as an industrywide bargaining agent. He demanded that the NRA replace the Bruere Board with an arbitration tribunal, mutually agreeable to both the Code Authority and the union, with all decisions final and binding. All these demands, Gorman maintained, could be met by revising the cotton code.[66]

Gorman began furiously to plan the strike, while at the same time working through government channels to prevent it by obtaining concessions to some of his demands. On 27 August William Green came to his aid by publicly calling on the Garrison Board to intervene and settle the outstanding issues, although the Garrison Board, established in July, had not assumed jurisdiction in textiles, steel, automobiles, bituminous coal, newspaper publishing, and petroleum because separate NRA labor boards already existed in those industries. The NLRB, established in the Department of Labor and not the NRA and operating under its own congressional charter, had aggressively followed the tentative policy path marked out by the NLB, particularly in its insistence that a majority of workers in a working unit had the legal right to bargain collectively for all employees. During the coming year, the board would begin to define and clarify that process.

Soon after its establishment, the Garrison Board became unhappy over the Bruere Board's laggard treatment of Section 7(a). For over a month before the strike vote was taken, the Garrison Board had been holding conferences with the Code Authority, the Bruere Board, and the UTW, in an effort to shift jurisdiction of Section 7(a) cases from the Bruere Board to itself. The Bruere Board, always sensitive to the Code Authority and its wishes, moved very slowly. After all, it only met monthly. The aggressive industry member, Benjamin Geer, was none too happy when he realized that the NLRB would take charge of the cases even without the Bruere Board's consent. On 16 August, Geer wrote to George Sloan, advising him that the Code Authority should consent with the stipulation that the NLRB's writ would be experimental only for a three-month trial period and should concern cases arising only at some future date. Geer believed the Garrison Board would get "mighty sick" of the problem soon. "I have a feeling, too," he wrote, "that they would soon discover that discrimination on account of membership in a labor union is a stock complaint and is always brought forward because of its appeal to the labor crowd in Washington and to the public in general."[67]

Robert Bruere believed that if the Garrison Board handled Section 7(a) cases, the effect would be to "crowd employers in the cotton textile industry into direct relationships with the United Textile Workers of America," a prospect that appalled him. George Sloan had told him, said Bruere, that the result "might be a revolt throughout the industry," and for the proper working of the code, that had to be avoided. Sloan, the Cotton-Textile Institute, and the Code Authority still controlled the labor board for the industry, and although it was ostensibly a government agency, via the delegation of power under the NIRA, it had, by its blatant partisanship toward the owners, lost any credibility it might have mustered to deal with the coming storm. Despite his reservations, however, Bruere agreed to allow the NLRB to assume jurisdiction in collective bargaining cases, for the sake of a "unified front," but he warned the NLRB that Sloan would refuse ever to meet with the UTW again, even indirectly as he had in June.[68]

The discussions between the Garrison Board and the Bruere Board over the jurisdiction of Section 7(a) cases merged into mediation attempts to ward off the threatened general strike. On 22 August, the Bruere Board met in special session to discuss the strike threat. Bruere stated that the board should "accept jurisdiction on the consent of the parties involved" to mediate in the strike. Bruere did not think that the board could "just remain passive," and

George Berry argued that "we should not allow ourselves to be lost in the shuffle." Benjamin Geer argued initially for a continued line of inactivity, but he soon agreed to drop his objections. "If I understand," he said, "we are simply making ourselves available in a positive way," by which he meant the old way.[69] It was a short meeting with no discussion at all of the UTW arguments or the issues that had been raised in the strike call. Later, on 29 August, the board assembled for a regular meeting and did not even mention the strike!

Meanwhile, even the employers ignored the increasingly irrelevant Bruere and his associates. On the same day the Bruere Board met to offer mediation, George Sloan made his first major statement about the proposed strike. Sloan interpreted the threatened strike as a violation of the June settlement which the UTW had made with the NRA, conclusive evidence, in his opinion, that the union could not be depended upon to honor agreements. Sloan took the position that the strike threat was an illegal attempt to change the code unilaterally and by force. As such, he considered it a strike against the NRA and not against the employers, and he stated emphatically that he would not meet in any conference with UTW officials. The Code Authority had tried to work "fairly" and with the interest of all elements at heart, he said. He denied the existence of stretch out in the industry, except for sound technological reasons which, in his view, had actually reduced the "demand for physical or nervous effort" which taxed "the nerves and sinews of a human being." He argued that the work week had decreased while wages had increased (technically correct, if only hourly wages were considered). He also contended that employment in the industry had grown. The strike was "not justified" and would "be a calamity to both workers and the public." The basic concept of the NRA and the "principle of peaceful cooperation between Government, Labor, and Industry" would be violated.[70] Refusing to negotiate face to face, Sloan had elected instead to oppose the UTW vigorously in the public forum.

On 24 August Gorman publicly rejected Bruere's offer to mediate, reviewing the UTW's long history of dissatisfaction with the Bruere Board and declaring that his union had no confidence in the board's ability to adjust the dispute. Gorman said that the Bruere Board had outlived its usefulness and should be abolished. At the same time, pursuing his strategy of government intervention, he expressed the belief that the NLRB had jurisdiction over worker and union complaints in the industry, its power being derived from Section 7(a). Lloyd Garrison, however, had decided that his board did not have official jurisdiction, since the cotton code had specifically authorized the Bruere Board. But administration pressure—from the NRA, Frances Perkins, and ultimately Roosevelt—forced him to relent and publicly commit the NLRB to enter the flurry of mediation efforts.[71] Naively, Garrison had in mind a great roundtable conference involving the NLRB, NRA officials, the Bruere Board, the Code Authority, and UTW leaders.

During the week between Saturday, 25 August, and Sunday, 1 September, when the strike was to begin, Gorman and Garrison met several times. Gorman agreed to the roundtable conference and even NLRB arbitration of the dispute, but only if the UTW secured some concessions from the Code Authority beforehand. Sloan refused to attend any such conference and even the Bruere Board debated whether to attend. Amazingly, in a special meeting the board's majority (Fox had now joined them) wondered if it had the legal right as a board operating under a code to discuss the strike with the NLRB, although Bruere did argue that "it would be wise to maintain a united front as a public service, quite apart from any other consideration."[72]

Sloan's adamant stand took the Bruere Board off the hook, and once again Gorman publicly requested that Roosevelt intervene personally, although how and for what purpose was not spelled out. Gorman argued that the UTW was not striking against the NRA but against the owners, and he expressed confidence that the workers would win if the strike occurred because of their "determination, solidarity, and a burning sense of outrage."[73]

Throughout the South, the mill owners stayed quiet, confident that even if the strike began, the union would again, as it had so often in the past, fall apart.[74] They knew it did not represent a real majority of the workers. William Anderson, spokesperson for the mill owners, announced their firm unwillingness to meet with any union members, and Sloan predicted that only 15 percent of the workers would leave the mills. The NLRB announced on 31 August that while it could not avert the strike, it "had no intention" of "ceasing efforts to bring about an early settlement of the issues."[75] Privately, Garrison wrote FDR that the differences were "profound and irreconcilable" and that "nothing can now prevent" the strike. But he advised the President that only after the strike had begun, to avoid the charge of breaking it, should he appoint a special impartial board under the authority of Public Resolution 44, to "prepare a concrete plan of settlement."[76] The UTW stood alone.

7

"We didn't have no backing—we shouldn't have done it"

THE GENERAL STRIKE, SEPTEMBER 1934

On 30 August the UTW announced that the cotton textile strike would be effective at midnight on Saturday, 1 September. The silk and woolen workers would also strike on the same day. The enormity of the UTW undertaking was reflected in the UTW's suggestion that perhaps a million workers would be idle. Since Monday was Labor Day, the full work stoppage would not actually come until Tuesday, 4 September, although many southern mills did not observe Labor Day. On Sunday, Gorman addressed the textile workers over the NBC radio network to explain the reasons for the strike. He would speak a dozen times on NBC. Sloan would often counter on network radio.[1] Mass meetings were held by the UTW throughout the southern cotton textile areas. Spirits ran high, but the secretary of the ACMA, William McLaurine, predicted that only a small percentage of the workers would leave their jobs. "I have great faith," he said, "in the final intelligence of the workers." George Sloan deplored the strike call and thought that "the leaders of strife beckon the operatives to misery, unemployment, and insecurity."[2] In Charlotte, North Carolina, however, when the UTW held a rally for the strike leaders on the eve of the strike, the meeting took on the spirit of a revivalist assembly. "We fight," said Roy Lawrence of the UTW, "for the Lord and for our families.[3]

The direction of what would be the largest strike in American history up to that time was in the hands of one man, Francis Gorman. Born in England and emigrating to the United States in 1903 when he was thirteen years old, he immediately went to work in the Rhode Island woolen mills. In 1922, he became an organizer for the UTW, and in 1928 he was elevated to a vice-presidency. In 1934, when he was forty-four years of age, his quick, nervous energy dominated the union. His popularity with southern organizers had driven McMahon to the sidelines. According to Jonathan Daniels, they appreciated in this small man "a soundness of judgment" and "a capacity for hard continuous work."[4]

Gorman had to plan a strike that spanned the East from Alabama to Maine. He divided the country into regions to decentralize the strike, while in Washington he would mount the public campaign and provide a continuous sense of a unified national strike. In the first week, for example, Gorman created an air of excitement by his announcement that he would send "sealed orders" to the locals. They were too secret to reveal to the press. It was nonsense, of course, but good theater. The "sealed orders" were merely short morale-boosting messages. Instruction Number Three, for example, sent on 4 September, had as its main line the admonition that "We can NOT fail this time or they will *drive us into slavery.*" It reduced the strike goals to a simple slogan: "Shorter hours! Higher wages! Reduce the working load! Recognize the union!" Instruction Number Five was even more to the point: "Hold the strikeline. We must stay out until victory is ours."[5] Anticipating that word of the strike would not reach unorganized and isolated mills, particularly in the South, Gorman borrowed a tactic used successfully by the UMW—the "flying squadrons." The term and the method caught the fancy of the southern workers and press. When workers left one mill shut down, they would form a cavalcade of trucks and cars, race to the next mill, invade it and call for the workers still at the machines to join them in the cross-country fun.

The flying squadron tactic was especially effective in the South, where mills were not clustered together in large cities. A mill with a relatively strong UTW contingent could exercise far more influence than might have been expected. The arrival of the cavalcade of cars and flatbed trucks with groups of workers hanging precariously to the staked sides and shouting encouragement to workers inside was a signal in the early September heat for an exodus of even unorganized workers from their machines. "Those cars and lines of cars," wrote Jonathan Daniels, "were something new and strange, wicked and terrifying. Or at least so manufacturers thought." Daniels remembered "the young women taunting the soldiers and the high laughter, like war," saying, "the people loved it . . . it was good to be young then, good to go in a tumultuous crowd and shout at the fence of the old man's house, good to climb into Fords and rush across other countries to join other familiar—unfamiliar young people in clamoring at the mesh wire of mill gates."[6]

In the Carolinas, where they principally operated, the flying squadrons ranged in number from a hundred people or so to one massive column of a thousand. In the Greenville and Spartanburg areas, the core of the South Carolina industry, the Columbia *State* saw the flying squadrons as "a horde of strikers" seeking "to unionize" workers after forcing the mills to close. A reporter described the impact at the tiny village of Greer, located between Greenville and Spartanburg: "Flying an American flag, the fast-traveling motorcade reinforced local pickets at Victor Mill here and the combined number of 1,500 to 2,000 strikers caused a night shift into staying away from work. . . . It then crossed Greer and some 35 strikers armed with clubs entered the front door of the Franklin Mill to shut it down." Managers got the strikers to leave peaceably, but the "entire night shift of 64, 40 of them women, responded to cries of 'come out,' and the mill stopped at 4:21 P.M." The incident was typical of the opening days of the strike in the Carolinas, with its half-mile-long motorcades, flags, signs, and cries of "come on out—we won't hurt you."[7] The Associated Press estimated that about fifty flying squadrons worked in the Carolinas on the first two days of the strike.

But Gorman paid a price for the flying-squadron gambit. The owners had maintained from the beginning that the strike was illegally aimed against the NRA, the code, and thus the government. The appearance of the flying squadrons forced the southern governors to bring out the National Guard to ring the mills with bayonets to protect the property and the right of nonstrikers to cross picket lines. The owners would claim that the flying squadrons had intimidated their workers into leaving the mills; the great majority of the millhands, said the manufacturers, wanted to work and would do so when their right to work was protected. The editor of the *Textile Bulletin* presented "As a typical example . . . one mill which employs more than 1,500 workers, of whom not more than 50 are union members. Those 50 played on two human weaknesses," said the *Bulletin*, "the fear of ridicule and the fear of bodily harm."[8] The editor of *Cotton* was more dramatic, asserting that "industrial chaos, hungry people, lost investments, bloodshed and unjust feelings and strife, must be the price paid by a people, a minority of whom have suffered themselves to be misled against their own interests, the remainder intimidated and threatened and deprived of their constitutional right to work, through force, violence, and threat."[9] The flying squadrons eventually worked to the owners' advantage because they aggravated violence, allowed the civil authorities to send the National Guard out, and justified the mills' deputizing large numbers of special guards.[10]

One of Gorman's most interesting achievements was his ability to create the illusion of a national strike, which dominated headlines for a month. He employed a public relations adviser, Chester M. Wright, who devised and arranged Gorman's radio talks. Gorman publicized the mostly mythical image of a powerful organization of regions, subregions, local committees, and, at the bottom, squads of ten local union members.[11] In actuality, the same old shaky UTW structure conducted the strike, with probably fewer than ten paid organizers in the entire South and small union locals representing only a fraction of most mills' workforce. In the beginning the spectacular success of the flying squadrons obscured the weakness of the union. No disciplined union existed in the southern mills in 1934. Gorman was the Wizard of Oz, a national voice in Washington, but behind the facade and the rhetorical smoke, the strike was neither national nor as well organized as most historians have assumed. In reality it was a series of spasmodic, uncontrolled local strikes and walkouts, and it should be seen as a series of events rather than as one cohesive event comparable to later strikes by national unions against integrated national companies or industries.

Indeed, after the first few days there existed a real question for many workers of whether they were on strike or locked out by the owners, most of whom did not make their usual successful effort to resume operations after a few days. The flying squadrons' success obscured the rather rational response of many workers to lie low until the trouble was over. Larry Wright, a North Carolina worker at an unorganized plant, years later remembered his own ambivalent feelings about the union, which had usually brought nothing but trouble to the workers. In September 1934 his supervisor instructed him to use a picker stick (a four-foot long hickory stick that is still part of a modern loom) to help defend the mill if the flying squadron came. But Wright told him: "In place of going out on that side of the building and getting me a picker stick, I'm going out on this side and find me a hole."[12] Ivy Norman, another North Carolina worker, remembered that she too elected neutrality: "I didn't know whether [the union] was good or bad, so I didn't mess with it."[13]

In the Carolinas, because of Monday's Labor Day, the flying squadrons did not appear until Tuesday, 4 September. Governor Ibra Blackwood made clear his stand of aggressive neutrality on 31 August, saying, "I am going to appeal to mayors, sheriffs, peace officers, and every good citizen to stand ready to be deputized to see that peace and order are maintained."[14] On the first day of the strike, as soon as the first flying squadron took to the road, Blackwood called out the Guard. But the squadrons often got to the mills first, and throughout South Carolina, by the end of the first day at least half of the state's mills had closed, with most of the others soon to follow, either by lockout or stoppage. At least a hundred mills were closed by the squadrons.[15] The second day of the strike in South Carolina was marked by reports of scuffles and confrontations between strikers and would-be workers. The Guard, reported the *State*, had been given orders to "shoot to kill" if necessary, and the sheriff of Anderson County, a big textile county, reported that he had deputized many textile workers to protect their mills and that he had several machine guns available to use if needed. Blackwood told the people of South Carolina that "mob rule and violence should not be permitted to menace our people." He urged each mill's workforce to vote, and if a majority wanted to work, the union should "withdraw."[16] The union had cried out for months to the Bruere Board for such a voting privilege.

On Thursday, 6 September, the most violent episode of the entire series of strikes occurred in Honea Path, South Carolina, a hamlet of less than three thousand people. At the Chiguala Mill, verbal clashes occurred between pickets and nonstrikers. A fistfight between two men broke out and "then suddenly shots from pistols, shotguns, and rifles blotted out the two-man fight and strikers, officers, and workers waged their intense but short-lived battle for supremacy of the situation."[17] Mack Duncan, then a seventeen-year-old nonstriking worker in the mill, remembered years later that the first shots had come from a nonunion worker who shot a union man who menaced him with an icepick. What actually happened and who was guilty of what was never decided, but after the brief outburst of firing and the frightened flight of pickets, guards, and workers, six strikers lay dead and over twenty wounded. Duncan remembered that he "got sick myself from seeing so much blood, and almost fainted."[18]

The next Saturday, over ten thousand workers attended the mass funeral of the slain strikers. In the sunlit field, George Googe of the AFL held aloft a bullet-riddled American flag from Honea Path and delivered an emotional sermon of support for the workers. Over the weekend South Carolina reeled from what had happened; the feeling of family that permeated the mill villages had been torn by the strike. Nevertheless, the union threatened that on Monday the squadrons would roll again. But on Sunday, Governor Blackwood declared that a "state of insurrection" existed in South Carolina. He put into effect "partial" martial law in the state, by which he meant in the mill villages and at the mill gates. Responding to the pressure, John Peel, the South Carolina UTW strike director, called the squadrons off, saying they would be "practically annihilated" and "slaughtered" if they continued. In its last massive act of defiance, the union held a parade in Columbia. Members and supporters marched four abreast carrying American flags to make their band of a thousand or so appear more impressive.[19]

From the very beginning, the effectiveness of the strike was difficult to ascertain because so many workers had obviously left the mills only after the arrival of the motorcades. The Associated Press (AP) ran daily counts of the workers striking, but its figures varied wildly and did not make clear the differences between striking and nonstriking workers who had left the plants. The AP's count at the end of the first day had 27,000 workers in South Carolina on strike, out of a work force of 62,000; 52,000 out in North Carolina, of 92,000 employed; 20,400 striking in Georgia, of the 60,000 working in the mills there; and 15,000 (the old Alabama strike) of that state's 38,500 workers. By the end of the second day of flying squadron activity, the AP reported 360,000 textile workers across the nation on strike. The highest number reported by the press was the *New York Times'* estimate of 400,000 at the end of the second week, with approximately half of the total being southern cotton textile strikers.[20] No-one, of course, had an accurate count.

Surprisingly, many southern mills, particularly if they were isolated from UTW-inspired flying squadrons, were never touched by the strike. In the Carolinas, by the end of the second week, the AP reported that 298 mills had closed, but that 254 were still operating or had reopened, with over 91,000 workers at the machines. In North Carolina the AP counted 210 mills closed, with 64,485 people not working; and 281 mills open, with 81,935 at work. In retrospect, many of the mills stayed shut after flying squadron visits because the owners were content to let the weak union's strike run its course without challenging the pickets at the mill gates.[21] The owners had no economic incentive to reopen the mills, and many owners, genuinely frightened and surprised by the effectiveness of the squadrons, were content, as were some of their workers, to lie low. Time was the owners' great ally. The number of workers actively participating in the strike was certainly lower than the inflated figures so often cited. After one tumultuous week, the strike in South Carolina had become a lockout as much as a strike, for the owners could have broken the deteriorating strike in the second week if they had moved aggressively to do so.

In North Carolina initial union enthusiasm ran high. John Redman, a UTW man, predicted on Labor Day that "there won't be a mill open below the Mason Dixie Line by Saturday."[22] In famous Gastonia County, on Tuesday, 4 September, only eight of forty-seven mills were able to withstand the arrival of a flying squadron, and close to three thousand workers staged a parade in the commercial section of Gastonia to show the town their strength.[23] On the first day of the strike, Paul Christopher, a young UTW organizer in Shelby, led one flying squadron in that area that closed twenty-seven mills by the end of the day.[24] Governor J.L.B. Ehringhaus did not move immediately to call out the National Guard, and the mills not guarded by the owners' private deputies lay vulnerable. At the end of the strike's second day, 5 September, Ehringhaus acted and mobilized the Guard, but Roy Lawrence, the North Carolina UTW leader, reported that "the calling out of the troops has not in any way hampered the ardor of the strikers." Nevertheless, as in South Carolina, the Guard around the plants lessened the impact of the motorcades, and on the picket lines and in the villages, North Carolina workers, like their sisters and brothers in South Carolina, split on the merits of the strike. One worker told the Charlotte *Observer* that if they send "one of those flying squadron stuff they will have to send over the National Guard to protect the flying squadron."[25] But North Carolina stayed free of major violence and, by the end of the first week, it was all over. Indeed, by the third week, well before a national settlement was achieved, many North Carolina mills had reopened behind the Guard's bayonets, and workers who had struck or left the mills under the impetuous enthusiasm of the flying squadrons began to drift back to the work floors.[26]

Georgia's pattern was different from that of the Carolinas. There UTW leaders did not stress the flying squadron. One column of some 250 union workers was formed in Newnan, and it closed twelve mills, but a year later Georgia UTW members expressed doubt that the effect had been positive. The squadron's picketing strikers frightened and intimidated other workers, and "its arrival at a mill was often the signal for an exodus of workers through the back door."[27] The Atlanta *Constitution* reported in big headlines on Wednesday that the strike, though widespread, was less than 50 percent effective and that many mills had really closed to avoid trouble. Gov. Eugene Talmadge, with a primary election only days ahead, refused requests by the owners to call out the Guard, arguing that "local authorities have enough legal means" to handle the situation.[28] On the second day, however, a gunfight broke out between strikers and mill guards in the North Georgia town of Trion, and the strikes in Georgia made national headlines a day before the one in Honea Path, South Carolina.[29]

At Trion, the strikers had badly beaten two nonstrikers clashing with the picket line; then a striker walked up to armed company guards and said, "Buddies, why don't you give up your guns and join our side?" When the guards refused, the strikers attempted to seize their guns; one of the guards, suddenly surrounded, fired his gun and was joined by other guards as the strikers ran. One worker was killed, and, although accounts differ, perhaps as many as twenty others were wounded. Minutes later, an injured guard lying down inside the mill was killed by a young boy who sprayed automatic pistol shots at him through an open window. On the same day two other pickets were shot and killed by guards in Augusta, and fights between strikers and nonstrikers closed a plant of the Bibb Manufacturing Company in Macon. Talmadge still refused to call out the Guard, with the primary election only five days away.[30]

On Wednesday, 12 September, Talmadge won the election by a landslide, and on 15 September, as he heard reports that flying squadrons were to be formed to close plants in Cartersville and the mighty Bibb in Columbus, he called out the Guard.[31] Under its protection, many mills which had voluntarily closed announced plans to reopen. A major confrontation between the Guard and a flying squadron took place on Monday, 17 September, at Newnan, where the Guards, operating under Talmadge's declaration of martial law, arrested over 128 workers. The Guard declared that the strikers would be treated humanely as "military prisoners." The strikers, some of whom were women and who were mostly in their teens or early twenties, took their arrests cheerfully. One worker told the *Constitution*, "We feel honored to go out with the National Guard rather than with the scabs."[32] The arrested strikers were interned at Fort McPherson, colorfully called a "concentration camp" by the press. When the national settlement came, they were quietly released. One woman called to her guards, "Goodbye, we had a swell time," and photographs showed the strikers happily waving to their captors.[32] Although one historian argued that Talmadge had "personally broken the back of the union in Georgia," it was apparent that well before the governor's delayed reaction in the third week of the strike, the strike had failed, as it had in the Carolinas. In Rockmart, Georgia, 18 September, over 1,500 workers, cheered on by its citizens, marched through the town, chanting, "We want work."[34]

What happened in the rest of the South by the third week of the strike had already occurred in Alabama by early September. The July strikes had not been spectacularly successful. And in North Alabama, mills with picket lines were soon surrounded by private guards, as the owners settled in to wait out the storm. In South Alabama the mills never went out, while in the North, as the general strike began the union stood still, losing strength daily. The workers had split tragically. Robert King of the Birmingham *News* described the struggle in Alabama: "Here, in many communities where a few months ago neighbors swapped news at the general store or over backyard fences and everybody was a friend, peaceful towns and villages are tense under the patrol of grim-faced men armed with rifles, shotguns, and pistols." He noted that "ominous machine guns bristle from vantage points, and strangers, who once were welcome within the gates of these towns and villages, are challenged by men who are suspicious of all but they know are 'one of them.'"[35] The early judgment of the obviously partisan Scott Roberts, president of the Alabama Cotton Manufacturers Association, who on 4 September called the textile strike "a complete flop," was not far from the truth. Although North Alabama stayed tense, the general strike changed the situation very little in Alabama. It continued to be an owner-controlled standoff.[36]

From his view in Washington, however, Gorman believed he had gained the respectability of a national strike. Whether from striking, seeking a "hole," or being locked out, the absent textile workers gained the headlines for a month. The strike had come to the attenuated New England industry in much the same pattern as in the South. On 10 September riots occurred in several New England towns, and people were hurt. On 12 September, amid much street violence at the mills in Rhode Island, four strikers were shot and killed. On 13 September, there was renewed rioting, and Gov. Theodore Green, who already had the Guard out, requested federal troops, a request FDR adroitly dodged. The Rhode Island strike, where some fifty thousand workers from many different kinds of textile industries merged, resembled those in the southern textile states. The union was not really in a majority position in the workforce, and an abbreviated northern version of the flying squadrons took out many plants that would have continued to run under ordinary circumstances. Enthusiasm for the strike came from the fear and frustration of workers in a dying industry rather than from a disciplined sense of the future, and the resulting strike was a mass failure.[37] But Gorman had achieved one important goal—creating the image of a national strike conducted by a national union carrying on centralized negotiations.

By the third week of the strike, cracks were all too obvious in the edifice he had built. Many southern mill owners who had closed their mills announced in a concerted manner on 15 September that they had plans to reopen despite union pickets, which they did slowly. On 10 September, for example, seventy-six mills were closed in Georgia, but by 19 September only sixty-two were closed and eighty-five were in operation.[38] By the third week of the strike, most strikers had exhausted their slender resources. Bobby Dean Jackson, historian of the Inman Mills of South Carolina, in 1967 interviewed one worker who vividly remembered the destitution of the families who had gone three weeks without pay. When the strikes ended, his family, although they had collected a cache of food in August, had only one can of condensed milk left in the kitchen and twenty-five cents in their pockets.[39] The UTW, unable to raise money, was incapable of furnishing relief, and despite the federal government's decision not to waver from its policy of providing relief to strikers if they qualified, local relief officials had little money, were mired in red tape, and, in the South, were often reluctant to extend aid to strikers.[40] The South's plentiful labor supply quickly furnished thousands of strikebreakers, and by 20 September the UTW's position was perilous. The jubilant predictions of victory in August were no more than distant memories, and the union admitted that "force and hunger" were sending its people back to work.[41]

THE SETTLEMENT

During the strike, Franklin Roosevelt was at Hyde Park, but that did not protect him from union pressure to settle somehow the labor relations issues which a year under the textile code had spawned. In August he had fended off reporters' questions about the union's claim that only he could prevent the strike. In his press conference of 15 August he said, "I do not think we are ready to talk about it at all. . . . We do not know enough about it yet." It was, he said, "complicated by the old differences between the northern textile people and the southern textile people," and "the thing is not crystalized yet."[42] Roosevelt as usual deflected the pressure, hoping that the NLRB mediation attempt would be a success. While Lloyd Garrison told the public that his NLRB would continue to work for a settlement, he privately advised FDR to look elsewhere and suggested a special one-shot mediation board. Garrison even included some possible names for the board. Among them was John G. Winant, a former moderate Republican governor of New Hampshire who had mediated a textile strike successfully in that state. Winant, said Garrison, had voluntarily called and offered his services. Also included was the name of Marion Smith, an attorney in Atlanta, Georgia, son of the former senator and cabinet member, Hoke Smith. Smith, although a corporate attorney, represented no cotton mills, was able, and was willing to serve.[43] As reports of the flying squadrons rolled into Hyde Park on 3 and 4 September, the President decided to act quickly to shift the focus of negotiation away from the White House.

In a press conference on 5 September, FDR talked to reporters extensively about the year's general strikes, and he read them Garrison's letter suggesting the appointment of a special board. During the conference he clearly indicated that he had done well to resist the early pressure to intervene in the July San Francisco general strike, saying, "Everybody demanded that I sail into San Francisco Bay, all flags flying and guns double-shotted and end the strike. They went completely off the handle." Roosevelt argued that the textile union leaders did not want the strike but had been forced into it by Norman Thomas (a reference to Thomas' speech before the textile workers' August convention).[44]

Soon after the conference Roosevelt appointed a special mediation board,

with Winant as chair, Marion Smith, and Raymond G. Ingersoll, a New York
arbitrator who was president of the Borough of Brooklyn. Officially named
the Board of Inquiry, the Winant Board, as it was known, was authorized
by the President's executive order "to inquire into complaints in the cotton,
wool, silk, rayon, and allied textile industries; to consider ways and means
of meeting such problems and complaints; and, upon request by the parties,
to act as a board of voluntary arbitration." Roosevelt's choice of Winant
demonstrated his personal fondness for the former Bull Mooser. Later FDR
would make Winant his World War II ambassador to Great Britain.[45] The
Winant Board faced "an almost impossible assignment," and a *New Yorker*
correspondent got to the heart of the matter when he noted that the board's
toughest problem, considering the economic roots of the strike, was to find
a way for textile workers to support a family on ten dollars a week.[46]

Meanwhile, Gorman and Sloan engaged in a war of press releases and radio
broadcasts, although it is unclear how widely broadcast their remarks were.
Certainly the press reported the verbal blasts. On 3 September Sloan released
a short statement to the press repudiating the UTW claims concerning wages,
code violations, and the stretch out. About this last, his particular target, he
claimed, "It is uneconomic for mills to expand work beyond the capacity of
employees, because of the higher proportion of inferior work that would result. Such a practice would bring its own penalty." Stretch out claims were
"without foundation."[47] Gorman, too, appropriated the press, and at the end
of the strike's first day he virtually claimed victory, saying, "The strike is moving with the impetus of a landslide and with the same irresistible force. . . .
Victory is assured at this hour."[48]

Neither Gorman nor Sloan advanced any arguments or facts different from
those that had divided the UTW and the Code Authority since the preceding
spring. Sloan's vigorous participation in the debate might be considered a
measure of the success that the weak UTW had achieved, in creating the impression of a national general strike. Sloan's defense of the industry's position
contradicted one of the major points he and the owners made — that the strike
was not against the owners but against the federal government. Roosevelt,
after appointing the Winant Board, remained gratefully insulated at his man-
sion on the Hudson. Although Steve Early, his press secretary, who remained
in Washington, often sent tidbits of information about the strike to Hyde
Park, none of them went beyond what Roosevelt could have learned from his
morning *New York Times.*

Governor Winant and his colleagues wasted no time in getting to work.
They assembled in Washington and worked long hours for the next eleven
days, assisted by such NRA staffers as Thomas Emerson and by a small, hastily assembled group of technical experts, most also from the NRA. The board
announced that at the beginning its sole purpose would be to gather information so that it could act with wisdom. Gorman, realizing what was hap-
pening in the South and acutely aware that time was his enemy, proposed

in a radio broadcast on 8 September that the Winant Board arbitrate the strike and that, pending arbitration, all the mills be closed "so that further murders of our fellow workers may be avoided."[49] On the same day Sloan announced that the strike was a failure and that he was "satisfied" with the strike trend. Replying publicly to Gorman's speech the next day, he declared that it was "utterly impossible" to accede to any request that all mills be closed, and he refused arbitration, noting that the Code Authority had no right whatsoever to make any settlement for an individual company.[50]

The southern owners, although in control of the strike and of the situation, after the National Guard units had nullified the flying squadrons, had found it "difficult to counter the adverse publicity" that they believed the strike had brought the industry.[51] Gorman knew that Sloan would turn down his request for the Winant Board to arbitrate, but he also knew that the public would see Sloan and the industry as blocking settlement of the strike.[52] Sloan had warmly welcomed the appointment of the board on 5 September and had pledged full cooperation, calling the board a "medium for enlightening the American public on the real situation as it exists today and the events which preceded."[53] Sloan then met secretly on 7 September with Winant and arranged for several major southern members of the Code Authority to come to Washington privately to meet with the board. Included in the committee were William D. Anderson, Charles Cannon, Thomas Marchant, and Benjamin Gossett. The manufacturers and the Winant Board met at the Cosmos Club. The cotton manufacturers were determined to fight on, viewing arbitration as totally unacceptable, and the conferences produced no movement to end the strike.

On 14 September, the explosive Hugh Johnson blasted the UTW in a speech to assembled Code Authorities at Carnegie Hall in New York. He denied that there were any sound economic reasons for the strike and claimed that it "was pulled in contravention of the solemn arrangements" of the NRA and was a political move on the part of radical elements in the country. He also charged that Norman Thomas, an articulate critic of the NRA, had instigated the strikes by a union whose word could not be trusted.[54] Johnson's charge was patently without foundation, but it served to encourage the opponents of the strike and weakened public support for the workers.

Giving up on arbitration and working rapidly, the Winant Board made its report to Frances Perkins on 17 September; she and Winant personally took it to Hyde Park to present to Roosevelt. The report enumerated the UTW grievances, and for the first time a federal agency recognized that the labor grievances might be valid, particularly the one regarding the effect of the production cuts.[55] Nevertheless, the report did not suggest any basic changes in code regulations or wages. The report proposed instead that the President create a Textile Labor Relations Board (TLRB) to operate under the authority of Public Resolution 44 rather than under the cotton textile code. The new board would replace the Bruere Board, and would have the authority to handle all Section 7(a) collective bargaining cases and cases involving other code provisions for workers in the cotton, silk, and woolen industries. The Code Authority would no longer have such responsibilities. The report recommended that, in order to determine the true economic position of the cotton, silk, and woolen industries and their ability to support higher wages and more employment, the Federal Trade Commission and the Bureau of Labor Statistics undertake extensive studies of these industries.

The Winant Board also suggested that, for the purpose of regulating the use of the stretch out system in the industries, a special study committee be created under the direction of the TLRB. The federal government had come full circle. The Bruere Board had started its ill-fated life as a special stretch out board! Before the special study committee, soon to be called the Work Assignment Board, got under way and reported, the Winant Board recommended that no employer should extend the workload before 1 February 1935, except in "special circumstances." With the strike collapsing as it delivered its report, the Winant Board urged that there be no discrimination by employers against those who had gone on strike, although the board did not find the UTW demand for recognition as the bargaining agent for all workers in the industry to be "feasible." Collective bargaining would have to be achieved on a plant-to-plant basis. Roosevelt was pleased with Winant's report. "It is," he said, "a good example of the practical way in which industrial problems can be calmly discussed and solved under a republican form of government."[56]

On 21 September, the President, armed with the Winant Report, finally intervened. He asked the workers to return to work and the owners to open the mills. "I want," he said publicly, "to express the very sincere hope that all employees now on strike will return to work and that all textile manufacturers will aid the government in carrying out the steps outlined." The Winant Board report would be the basis of settlement.[57] The next day the UTW Executive Council voted to end the strike. "It is our unanimous view," the council stated, "which we shall support by our further statements, that the union has won an overwhelming victory, that we ought to terminate the strike as no longer necessary and that we now go forth in a triumphant campaign of organization."[58] George Sloan merely promised to give the Winant Report serious consideration, but the UTW, faced with a crumbling strike, on 3 October 1934 formally accepted Roosevelt's proposal for ending the strike. The UTW letter to Roosevelt agreed specifically to a truce for six months, during which time the union would cooperate with the new TLRB and the NLRB and permit no stoppage of work in protest against their decisions. The labor leaders "hoped" that the textile manufacturers would also agree to work out a settlement along the lines of the Winant Board findings.[59]

Unlike the union, the Code Authority, never formally accepted any settlement, although Sloan publicly stated the willingness of the industry to cooperate with the new TLRB and to avoid retributive action against workers who had struck. On 1 October 1934 the Code Authority sent to all members of the CTI a report on the strike, the union demands, the Winant Board's recommendations, and the Code Authority's position. At best, the Code Authority offered a rather chilly hand to the new TLRB and any special stretch out committee. On the key issues of collective bargaining and wages it remained firm, arguing that the UTW represented at best sixty thousand paid-up members. The Code Authority had no intention of recognizing the UTW as an industrywide bargaining agent. On another issue, soon to become the top union concern, the Code Authority recommended to the industry "that as work becomes available, the mills reemploy workers who did not engage in lawless violence."[60]

The industry's attitude toward the end of the strike was expressed in a letter from Sloan to Benjamin E. Squires, the executive director of the new TLRB. "As you know," wrote Sloan, "the strike was called off by the UTW without any consultation or agreement by it or by the government with the industry or any of its members." According to Sloan, there was nobody who was "authorized to speak for any mill in the matter of labor relations." To clarify the Code Authority's request that nonviolent strikers be rehired, he said, "It did not occur to the Code Authority that work should be made available to the strikers by discharge of any bona fide workers who were employed at the close of the strike, whether or not they had been employed prior to the calling of the strike." He cited an NLRB ruling that upheld his position.[61]

Rugged individualism still reigned in the rolling hills of the Piedmont. The industry stood committed only by Sloan's public statement and the private views of leading manufacturers to a Code Authority that depended for its power only on the legal uncertainties of the NRA. Individual mill owners had not promised not to discriminate against workers who had struck nor to cooperate with the TLRB and the various investigative bodies established by the government. Nothing existed on paper binding any individual company whatsoever. And the Code Authority had lost something in the strike. The Bruere Board departed, replaced by a more independent TLRB with a stretch out study on tap. More importantly, the partnership principle fought for so hard by the CTI had been weakened by the mill owners' hard fight against collective bargaining.[62] The UTW challenge had been defeated by the mill owners of the South and their lockouts, not by George Sloan and his press releases. In the months to follow, the mill owners would increasingly revert to the cherished independence that the NRA now seemed to threaten.

The union had been badly beaten, and the UTW officials had little choice in their heartbreaking surrender. Gorman had carried on his smoke-and-mirrors act for days, but from the beginning it had been a chancy affair. The initial thrust of the flying squadrons had very quickly given way to a cat-and-mouse game, with the owners as the victorious cat. By the end of the second week, many southern mills had reopened with new workers or with old ones sheepishly coming back. Kasper Smith, a southern worker, remembered in the 1970s the surge out and the excitement of the picket lines and the stirring labor songs. But he also remembers that "they had no business striking down South because they were weak here. We didn't have no backing . . . we shouldn't have done it. The South hadn't even begun to organize well by then." "We were," he said, "85 percent union here [in his own mill] that closed those mills down. But when the strike was over everybody hurried back to the company side."[63] The union's loss of the South meant the strike was over, and it seemed good union strategy to call it off and salvage the wreckage.

By accepting the Winant Board proposals, the UTW hoped to present the image of a public-minded union to contrast with that of the selfish employers. Gorman had also become genuinely worried about the safety and welfare of union workers. The frequency of clashes with other workers at the picket lines, the loss of life, the workers confronting bayonets—none of it was to his liking. He also knew that the union workers had reached the end of their slender economic resources and could endure no more. The UTW tried to believe that the end of the strike had really been a settlement that offered some gains. At least Robert Bruere was gone, and there was the hope of a more impartial board ahead. Stretch out would be studied once more, and the Code Authority's mid-October acceptance of the Winant Board's freeze on stretch out until the Work Assignment Board reported could be used to the union's advantage. All in all, Gorman argued, the UTW had pushed as hard as possible: "We went as far as we could, short of starting a revolution." Stoutly defending the strike against its critics, he contended that the general strike had had a positive effect, although none of the strike demands had been met directly by the mills.[64] The strike ended the old style of union organizing by awakening the textile workers to the necessity of building a permanent union with organization protected through written contracts, and Gorman believed that the strike developed the leadership needed to accomplish this goal.[65]

Gorman's defense convinced neither contemporary participants nor later judges. Kasper Smith, the same textile worker who remembered the excitement of the strike, also remembered its conclusion—defeat and return to the mills, on the owners' terms. He lost his job two weeks after returning to the mills and waited several months, as unionism faded, to go back to weaving. "I think," he said in the late 1970s, "what happened in 1934 has a whole lot to do with people not being so union now."[66] The UTW's real mistake in fall 1934 was insisting that the strike and its inconclusive settlement were a success rather than the opening round in a continuing offensive. Gorman boldly told the October 1934 AFL meeting that the UTW was stronger than it had ever been before, and he called the strike "one of the most amazing victories ever recorded in the annals of the A.F. of L."[67] Roy Lawrence of the UTW asked the cotton textile workers in North Carolina to go back to work "as a victorious army, conscious of their strength, the justice of their cause, and the solidarity which has bound them together in this memorable struggle and will continue to bind them in the future."[68] But the workers perceived that the new array of boards and studies had really gained them little in immediate terms, and they were bitter over UTW claims of victory. Franz Daniel, a longtime textile organizer, said in 1960 that the memory of what he called the "deception" by the UTW leaders still lived on in the textile towns.[69]

The strike's enduring significance lay in the bitterness of the workers and the resulting roadblocks in the quest for effective unionization and collective bargaining. Milton Derber and Edwin Young wrote that in the South "the touchstone of southern unionism . . . was the cotton textile industry, and the failure of the great textile strike of 1934 . . . symbolized at least a temporary parting of the way between the South and the rest of the nation as far as unions were concerned."[70] The key word is "symbolized." Elsewhere in the South unionism also failed, in such industries as lumber, furniture, chemicals, and food processing. The smashing of the young UTW locals in the South sent a message throughout the southern crescent, and the unions retreated. After the defeat of textiles, wrote George Tindall, "their southern campaigns," assumed "the character of guerrilla actions punctuated by occasional victories."[71]

The strike highlighted the inability of the NRA labor policy to create a stable pattern of labor relations characterized by collective bargaining. As in other strike situations in 1934, government boards had proved unable to avert the strike and equally powerless to compel or arrange an equitable settlement. The union needed assistance from the New Deal and did not get it. In the South, the labor problems of the cotton textile industry continued to be handled under the cotton textile code provisions, discredited though they were. The New Deal still had not interpreted the meaning of Section 7(a) for the textile workers. A key question remained unanswered: Was collective bargaining guaranteed by the federal government, or was it a right that had to be earned in grievous conflict? A clear answer to this question emerged from events in the cotton textile industry in the months after the strike.

"Baffled and betrayed"

THE TEXTILE LABOR RELATIONS BOARD, THE UNION, THE INDUSTRY, AND THE END OF THE CODE, 1934-36

Roosevelt, having secured the UTW's offer of a truce under the terms of the Winant Board's proposals, moved quickly to put the agreement into effect. On 26 September, using the authority of Public Resolution 44, the President appointed the new Textile Labor Relations Board (TLRB). The board, which would operate under the Department of Labor, consisted of three impartial "special commissioners": Walter P. Stacy, chairperson, a retired North Carolina judge; retired Admiral Henry A. Wiley; and attorney James A. Mullenbach. The three men already sat as the Steel Labor Relations Board, improvised in reaction to labor problems in another industry. Textiles would be just another chore. Roosevelt authorized the TLRB to investigate alleged violations of Section 7(a) in the textile industry (cotton, silk, woolen, and rayon), to arbitrate questions voluntarily submitted, and to exercise "other" functions authorized by the various textile codes. The TLRB would assume all the general enforcement duties of the Bruere Board, including the "adjustment" of labor complaints and disputes. The President made the TLRB's decisions subject to review by the NLRB, a condition that the UTW wanted.[1]

The President also ordered the two investigations of the cotton textile industry which the Winant Board had suggested. The Bureau of Labor Statistics was to prepare a report on hours, earnings, and working conditions in the textile industries, and to report on the various occupational classifications of labor and their wage differentials. The report, compiled outside the NRA and beyond the reach of the industry, was obviously seen as an impartial answer to the economic questions raised by the strike. Similarly, the second investigation, to be made by the Federal Trade Commission, would be an impartial report on the general economic conditions in the industry. The FTC's task was to get to the heart of one of the strike's basic issues—could the industry pay higher wages and have a shorter work week in light of its real labor

costs, profits, and investment? In the President's plan, further study and report had replaced the original UTW strike goal of negotiation through collective bargaining.

The TLRB was relieved of the problem of stretch out when Roosevelt
amended the cotton, silk, and woolen textile codes on 16 October to provide
for the appointment by the TLRB of three boards to deal with that complicated problem. On 30 November 1934 the President ratified the creation of
boards for all three industries. Each of the three boards was to be an autonomous unit, composed of an impartial chairperson, an employee representative, and an employer representative; but they were to function in administrative conjunction with the TLRB. The Cotton Textile Work Assignment Board
(CTWAB) consisted of William A. Mitchell, chair, Geoffrey L. Brown, employee representative, and Earl R. Stull, employer representative. The board's
assignment from the TLRB was to survey cotton mills to determine proper
workloads and to investigate alleged increases in work assignments after the
adoption of the cotton textile code.[2] The hope was that the board could sci-
entifically determine the workloads across the wide spectrum of the industry.

The UTW had stridently demanded solutions, but all it got from the New
Deal was more boards. The Code Authority merely acknowledged the boards
and promised cooperation, although Roosevelt's 16 October amendment of
the cotton code gave the new boards the same government sanction the Bruere
Board had possessed. The new arrangements, however, did weaken the Code
Authority, for the federal partner assumed more direct responsibility in labor
relations. The new arrangements, however, were unclear. Although the code
remained intact, people wondered how the new boards would interpret their
charges. But as one journalist noted, Roosevelt's quick action in establishing
a new complaint and dispute network had "aroused the greatest enthusiasm
and optimism among the leaders of the strike."[3]

THE TLRB AT WORK

From the beginning the TLRB was a more professional board than the
Bruere Board. Its members, well paid at $8,000 per year, were fulltime
bureaucrats. The board assembled a new staff to meet all its responsibilities
in textiles. At one time, with the work assignment boards for three industries
functioning simultaneously, the staff consisted of over ninety people. But as
those boards finished their investigative work, the TLRB's permanent staff
never numbered more than thirty-seven, despite overseeing the labor relations aspects of codes covering 1.3 million workers in 6,658 plants with an
invested capital of nearly $5 billion.[4]

The relationship of the TLRB to the senior board, the NLRB, had to be
worked out. Before the strike, the NLRB had not assumed responsibility for

enforcing labor provisions in industries in which a code provided for a labor board. Nevertheless, pressure on the NLRB to move collective bargaining along via interpretation of Section 7(a), and the rules it and the earlier NLB had developed, dictated that the TLRB and the NLRB continue the discussions over jurisdiction that had begun with the Bruere Board before the strike overwhelmed them. The TLRB had the same statutory power as the NLRB, but the NLRB insisted that the TLRB follow the NLRB's lead in interpreting Section 7(a). This the TLRB quickly agreed to do.[5] Overwhelmed at first by complaints from workers that they had not been rehired by owners after the strike because of union activities, the TLRB turned to the extensive network of the NLRB for help, by using its field agent system and regional boards. But on 13 November, the NLRB informed the TLRB that it was turning all textile cases over to the TLRB for original jurisdiction, regardless of the nature of the complaint.[6]

With its limited resources and wide responsibilities, the TLRB never established an effective field investigation system. As NLRB support diminished, the TLRB decided to turn to the Code Authority for help. On 18 December 1934 Sidney Munroe, George Sloan's assistant in the CTI and the Code Authority, met with Admiral Wiley and Walter Taylor, a TLRB staffer, to arrange the cooperation. TLRB member Col. Frank Douglass, who had replaced the recently deceased James Mullenbach on the board, wrote Sloan on 21 December 1934, officially authorizing the procedure. Sloan's reply of 24 December accurately noted that it was "very similar to the method followed by our field setup in the past."[7] The Code Authority's three-person field staff would once again investigate the numerous complaints of wage and hour violations of the cotton code, leaving Section 7(a) cases and stretch out complaints to the TLRB.

The TLRB, sensitive to past union criticism of this delegation of power, claimed in February 1935 that it had first cleared its plan with Thomas McMahon and Francis Gorman of the UTW, who approved the use of the Code Authority as long as the complainant was notified of the result of the investigation. The TLRB also believed "that manufacturers in the textile industry were more willing to adjust matters presented to them by representatives of the Code Authority than they were with government authorities."[8]

The TLRB actually referred only selected cases to the Code Authority, preferring to use its own staff in cases where there was a high probability that the complaint was valid. Telfair Knight, general counsel of the TLRB, argued that the system worked out was significantly different from that used by the Bruere Board. The TLRB acknowledged each complaint, and the complaint was "continuously followed up and handled" by the board's staff until "final adjustment was reached." Knight claimed "considerable success" for the method, saying that no complaint was closed until the complainant was satisfied.[9] TLRB member Frank Douglass later argued to Frances Perkins that the procedure had not been adopted in deference to the Code Authority, but had been instigated by the board and was subject to the board's discretion. Like Knight, he pointed out that the board was always careful to seek UTW cooperation.[10] The December agreement also furthered the aims of the TLRB to bring peace to the industry. Benjamin Squires, executive director of the TLRB, conveyed to Charles Cannon, president of the huge Cannon Mills, the board's belief "that lasting peace is more likely to obtain by joint consent than by formal rulings."[11]

The procedure the TLRB used for adjusting controversies in the textile industry followed the well-worn route of the Bruere Board, minus the mill committees and state boards. First, an investigation was made either by the Code Authority or the board's agents. By winter 1935 the TLRB had three agents in the South.[12] The overworked field staff attempted to settle complaints by mediation and conciliation. Only as a last resort would there be a formal hearing and decision by the board. If the complaints were sustained and the mill continued its practices, the case could be forwarded to the Compliance Division of the NRA for enforcement. The TLRB divided complaints between two investigative divisions. One division handled complaints of discrimination because of union membership. The other division handled wage and hour complaints arising under the codes. In addition to these two divisions, the board supervised the work assignment board investigating stretch out.

Symptomatic of the evolving nature of the New Deal labor policy, the TLRB had no bureaucratic procedures to deal with union representation and majority-rule collective bargaining, although, unlike the Bruere Board, its field agents were not antiunion. On 16 October 1934 one of its first field investigators, Carl Gill working in Georgia, severely criticized the Bibb Manufacturing Company in his report. "The criticism I offer against this company," wrote Gill, "is that it makes no pretense of engaging in collective bargaining even to the extent of talking with a shop committee or representative of the union. Anderson [the president] et al. are desirous of breaking the union."[13]

As the TLRB organized its staff and sorted out its duties, workers in the South, particularly those who had stood openly on the union side, faced a new problem — triumphant local owners who meant to make the most of their victory over the strikers by locking them out or blacklisting them. Many strikers found their jobs filled by strikebreakers. The *New York Times* reported on 29 September that the "South is unreservedly pleased that the textile strike is over," but the "issues raised by it here have not been settled and will be difficult to settle in the future." The *Times* said that the strike, despite the issues of wages, hours, and stretch out, fundamentally "grew out of the basic struggle over unionism" and that "union recognition is still a fighting issue with many of the mill managements." Thousands of workers, said the article, were not back at work.[14] *Newsweek*, using what it termed "impartial estimates," reported that eighty thousand workers "found Southern mill gates locked against them when they sought to return."[15] Roy Lawrence, textile organizer, said that in his state some ten thousand workers sympathetic to the union were unable to return to the mills. Conditions, he said, were worse than ever, with the mill owners "doing just like they have always done."[16]

The TLRB, flooded with complaints of discrimination against union members, sent a short letter on 17 October to all mill managements asking them not to discriminate by refusing to rehire union members and to refrain from evicting union strikers from the mill villages. Such actions, the board argued, would prevent a lasting peace.[17] But less than two weeks later, a UTW letter claimed that discrimination against former strikers by lockouts and evictions from the mill villages were still widespread, particularly in the South. Gorman told his listeners in a radio address that he feared another national strike might be imminent and announced that "strike sanctions" would be granted to every local facing discriminatory post-strike practices. He reported that twenty-five thousand workers had lost their jobs, fifteen thousand of them in clear cases of discrimination. "We do not want a renewal of conflict," he said. "We want progress through the peaceful machinery proposed in the report of the Winant Board."[18] A month later, Gorman still claimed that two hundred mills (about a fifth of all in the industry) still practiced discrimination against UTW members and that the TLRB investigators had been helpless to prevent it.[19]

Martha Gelhorn, one of Harry Hopkins' informal reporters, visited the Carolinas in the aftermath of the strike, and one of her reports provided a vivid description of the workers' lot in Gastonia, N.C. She reported that she had been talking to mill workers and as many local union presidents as she could find. There was, she told Hopkins, "widespread discrimination" against union workers. They "live in terror of being penalized for joining unions; and the employers live in a mingled rage and fear against the imported monstrosity: organized labor." The owners were to her "strangely hysterical about unions." Many of the mills had not reopened after the strike or operated only two or three days a week, and Gelhorn found the economic plight of the workers wrenching—especially that of the union presidents, all of whom had been fired and evicted from the mill villages. "These men," she wrote, "are in a terrible fix." But to her surprise, she found little violence or hostility, only a "kind of contained and quiet misery" with a continued faith in FDR and hope that the TLRB "will do the just thing." This first-time visitor to the cotton textile South told her boss, "Gastonia County is my idea of a place to go to acquire melancholia."[20] Another journalist surveying conditions in the South said, "It certainly looks to be a long, cold winter for the jobless strikers."[21]

The TLRB had expected that the employers would rehire all the strikers without discrimination. "The strike," said the board in a November telegram to all mills, "cannot be satisfactorily ended and peace restored to the textile industry until all workers who left the plant during the strike, and who did not engage in lawless violence, are returned to their former positions. This is a fundamental issue which must be met."[22] A few days later, executive director Benjamin Squires wrote to Sloan, noting that it had been weeks since the termination of the strike "but the Textile Labor Relations Board is still receiving numerous complaints that strikers are not being rehired and that many are being evicted from company houses." The TLRB urged employers "to reemploy those who were in the mills before the strike without further delay, and without discrimination."[23]

Sloan replied to the TLRB that the Code Authority had never entered into any formal or informal agreement to settle the strike and thus had no obligation to support the Winant Board report. Sloan reminded the TLRB that the Code Authority had suggested to the industry that it reemploy workers who had left their jobs, if they had not engaged in violence, but he insisted that there was no obligation to rehire workers if there was no work for them. Many former strikers were idle, he declared, because the industry, with orders slack, had no jobs for them. Furthermore, the industry refused to discharge people who had taken jobs during the strike and replace them with former strikers. Sloan, citing the Code Authority's repeated requests to the industry to avoid discrimination, denied that any massive effort at discrimination was occurring, except in cases of workers who had engaged in known violence on the picket lines. "In any event," wrote Sloan, "I think that it is clear to you that it is a matter for each individual mill and that there is nothing in the Code Authority and nothing in the recommendations of the Code Authority which warrants my urging a mill to decide this question of policy one way or the other."[24]

David Clark, editor of the *Textile Bulletin*, admitted that many employers were trying not to rehire union members. That was their right, said Clark, and essential for their "own protection, the protection of loyal employees, and development of future harmonious employment relations."[25] Clark advised all southern manufacturers to ignore the TLRB and hire whom they wanted. William Anderson declared that "no recommendation made by the Winant Board, no statement by the President concerning the reemployment of strikers, and no law of the land" could make him replace a "loyal worker" with a striker.[26]

As a matter of fact, the TLRB had not recommended that strikebreakers should be replaced with workers who had gone on strike. The board in its first decisions upheld the right of a company not to replace strikebreakers with employees who had worked in the mills before the strike. What the board insisted upon, however, was that workers applying for jobs not be rejected because they belonged to the UTW or had participated in the general strike. Such rejections, said the board in the few cases that reached it, constituted unfair labor practices.[27] Of forty-six discrimination cases decided by the TLRB up to 2 May 1935, thirty rulings favored complaining workers, while sixteen favored employers.[28] Discrimination cases occupied much of the board's time, and by January 1935, it had received more than sixteen hundred discrimination complaints involving 579 mills. Hearings had been held in fifty-two cases, nineteen before regional boards of the NLRB, twenty-three before field examiners of the TLRB and ten before the TLRB itself.[29]

The TLRB, while devoting most of its time to cases of discrimination, also tried to further the principle of collective bargaining, something the Bruere Board had ignored or undermined with its mill committee system. The TLRB insisted upon the NLRB principle that for collective bargaining to be genuine, every reasonable effort to reach an agreement had to be expended. But it never succeeded in establishing the majority-rule principle in the cotton textile industry, although in two cases it did hold referendum elections for the choice of employee representation.[30] In general, the board made no progress in bringing collective bargaining to the cotton textile industry. The pattern of the TLRB in collective bargaining followed closely that of a sister board, the Bituminous Coal Labor Board, where during the same time period, only the economic power of the United Mine Workers could make Section 7(a) effective in a few instances, despite the efforts of the coal board to bring it about.[31]

In attempting to carry out its duties, the TLRB encountered considerable resistance from employers. Field agent D. Williams reported to the board in February 1935 that "there is evidence of a combination of mill owners in Georgia to oppose to the limit the principle of collective bargaining, and they are not likely to stand for anything which appears to be even remotely connected with it."[32] Thomas M. Marchant, well-known southern manufacturer, asserted as early as October 1934, "The investigators being sent into the South are causing considerable disturbances, and really make it almost unbearable for the mill executive."[33] By spring 1935, when the NIRA was deemed unconstitutional, the board was engaged in three federal court actions to make companies obey the code. Nevertheless, Telfair Knight, counsel for the TLRB, wrote in May 1935 that persistent persuasion of the employers by the board had resulted in many cases of employer cooperation without legal action. Knight said that of 110 cases heard by the board up to that May, it had been necessary to refer only 10 of them to the Compliance Division of the NRA, and only seven Blue Eagles had had to be removed in all the textile industries under its jurisdiction.[34] On the other hand, the UTW accurately claimed that the TLRB could never enforce its decisions on discrimination cases adequately nor even deal with most of them. An employer desiring to flout the TLRB's authority would have found it easy to do. The board's ranks were thin; its goal was industrial peace, not collective bargaining.

The TLRB did settle a considerable number of labor complaints. From September 1934 to May 1935, the board received from all its textile industries 4,374 complaints from thirty-five states, involving 1,407 mills and 128,806 individuals. During the same period, the board claimed it adjusted 127 strikes, 38 of them in cotton, and conducted over 135 separate hearings. Prior to the suspension of the cotton code in May 1935, the TLRB received 2,847 complaints from the cotton industry involving 707 mills and 77,325 workers. Of these complaints, 2,881 were adjusted to the satisfaction of all parties, said the TLRB. In the South the greatest number of these complaints—1,683 of them—involved discrimination complaints or violations of Section 7(a).[35]

The UTW went from acceptance of the TLRB to outright attack. Despite the board's inability to halt the lockout of former strikers, as late as January 1935 the union still had kind words for the board. "The Textile Labor Relations Board is going straight ahead," it said, "and no honest criticism can be laid at its door so far as the outcome of its work is concerned at this time."[36] By early February 1935, the union had radically changed its view on the board's mixed record, as the TLRB's inability to enforce its decisions became clearer. The UTW complained about the number of investigations, the followup of complaints, and the continued failure to deal with discrimination against union members.[37] In 1936 Gorman called the TLRB "a bitter disappointment. Thousands of discrimination cases came before the board—and few were ever decided in our favor." He said the southern employers "laughed out loud at the decisions when they were in our favor," while the "workers were kept starving in the streets in open defiance of the government."[38]

When the NIRA was declared invalid in May 1935, the TLRB was left without legal status. By then its credibility with the UTW had dropped to low levels, and the union had stopped cooperating with the board. On a southern tour in spring 1935, Gorman told a gathering of North Carolina cotton textile workers, "We are tired of being born in company homes, tired of being raised in company shacks, tired of being entertained on company playgrounds, tired of being educated in company schools, tired of buying company coal, and tired of being buried by company undertakers." The workers, he cried, felt "baffled and betrayed" as the "textile mill management have openly repudiated their own code."[39] Despite the board's rapidly eroding effectiveness, after the Supreme Court's adverse NIRA decision Roosevelt, by simple executive order, extended the TLRB until 30 November 1935, at which time the board and part of its personnel were transferred to the Textile Division of the United States Mediation and Conciliation Service. But in May 1935 the board ceased all activities related to the defunct cotton code, although it continued as a voluntary mediation and arbitration board until it was abolished on 31 July 1937.

THE UTW: A LOSING STRUGGLE

For some time after the general strike, the UTW kept to its strategy of claiming victory. Immediately after FDR set in motion the Winant Board recommendations, the union circulated a little propaganda sheet to the workers which called the strike a "real and smashing victory." The union also reported that it had "launched an intensive organizing campaign on every front, using new and effective methods to bring together the entire strength of the workers in one competent solid organization under the banner of the United Textile Workers."[40] The UTW flyer spoke of a new spirit in the South. "In that month of September, 1934," it said, "there was born a new consciousness of unity—unity of interests, unity of skill and knowledge—which is a real thing, unity of action, and unity of accomplishment." The textile workers in the South, the UTW claimed, "are on the offensive. They are becoming articulate. . . . They are rising in resistance to conditions of exploitation that have existed for two centuries" and are "organizing and combining, and challenging the South's most feudal system."[41] Gorman even wrote to young Paul Christopher, the UTW organizer in North Carolina who daily saw defeat, that the "bitter opposition in the past of a number of employers to our organization" was "because they feel we are on the verge of obtaining decent conditions."[42] In January 1935 Gorman even threatened another strike, hinting of plans for a spring push to create an alliance between unions in the textiles, petroleum, steel, automobiles, and tobacco industries.[43]

The union, by assuming its stance of victory and speaking of the inevitability of organization, sought to keep by brave words what it thought it had achieved in the pre-strike code months. The UTW leaders took to the road to achieve at least a rhetorical triumph. Early in 1935, in speeches in Newberry, S.C., and Columbus Ga., Francis Gorman called for a "new deal in the southern textile industry" as he summed up the result of the strike before "immense throngs," according to the UTW. "Mill workers came from many mills, and wild cheers and shouts greeted his appearances in the halls," demonstrating enthusiasm "such as seldom witnessed before an assembly of southern industrial workers."[44] In February 1935 the UTW's chief southern organizer, John Peel, told the UTW leaders that "the union is making rapid strides in the South and this in the face of the most terrific and despicable opposition ever attempted by the avaricious employers."[45] Thomas McMahon also toured the South, winding his way through the Piedmont towns in early summer 1935. The union paper reported that "monstrous crowds have greeted McMahon on his swing through the Southland." It said "Not before has an official of the United Textile Workers of America been greeted by more enthusiastic audiences." Unionization, the paper claimed, "is taking root in a firm and deep soil that gives promise of resisting the combined efforts of industrialists to destroy it."[46]

The conditions that brought about the 1934 strike still existed. The TLRB indicated that small, spontaneous walkouts in the 1929 style continued, with its year-end report in June 1936 reporting 217 strikes nationwide involving 66,730 workers. A year later, it reported 101 strikes involving 35,242 workers, some of them southern cotton textile disturbances.[47] John Peel reported in 1936 that since "the general strike of 1934, there have been numerous strikes throughout the South, some of six to nine months duration." Some walk-outs had resulted in "great progress," with "working agreements" with "quite a number of mills."[48]

The union reported in September 1936 that "during the past two years we have had close to 100 strikes throughout the Southern District and with the exception of a few cases pending settlement before the National Labor Board, all have been settled amicably and in many of the settlements workers are now enjoying closed shop working agreements." In that month the UTW claimed "over three hundred prosperous locals in the Southern District." It explained the apparent loss of membership by describing the wild 1933–34 gains in membership as "a mushroom growth with just about as much back-bone as a mushroom."[49] In spring 1936, McMahon was back in the South again claiming it as his "best trip," with much "enthusiasm," "spirit," and more "earnestness" than he ever remembered. He claimed that 104 locals existed in North Carolina alone.[50] "Throughout the South," said organizer Peel in May, "a splendid spirit prevails among our membership, and the morale generally is better than for some time."[51]

But the bravado and optimism did not reflect the southern reality. The UTW's pre-strike membership in the South, always tentative, was melting away. The 1934 strike's failure to gain immediate benefits severely damaged the union. More boards and further studies were not tangible gains for workers in the mill villages, who saw the harsh vengeance taken upon strike leaders—loss of employment and eviction from the village, the crucible of family culture. Remembering the despair of his fellow union organizers, Franz Daniel, or-ganizer for the Amalgamated Clothing Workers Union in the South in 1934, said, "When those mill workers went back defeated, those of us working lost heart."[52] The Textile Workers Organizing Committee later criticized the UTW leaders for their failure in the 1934–36 period. The leaders' "vision of power grew," said the CIO organization, and "they mistook sentiment for organiza-tion." Their participation in NRA councils and boards "lent a sense of reality to their illusion."[53]

The union had not been able to break the twin barriers to organization presented by the economic matrix of the industry and the worker culture of mill and village. Mildred Shoemaker, a former cotton textile worker in the 1930s, remembered in 1979 that in her Burlington, N.C., mill, not many work-ers supported the union or the strike of 1934. As soon as the National Guard arrived, "the next morning we went in." Pickets yelled at her, but she yelled back, "I got two little children. I've got to work." She thought the strike lead-ers were "hoodlums," anyway.[54] Although her husband joined the union, Mareda Cobb, a Bynum, N.C., worker in the 1930s, was always against it, be-cause "I always knew that North Carolina would never strike. I always had that in my head, and they ain't never. And that's what it takes. You've got to stick together to win anything, and they won't do it." Mrs. Cobb was not sure why textile workers in the South would not "stick it out." Perhaps, she thought, "they wanted the benefits" from unionism, "but they didn't want to pay union dues."[55] They also received little help from the New Deal's hesitant and ambiguous labor policy which proved to be an ineffective lever against the dead weight of the southern industry.

Immediately after the strike, the few remaining UTW organizers in the South were cut back from a full salary to only three weeks' pay per month. Not until January 1937 did Paul Christopher, for example, return to his full-time salary of thirty dollars a week. Christopher often faced financial difficulty. He even tried to go back to the mill as a weaver but found himself blacklisted. His UTW work epitomized many of the UTW problems in the post-strike cotton textile towns, and his reports in 1935 and 1936 indicated that much of his time was spent investigating cases of discrimination against union members, and arranging affidavits and testimony of workers for the TLRB and the emerging second NLRB. He appears to have directed only one cotton textile strike, in February 1935 at Shelby, N.C., his base. His weekly reports show him spread too thin, dashing madly around his large North Carolina area, thickly dotted with mills and villages, talking to small local union meetings, interceding at mills to mediate work floor complaints, lobbying local politicians for labor's causes, and entering mill villages to win workers to the union.[56]

An isolated organizer in a widely dispersed and often hostile territory, Christopher kept the faith. Early in 1936 he reported to James Starr, secretary-treasurer of the UTW, that no local unions remained active in Charlotte, N.C., but he hoped to revive them. In March 1936 he expressed the belief to John Peel, his superior in Greenville, S.C., that "the textile workers in and around Durham can be organized again if a man will be stationed there for awhile."[57] But the UTW had no strategy, no target, leaving Christopher aimlessly spinning his wheels, trying to achieve his central task without a coherent plan. Despite his intelligence and drive, he failed to organize even the Cleveland Cloth Mill in Shelby, where he had once worked. On 22 April 1936 he wrote to Peel, "Sure, I'm trying to tell the workers that the only way to stop it [stretch out] is to organize, but it doesn't seem to have an effect. I haven't signed up a single member and I worked the village thoroughly yesterday and am going to work again today."[58]

Late in December 1936 a Christopher letter to Francis Gorman got to the heart of the matter. He reported that the union's fight against discrimination against union members had been a disastrous failure. At the Pamona Mills in Greensboro, N.C., when the mills had reopened in 1934 under National Guard protection, thirty union members had refused to go back until the union had officially stopped the strike. They were dismissed and, Christopher wrote, "We were never able to get them back to work. Consequently, the organization dissolved and we've never been able to get anything going there since, or in Greensboro either, for that matter." Christopher asked Gorman for money to start a small newsletter to give publicity to whatever successes the UTW had had in North Carolina, so as to give the workers a sense of union identity and accomplishment. Christopher told Gorman, "We can't expect much headway anytime soon by appealing to only the common-sense intellect of the workers; we must repeatedly get their emotional attention and interest."[59] Nothing came of Christopher's ideas.

The UTW did not, of course, vanish from the southern mill towns. State federations of textile workers, for example, continued to meet in 1935 and 1936 in North and South Carolina. In South Carolina, locals, considerably smaller than in pre-strike days, carried on union activity at a number of mill towns, and the short, angry walkouts that occurred gave opportunities to the local UTW members to attempt to recruit members. But the fire and dash of the flying squadrons was long gone. The South Carolina locals in 1935 and 1936 were more or less dormant and much smaller than the code-swollen units of 1933–34.[60] In a post-1934 local in a Spartanburg mill, the union "had no program. Members just met, idled away their time as in a social club, and then drifted back to their homes. Sometimes a representative from the national organization would visit the groups and attempt to steer the union on a more definite course, but local leaders still resented this as interference."[61]

By the end of the long attrition period after the 1934 strike, the UTW had, in April 1937, only 37,588 members nationally, with another 17,599 workers in separate federations in the hosiery industry and 15,692 in dyeing. The UTW's paid-up members numbered only 557 in North Carolina and 726 in South Carolina. Surprisingly, Alabama still had 3,744 dues paying members, but Georgia had only 445.[62] The dramatic decline in numbers meant that by 1936 the southern locals were hollow organizations and that the UTW possessed no power in the industry after three years of the New Deal.

The owners also took inventory after the 1934 strike. The largest trade organization of southern mill owners, the ACMA, held a special meeting in Greenville, S.C., on 17 October 1934 to reassess the cotton code. Some 350 southern manufacturers attended the meeting and expressed their resentment "against the ever-increasing encroachment of the national government in the field of business and especially in the cotton textile industry." The ACMA stated that it would oppose "any activities of the government agencies" that would "tend to set aside the right of self-government provided for in the code and to substitute federal relations therefor." The cotton mill owners passed other resolutions that deplored mob violence in the form of flying squadrons; pledged continued support for George Sloan and the Code Authority (an attempt to quiet rumors that some southern manufacturers were unhappy over Sloan's supposedly conciliatory meetings with the Winant Board during the strike); opposed the cotton processing tax of the AAA, as well as any change in code provisions covering maximum hours of labor and machine load limitations; and asked the administration to arrange trade agreements with foreign countries to prevent any further reduction of the export of cotton goods. William Anderson of Georgia called the meeting the "most harmonious ever held by the organization."[63]

The ACMA also adopted a ten-plank labor relations platform circulated by the National Association of Manufacturers. The platform, repetitious and lengthy, tolerated unions as long as there were no strikes, no rules or contracts, and few members. It particularly damned collective bargaining as expressed in liberal interpretations of Section 7(a), claiming, "Minority groups should have the right to negotiate with their employers, and any provision that a majority group must be the sole spokesman for all would be unsound, untenable and contrary to the American theory of government."[64] The southern manufacturers still supported the economic provisions of the code, but they maintained that the code had no jurisdiction over their labor relations.

The general strike had strengthened the manufacturers' resolve to keep the UTW out of the South. One southern manufacturer warned that unless "zealous union leaders are checked they will carry on their ruthless campaign under feigned government action until a bloody revolution and an overthrow of the government will be the consequence."[65] Southern employers, encouraged by the defeat of the strike, became even more vociferous in their denunciation of unionism. One South Carolina manufacturer, Waite Hamrick, Jr., summarized the survivalist attitude of the owners in a 1935 interview with an investigator from the TLRB. Said the investigator, "He also stated that the government had their chance; the Cotton-Textile Institute had their chance, and now he wanted his chance without outside interference." He "would close down rather than submit to the workers."[66] William Anderson, ACMA president, blasted the union at the April 1935 meeting, claiming that workers were "in better shape today than they have ever been." He said that attacks calling textiles a "paternalistic industry" were nothing but attacks from "muckrakers, the uplifters, and the sob-sisters."[67] A young undergraduate student at Vassar, after interviewing industry leaders in 1935, wrote that "there is to be no more playing with academic theories of the balance of power between capital and labor, collective bargaining, majority representation." The "keynotes" in 1935 would be "efficiency, coordination, profits."[68]

In 1935, reports of the investigation that Roosevelt had initiated in fall 1934 began to be published. Three of the FTC reports dealt with economic conditions in the cotton textile industry.[69] The reports contained something for everyone. Industry and union alike saw them as justifying their pre-strike arguments. Some mills made money, others broke even, and some lost money, said the FTC, although in general 1933 had been a good year, the same old problems arose in 1934. The Bureau of Labor Statistics released two reports on wages in the cotton textile industry. Statistics in the reports supported both the UTW argument about the impact of short hours and the owners' arguments that hourly wages had increased and that there had not been a widespread violation of code wage standards.[70] The industry, however, largely ignored the reports or tended to emphasize the statistics that were favorable to management. Sidney Munroe, CTI secretary in 1936, argued that the reports totally vindicated the industry's position in 1934.[71]

The UTW was further damaged by the delay of the Cotton Textile Work Assignment Board (CTWAB) in finishing its investigation of the stretch out. The CTWAB had difficulty in assembling technical experts and in designing its study. While it plodded along, reports to the Department of Labor from the South indicated that manufacturers there were consistently using the stretch out to gain a small competitive edge despite the equalizing tendency of the cotton textile code.[72] The report, dated 26 April 1935, was not finally released until 12 May. The CTWAB concluded that machine assignments were not excessive in the "great majority of cases," even though "a few" companies had set up excessive workloads.[73] Of the some 1,200 cotton textile mills in the country, 249 had had stretch out complaints filed against them. The board had investigated 36 mills and found excessive workloads in only 11. Thus, the report argued, "it can be assumed" that only 6.5 percent of the cotton mills had excessive stretch out.[74]

The CTWAB was "convinced that it would be unwise and impracticable to attempt to set up standards of machine assignments in the cotton textile industry, expressed in the number of machines to be tended." The board reported that, with over six hundred variables to be considered in deciding the degree of worker effort involved in a machine load, the only fair way to determine workloads was by individual mill studies, and it recommended a "permanent" group to serve as a "factfinding board" as the mills and the workers in them individually worked their way to a fair load. In a masterpiece of bureaucratic reporting, William A. Mitchell, chair of the CTWAB, wrote to Frances Perkins that "since we have found some existing excessive work assignments and workloads, as well as several threatened strikes against alleged excessive work assignments and workloads, and since there is the probability of continued installation of improved machinery, methods, etc., and use of better materials, as well as registering of protests in the past of employees against increased work assignments involved in such installations, we feel there is urgent need for a permanent Cotton Textile Work Assignment Board."[75]

The UTW reacted angrily to the report. Gorman wrote to Mitchell to say that the UTW could not "agree that work assignment is solely an engineering problem to be settled by mathematical mearsurement of workers' effort." Gorman wrote, "The workers in the cotton textile industry have been betrayed by the representative of the employees and the *impartial* chairman of the Work Assignment Board, who have signed employer-dictated recommendations."[76] John Peel, UTW southern chief, thought that "if the manufacturers had been given the right to write the report they could not have made it more favorable to themselves." He called it "incomprehensive, unjust and unfair to the employees." He charged that workers had been preelected by management to talk to the investigators of the board and that it had not been "a fair and impartial investigation." [77] Like the other reports, this one too sank quickly from sight.

By spring 1935, the UTW had completely lost whatever faith it had once had in the Cotton Textile Code. Another three month's production cut, ordered on 26 March 1935 by the Code Authority, infuriated the union. On 1 April 1935, Gorman urged Congress to initiate an inquiry into the textile industry. He called for "thorough and merciless investigation of this industry, its capital structure, and its methods of operation and selling." He demanded the "compulsory elimination of obsolete machinery." The union leader once again called for a thirty-hour week but "with drastically increased rates of pay, elimination of the North-South differential and a restoration of the differentials between minimum rates and skilled rates to their pre-Code ratio." He wanted the old code scrapped and the "imposition of a new code, with labor sitting in equal number with employers on the Code Authority and all subordinate boards." Following the old partnership ideal, Gorman pleaded for "a joint government-labor-management study of marketing and market extension." He argued that Congress should mandate the majority rule in collective bargaining conducted with secret ballots and, above all, he asked that Congress order the Department of Justice to punish violators of orders of the TLRB or the NLRB. [78]

The UTW, weak and impotent, was still determined to follow its policy of cooperation with the New Deal and hoped that a new federal labor policy could bring about a unionized industry. The manufacturers, Gorman told a crowd of workers in North Carolina, had violated their own code and handed the workers "a raw deal instead of a New Deal." [79]

CRISIS IN THE INDUSTRY

The manufacturers paid no attention to Gorman's new plans for the industry. For months they had been struggling with another crisis, a severe business slump. Donald Comer, with only half of his spindles operating and half of his workers laid off, informed George Sloan in December 1934 that he could not attend the monthly meeting of the Code Authority because business conditions were "so distressing that I feel it is of prime obligation to devote every minute of my time trying to hold the ends together here." [80] The year-end assessment of the industry in 1934 was very gloomy. The *New York Times* reported that the industry as a whole had operated at a loss for the last six months of 1934. [81] The slow deterioration of the business, which had developed after the code boom of 1933, accelerated in winter 1934–35. The stronger, better-managed mills made profits, but scores did not.

On 10 March 1935 the *New York Times* reported that for "a space of nearly two months now demand has been at a practical standstill, prices have dipped steadily, and the pressure exerted on manufacturers has brought many to the breaking point."[82] William McLaurine, ACMA secretary-treasurer, invoked the same dismal theme at the group's annual spring convention, saying, "It is useless for me to try to tell you the stress of operating capital, processing tax money, and many other trials that many weak mills have had."[83] George Sloan reported that since fall 1934, over seventy-one cotton mills had closed.[84] Meanwhile, in New England, the sharp recession devastated the region's cotton textile industry. By April 1935 twenty-two mills had closed in Rhode Island, and New Englanders pressed for removal of the North-South wage differential.[85] For the owners, marketing, not labor relations, was the crisis area in the industry.

On 25 February 1935 NRA concern over the economic crisis of the industry moved it to appoint a special committee, the Textile Planning Committee (TPC), to study thoroughly the crisis situation in the cotton, silk, and woolen industries and to consider code changes.[86] The TPC was composed of Sidney Hillman, president of the Amalgamated Clothing Workers Union; Leon Henderson and Arthur D. Whiteside, both members of the National Industrial Recovery Board, which had replaced Hugh Johnson as administrative head of the NRA; and Prentice Coonly, a division administrator of the NRA. The committee was charged by the NRA with formulating a long-term program to address the labor problems that had bothered NRA officials for so long, as well as to recommend temporary or emergency steps to address the economic depression in the industry.

The TPC began its work at once with a roundtable conference on 26 February 1935 between the committee and TLRB members Henry Wiley and Frank Douglass. The group discussed the system of handling labor complaints that routed those concerning wages and hours to the Code Authority, and the TPC suggested that the system "might lead to subsequent criticism." It set in motion plans for the TLRB to assume all field investigation responsibility for all complaints. The very next day, the TPC met with George Sloan and some Code Authority members and pursued the same subject. As usual, the Code Authority defended the system as the only way to get employer cooperation, but it too would eventually accept the idea of another field investigation network.[87] The Code Authority actually welcomed the TPC as one sign that the vacuum created by Johnson's fall from power would be filled. The Code Authority, wanting to lobby the committee for its economic goals, was willing to give in on the unimportant complaint system.[88] In April 1935 the TPC, in the tradition of New Deal planning, was enlarged to twelve members, the new members coming from the Code Authority itself and other NRA offices. The committee was still deliberating at the time the NIRA was struck down by the Supreme Court.

The crisis in the industry, and political realities, produced another study group. On 18 April 1935 New England governors petitioned the President to investigate the "critical and serious permanent problem of the textile industry."[89] Roosevelt turned to Secretary of Commerce Daniel Roper, who suggested a cabinet committee to consider the problems of the processing tax, the North-South wage differential, the import-export problem, and the depressed price structure in the industry.[90] Consequently, the President politely requested Roper, Secretary of State Cordell Hull, Secretary of Agriculture Henry Wallace, and Secretary of Labor Frances Perkins to be "good enough to constitute yourself into a committee to supervise a study of the cotton textile situation."[91] The secretaries quickly formed a working committee of subordinates consisting of a representative from each department and one from the U.S. Tariff Commission.[92] The cabinet committee actually took its work seriously, holding several meetings with manufacturers, labor representatives, and public officials. Its report on the destructive economic structure of the industry took weeks to prepare. When it finally appeared, a sharp business upturn in the industry made its findings already dated. The cabinet committee report, in its only significant comments on labor and the code, found that code provisions had raised hourly wages in all branches of the industry and that the forty-hour week had resulted in increased employment, but that the code had resulted in no significant increase in total annual income per worker, except where continuous employment could be furnished.[93]

In 1936–37, well after the demise of the cotton code, another abortive effort was made to achieve a measure of federal control over, or at least to "rationalize," the industry. The effort this time came not from the industry or the administration, but from Congress. Henry Ellenbogen, a Democrat representing a textile district in Pennsylvania, in 1935 drafted what he called the National Textile Bill. The bill would have created a seven-member commission to control the textile industry just as the Code Authority had envisioned itself as doing. Ellenbogen's National Textile Commission would have decided and enforced minimum wages as the Code Authority had done, but it would also have guaranteed collective bargaining, regulated work assignments, and supervised production controls. It all looked like a rerun of the cotton code, with fairer treatment of labor. It was, of course, part of the effort to create little NRAs after the big one had fallen apart.

When the bill bogged down in the House Labor Committee, Gorman sent a long letter to FDR on 20 May 1936 begging his intervention. "We have been handicapped in our organizational work in the South by vicious opposition of the employers," he told the President amid careful economic arguments for the bill, "and we believe that something should be done by the Congress in behalf of over a million workers." FDR replied that he was "presently aware of the unfortunate condition in the textile industry" and would consult "with some leaders in Congress" about the bill.[94] Although the bill was rewritten again in 1937 to strengthen its interstate regulation language, it never had any chance of passage. On 21 May 1937 the full committee of the House Labor

Committee voted to table the bill until another federal measure for control of maximum hours and minimum wages in all interstate industry could be fought out—the Fair Labor Standards Act.[95]

THE END OF THE CODE

Southern manufacturers' criticism of the NRA was widespread in the last few months of the agency's existence. The labor problems of 1934 and the economic crisis of that winter had sapped the manufacturers' enthusiasm for cooperation with the government and the Code Authority.[96] George Sloan, on 3 February 1935, wrote to Donald Richberg, the President's man in the NRA after Hugh Johnson's departure, that any attempt to extend the NIRA industry by industry rather than through a blanket process would plunge the cotton textile industry into "the chaos of the first six months of the job," and he predicted that the industry "would not again go through with it." Sloan thought that opposition against extension of the NRA, which FDR had proposed early in 1935, was strong and that the Code Authority had to "meet the opposition squarely and overcome it."[97] By May the Code Authority had begun a major campaign to shore up support for the code. Goldthwaite Dorr, the temporary president of the CTI who replaced Sloan when the latter resigned, defended the NRA and its codes in a major talk to the U.S. Chamber of Commerce as a major success in reining in mindless, destructive competition. "Some collective regulation of competition," he said, "is essential to the continuance of the system in modern industrial life and is in the public interest."[98]

When the Supreme Court actually killed the NRA and the cotton textile industry had to operate without a code, the industry felt a mixture of relief and apprehension. The code had been supported by a majority of the manufacturers. As late as 1937, for example, William McLaurine, ACMA secretary-treasurer, told the group's annual gathering that a large part of the industry was "convinced the forty-hour work week for labor, the eighty-hour week for production machinery, the minimum wage, and the elimination of persons under sixteen years of age from employment are fundamental and vital principles for the industry to observe."[99] The fundamentals of the code had become standard in the industry. The industry wept no tears for Section 7(a), but for competitive reasons it wanted to retain compliance with the four items McLaurine mentioned.[100] The day after the NRA was declared invalid, Donald Comer believed it was inconceivable "that the textile industry will go back to the old days of unrestricted competition." Years later, Comer still praised that first code for banishing long working hours and child labor.[101]

In June the ACMA called a special meeting in Charlotte, North Carolina, to discuss how to salvage something from the wreck of the NRA. Over three hundred manufacturers, representing well over half the capacity of the southern industry, attended. The Charlotte *Observer* reported that the mill officials were determined to secure the "beneficial principles" of the former code.[102] The mill executives unanimously passed a resolution recommending no changes in the conduct of the cotton textile business, and they agreed among themselves that the wage and hour provisions of the former code should be followed voluntarily. The Charlotte *Observer* argued that "the textile industry either must face the necessity of carrying on upon this basis or facing chaos such as it has never known."[103] Two ardent Code Authority members, Donald Comer and William Anderson, wrote to every member of the ACMA in July 1935 that it would be "wonderfully wise" to have voluntary agreements on the minimum wage, maximum hours per shift, and minimum wage, but they doubted that there could be any agreement on machine hour control.[104]

The UTW reacted with alarm. Not even the TLRB remained to serve as a crude shield against the owners. Francis Gorman was on a tour of the South when the Supreme Court announced its decision. Just days before the action, he had enunciated his fear that if the Court struck down the code, the South would be plunged back into the dark ages of sixty-five-hour work weeks, with no minimum wage. He said that "all available" UTW organizers would be "hurled into the South" to stem the expected drive for pre-code standards. "The message I have tonight is for our unions, and it is this," he telegraphed the southern locals. "Do not give an inch. Strike instantly if any destruction of standards is attempted. Be prepared for any action."[105] But the UTW was a molehill, not the mountain it had been in summer 1934. Gorman's call for southern workers to rise as one in protest had a hollow ring. In fact, the union would throw what little clout it had into a pragmatic attempt to win passage of the Ellenbogen Bill, as a replacement for the defunct code.

On 5 July 1935 William McLaurine urged southern mills to keep to the code guidelines. "The nonconformers," he wrote, "are destroying markets, inviting labor troubles, inviting legislation," and proving "the inability of the industry to govern itself." On 10 August he warned ACMA members that "chiseling on wages and hours was dangerous" and would add "chaos to confusion."[106] Although constant rumors and reports reached the TLRB that some mills in the industry were indeed paying less and increasing work weeks, the CTI claimed that the violators represented less than 10 percent of the mills.

Late in 1935 the CTI announced that it had drawn up a formal pledge which would be sent for signature to the executives of twelve hundred cotton mills. The pledge was a statement that the mill agreed to exceed neither the two forty-hour shifts a week nor the forty-hour maximum work week for employees. The mill also guaranteed to pay the old code minimum wages and to employ no child labor.[107] The pledge was reminiscent of the old "55–50" pledge taken before the NRA came into being. The CTI never released figures on the number of executives who signed the pledge, although in June 1936 the new president of the CTI, Claudius Murchison, argued that "the cotton mills as a whole have been maintaining [it] voluntarily," although he admitted to some "departures" as to hours of operation.[108] It was all a tempest in a teapot, anyway. By the late 1930s, with the return of good business, most mills added a third shift and went to the forty-hour week, and by 1938 the Fair Labor Standards Act obviated the need for voluntary agreements.

Gorman's fear that the mills would rush back to the standards of the 1920s was not well founded. A partisan AFL study late in 1935 reported that departure from code standards in the cotton textile industry affected 208,680, or well over half, the employees in Georgia, North Carolina, and South Carolina. The study said that 119,650 employees had lengthened hours, with a "considerable number" of mills returning to fifty-five hours a week and a few mills even adopting the sixty-hour standard.[109] Scattered complaints in TLRB case files indicated that there were mills that reverted drastically, but the larger AFL numbers are suspect. A more impartial study conducted early in 1936 by the Federal Contract Division, Department of Labor, surveyed firms holding federal contracts and found that 189 companies with 106,747 employees retained both code wages and hours, while 78 firms with 20,934 employees retained either code wages or hours. Only 109 firms employing 33,951 employees conformed to neither code wages nor hours.[110] Because of a stronger competitive position the larger the firm, the higher the probability that code standards were in force. The statistical charges flew back and forth in 1935 and 1936, but clearly the code standards, by and large, were being maintained.

Any sentiment in the industry for some legally binding provisions similar to the cotton code was dampened by increasing economic prosperity in the last half of 1935. By 1936, southern mill income generally had reached 90 percent of the 1929 level.[111] The industry had weathered the crisis of 1934–35, and most mills showed profits in the last half of 1935.[112] The CTI received an invitation in December 1935 to meet with an administration-sponsored Council for Industrial Progress, to work out plans for voluntary cooperation to carry on old NRA codes. Claudius Murchison, CTI president, rejected the invitation. Increasingly, as the bittersweet memories faded, cotton textile manufacturers became disenchanted with the idea of partnership with the government, not to mention labor. By 1935, many believed that the NRA, with its emphasis on the economics of scarcity and cooperation, had actually retarded the return to prosperity. The trade journal *Cotton* argued that "the country is ready to reemploy millions, but only as conditions for investment are made more reasonable." The *Textile Bulletin*, in its 1935 New Year's message, wrote, "We wish for the textile manufacturers more PROSPERITY and less NRA."[113]

By late 1935, the industry no longer leaped at the prospect of help from without. When he rejected the invitation to join new efforts at self-government, Murchison said that the industry would rely on its own initiative; it was no longer interested in "leaning on the broken crutch of legislation."[114] In 1941, Goldthwaite Dorr, on the CTI board of directors, recalled the code years as the industry's "most dramatic experience," but one accompanied by "disappointments and disillusionments."[115]

The cotton textile code had not solved the major problems of the industry, and its basic structure remained unchanged. The important production and distribution functions were still widely separated; and production cuts and prohibiting installation of new machines, the latter a dubious proposition, had not been effective in reducing the industry's capacity to overproduce. Other desired economic objectives of the code were achieved either for only a short time or not at all. The Code Authority never even got close to controlling prices. Prices of gray goods were not generally influenced by the code, because of the tremendous number of variables that helped to determine prices. The demand for cotton goods, following the level of general economic activity, never approached pre-1929 levels in the 1933–35 period. In 1934, over half the cotton textile companies recorded a net deficit; and in 1935, despite the second-half comeback, net profits for the industry as a whole shifted from a deficit of $2.1 million to one of $4.0 million.[116] The code thus had failed in its most basic economic goal — to make the industry profitable.

By itself the code had little chance of success without the exercise of draconian measures, impossible to enforce in such a widely-owned industry operating in the private marketplace. Only a radical reorganization, with a drastic reduction of spindles and looms in place, would have created a profitable industry in 1934–35. In the years ahead, profitability lay in economic consolidation, technological progress, and increased demand. The early New Deal, as so many scholars have noticed, moved too sluggishly to create an economic climate within which the code's economic objective could be obtained.

Workers benefited from the code, even if the attempt to organize had failed badly. Child labor received a fatal blow. The forty-hour week and a minimum wage became dominant in the industry even before they were codified in the Fair Labor Standards Act. Employment increased slightly in 1934, by about twenty thousand workers, and decreased slightly in 1935 from the final 1933 figures. Hourly earnings increased from an average of 30 cents an hour in 1933 to 34.6 cents in 1935, although, because of production cuts, weekly wage earnings at the end of 1935 stood at only $13.31 a week, compared to $12.51 in 1933[117] Prosperity and gains in real income eluded the workers, but the value of working less should not be underestimated. The reduction in time worked is the dominant positive outcome remembered by older workers. And the long struggle in NRA forums and study groups over conditions on the mill floors paid off in renewed employer concern for these issues in the late 1930s.

The NRA era saw the largest union membership that had ever existed in the southern cotton textile industry. Despite the determined opposition of southern employers, the UTW grew large enough to believe that it could challenge the owners on an industrywide basis. The failure of the 1934 general strike and its aftermath sapped the union, which remained a burntout shell until 1937. In Section 7(a) the federal government in 1933 inadvertently set off a growth spurt for unionism, but Section 7(a) did not provide the coercive power needed to bring about collective bargaining in the southern cotton textile industry. The New Deal had neither the stomach nor the support required for such a revolution.

Collective bargaining was only a pleasant dream for the unions and a nightmare for the owners. If the UTW had been strong enough to force its demands on the industry, the labor boards of the New Deal — the Bruere Board and the TLRB — could have provided proper channels for restructuring labor relations. But legislation by itself could not bring about a unionized industry. Just before the NRA passed away, a letter to FDR signed by "A Helpless Textile Worker" arrived from an employee of the Bibb Manufacturing Company in Macon, Georgia. It eventually found its way to the TLRB. The workers, said the letter, "are being treated worse than slaves of olden times. I believe when the NRA fails to rule the manufacturers that it will cause a terrible war to be right here. . . . Please help us in some way is my daily prayer."[118] But expediency and conformity to existing power relationships, not prayer and idealism, marked New Deal labor policy in the industry between 1933 and 1936. The owners had power; the UTW did not. And proponents of new labor legislation had to address that very real discrepancy.

"Son, we're short on speakers and we're plumb out of strikes"

THE WAGNER ACT AND THE TWOC, 1937

The imprecise meaning of Section 7(a) had created problems from the very beginning. Even if unions had achieved the principle of majority-rule collective bargaining through the labor boards, the cumbersome and wholly ineffective NRA enforcement policy allowed employers to continue to resist without fear of penalty. Under Section 7(a) there had been no way to prevent either the establishment of company-dominated unions or employer discrimination against union members. In spring 1934 Sen. Robert Wagner (Democrat of New York), in an attempt to strengthen Section 7(a) and to codify the rudimentary principles of collective bargaining emerging from the confusion of NRA boards, introduced a bill which defined unfair labor practices by management in concrete terms and which would have established a federal labor board to enforce the right of majority-rule collective bargaining. The bill died. FDR, still committed to the NRA model, feared such an assault on government-business cooperation. Congress, bending to administration-backed compromise, passed Public Resolution 44 as a substitute. The resolution enabled the President to appoint labor boards such as the TLRB and the first NLRB, independent of the NRA Code Authority, to interpret and administer Section 7(a) principles, as well as to act as boards of mediation.

Faced with the invalidation of Section 7(a) after the NRA ended and fearful of a resurgence of the labor unrest that had characterized 1934 labor relations, Congress turned to Senator Wagner, who had reintroduced his labor bill in February 1935, well before the death of the NRA. Without much debate and with only scattered protests from southern congressmen and conservative Republicans, the bill, cosponsored in the House by William Connery of Massachusetts, passed the Senate 63–12 and the House by voice vote. FDR signed the bill on 5 July 1935. Wagner's success could only be explained by the absence of any cohesive White House thinking on labor policy. With little organized political power in 1935, labor was relatively uninvolved in the bill's development. Business quickly drummed up opposition, but the bill was a triumph for Senator Wagner and a small group of bureaucrats and intellectuals.[1] Once again the New Deal had produced legislation guided more by recent experience than by some grand design.

The Wagner Act, grafting ad hoc NRA experience onto the private laissez-faire tradition, stated clearly that workers in interstate commerce were to be protected by the federal government in exercising their right to organize and bargain collectively through freely chosen representatives. To implement that principle, the Wagner Act stipulated that the representative of the majority of workers in a bargaining unit should have the power to speak for all the workers, thus establishing firmly in law the fragile policies of some NRA labor boards. The NLRB, established by the act, would hold elections to determine if a majority of workers wanted to bargain collectively through an agent or union of their choice.

Five unfair labor practices by employers were defined and forbidden by the act: (1) any interference, restraint, or coercion of employees in the exercise of rights guaranteed; (2) domination of or interference with the formation or administration of a labor organization, or with the contribution of financial or other support to it; (3) discrimination to encourage or discourage union membership, except that closed-shop contracts were legal if made with a union representing the majority of employees in an appropriate bargaining unit, and without legal assistance by the employer; (4) discrimination against an employee for filing charges or testifying; (5) and refusal to bargain collectively with the legal representative of employees in an appropriate bargaining unit. All these practices had been common weapons in the battle against the NRA labor policy.

The NLRB, composed of three labor-relations professionals appointed by the President, established a system of regional offices to assist it in carrying out its duties. The board was to investigate, hold hearings, and issue decisions and orders, but its orders were not self-enforcing. If a cease-and-desist order or an order remedying an unfair labor practice was ignored, the NLRB could petition a U.S. Court of Appeals for enforcement of its decision. Similarly, any employer or interested party could petition the appeals court for review. Until the court acted, an employer could violate the NLRB's order without penalty, but after the court ruled on the case the firm could be held in contempt if it persisted in violating an order. With the Wagner Act, the evolution of New Deal federal labor policy had ended. The common law of the NRA boards had become statute law. Collective bargaining in good faith under federal procedures and standards was the law of the land.

Most employers, not surprisingly, had strongly opposed the new act. But the immediate impact of the Wagner Act in advancing unionization in mass-production industries such as steel, automobiles, and textiles was negligible. The reason was clear. Corporate management throughout the country was convinced that the law would be declared unconstitutional by the conservative Supreme Court that had dealt with the NRA.[2] The NLRB met this attitude so consistently that it felt compelled in its first report to attack the 150-page brief issued by the National Lawyers Committee of the American Liberty League on 5 September 1935.[3] The league's document, widely publicized and widely distributed (some forty thousand copies), had assaulted the NLRB, calling it unconstitutional, even before the board began to function. Employers ignored the act or consciously delayed and impeded the operation of the NLRB in any way they could, and in 1939 Sidney Hillman argued that "no-one paid any attention to the law for two years after Congress enacted it. High-priced counsel advised their clients to disobey it. They told them it would never get by the Supreme Court."[4] That attitude predominated throughout the South. In 1939 Yelverton Cowherd, a southern CIO official, said that during 1935–37 southern employers "adopted a policy of absolute ignorance of the Wagner Act."[5] The NLRB itself moved with exceptional caution, engaging in a two-year legal battle before it could move with assurance that its word was law.[6] The unions, often finding little encouragement from the NLRB, resorted to the law in those first two years as a last move, because they too suspected that it would be struck down by the Court.

The Supreme Court revolution of 1937 ended this cold war, and on 12 April 1937 the new Court upheld the Wagner Act. Malcolm Ross, an NLRB staffer, remembered 12 April as the real start of labor relations under the act. "That a few employers at once complied," he wrote, "only made the others feel worse. For three years the bile generated to defeat the act had accumulated to the point that no employer could at once rid it from his system."[7] Nevertheless, the NLRB reported that "the effect of the action of the Supreme Court was instantaneous," and the board soon established itself and its procedures across the nation in a way that no NRA board had ever done.[8] During the first five years, the NLRB acted in nearly thirty thousand cases involving 6.5 million workers, two-thirds of the cases being concerned with unfair labor practices and a third of them with elections for majority representation. Nine of ten cases were settled, and 280,168 strikers were reinstated. The board claimed to have settled 860 threatened strikes involving 202,417 workers and conducted some 3,492 elections, in which 1,261,130 votes were cast.[9] The New Deal finally had a lasting labor policy, which, with two major amendments, would remain the law of the land for decades.

THE WAGNER ACT AND
THE SOUTHERN COTTON TEXTILE INDUSTRY

With the Court's confirming action, the New Deal labor policy appeared to have come of age. The New Deal had just been returned to government for another four years in an overwhelming victory at the polls, and the labor movement, seeing itself reinforced by a sympathetic administration, looked to the future with unprecedented enthusiasm. By 1937 there had been two years of steady economic growth, and increasingly management had begun to accept collective bargaining, however distasteful.[10]

The victory of the Wagner Act, though, was not the end of the contest. Businessmen were not any more convinced in 1937 than they had been in 1933 that unions were a desirable addition to industrial America. Although many business people and organizations accepted the Wagner Act after 1937, they never gave up their fundamental objection to the legislation or their hope for its amendment or repeal. As the reality of the new era in labor relations asserted itself after 1937, the Wagner Act became the most bitterly fought of all New Deal legislation. In the 1940s, it provided the top agenda item responsible for the Republican Party's rebirth. As *Fortune* said in 1938, "[The act] prejudges the employer to be a scoundrel without rights in equity. It penalizes him for even a mild expression of personal opinion, but it provides no penalties for fraud, coercion, or violence on the part of the hotheaded labor majority." The NLRB, said *Fortune*, "is at one and the same time judge, jury, and prosecutor, and provides no real opportunity for an impartial review of the board's decision." The magazine continued the condemnation, declaring that the Wagner Act "violates the right of free speech, the right of property, the inviolability of a contract. It promotes lawlessness, destroys discipline, and encourages strikes against society. It is a dangerous intrusion of radical bureaucracy into private enterprise."[11] The relationship between management and the NLRB would be forced and unhappy.

The reaction of the southern cotton textile manufacturers to the Wagner Act was similar to the reaction of manufacturers elsewhere, but more forceful. Southern businesses accepted the recovery program of the New Deal, but generally they rebelled with violent language against its reform measures.[12] By 1935, after the NRA's death, the southern cotton textile manufacturers were opposed to any kind of federal activity that attempted to control or regulate business. They contended that recovery had been accomplished, business was "sound," and they could exist without any federal help. Further, they asserted that national legislation was unnecessary and unconstitutional; an active New Deal would only retard the nation's economic recovery.[13] William Anderson, a strong industry voice from Georgia and formerly a staunch member of the Code Authority, attacked FDR as being in the "grip of a bunch of Socialists and Communists" who preyed "on his weaknesses." The AAA and the NRA, said Anderson, "were written by the immature, callow, Socialistic, and Communistic hot dogs that Professor Frankfurter and others filtered into the various departments."[14]

By 1937, the New Deal and all its works were anathema to many cotton textile owners. They constantly attacked the Wagner Act. In August 1935, the CTI had advised the industry that it was impractical for the CTI, as some members had requested, to secure an injunction against the operation of the act, but it encouraged individual companies "to raise in court any question as to the validity of the law and the propriety of the board's action under law." The CTI thought "there would be serious questions as to whether it is constitutional as to a regulation of labor relations in manufacturing industries."[15]

Initially, the industry ignored the law. Robert R. West, president of Riverside and Dan River Cotton Mills, said the act was "ill natured legislation designed only to express an opportunistic social philosophy."[16] *Cotton* declared editorially that the Wagner Act, if allowed to stand, practically turned "labor relations in American industry over to organized labor."[17] J. Warren Madden, chair of the NLRB, said in 1936 that employers in the textile industry were resisting all efforts of the board to enforce the NLRA and that orders issued by the NLRB were not followed by the manufacturers.[18] Rep. Kent Keller (Democrat from Illinois), who conducted the hearings at which Madden testified, reported that southern mill owners were more adamant in their opposition to collective bargaining than employers in other sections of the country.[19] In 1937 the *Textile Bulletin* argued that the Wagner Act was "unrighteous, unsocial, unwise, unmoral and un-American," and in 1939, the editor called the NLRB "the most contemptible political organization since our government was founded."[20] In a more practical response, many of the mills in the South established company unions in 1935, in order to sign union agreements and legitimate their claim that they were engaging in collective bargaining.[21]

Louis Stark, labor reporter for the *New York Times*, visited the South in fall 1935 and discovered the strategy of the cotton textile employers to defeat the Wagner Act. "Cotton textile manufacturers opposing the Wagner Industrial Relations Act," he wrote, "will refuse to conduct elections among their employees if ordered to do so by the National Labor Relations Board and will seek federal injunctions should such mandates be received." The effort to defeat the NLRB in the Carolinas, Georgia, and Alabama would take three forms. "First," wrote Stark, "the mills will fight at public hearings called by the board on petitions filed for elections. Second, if elections are ordered the case will be immediately taken to the courts to delay further action pending scrutiny of the Wagner Act before the Federal Supreme Court. Third, in the event that the labor board . . . certifies that a local of the United Textile Workers Union is the accredited agency for collective bargaining as the result of an inquiry of its own and without an election, the manufacturers will either refuse to bargain with the union committee or will 'just sit,' deny all demands, and insist that they have complied with the law by receiving the union committee."[22] The NRA labor boards had proven to be contented tabbies, and the southern mill management thought the new cat could be domesticated as well.

The UTW enthusiastically supported the Wagner Act and made the obligatory optimistic pronouncements. While the bill was still making its way through Congress, Francis Gorman called it "one of the great and farsighted economic social proposals that has ever been advanced."[23] Soon after the bill was signed by FDR, John Peel, chief UTW southern organizer, announced that the union would begin to use the NLRB as soon as possible.[24] Despite its private fear that the courts would not uphold the Wagner Act, the UTW brought cases before the board in 1935–36, and in every case the board upheld the union's arguments. Prior to April 1937, NLRB cases initiated by the UTW demonstrated the full range of employer resistance, including simple refusal to have an election or meet union representatives, creation of a bogus company union to create the illusion of collective bargaining, mass firings of workers who engaged in union organizing, and coercive intimidation of workers and organizers. In one case the NLRB was moved to take special note of "recurring labor strife" in the cotton textile industry, noting that in the last four months of 1934 and the first seven months of 1935, there had been ninety-four strikes and lockouts in the industry and that "interference with organizational activities by employers, and the failure of employers to recognize the organization of employees, has been a constant source of unrest."[25] But mills refused until spring 1937 to comply with the orders and fell back on the legal delaying tactics that *Times* reporter Stark had predicted.

The resistance of the industry, of course, was duplicated in many other industries North and South, and once the legal status of the NLRB was decided by the Supreme Court, southern cotton textile employers as a group, like employers everywhere, dropped their attitude of outright defiance.[26] Frank DeVyver wrote in 1939 that many southern employers began to comply with the Wagner Act after the Supreme Court decision, even though their disdain for the act had not diminished.[27] William McLaurine, ACMA secretary-treasurer, contended in 1938 that the southern cotton textile industry had cooperated fully with the Wagner Act. The industry, he asserted, had "endeavored not only to comply with the letter of the law but with the spirit of sound social economics and industrial progress."[28]

But on the firing line the UTW detected little softening of attitude even after April 1937. Francis Gorman claimed the Supreme Court decision meant little to the southern manufacturers. Soon after the decision he stated that the UTW could find "no great change" in the attitude of the companies toward organization.[29] Virginius Dabney and Stetson Kennedy, two contemporary southern journalists, also believed that the validation of the Wagner Act did little to shake the southern employers' will to fight the act and the NLRB.[30] In fact, the manufacturers' acceptance of the Wagner Act, even in the narrow legal sense, was shallow, and they remained deeply "hostile" to the very concept of collective bargaining.[31] The range of NLRB cases and the persistence of employer resistance indicated that the southern textile employers accepted the consequences of the Wagner Act only when legally coerced to do so; the strategy outlined by Louis Stark in 1935 remained in effect throughout the 1930s.

Though still smarting from the Bruere Board's failure and the end of its brief affair with the TLRB, the UTW put its faith in the Wagner Act. In June 1935 the union predicted that the act would "unquestionably" stand "as one of the great milestones in the progress of this country, and in placing industrial workers on an equal footing with the close and compactly organized employers."[32] But the bad news of employer resistance could not be ignored by the union. By the end of 1935 John Peel reported to the union leaders that the employers had taken a decided stance against the New Deal and its philosophy. The workers, he said, found it difficult to use the Wagner Act in the face of such determined resistance. Peel thought that the attacks on the New Deal by southern textile manufacturers were in reality "only a subterfuge to cover their real fight" with labor.[33] Early in 1936 UTW organizers reported a southern proliferation of company unions calling themselves "Friendship Associations" and "Good Will Clubs," and organizers found that despite the Wagner Act "everybody is afraid to join" a real labor union.[34]

Labor organization actually became more difficult for the UTW as the employers' opposition to the entire New Deal program stiffened. Paul Christopher's experiences in his North Carolina UTW district illustrated the problems. Christopher thought the 1934 strike had been a dismal failure, and in Christopher's eyes, the new labor legislation changed little. He wrote to Thomas McMahon that all the union had "gotten from the Department of Labor was rather bitter pills when we tried to get something substantial." Stretch outs, wage reductions, and discrimination against union members continued in Christopher's area, despite his efforts to cooperate and bargain collectively with management.[35] Christopher discovered in the first two years of the Wagner Act that southern millhands had lost what little faith they had had in the UTW. They did not expect the union and the government to improve their wages or make the mill floor a better place to work. They had embraced the NRA and received little in return. Workers had to organize to take advantage of the Wagner Act, but many of them were too disillusioned and skeptical to follow the UTW lead. After the wreckage of 1934, the workers kept to the old ways of paternalism and the mill village enclaves.

The success or failure of labor organization depends on the power of the union to obtain concessions from the employer. The NLRB argued that the Wagner Act facilitated the union's use of such power, but the act was not a substitute for union power.[36] The New Deal's mature labor policy remained very much in the tradition of Progressive reform rather than radical change. By 1937 Francis Gorman had realized that New Deal legislation alone would not bring unionism to the southern cotton textile industry. "Yes," he said in that year, "I think organization is more necessary than legislation from the standpoint of permanency. I think both are essential, but the fact remains that we have not and cannot, owing to the opposition of the employers, and their unwillingness to accept the organization as a constructive force — we cannot create those organizations, and in the meantime, of course, everybody is suffering."[37] The failure of legislation to help the UTW build an aggressive and self-reliant organization of workers prompted union leaders by 1937 to seek a new solution — one that they hoped would create the economic power needed to make the New Deal answer to the labor problem work for them.

THE TEXTILE WORKERS ORGANIZING COMMITTEE

Shortly after the 1935 AFL convention, in November, a group of labor leaders led by John L. Lewis formed the Committee for Industrial Organization. Their action was the culmination of a long conflict within the AFL over the appropriate form of union organization for America's large factory industries. Efforts to reconcile the new group's unions and the AFL failed, and in 1938 the new committee became the Congress of Industrial Organizations (CIO). The American labor movement was divided.[38] As early as 1934, Thomas McMahon and the UTW had called for industrial unionism throughout the AFL, and McMahon was a charter member of the Committee for Industrial Organization. McMahon had the full support of the UTW's executive council. Craft unionism made no sense in the textile industry, and the UTW had abandoned it long ago. "We stand," declared the executive council of the UTW, "four-square behind the organization [C.I.O.] in its progressive, militant courageous effort to bring within the folds of organized labor, the millions of unorganized workers in basic, mass-production industries."[39] The 1936 UTW convention approved the entire course of action taken previously by its president and executive council. Because of the UTW's continued affiliation with the CIO, in April 1938 the AFL officially expelled the UTW.[40]

Throughout 1936 the UTW looked to the CIO for help in mounting a vigorous campaign in the textile industry. Although the CIO was deeply involved with organizing campaigns in the steel and automobile industries, it could not long ignore the challenge of textiles. In August 1936 the UTW leaders formally asked the CIO to collaborate in a joint organizing campaign in the South. Occupied elsewhere and perhaps fearful of the mess in textiles, the CIO delayed its response. But in December 1936, John Brophy, the CIO director of organization, attended a UTW executive council meeting which discussed both the need to organize the entire textile industry and an offer from the Amalgamated Clothing Workers Union (ACWU) to undertake joint projects with the UTW. The UTW desperately needed any help it could get. In 1936 John Peel had only eleven paid organizers for the entire South, three each in North Carolina, South Carolina, and Alabama and two in Georgia.[41]

Following Brophy's conference with the UTW, a renewed union effort began to take shape. Long under fire within the UTW, virtually eclipsed by Gorman, and seen by the CIO as ineffective, Thomas McMahon resigned from the UTW presidency in February 1937 to become head of the Rhode Island Department of Labor. Francis Gorman succeeded him as president. Gorman had been carrying on an intensified discussion with Brophy and with Sidney Hillman, of the ACWU and the CIO, about the possibility of UTW-CIO cooperation. Hillman was concerned about any venture into southern cotton, which he thought of as "America's industrial backyard."[42] But he recognized that the effort had to be made. The negotiations culminated in a UTW organizing contract signed on 9 March 1937 by Gorman of the UTW and John L. Lewis, Charles Howard, and Sidney Hillman of the CIO.

The UTW had hoped that the two organizations would cooperate on an equal basis. It wanted money and organizers, under the UTW's direction, but the CIO had different ideas. The CIO agreed to finance an organizing campaign in all branches of the basic textile industry, but it wanted to abandon the federation ideal of the UTW and create one large umbrella organization similar to its Steel Workers Organizing Committee. Although the UTW remained in existence, the agreement created the Textile Workers Organizing Committee (TWOC) to do the job of organizing. Under the agreement—negotiated in Washington between a supplicant UTW president and more confident CIO leaders—the CIO was given the power to carry on any subsequent reorganization of the UTW that might be needed when the TWOC disbanded. The TWOC officers were to be appointed by Lewis, the CIO chairperson, subject only to the provision that two members of the top hierarchy would be chosen from the UTW. The UTW treasury, such as it was, was to be turned over to the TWOC. All UTW officers and staff would be paid by the TWOC and were placed under its jurisdiction and orders.[43] The agreement was publicly announced on 19 March 1937 by Sidney Hillman, who set the tone for the upbeat press releases that became a characteristic feature of TWOC public relations. Hillman announced a goal for the South of three hundred thousand new union members.[44]

Under the agreement, the TWOC left the old union no identity whatsoever.[45] The CIO leaders had little respect for the UTW and its faction-ridden organization. In their own CIO analysis of the union on the eve of negotiations, they saw it "saddled with factional fights, incompetent organizers who eat up what few dollars finally reach the UTW treasury, a president who has not the confidence of any of the dominant leaders of the different Federations." The CIO said that the UTW "stands still, doing nothing, and tries to borrow enough money to meet its current payroll."[46] In accord with such a harsh judgement, the CIO forced the UTW to give up its sovereignty. When Francis Gorman defected back to the AFL in late 1938, he attacked the agreement, claiming that the CIO, in its arrogance and ignorance of textile unionism's problems, had ignored the UTW's protests at the time and that the UTW had had no choice but to accept an agreement "presented to them already drawn up."[47] The criticism was that of an unsuccessful and alienated UTW leader. In March 1937, the union was delighted to be caught up in the glamour and excitement of the CIO. In a 15 March letter to all UTW locals, Gorman enthusiastically endorsed the CIO takeover, saying, "For the first time in the history of our organization, we are in a position to tackle the job of organizing the textile industry."[48]

Immediately after signing the agreement on 9 March, Lewis appointed Sidney Hillman TWOC chairperson, and Hillman used the days before the official announcement on 19 March to gather the union forces and put together an organization and a plan. Len DeCaux, borrowed from the CIO to help with publicity, remembered that Hillman's model was the steel industry. "In planning, financing, direction, Hillman deliberately followed the SWOC [Steel Workers Organizing Committee] pattern," said DeCaux. "TWOC, like SWOC, was to be run from the top—by Hillman. His ACW—like UMW in SWOC—would supply most of the money, leaders, key organizers."[49]

Hillman's associates on the TWOC were Charles Weinstein of the Amalgamated Clothing Workers, Thomas Kennedy of the United Mine Workers, Charles Zimmerman of the International Ladies Garment Workers Union, and Thomas F. Burns of the United Rubber Workers, although the last three were never active in the drive. From the UTW, Hillman chose Francis Gorman and Emil Rieve, president of the Hosiery Workers Federation of the UTW, who worked out of Philadelphia.

Although its greatest obstacle was the southern cotton textile industry, the TWOC had no southerners at all on its highest council. Hillman, from the very beginning, shied away from the South, with its diffuse textile industry. He established TWOC headquarters in New York City, his own base of operations, far removed from the Piedmont mills and their distinctive southern workers.

Hillman carefully cultivated the impression that he personally directed the TWOC drive on a day-to-day basis.[50] As the few remaining minutes of the few TWOC meetings in New York City indicate, in actuality Hillman functioned more as the remote chairman of the board.[51] Hillman's major contributions were the role of national figurehead, the March planning, the gathering of money, and an occasional inspirational speech. He would never establish a southern presence. Although the official announcement stressed the TWOC as a CIO organization, especially significant as one big textile union embracing all textile workers and all industries, the TWOC's organization and efforts were different in the South and the North. Hillman divided the country into eight regions. The South was divided into two regions, the Upper South and the Lower South, and the rest of the country was divided into six much smaller regions. In the North, ACWU men headed five of the six regions. The Lower South, which included all of North and South Carolina, Georgia, Alabama, West Tennessee, Mississippi, Louisiana, and Texas, contained the southern cotton textile industry. A. Steve Nance, a Georgia typographical union leader and president of the Georgia Federation of Labor, headed the region. Leadership of the Upper South—Virginia, West Virginia, and the synthetic fiber industries of Asheville, North Carolina, and East Tennessee—fell first to veteran UTW leader John Peel and then, quickly, to another UTW man, Roy

Lawrence. Evidently the decision to make Atlanta, rather than a city in the Carolinas, the center of union organization rested on Nance's widespread popularity. Lucy Randolph Mason, TWOC publicist, thought Nance "was respected, trusted, and loved by more people in Atlanta than any other man."[52] Under Nance, Hillman inserted Franz Daniel, a southern ACWU organizer, to serve as field agent coordinator and to handle strike situations.

Of over 600 organizers TWOC hired, only 112 were assigned to the two huge southern regions, with 42 going to the Upper South to concentrate on synthetic fibers rather than cotton.[53] According to one account, Nance originally had only 30 field organizers to cover the area from North Carolina to Texas,[54] while another source indicated that Nance had perhaps 50 organizers in 1937.[55] Whatever the numbers, he had more organizers than any of his predecessors. Most of the southern organizers were southern-born, and many had old UTW ties. For example, Paul Christopher, in his late twenties, found himself traveling throughout the South as a major union organizer. H.D. "Red" Lisk became a major leader in North Carolina. Both Lisk and Christopher came from mill families. The TWOC also reached out to southern-born reformers. In summer 1937 Lucy Randolph Mason, of correct southern lineage, moved from New York to Atlanta to serve as Nance's publicity director. Dr. Witherspoon Dodge, a young Methodist minister, joined TWOC as a field organizer in Georgia. Myles Horton, the famed founder of Highlander Folk School, at times worked for TWOC. Every effort was made to give a southern cast to the TWOC, to counter the radical image of the CIO, with its New York headquarters run by Sidney Hillman, and to avoid the charge that a northern union was invading Dixie.

Despite the cosmetic southernization of TWOC's Atlanta office, the basic overall organization and allocation of TWOC resources reflected Hillman's decision to win the North first.[56] Certainly, the ideal, the goal, was to ride the 1937 crest—the reelection of FDR, the Wagner Act, the growing union success in other industries—to a quick victory and create at least a northern fortress. But the strategy was diluted by the smaller yet still considerable southern effort. The TWOC decision to decentralize and carry on a campaign in every textile industry, and at every factory if possible, was a crucial but potentially disastrous move.

The UTW stood at the brink of insolvency when the TWOC was formed. That fact alone dictated Gorman's acceptance of CIO dominance. Hillman's prestige and the backing of John L. Lewis were also important factors. Hillman's ACWU contributed a princely $800,000 over the life of the TWOC, and the UMW gave $198,000. In contrast to the situation in 1934, now textile workers had support. Financial aid came from several other CIO unions, and as TWOC membership increased, local dues became important. From March 1937 to May 1939 TWOC spent over $2 million. Next to the campaign in steel, TWOC's was the best-financed CIO organizing drive of the 1930s. Although TWOC organizers tended to be young and idealistic, their average salaries of twenty-five to thirty dollars a week made them some of the best-paid workers in the mills.

"Never," said one sympathetic journalist, "was a great organizational drive prepared with more care than that of the TWOC."[57] Hillman planned to follow a course of action that focused on "education, organization, union contract, and responsible collective bargaining," putting the New Deal to work in the mills.[58] The TWOC would expend great effort to explain the mutual benefits for both employers and employees that would accrue from collective bargaining and cooperation between labor and management, the two distinguishing features of Hillman's work in the apparel industry. Hillman promised a policy of responsibility on the part of the TWOC, one that would avoid strikes. "We are going to present," he declared, "a constructive program which needs from management as much organization as from labor."[59]

The no-strike-if-at-all-possible strategy flowed from the consequences of the 1934 strike as much as from Hillman's philosophy. Nance glowingly supported the policy. He told journalist Jonathan Daniels that he had just gotten a telephone call from a mill worker who said, "if you'll send us a speaker, I think we can have a strike." Nance told Daniels that he replied, "Son, we're short on speakers, and we're plumb out of strikes." Nance explained to Daniels that he wanted contracts, not conflicts.[60] Achieving that goal would be difficult in an industry with such strong-willed owners as southern cotton textiles had. Also the workers were often impatient with subtle approaches and the long delays involved in collective bargaining. Paul Christopher, working at the Bemis Bag Mill at Bemis, Tennessee, barely restrained the workers from a destructive walkout. "It's hard," he wrote fellow organizer Franz Daniel, "to try and discipline workers to pursue the policy we have outlined, when the company is taking every advantage of our peaceable attitude to impose additional injustices and hardships on our members."[61]

TWOC planned to run a campaign centered around the use of the Wagner Act, targeted against vulnerable or receptive mills. Hillman hired Solomon Barkin, an economist previously employed at the U.S. Department of Commerce, to compile economic information on the industry and to provide answers to key questions that would arise when the time for contracts came.[62] What had been the history of the previous organization at the mill? Who were the best-known union men and women among the workers? Who owned the mill? Was the mill profitable? To avoid the boom-and-bust cycle that in the past had so grievously wounded worker morale, the NLRB would be used extensively. One TWOC publication in the South called the law an impenetrable "armor for the honest toiler, paving his road to economic and social liberty."[63] Steve Nance informed his organizers in July 1937 that "strikes are seldom necessary, because we can prosecute discrimination cases and refusal to bargain collectively before the National Labor Board just as easy with the workers at work. The same applies to negotiations as to wages, hours, and working conditions through a contract."[64]

Local unions, under the original TWOC policy, were to be chartered only after the union succeeded in winning a contract from the mill, so as to establish a lasting union. The workers would pay no dues or initiation fees, but would merely sign a pledgecard designating the TWOC as their bargaining agent.[65] The TWOC's methods both undercut the often-repeated charges of manufacturers that union leaders organized only for dues, and eliminated the difficulty and expense of establishing a local until a stable base could be secured by a written contract under NLRB rules. The system was partially abandoned in 1938, however, when TWOC discovered that, despite NLRB election victories, the employers refused to bargain and sign agreements. TWOC concluded that local circumstances should govern a decision to establish or not to establish a functioning union. Under the TWOC plan, all new locals became TWOC locals and not UTW locals, and existing UTW locals were urged to recharter under the TWOC banner. Many did so within two years.[66] In spring 1937, then, the TWOC planners had put in place a new union, new dollars, new or newly adapted leaders, and a new strategy to make use of the Wagner Act. The textile unionists now hoped to control events rather than being controlled by them, as they had been in 1929–31 and 1933–34.

THE INDUSTRY RESPONSE

Cotton mill executives reacted calmly to the news of the TWOC founding and its impressive plans. "We will not organize against the CIO threat," said Claudius Murchison, new CTI president, "but we will concentrate action with respect to improved wages, shorter working hours, elimination of child labor, establishment of a code of fair competition, all of which looks to the greater stability of the industry and a return to prosperity." Nevertheless, Murchison signaled the industry's determination to continue to resist unionism. Every mill would participate in the struggle. The industry's "first answer to the challenge of the CIO" would be to battle it in every mill in the South.[67] Murchison soon received a belligerent tirade from William D. Anderson against the New Deal and the new unionism. "I propose," complained Anderson, "to 'organize' against the CIO threat, and I hope many of my friends in the textile industry will join me in such an organization."[68] More practically, many southern mills moved quickly to take the wind out of the CIO's sails. Immediately after Hillman's official announcement on 19 March, which came after several days of news stories, numerous southern mills raised wages up to 10 percent. In South Carolina, over 95,000 workers received wage increases of from 5 to 10 percent. The Associated Press reported on 31 March that 294 mills had increased wages, affecting 199,255 workers.[69]

Harry Reimer, correspondent for the textile industry's *Daily News Record*, reported that mill executives, particularly in the South, would not accept the

TWOC without a fight. Reimer pointed out that manufacturers had "resented efforts of labor organizers in the past as an unnecessary intrusion," and he now predicted that many would fight to the "last ditch to save themselves and their organization from unionism."[70] The Raleigh *News and Observer* also feared the worst and asked for the best statesmanship North Carolina could muster to avoid a conflict that would "cost much in blood and money, in bitterness and antagonism, in division and destruction."[71] An observer in the *Christian Century* also foresaw a mighty southern reaction to the CIO invasion. "The average outsider," wrote J.H. Marion, Jr., "can scarcely realize with what suspicion, fear, and resentment the ruling classes in the South have regarded the whole labor union movement. Unions to many good people are nothing but rackets, and their leaders an unscrupulous crowd of gang-sters. . . . The CIO may yet discover that compared with southern textiles, steel was a playful kitten."[72]

Employer confidence in the face of the threatened CIO onslaught came in part from improved economic conditions in the industry, which had made possible wage increases and increased employment. After the depressed conditions of winter 1934–35, most mills made profits in 1935. In 1936 business improvement accelerated, and the industry operated at a high level of production. The momentum carried over well into 1937. In the South, cotton goods had gained nearly 30 percent in dollar value—a figure well above the low rate of inflation in the period. The South also continued to increase its share of the industry at the expense of New England. It gained 57 new mills in the 1935–37 period, bringing the total to 766 spinning and weaving establishments.[73] For cotton textiles 1936 was a good year, and the *Textile Bulletin* reported in December that the "long trend outlook for cotton textiles is gratifying."[74] In spring 1937, the "depression blues" was a song of the past.

The euphoric mood of the industry in winter and spring 1937 altered abruptly as a sharp recession, the famous "Roosevelt Recession," hit American businesses in fall and winter 1937–38. The recession, usually seen as a consequence of New Deal budget-balancing policies, quickly appeared and then disappeared when the New Deal turned on the spending spigots again in 1938. The *Textile Bulletin* reported in January 1938, "For the cotton textile industry the first six months of 1937 represented the crest of the Recovery period. All previous records of output were surpassed."[75] But business activity began to slide downward in September 1937 and touched bottom in June 1938, attended by falling industrial activity, a declining stock market, and rising unemployment. In May 1937, employment in the southern cotton textile industry stood at 468,000, but by November 1937 it had dropped to 399,000.[76] Fortunately, the recession was short. The cotton textile industry was operating at 81.9 percent of capacity by November 1938, compared to 69.8 percent in November 1937.[77] Prices, however, were slow in rising after the sharp drop in fall 1937, and the southern cotton textile industry was slow to regain the high profit margin that had existed just before the 1937–38 recession.[78] Consumer demand lagged slightly behind the recovery, and despite a reduction in spindles in place, the industry still managed to produce more than it could sell.

Unfortunately for the TWOC, the short recession coincided with its ambitious plans. Shortly after it began its southern drive in earnest, the recession started and mills closed, not because of unionism and its threat but because of business conditions. Many workers, remembering the discrimination and joblessness visited upon the mill villages after the 1934 strike, concluded that a cause-and-effect relationship existed between the TWOC activity and the unemployment and closed mills. Paul Christopher informed Francis Gorman late in 1937 that the recession had devastated the industry in his state, South Carolina. "There must be about 25 percent who are completely out of work," he wrote, "and the others are working about half-time." Wage cutting and the stretch out, which had been "frozen" in the recent good times, returned, but any effort by the TWOC to counteract such trends by strikes, he thought, would create serious disorder because of the concern over jobs.[79] In early 1938 Christopher reported to TWOC that "in the Piedmont section of the two Carolinas we have thousands of workers totally idle and other thousands working only part-time." The same conditions prevailed in April, although Christopher reported conditions worse in Alabama, with operations curtailed in most mills and about half the workers laid off.[80] A sympathetic James Starr, UTW secretary-treasurer, in reply to Christopher's lament, summarized TWOC's plight and bad timing: "It is not an easy matter to organize workers, whether they are in textiles or any other kind, when they are walking the streets looking for jobs, many of them suffering the pangs of hunger."[81]

By summer 1938, however, economic vitality was flowing back into the Piedmont mills. Indeed, as early as January 1938, the *New York Times'* economic reporter had predicted a return of profitable operations for southern mills. Inventories had been depleted by the very slack fall production schedules, and prices had begun to turn up.[82] Throughout 1938, production and profits rose. The ever-colorful president of the Bibb Manufacturing Company became ebullient by early 1939, exclaiming, "It looks as though the goose is going to hang high again."[83] Despite the recent recession, by 1940 the industry was experiencing a prosperity it had not enjoyed since 1919. In December 1940, the *Journal of Commerce* claimed that virtually every mill would show a profit for the last half of the year. The fear of war in Europe in 1939 had sent many South American buyers to American mills, and stepped-up defense preparations in the U.S. had strengthened domestic demands. By 1941, most southern mills had instituted around-the-clock production to meet the demand. Approximately 50 percent of the textile industry's output in August 1941 was going to defense.[84] In summer 1941, the president of the Alabama Cotton Manufacturers Association reported, "For the first time in the history of America, the consumption of cotton is approaching a rate equal to the production of cotton."[85]

The economic vicissitudes of the industry created problems for TWOC. The recession sapped worker motivation, and the sharp rise in economic prosperity between 1938 and 1941 gave management confidence and strengthened its determination to keep the union out of the mills.[86]

"You do not work for me and to hell with the CIO"

THE TWOC AND THE NLRB, 1937–41

The TWOC drive got under way by April 1937, but Hillman, following a North-first policy, made the various textile industries in the Middle Atlantic and New England states, rather than southern cotton textiles, his primary objectives. The UTW provided a base to build on in the woolen, silk, and synthetic fibers industries, and the TWOC made real progress by early fall. It claimed, for example, that 75 percent of the workers in the silk and rayon industries had been organized or had signed pledge-cards. On 15 May 1937 the TWOC claimed bargaining rights for 81,000 workers, and by 30 September the number had risen dramatically to 215,000.[1] In many cases in the North, actual working contracts followed bargaining rights, particularly in the hosiery industry, where there had previously existed an active hosiery workers union as a federation of the UTW. In the southern cotton textile industry, however, there was little for the TWOC to build upon, particularly given the hostile reaction of the owners and frequent indifference of the workers. The TWOC found itself under attack from all sectors of the southern community. "In tackling cotton," wrote one journalist, "the CIO is incurring the active opposition of all combined interests of southern capital, for southland is Cottonland in field and factory. Industrialist, banker, utility magnate, plantation owner, merchant, newspaper publisher—all . . . aim to halt the CIO tenant union in the cotton field, and textile union in the cotton factory."[2]

An irrational southern outcry greeted the CIO already tainted in southern eyes by radicalism, race-mixing, and communism. Louis Adamic, who had been out of the country, arrived back late in spring 1937 and was immediately struck by the hate campaign directed toward the CIO, primarily because of sitdown strikes in the North. Even for intellectuals, he said, "labor was going too far too fast, employing dangerous methods and weapons," even if there were no "communists manipulating it."[3] The sitdowns shocked even liberal southerners and increased their alienation from unions as institutions for southern reform.[4] Lucy Randolph Mason, who had recently come South to influence educated public opinion in favor of the TWOC, reported to Sidney Hillman that the ignorance of unionism and the CIO in the South was "incredible." "TWOC," she wrote, "is regarded by many people who thought they were in sympathy with organized labor as a dangerously radical and subversive movement."[5]

Throughout the South, at virtually all CIO organizing activities, angry receptions awaited the organizers. Sheriff James R. Hicks, Jr., of Macon, Georgia, declared, "We don't need the CIO workers here to stir up trouble"; announced a twenty-five-dollar reward for identification of any CIO representative distributing leaflets; and vowed "to put them under the jail."[6] In Moorehead City, North Carolina, a gang of "citizens" led by their mayor, H.S. Gibbs, physically ejected TWOC organizers from the front of a shirt company.[7] Even in such a large city as Memphis, Tennessee, Mayor Watkins Overton warned that "imported CIO agitators, Communists, and high professional organizers" would not be tolerated. Their tools, he said, "are violence, threats, and un-American policies."[8] In a peculiar twist, the *Textile Bulletin,* in its sustained editorial attack on the TWOC and its parent CIO, linked both to Hitlerism. "This dictatorship," said the *Bulletin,* "wants mass action, mass thinking, mass principles of life and living, regardless of economic conditions and environmental necessities. . . . The CIO is definitely a step in the fascist plan. . . . It is not a fight for wages and hours and improved labor conditions. This is only the dress up front."[9]

Even the Ku Klux Klan, bringing its hoods out of closets, found the CIO a ready target. In 1937 activity by scattered Klan groups was particularly noticeable in South Carolina, although less so in Georgia and Alabama. The Klan did not actively take the field, except in a few cases of isolated violence, but confined itself to public statements claiming that the TWOC and CIO were "controlled by communistic foreign ideas."[10] Although the Klan actually hoped to use the TWOC as an issue to gain members, its opposition to the TWOC was only a minor irritant, or as the *New York Times* reported, "only the rattling of an old skeleton."[11] But the Klan's ghostly reappearance gave evidence of the deep southern hostility to the very idea of the TWOC as the prelude to "one big union," particularly given that people with foreign-sounding names led it. The *Textile Bulletin* noted that Hillman "has been very successful in dominating the foreign-born employees who operate the clothing factories of the North, but will find it different when he tackles the Anglo-Saxons who operate the cotton mills of the South."[12] Because of its CIO connections, the TWOC became associated in the South with Yankees, Jews, and Communists.

The employers, particularly in 1937, used discriminatory discharges, threats, evictions from mill-owned houses, labor spies, physical disruption of meetings, company unions, and cooperation from local government officials to deprive organizers of their civil liberties. In any case, southern workers were not eager to join the union. Many of the mill areas in South Carolina were saturated with evangelists who preached against the CIO, as meaning "Christ is out." The TWOC charged that the preachers were often paid by the owners. Although proof is hard to find, a cynical observer in 1937 noted that the evangelists "all had new tents and cars."[13] It was an old story for organizing campaigns in the South. Between 1936 and 1939, nineteen southern union organizers and workers were killed.[14] Organizers were frequently beaten by company deputies, irate citizens, or nonunion workers. On a few occasions, TWOC organizers were forced to carry on their organizing work in secret because they feared violence. Local authorities seldom would agree to protect the organizers' rights to move about freely. On a few occasions police officials permitted violence toward union organizers to occur in their presence. Local judges and juries dismissed TWOC appeals for relief. In her personal history of CIO organizing efforts in the South, Lucy Randolph Mason devoted twenty pages to such physical intimidations of CIO organizers between 1937 and 1940.[15] One Georgia delegate to a TWOC convention in Philadelphia bitterly described his reaction to southern resistance: "I saw the Liberty Bell, but when I looked at it, I thought that if I took it with me it would be smashed in pieces the minute I crossed the Georgia state line."[16]

The charge of Communist influence hurt the TWOC. The AFL leaders in the South, George Googe and Holt Ross, were often guilty of making this irresponsible allegation in the bitter battle between the estranged laborites. In May 1937 George Googe cried that the CIO was "using communistic strategy and being aided and abetted by communistic organizations directed by the third International in Moscow."[17] The AFL hoped to make itself appear to employers as the lesser of two evils by associating the TWOC with radicalism. Dr. Witherspoon Dodge, the fiery professor and TWOC union organizer, replied to such charges in caustic language: "I happen to be from the deep, dark, and dismal South, where everybody nearly is a communist to the dumb-hided ignoramuses, who dictate to us what they call public opinion from blind, glass-topped mahogany tables and editorial chairs, and unfortunately, frequently from blind pulpits. To have an original idea in the South is to be a Communist in the eyes of about 90 percent of the people."[18] A. Steve Nance tried in July 1937 to brush aside the charge of Communism, saying, "This has been the stock argument of all the self-appointed witch-doctors who want to restrict freedom of speech, press, and assemblage behind a scare of real bogey-man that has never and never will exist in the South."[19] But the frivolous charge stung and stuck. As late as 1941 the Textile Workers Union of America, successor to the TWOC, found it necessary to pass a resolution excluding Communists or Fascists from membership.

Aside from crude antiunion tactics, management throughout the country was poorly prepared for the depression and particularly for the New Deal in labor relations. Most managements had had no experience with modern personnel techniques or with collective bargaining, whether with company unions or organized labor.[20] The southern cotton textile owners, though, learned fast, and by the late 1930s had become much better managers with regard to labor relations. The successive challenges of the 1929–31 and 1933–34 cycles of unionism, combined with the 1937 TWOC threat, forced the owners to abandon the simple nineteenth-century paternalism, which many had long ago discarded, anyway, and begin to adopt modern management techniques.

Labor economist Frank T. DeVyver interviewed some owners in 1937 and reported an increased awareness of the need for better labor relations. "Whatever their attitudes toward organization, he said, "southern mill men are managing labor with more firmness than formerly. The possibilities of organization, as much as organization itself, was responsible for this situation."[21] By 1938, most southern mill owners soft-pedaled the use of efficiency systems and instead, the *Daily News Record* reported, relied more and more on "plain common-sense management."[22] The TWOC threat created, according to one reporter, "a constant exchange of information between mill owners, principally by telephone" to develop owner strategies to defeat unionism.[23] In February 1938 William McLaurine of the ACMA reminded the owners that unions might not "be necessary if the new ideas of industrial relations as incorporated in the plans of management are handled intelligently."[24] Solomon Barkin, the union researcher, sensed in 1950 that the cotton mill owners had mastered a variety of personnel tricks which represented a shift from what he called the earlier "welfare" techniques of paternalism to a newer "humanistic" approach stressing communication, conscious group identity, individual counseling, and clear work policies. Nevertheless, Barkin still saw the approach as one designed "to induce the worker to accept or adapt himself fully to management's code of values and management's goals."[25] To defend themselves against TWOC intrusion, the owners learned to use the stroking hand as well as the fist.

Formidable opposition did not prevent the TWOC from actively setting its organizing drive in motion in spring 1937. The task was enormous. Samuel McClurd of the TLRB, still active as a Department of Labor mediation group, reported that the TWOC faced a situation very different from the one the CIO had faced in steel and automobiles. No single corporation dominated even an important fraction of the industry. Every mill was run as a separate unit. Even mill chains operated their different mills autonomously. "Furthermore," wrote McClurd, "there is no existing machinery through which the industry as a whole can be negotiated . . . the union must deal with the individual plant management."[26] The TWOC would have to organize house by house in the village and mill by mill in the Piedmont—and do its work among individuals who in the last three years had overwhelmingly rejected the UTW and whose culture impeded unionism. The hope of a fast start faded quickly, as the TWOC directors in the South, Steve Nance in Atlanta and John Peel in Roanoke, Virginia, found it difficult to gather competent organizers. A field agent for the TLRB reported in late March that "everything is in an uproar and no-one seems to know exactly what will be done."[27]

Slowly, priorities were sorted out. Hillman, according to Solomon Barkin, planned for the southern cotton textile drive to have "considerable autonomy," to be adapted "to the southern needs," and to be run by Nance out of the Atlanta office, with Peel concentrating on the rayon industry of the Upper South.[28] The common image of an all-powerful Hillman, directing the southern push, was a complete fiction. Very few meetings of the TWOC took place at the New York headquarters. The cotton campaign was run from Nance's six-room headquarters in downtown Atlanta. Nance did follow one Hillman directive; he tried, as best he could, to keep his organizing staff southern and non-Jewish, with few foreign-sounding names. "One thing they cannot charge against us," he told a New York reporter, "is that we are foreigners, Reds, outside agitators, or damn Yankees." Nance emphasized his own Revolutionary War and Civil War heritage to the reporter and boasted, "Virtually every one of our officers and organizers likewise is of southern birth and upbringing. This is strictly an American and a southern movement, and any statement to the contrary is so much tommyrot."[29] By midsummer, Nance assembled a force of about a hundred such people. Paul Christopher, for example, exulted on 14 July 1937 that the TWOC had thirty-six organizers in the Carolinas alone.[30] For the first time, a significant number of women organizers were also at work, one with the exquisitely southern name of Eula May McGill.

The organizers concentrated on obtaining pledgecards, as planned at the March meetings, and they quickly decided that seven workers were enough to form a local union. As early as May 1937, Nance claimed that a hundred thousand workers in his district had signed TWOC pledgecards, but signing a pledgecard was quite different from becoming a dues-paying member and working under a TWOC contract. The *Journal Of Commerce* sent a special correspondent to the South in summer 1937 to evaluate TWOC claims that about a third of the cotton workers had signed pledgecards. The reporter found that the claims were not "exaggerated," with even the TWOC amazed at the response, but the correspondent also reported that the workers had signed with little commitment. One North Carolina worker summed up the general attitude when he said, "There's no charge to join up. We've got nothing to lose and maybe something to gain." The reporter for the *Journal* believed, as the AFL predicted, that the TWOC could not hold the pledged workers in any industrial dispute and that many workers would drift away after the unimportant act of signing the pledge.[31]

In 1937 TWOC literature in the South exuded confidence and stressed Hillman's arguments regarding the rationality of unions and the mutuality of interests between workers and owners. TWOC portrayed itself as a strong organization with the money and leadership needed to create the region's first stable textile union, capable of securing better pay, economic security, and improved working conditions. Gaining respectability, however, appeared to be its initial goal. One of Lucy Randolph Mason's first acts as Nance's publicity director was to send a letter to 425 southern ministers explaining TWOC's moderate, practical goals. Hillman reinforced all this by arranging a meeting with FDR and Frances Perkins on 31 March 1937, ostensibly to discuss the pending wage and hour legislation. After the meeting he touted TWOC to reporters, telling them that TWOC hoped "to make headway through the cooperation of employers," and that it thought the matter could be settled without strikes. "I believe," said Hillman, "that the management will cooperate with the workers. The response has been generally good."[32]

Full of such optimism during summer 1937, TWOC organizers hawked their pledgecards, and on 1 July 1937 TWOC's southern newsletter told those who had signed pledgecards that "textile workers have joined the TWOC movement by the tens of thousands in the South and are continuing to join every day."[33] On 12 July 1937 the *Union News Service* reported that "membership cards were flowing into TWOC offices in North Carolina and Alabama at the rate of a thousand a day" and that over three hundred thousand workers were in the TWOC.[34]

The summer 1937 pledgecard drive emphasized the Wagner Act. In fact, the purpose of the pledge drive was to begin the process of collective bargaining that the act protected. A key TWOC pamphlet sported the large headline, "U.S. is for US," and promised that nothing could stop the TWOC. The pamphlet emphasized, "your right to join this great union movement which is sweeping the country and has the approval" of Congress, the President, the voters, and labor everywhere. In a large box was the Supreme Court's opinion upholding the Wagner Act: "Employees have a clear right to organize and select their representatives, as the company has to organize its business and select its own officers and agents. . . . Union is essential to give laborers an opportunity to deal in equality with their employer." "JOIN THE UNION NOW!" the pamphlet urged in big letters. "You can do so without fear for LAW and POWER are on our side." Smaller sections in the leaflet stressed the right of collective bargaining under the Wagner Act, presidential and congressional support, and the power of the CIO to protect workers. It was now safe to join a union, the pamphlet urged; employers had to bargain in good faith. The last page of the leaflet had the pledge to be signed, authorizing the TWOC to act as the bargaining agent.[35] The midsummer pledge drive would begin the march toward collective bargaining contracts, and Nance attempted to create the illusion of an army of workers rushing into the union.

The glowing reports of pledgecard signings represented nothing but public-relations fluff. After the initial surge in late spring and early summer, TWOC hit a wall of resistance. The barriers to effective unionization in the mills were as high as ever. It was a long road from pledgecards to a union powerful enough to compel collective bargaining. In South Carolina, TWOC lost its momentum even in pledgecard signing by early August 1937, as it depleted the ranks of workers already receptive to unionism.[36] According to Solomon Barkin, by August 1937 the national campaign had garnered 133,939 pledgecards, with 61,093 of them in cotton. Of the 61,093 pledges, 48,839 were in the Lower South and only 5,576 in the Upper South.[37] By TWOC's own statistics — probably inaccurate, given the highly decentralized and rather chaotic nature of the summer campaign — less than a fourth of the cotton textile workers had signed a pledge.

Throughout the 1937 campaign, the national TWOC office in New York tried to keep its organizing force in the field informed and optimistic by publishing a newsletter for regional directors. Painfully clear in its pages was the lack of real progress in cotton textiles and even in other textile industries in the South. Not until midsummer did the newsletter provide a detailed explanation of how unions could gain access to the NLRB's majority-rule election process. The 11 September 1937 newsletter listed twenty-six election cases pending before the NLRB, and twelve involved southern cotton mills. The 15 October 1937 letter bragged of a perfect score in representative elections, but there was no sense of any significant number of contracts in cotton textiles, only a small mill here and there.[38]

Although TWOC made solid progress in 1937 in the northern-based industries of silk, carpets and rugs, finishing, synthetic yarns, and woolen goods, by late 1937 it had failed in the South. By August TWOC had only sixteen written contracts in mills of all sorts in the South, covering 17,500 workers.[39] By October TWOC had won contracts in nine southern cotton textile mills, covering only 5,000 workers and 346,476 spindles, 2 percent of the total active spindles. It had active negotiations under way with only 4 percent more of the industry.[40] The *Daily News Record* estimated that nationally TWOC membership in October was only 84,000, out of a total workforce of over 1,000,000; the great failure had been in cotton textiles, where about one-fourth of TWOC's effort had been expended. Hillman, the correspondent thought, had underestimated the problems of the South. The article noted, "The experience of TWOC organizers in working among the southern textile operatives, the attitude of the public, the press and the pulpit, and of county, township, city and village peace officers" forced the union to confront "factors of a type quite different [from those] heretofore encountered by Sidney Hillman in his work with North and East." The South had "a different psychology, a different temperament." The writer observed that TWOC had "not yet taken steps to join the issue with any recognized key mill in the South" and that until that was done, the organizing campaign had to be counted a failure.[41]

In 1937 TWOC failed at the grassroots level, in the cotton mills, and not in its conceptual planning. Paul Christopher's work as a district TWOC organizer demonstrated the simple failure of the workers to respond to the TWOC message. Christopher did everything right. A South Carolinian, born of cotton mill workers, raised in mill villages, himself a mill worker for eight years after he dropped out of Clemson University for lack of money, Christopher worked diligently in North Carolina and throughout the Lower South. He visited homes in the villages, stood at plant gates with leaflets, even engaged in bargaining talks and conducted an intelligent strike. He often bore the brunt of TWOC impatience, and even in this much-praised drive he was yanked from place to place with no fixed long range target, due to a shortage of organizers and money. Despite Christopher's efforts, nothing could make cotton textiles conform to that New Deal image of "labor on the march."[42]

Christopher's colleagues met the same fate. In 1937 the state staff of eight organizers in South Carolina got only one formal contract covering only 1,200 workers in five mills, although it gathered over 12,000 pledgecards. In the same year in Alabama, the ten TWOC organizers got only 4,800 pledgecards and four contracts covering 2,500 workers. In Georgia, with thirty-four organizers, TWOC turned up about 12,000 pledges but only three contracts involving slightly over 1,000 workers. The North Carolina movement did no better—over 20,000 pledges from the state's large workforce but only one contract for a meager 450 workers.[43] While TWOC in 1937 made solid gains in the North in other textile industries—429 contracts covering 155,960 workers—it bogged down in the cotton textile heartland, where suspicious workers waited and watched. As telling evidence of worker apathy even in the few places where it won contracts, TWOC never pressed hard for the closed shop but rather, because of the workers' dislike of paying dues, went for a dues checkoff and the preferential union shop.[44]

The southern mill workers wanted quick results and hard evidence of gains, but nothing in the Wagner Act made either a certainty. Lucy Randolph Mason recognized the problem when she wrote Hillman on 2 October 1937 urging an increased CIO effort involving other industries in the South. She was impressed by the real grievances of the textile workers and "by the determination and enthusiasm of union members," but they needed quick help to "lessen the concentration of opposition to TWOC and give it more moral support."[45] The help from the New Deal's collective bargaining policy was neither quick nor particularly useful in the situation that TWOC faced. TWOC reported that from March 1937 to May 1939 it filed some 450 separate complaints with the NLRB or its regional offices charging unfair labor practices, most of them by southern cotton textile manufacturers.[46] The complaints alleged various kinds of interference, ranging from interference with the work of organizers and intimidation of workers to keep them from joining the unions, to outright refusal to bargain with properly certified bargaining agents. After its pledgecard campaign, the union had moved aggressively to translate the pledges into effective bargaining units. By September 1937 it had used the NLRB to conduct fifty-eight elections in the South in all kinds of textiles and reported that it had won all fifty-eight.[47] But it quickly discovered that winning a bargaining election was only the first step in a long, involved process.

The decisions and orders of the NLRB for the late 1930s, filling over twenty volumes, in every reporting period include one or more cases involving a southern cotton mill. Distressingly, many of the cases merely chronicle the same unfair labor practices. Of all the cases, one stands out as illustrative of the TWOC era. In and around Gaffney, S.C., a small Piedmont town, the Hamrick family owned and operated three separate cotton spinning and weaving mills—Alma Mills, Limestone Mills, and Hamrick Mills—together employing almost two thousand workers. The mills were typical of those in the Piedmont in the 1930s. Waite Hamrick, son of the founder, was the president and treasurer of all the mills, while his brother Lyman was secretary and manager of the Alma Mills and vice-president of the other two. Taylor Best, the TWOC organizer who first worked the mills, collected pledgecards from what he considered a majority of the workers at the Limestone Mills. He approached Waite Hamrick in 1937 to attempt to prove that TWOC represented a majority of the workers. Best reported later that after a brief initial meeting, Hamrick refused to have any discussion with him. Hamrick told Best, "You do not work for me and to hell with the CIO."[48]

The three mills had a long history of antiunionism. The UTW had begun organizing in the mills in Gaffney in August 1933 but never established anything beyond a sometimes-active local for a minority of the workers, although all three Hamrick mills were shut down during the 1934 general strike. The management met with the local UTW president, J.H. Palmer, in October 1934, and the mills resumed production, although Palmer reported that "many of the grievances were not adjusted." In February 1936 the workers at the Alma Mills walked out over the crude implementation of increased workloads—stretch out—and soon, in April 1936, the workers at Limestone Mills joined them. Eventually Waite Hamrick met with Palmer, still the UTW local president and nominal leader of the strike. Nothing was settled, but the striking workers, destitute after such a long siege, returned to work in August 1936 under company terms. The UTW, to the extent that it had attempted to give directions to the worker protest, had failed once again, and the local became inactive.[49]

Throughout 1937 TWOC worked hard in Gaffney, but the mill owners' hostile reception and the memory of the strike failures of 1934 and 1936 made signing the workers difficult. In November 1937, after weeks of organizing work, TWOC in frustration filed in the regional NLRB office at Atlanta charges against all three mills, alleging intimidation of workers who had signed TWOC pledgecards. Not until spring 1938 did TWOC feel confident enough of support by a majority of the workers to strike for an election at the mills. The elections, however, were then postponed, at TWOC's petition, because the Hamrick management, by alleged unfair labor practices, had initiated a fight to undercut the TWOC majority that was building in the three mills. Because all three mills were owned and operated by the same management and because of their proximity to each other, on 3 October 1938 the NLRB joined the three mills together into one case. Charles Feidelson, regional director of the NLRB's tenth region, reported that his field investigations during the summer had determined that "occurrences" in all three mills were "such as to show them to be a part of a designated campaign against the organization of the workers into the Textile Workers Organizing Committee."[50]

The NLRB's final report and the transcripts of the various hearings detailed a determined effort to drive off the TWOC organizers and to prevent the workers in the three mills from joining TWOC.[51] In order to eliminate the danger of a TWOC election victory, the Hamricks formed three company unions: the "Square Deal Club" at the Alma Mills, the "Free Fellowship Club" at Limestone Mills, and the "Good Fellowship Club" at Hamrick Mills. The workers were pressured to join the clubs and to sign a pledge denying the right of any other organization to represent them. Soon after the NLRB ordered the spring 1938 election, a worker lurking outside the office of president Waite Hamrick at the Limestone Mills overheard a conversation between Hamrick and five overseers and section hands, in which the men plotted to "bust" up the TWOC.

"Hell," said one man to Hamrick, "we can stop it if it takes a little knocking." Hamrick replied, "Just go to it"; he would back them all the way.

A battle between the clubs and TWOC erupted. On 29 May 1938 a union rally led by Witherspoon Dodge opposite the Alma Mills was broken up by thirty to forty Square Deal Club members, most of them supervisors of some sort, armed with "rocks, boards, and hose pipes." Union people were knocked down, and Dodge wisely had the gathering disband, in disorder. The next day TWOC petitioned for a postponement of the elections and filed new charges of unfair labor practices.[52] Waite Hamrick contacted a local evangelistic preacher, D.E. "Preacher" Parker and, according to testimony, financed a lot for a future church site as well as giving Parker a check for $500 to "preach against the CIO." The NLRB believed "Preacher" Parker to have been an effective antiunion agent.[53] The Hamricks closed the Alma Mills on 27 May 1938, allegedly because of business conditions, but on 5 July 1938 some fifty company club members gathered at the Limestone Mills gate at the morning shift to threaten and single out for abuse workers who had signed TWOC pledgecards. Credit at a company store began to be routinely refused to TWOC sympathizers.

Particularly telling were individual cases of discrimination and hardships visited by the company and its antiunion employees on TWOC members. When the Alma Mills reopened after several weeks, leading TWOC workers were not rehired and were evicted from company-owned houses. The local TWOC officers sent a letter to the NLRB on 12 April 1939, praising the work of C.W. Whittmore, the NLRB trial examiner, but arguing that "Mr. Whittmore heard only a small part of the suffering, hardships, and sickness caused by the company discharge and throwing these people out of company-owned houses, to final shelter in car sheds, out buildings or wherever they could find a place to stay."[54] The threats continued even after the regional hearings in December 1938 and January 1939. After testifying, Hillard Coker, a union worker, was accosted by a well-known company supporter, "Buck" Perry, who put a knife across his throat and said, "After the Court leaves here, I will stomp you, God damn it, until you can't see."[55] The NLRB used thirty-seven pages in its formal decision to document individual cases of violence, discriminatory firings, and work floor harrassment directed against union workers, all orchestrated and controlled by the company.[56]

The board's decision totally favored the union, finding the mills guilty of arranging assaults on union members and union meetings, coercing employees to resign from the union, supporting and encouraging an antiunion religious campaign among employees—all activities that the board saw as major unfair labor practices under the category of interference, restraint, and coercion. The three mill clubs, said the board, constituted illegal and unfair labor practices because they were company financed and led by supervisory employees, and they met on company property. The board identified thirty clear cases in which workers were discharged or refused employment because of union activity.

Although the Hamricks lost the battle, they really won the war. The time needed to win minor victories devastated the TWOC and its effort to create majority bargaining units. The TWOC had worked for over a year to build a possible union majority. After the postponed spring elections of 1938 and the efforts by the company to "bust" the TWOC, it was not until December 1938 and January 1939 that the formal hearings on the union charges were held. Meanwhile, the company consolidated its nonunion operation. The trial examiner found against the company on 3 April 1939, but the company appealed to the NLRB, and it granted a hearing to the company in Washington on 21 November 1939. The union, alleging that the company had suborned perjury in the Gaffney hearings, had a further hearing before the NLRB in Washington on 5 December 1939, and the board then ordered another hearing on 22 January 1940 at Spartanburg, South Carolina, and on 23 and 24 January at Gaffney, where several workers admitted to their perjury. On 2 February 1940, the NLRB agreed, at the mills' request, to delay its decision because of the mills' charge that C.W. Whittmore, the trial examiner, was biased against the companies. Finally, on 6 April 1940, the NLRB issued a preliminary finding of fact and law against the mills, but the mills disagreed on 20 April 1940 and asked for another hearing. The board granted two hearings in Washington on 1 and 16 May 1940. The final decision, the one printed, came on 29 May 1940. The penalty was reinstatement of a handful of workers, back pay, and the usual posting in the mills of the notification and cease-and-desist orders. The union, meanwhile, had to start all over in its quest for majority-rule collective bargaining.

Incredibly, the case still dragged on after this. The company took the board's decision to the federal district court, lost, and then dickered with the NLRB over the amount of back pay that the board had set—a total of $32,000, to be divided among the wronged workers. Over union objections, the NLRB negotiators finally agreed to half that amount. In open defiance, which the NLRB ignored, the company, although it rehired a few of the workers, refused to rehire two because they were "obnoxious" people. The federal court agreed to the halved settlement in October 1940, but the company did not pay some workers until July 1944.

No wonder a union member, M.E. Underwood of Gaffney, probably an employee of the Hamrick Mills, wrote in 1940 to Charles Feidelson of the NLRB Atlanta office (with copies, she claimed, to FDR and John Lewis) that she was frustrated because of NLRB inactivity some fifteen months after the board's first hearings in the Gaffney cases: "I am going to say that I am going to have to turn in my union card to them [the company] because I cannot afford to lose my job and starve to death waiting for the NLRB to hear my case."[57]

The Gaffney case, while interesting because of the lengthy printed space the NLRB gave to it in an attempt to be specific as to what constituted unfair labor practices, was not unusual in its pattern of unintentional but awkward delay simply to get a judgment of unfair labor practices. Another case, that of the Highland Park Manufacturing Company of Charlotte, N.C., began with a TWOC complaint on 31 April 1937 alleging discriminatory firings of TWOC activists. Hearings on the charges were not held until 9–11 December 1937; the union complaints were not formally upheld until 12 February 1938, and then only in part. But the mill only increased its antiunion activities. The union filed six new charges between 3 March 1938 and 3 February 1939. A summary of the case prepared on 18 February 1939 by NLRB staffer Sumner Marcus included the regional director's report "that the Union (TWOC) has disintegrated and that its previous majority has been reduced to a handful of members."[58] The company then agreed to cooperate with the NLRB, and on 20 November 1940 one worker received $150 in back pay.

TWOC's publications made passing mention of many similar NLRB elections and cases prosecuted by the TWOC between 1938 and 1941.[59] The union dutifully proclaimed every one of them a blow for progress, no matter what the length of the process, but the victories were often meaningless. The TWOC campaign in southern cotton textiles in 1937 and after and its use of the Wagner Act dramatically demonstrated that federal legislation was not a substitute for union power and that the legislation by itself did nothing to create union power.

A SECOND LIFE FOR THE TWOC AND A NEW UNION

Lucy Randolph Mason realized that the 1937 efforts had failed. In a report to Sidney Hillman in January 1938, she praised the "courage and persistence" of the union workers whose ability to keep working "in the face of their poverty and privation" was "inspiring," but for Mason the lesson of 1937 was that only a "long campaign" lay ahead, with "persistent, quiet digging in" as the "only way to build a southern labor movement."[60] Franz Daniel, second in command of the Deep South, said years afterward that the 1937 recession struck a fatal blow at an already difficult task. All the economic pressures on the manufacturers to avoid interruptions of production were removed by full warehouses and slack orders, and workers were even more reluctant to take the risk of joining a union when short time and lay-off periods had come to the mills. Daniel believed that in late summer 1937 TWOC should have retrenched and concentrated its full power on strengthening already established locals.[61] TWOC also had to cope with the illness and subsequent death in April 1938 of Steve Nance, the respected leader. Previously, in late October 1937, Sidney Hillman had suffered a severe attack of pneumonia and had to spend the winter in Florida, unable to return to New York until April 1938. Both events, although important, were not as crucial to TWOC's failure as its inability to break through in the mill villages. Hillman's contribution to cotton textiles had always been as money raiser and national symbol, while Nance, though popular within the union bureaucracy and in the state of Georgia, was an AFL typographical unionist with few personal contacts in the crucial Carolinas. He was quickly replaced by Roy Lawrence, an old UTW leader.

By the time Nance and Hillman left the fray, TWOC had already failed. Paul Christopher saw clearly the task ahead in late winter 1937–38: "I believed that when the TWOC took over we were on our way to quick organization in the textile industry and that militant, permanent and intelligent local unions would be the result. Many moves and obstacles have retarded our progress and lengthened the road to our goal, but I hope to see the desired organization functioning in my generation."[62] By winter 1937–38, TWOC had lost its momentum. From April to July 1937, TWOC averaged $123,498 a month in income from its two principal sources, dues from its growing membership and contributions from ACWU and other CIO unions. The average fell to $112,807 in August to October 1937. In November 1937 to February 1938, it fell to $101,988, with $42,252 coming from TWOC itself and $57,236 from other CIO unions. But ACWU contributions in the last period came to only $2,500, down sharply from the $50,000 monthly average in late 1937.

Although operating with less money, TWOC in 1938 still had significant resources. What was important was the withdrawal of a disproportionate amount of those resources from the southern cotton textile industry, where the TWOC had lost so badly. In April 1937 the TWOC organizing staff in the cotton district of the Lower South reached its peak number, 112. Even in October 1937 the organizing group had dropped to 85, and by March 1938 it had been almost halved, to 44. Further adding to the 1937–38 winter blues, TWOC, having gained during all of 1937 only sixteen contracts covering not

much more than twenty-one thousand workers, had insufficient power to re-
new six contracts that had expired.[63]

Still, TWOC was prepared to continue its work in the mill villages and
at the plant gates in 1938. In winter 1937–38 it continued its policy of avoid-
ing strikes, although not always successfully. The few it did undertake almost
always ended in failure. Much of the organizers' time was spent running from
place to place investigating disputes over stretch out or worker reports of
discriminatory firings. Even so, they won most of the elections they organized
and were particularly pleased with victories in Huntsville, Ala., at the long-
troubled Merrimack Company, as well as a victory at the Erwin Mills in Durham, N.C. By March 1938 their report listed 7 fully functioning new TWOC
locals in Alabama, 4 in Georgia, 7 in North Carolina, 4 in Virginia, and 3
in South Carolina. TWOC had absorbed 152 UTW locals nationally, 37 of
them in the Deep South cotton region.[64]

In June 1938 a report to one of the very infrequent national TWOC executive council meetings, probably prepared by Solomon Barkin, listed TWOC
gains and losses in its first year. The report emphasized problems more than
victories. It bemoaned the continuing difficulty of collecting dues from workers who treated this obligation in a "slovenly" manner. The report argued
that organizers had been poorly trained: "Too many are imbued with the spirit
that the signing of pledge cards finishes their jobs." The report was an ad-
mission that, despite "great hope" and a "sweeping beginning" and the
establishment of a "foothold," TWOC had failed in the South and that "special efforts have to be bent upon its organization."[65]

As the economic situation in southern cotton textile business improved,
Hillman announced in June 1938 that "a renewed organizing drive in the
South" would be built around the consolidation of gains made through the
NLRB cases.[66] With its trimmed staff, the TWOC abandoned the rush to get
names on pledgecards and attacked the problem of establishing the TWOC
as a permanent union. In November 1938 Solomon Barkin characterized the
summer's effort in the Lower South as a continuation on "the original broad
basis," but he admitted that the area was so "vast" that attention had been
given to a limited number of mills where the TWOC had carved out some
semblance of a niche for itself. He characterized the entire 1938 summer drive,
north and south, as one of "developing and maintaining the organization
which has been built."[67] Hillman still attempted, however, to build a public
image of another CIO victory. In July 1938 he "expressed pleasure" at progress
in the South, without specifying when and where.[68] On 11 July more than
125 TWOC representatives from both Upper and Lower South regions met
with Hillman in Charlotte, N.C., at the heart of the Carolina textile belt,
to discuss further organizing efforts. Hillman claimed at a press conference
that the TWOC, using over two hundred organizers, had over 130,000 members in the South, and had won forty NLRB elections.[69] He did not point
out that winning an election did not mean either the establishment of an

effective union or the signing of a contract. His membership figures must have included almost all who had ever signed a pledgecard. By the end of the summer, the *CIO News* was once again reporting TWOC success. "Its campaign in the South," said the paper, "has been hailed by liberal leaders of that area as the most significant effort" ever; TWOC had won an "amazing number of Labor Board elections."[70]

The real story was one of hard slogging. A few new contracts were won after months of effort, but contracts were also lost. TWOC's greatest activity centered on pursuing the several NLRB cases, such as that involving Alma Mills. From 1937 to 1941, in the four states of North and South Carolina, Georgia, and Alabama, in *all* textile industries, TWOC won twenty-one new contracts but lost eleven, gaining by 1941 only ten active contracts, most of them not in cotton.[71] The *Daily News Record* paused in fall 1938 to assess the TWOC efforts in the South, interviewing at length Harry Ashmore, a southern journalist who had paid close attention to the union. Ashmore said that the "drive had bogged down." He estimated that TWOC had only three signed contracts in cotton mills, covering less than five thousand workers, although they had negotiations pending in over ten mills where they had won elections. According to Ashmore, "The opinion of most observers today is that the TWOC has not done as well in the South as its sponsors hoped when they started two years ago. The innate stubbornness and previous experience of the southern workers, the united opposition of the owners, and the general antipathy of the public has made for tough sledding."[72] The glum minutes of the TWOC Advisory Board's first meeting in New York City in the same month support Ashmore's conclusion. Roy Lawrence, director of the crucial Lower South region, reported "no spectacular progress had been made in his area." Hillman made only a cameo appearance before the group, and the minutes said that "while he did not view the situation with pessimism he would like to see a little more done."[73]

When the TWOC push started in 1937, the editor of the *Textile Bulletin* had predicted failure. "As we have traveled over the Southern areas," he said, "we have been impressed by the fact that so many employees look with suspicion upon the CIO movement." The editor concluded that the workers were content: "The work is regular, the wages are good and getting better, the hours are reasonable." And the workers and management "enjoy candid relationships. They were born in the same environment and grew up together."[74] Actually, employer stubbornness and vigorous countermeasures had hurt the TWOC as much as worker indifference, suspicion, and apprehension. Beyond such obvious tactics as renewing forms of paternalism, firing workers for union activity, intimidating organizers and workers with violence, harrassing union workers on the job, and inciting community resistance, the owners took full advantage of the wide latitudes of employer resistance permitted by the Wagner Act. Mill owners, reported Harry Ashmore, adopted a "Ghandi-like passive resistance" where collective bargaining was concerned."[75] Lucy Randolph

Mason remembered that by the time "a worker's charges had been dragged through the courts for many months, his union zeal was dampened."[76]

TWOC argued in 1939 that southern employers who faced a certified union indulged "in endless discussion to circumvent any possibility of agreement. Yielding on very minor points, they refuse to settle esstential questions, through delay and extended negotiations, in the hope of either weakening the unions, or wearing down its resistance."[77] Two years later, the Textile Workers Union of America, successor to TWOC, complained of the same thing, claiming that "the employers have indulged in the most procrastinating tactics and have circumvented every attempt at collective bargaining."[78] The weakness of the Wagner Act in securing collective bargaining contracts was quickly exploited by the seasoned and alert Piedmont managers.

The protracted union struggle with the Erwin Mills, a cotton textile company in Durham, N.C. that operated typical mills there and in Erwin and Cooloomee, N.C., vividly documented the way a company could drag out the process of collective bargaining. TWOC began its pledgecard drive at all three mills early in 1937, and on 30 November, believing it had a majority of workers in all three mills, it petitioned the NLRB for an election in each mill. The company, whose president, Kemp P. Lewis, had been a member of the NRA Code Authority, did not commit unfair labor practices in the heavy-handed style of the Alma Mills group. Accordingly, the case went through the NLRB process smoothly. Elections were held on 9, 10, and 11 February 1938, with TWOC winning handily at two plants, 1,468 to 243 and 786 to 219, but squeaking through, 958 to 813, at the third. On 14 April 1938 the NLRB certified the TWOC local as the legal bargaining agent for the workforce at Erwin Mills.[79]

But the company had firm ideas about collective bargaining, even though it had lost the election. W.H. Ruffin, the secretary-treasurer of the mills, in summer 1937 outlined the company strategy in a memorandum. It would always treat the union officers "firm but courteous." No fear of a strike or shutdown would ever, said Ruffin, "move us from sticking to our fundamental principles." Ruffin proposed that the company work only toward a detailed contract, "with negotiation and signing delayed as long as possible."[80] At the same time Ruffin prepared a list of "Things Not to be Granted." It included the closed shop, the preferential shop, checkoff dues, straight seniority, binding arbitration, abolition of piece-rate pay scales, vacation with pay, an increase in wages, and an agreement to negotiate later anything not definitely in the contract. Under "Things Which Might Be Granted," Ruffin put seniority with provisions, time-and-a-half for overtime, the forty-hour week, agreements to continue the present wage scale (unless it was economically necessary to change it), and recognition of the union as the exclusive bargaining agent. Under "Things to Insist on Getting," Ruffin listed exclusive rights to manage the plant, union agreement to refrain from coercing nonunion employees to join the union, exclusive control of workloads through a fair timed system, and unquestioned right to install new labor-saving machinery.[81]

After the TWOC election victory, the company began its meeting with the bargaining groups. The various contracts submitted by the company in the few very formal and brief meetings held in 1938 embodied Ruffin's suggestions. The company's first contract proposal of 24 March 1938 demanded no closed shop, the unrestricted right to shut down the plant at any time, and the right to change machine loads at will, which would be in "the best interest of both the company and its employees." Employees had to agree to give "a reasonable day's work" and accept the use of scientific work studies from "time to time." The workload would be set "on a basis of fairness and equity consistent with quality of workmanship, efficiency of operation, reasonable working capacities of normal operatives." Wages and the various ways they were decided would remain unchanged. Layoffs would not be based on seniority but on productivity, although in cases of comparable merit, mill village residents would be given employment preference. The company agreed not to discriminate against union members in hiring or firing. In its first contract proposal of 8 March 1938, TWOC had requested strict senority rights, a 15-percent across-the-board wage increase, and the closed shop. Regarding workloads, it called simply for no stretch out and changes to come only after mutual agreement. In reply to the company's firm proposal of 30 August 1938, TWOC spelled out in greater detail the possibility of workload changes through timed studies, but in cases of worker disagreement it called for binding arbitration. Also, along with a request for a 15-percent pay increase, the TWOC asked for one week of paid vacation.

The company, which had no intention of reaching an agreement with TWOC, brushed aside the TWOC proposals. The company had decided to defeat the union contract efforts by negotiating with a worker grievance committee it had set up at the mill level rather than with TWOC organizers.[82] Thus, the workers would be satisfied that their grievances were being considered, and the company would not be burdened by a formal union contract. The company did not reply to TWOC's August 1938 offer until 14 February 1939, at which time it suggested virtually the same contract it had first offered, a contract the TWOC had refused because it contained no wage increase or workload protection. TWOC and the company exchanged contracts on 4 March 1939. The company contract contained the same old proposals, although it spelled out in greater detail how the union could not discriminate against or recruit nonunion members in the workforce. In its new offer, TWOC dropped its demand for straight seniority; agreed to the technological necessity of setting workloads through scientific timing; asked for arbitration of workload disputes, although the decision would not necessarily be binding; and, in a desperate bid for a contract, abandoned its request for a wage increase! The company "almost approved" the new proposals but decided to call off the "negotiations" temporarily.[83]

The company's sparse notes on its TWOC negotiations indicated that on 7 March 1939 one of its plant managers reported that TWOC had submitted the company's 4 March proposal to the workers at "various" plants, and the workers had rejected it unanimously. The company then met on 28 March with Roy Lawrence, TWOC's Lower South director, to discuss the contracts but agreed only to meet again on 4 April. On that date, according to the company, Lawrence agreed to the company's demands regarding noncoercion of nonunion workers and appeared to come close to accepting the company's contract. But the next day a union committee came to the company and told it that Lawrence had instructed them to refuse the contract. On 18 April 1939 the union committee formally rejected the company's latest offer.[84]

Throughout April and May company officials often met with its grievance committee, which it called "the Durham CIO Shop Committee," to discuss workloads, but the policy of local bargaining was severely tested when the committee presented a list of grievances to president Kemp Lewis on 8 June. The company diary noted briefly, "They say they keep bringing grievances up but we do not do nothing about them."[85] On 9 June, 250 courageous workers, well less than a fourth of the workforce, left their jobs at the Durham mill over the issue of continued seniority rights for laid-off workers who had been rehired. The mill continued to operate, and Lewis continued to meet with the grievance committee. On 16 June he met with Herbert Eby of the NLRB field staff, who argued that the workers had retained their seniority rights to certain jobs. The company then agreed in part, and on 19 June the company diary noted that "everyone" was back to work, the "mills opening up as usual" with "no bad feelings evident." The grievance committee, perhaps grateful for the company's compliance, agreed to a study of workloads, allowing the company to "immediately bring the Engineers in for the work."[86]

For the rest of 1939 and during 1940, the management met at various times with worker committees in all the mills, committees that it knew were led by TWOC affiliated employees. The committee reports showed the variety of complaints workers had over job assignments, piece rates, break time, and work discipline. Lewis, relying on the grievance system to satisfy the workers, had broken off formal negotiations with TWOC organizers in April 1939. Again uncertain of its strength, despite the hard-core union group in the Durham mill, the union turned to the NLRB for support. TWOC had been replaced by its successor, the Textile Workers Union of America (TWUA). TWUA let the issue languish in summer 1939, but in the fall it initiated a refusal-to-bargain case against the Erwin Mills. Lewis temporized by agreeing to bargain again, but nothing happened. On 11 March 1940 some union workers left the plant over what the company called a workload dispute, although the TWUA called the walkout a protest against the refusal to bargain. Once again, most workers stayed on the job, and the mills continued to produce. The union quickly called off the strike. The company played rough, and Lewis wrote to his New York labor lawyer that he had replaced over two hundred strikers with new workers. According to Lewis, the workers replaced were "a good many of the radical and dissatisfied ones," and he would be surprised "to hear anything more from the union for sometime."[87]

On 19 August 1940 NLRB field man Herbert Eby and Henry Adams of TWUA met with company officials, although Lewis absented himself. TWUA charged that Erwin Mills had refused to rehire 428 union workers and had refused to bargain for two years. Company officials reported to Lewis, "We denied both accusations." But on 19 September 1940 Lewis agreed to negotiate again if there were another certification election for the TWUA.[88] Under pressure from the NLRB, the Erwin Mills management met with TWUA negotiators on 14 January 1941. The NLRB ordered another election at the mills, which TWUA won in April 1941. After winning its first election in February 1938, the union, by winning a second time in April 1941, could once again begin bargaining in good faith with Kemp Lewis.

Amazingly, the company finally signed the written contract that Ruffin had so feared in 1937. On 3 May 1941 TWUA obtained a contract for the one mill at Cooleemee, covering about a thousand workers. The agreement permitted scientific workloads and nonbinding arbitration over workloads. There was to be no closed shop, and the contract, immensely favorable to the company, made no mention of wages. In a separate agreement, the union and the company agreed to a 2.5 cents per hour wage increase for all three mills. Negotiations also began for contracts at Durham and Erwin, but the company balked again. Eventually, in a complex set of negotiations and hearings, as well as another unsuccessful union strike at the Durham Mill, the National Defense Mediation Board mandated a contract.[89] A determined company had fought TWOC to a standstill in the bargaining process so loosely defined in the Wagner Act, and even a seeming union victory obtained little result in the end.

Battered by the forces against it — worker and industry history, the recession, unfair labor practices, the more subtle refusal to bargain, and a resurgent modernized paternalism — by early 1939 TWOC more resembled the UTW in 1935 than a militant union on the march. Solomon Barkin reported to the second meeting of the TWOC Advisory Group in January 1939 that "no new drives have been recently undertaken." The big debate concerned how to transform the TWOC into a new union, something the group, largely southern, wanted to do, even though it probably meant the end of monetary support from other CIO unions.[90] Organizers' wages had been cut by a fourth in fall 1938, and early in 1939 they were cut in half again, to fifteen dollars a week. The enthusiasm of 1937 was gone.

With organizing activity severely hampered, the major undertaking of early 1939 was a series of state-wide TWOC conferences to bolster the spirits of the committed. The North Carolina conference claimed 500 delegates from 150 mills, while the South Carolina conference reported that 400 delegates from 45 "textile centers" attended.[91] Nevertheless, in the spring the *Daily News*

Record reported that TWOC was "resting on its oars" and that scarcely "any organizing activity" was taking place.[92] Fiery speeches and resolutions of vigorous support for the Wagner Act were the order of the day, but surely among some of the delegates at those conferences there must have been a keen awareness that, despite all the New Deal activity of the last few years, the southern cotton textile industry was not significantly unionized.

During the closing months of 1938 dissension within TWOC contributed to its woes. Francis Gorman, assigned a position subordinate to Hillman, had been dissatisfied from the start. No longer the chief voice in textile organizing, Gorman discovered that he was not even a chief aide to Hillman. The CIO leadership considered Gorman a liability because of his strong association with the abortive general strike of 1934. Gorman sat out the TWOC campaign merely maintaining the old UTW office in Washington. When Hillman became ill in November 1937, Emil Rieve of the American Federation of Hosiery Workers carried on TWOC's day-to-day activities. By fall, realizing that Rieve would eventually become permanent head of TWOC and even perhaps of the union that was to replace it at some future date, Gorman decided to make a play for a return to leadership.

In a show of petty union politics and intrigue, Gorman made common cause with Joseph Sylvia in Rhode Island, the leader of the former Woolen and Worsted Federation (WWF) of the UTW. Sylvia, also shunted aside by TWOC, filed a legal suit against TWOC in spring 1938, charging that it had illegally seized WWF funds in the March 1937 TWOC-UTW agreement. When a lower court ruled in Sylvia's favor in November 1938 (the decision was reversed on appeal), Gorman determined to act. On 13 December 1938 he called the TWOC-UTW contract invalid and advised all former UTW locals that they were no longer under TWOC control. On 14 December 1938 TWOC expelled Gorman. Significantly, he and Sylvia turned to the AFL for help in remaking the UTW, and in February 1939 the dissident textile leaders had the UTW reinstated in the AFL as the United Textile Workers-AFL (UTW-AFL). This union had only 1,500 members, but it soon gained more members from some new contracts and a few defections of old UTW locals and leaders from TWOC. In 1941, though it claimed 42,000 members, the UTW-AFL was little more than a paper union.[93] It made no inroads into southern cotton textiles, and TWOC denounced Gorman as a "pathetic little 'Napoleon' without an army."[94]

The breakaway by Gorman and his few followers served to remind TWOC of the need to formalize its relationship with the old UTW locals still under its jurisdiction. Accordingly, TWOC arranged a five-day constitutional convention in Philadelphia in May 1939, and, accompanied by considerable hoopla, the 302 locals of the TWOC merged with 126 former UTW locals to form a new union, the Textile Workers Union of America (TWUA-CIO), with Emil Rieve as president. The new union claimed to represent 424,000 workers, but paid membership was probably only a small percentage of that figure.[95]

The founding of the new union officially ended the life of the Textile Workers Organizing Committee. The report which TWOC presented to the TWUA convention left little doubt that the organizing committee considered its efforts in the South to have been successful. Despite the absence of many tangible gains, TWOC looked to the future. "The 'New Deal' program," it claimed, "had planted the seed for a more liberal South. The TWOC and the entire Southern labor movement have joined to cultivate these seedlings in order to reap a really liberal industrial society, founded upon free collective bargaining." TWOC argued that "there are signs that the cotton textile employers are loosening their holds on politics, churches, thought and life in the South. In place of the cotton feudal system, slowly the new liberal South is building a genuine democracy founded on recognition of the rights of workers." And TWOC claimed it was "planted solidly in the South. Its leadership is recognized as intelligent and responsible."[96] Roy Lawrence, the Lower South director, counting workers under contract and the total employed in plants where TWOC had won bargaining elections, claimed that TWOC represented 62,000 southern workers in eighty-seven plants (he lumped the Upper South region with the Lower South). Lawrence also claimed an additional southern membership of 85,000 workers in sixty-four plants and eighty-five active locals. Lawrence's figures bore little resemblance to the figures released in a major TWOC report on 15 May 1939. He must have still been using pledgecard figures.[97] Sidney Hillman took heart in the shaky figures, however, and he told the delegates, including over one hundred southerners (a third of them women) that "by your next convention you will represent a 100 percent organized industry."[98]

The speakers at the convention paid proper homage to the New Deal's Wagner Act. Roy Lawrence refuted rumors that the southern organizers were unhappy that the Wagner Act had proved to be ineffective in accomplishing the first simple task of getting workers into a union. Anyone who maintained that, he declared, was a "plain bald-faced, unadulterated double distilled, damnable liar."[99] But John L. Lewis, ever the realist, told the assembled textile workers that the "law of the jungle obtains in the textile industry, the law of tooth and fang" and that "the only protection you have today and the only protection you will have tomorrow against that continued exploitation and against the economic and social debasement is your union, this union here."[100] Lewis understood that the success or failure of a union lay in its power to gain concession and cooperation from an employer, and nothing in the Wagner Act itself required employers to make those concessions.

At the Philadelphia convention, everyone recognized the importance of organizing the South, and on the fourth day southern delegates moved to the platform of the convention hall and staged a demonstration with songs and speeches. Plagiarizing FDR, the delegates' resolutions, offered immediately after the rally, called the organization of the South the union's "No. 1 task." But the TWUA really had few resources. In 1939, it had less than thirty active organizers throughout all of the South. Once again the textile workers turned to the CIO for help.[101] On 16 December 1939 the CIO sponsored a conference of southern union leaders to coordinate a new drive planned for early 1940.[102] The TWUA's new president, Emil Rieve, a polish-born hosiery worker from Philadelphia, was chosen to lead the organizing, which would encompass not only textiles, but rubber, oil, and steel as well. The TWUA magazine reported that Rieve and the CIO leaders did not underrate the "obstacles in the way of CIO progress in the South," but Allen Haywood, the CIO director of organization, countered, "I know we can organize the South in spite of the obstacles we have to face. We've done it in other sections. With hard work and cooperation, we can do it anywhere we try."[103]

But the new CIO plan fell flat in cotton textiles. The old problems and the old patterns endured. No new money flowed to TWUA, and the organizing force stayed the same. If anything, TWUA was more cautious than TWOC, and its organizers tried to avoid conflict with management. "The least important method of compelling recognition," the executive council stated in 1941, "was through strikes."[104] The union worked hard to develop strong grassroots locals before even initiating New Deal collective bargaining policies. "Perhaps," a union editorial said early in 1940, "we've come to depend too much on the New Deal . . . the Wagner Act is the beginning and not the end."[105] Still, the NLRB process was the only game in town. By May 1941 TWUA won by election the bargaining rights in fifty-one southern cotton mills. Contracts were secured in twenty-nine cases, but in the remaining mills, the union failed to secure a contract. TWUA faced the same tactics that had defeated TWOC. In the North, as of May 1941, TWUA had brought before the NLRB only one complaint of unfair labor practices by a cotton mill management, while in the South it brought twenty-four such cases and won in twenty of them. But the opposition took its toll on the union. Of the twenty-nine new contracts secured from 1939 to May 1941, only sixteen were still in effect on 31 May 1941. By May 1941 TWUA had only twenty-three active contracts in the southern cotton textile industry, covering 17,000 workers. Only seven of the contracts had been secured without the use of an NLRB election.[106] TWUA, like TWOC, had failed to organize the southern cotton textile industry.

In April 1939 the *Daily News Record* summed up the reasons for TWOC's defeat, listing strong employer resistance; TWOC tactical and organizational mistakes, such as reliance on the pledgecard campaign; and the uncertain ways of the Wagner Act. But the article stressed that the "real reason," the "only clear answer," was the workers' failure to receive the message. The workers were the "utter despair of the union organizers."[107] In October 1939 TWUA sent Solomon Barkin, its director of research, on a two-week tour of the South to help plan the union's 1940 drive. Barkin wrote a report that included a harsh view of the southern workers. The worker was a "small-town, suspicious, individual" who was "extremely provincial — completely isolated," knowing only "his own mill." The southern workers, who lived in "hovels," were unconcerned over increasing their wages and creating "high standards." They were, to Barkin, "explosive and unpredictable." He reported that "building unions" in such an environment was a "community problem."[108] Barkin's solution was something he called a "demonstration center," but the strategy he suggested was really nothing more than the old TWOC strategy of 1938 — work in a few strong places to build a record of using collective bargaining to achieve tangible improvements and so demonstrate the benefits of unionism.

The policy, which represented about all the union could hope to do with what it had to work with, failed TWUA as it had TWOC. Still, in some unintended ways, TWOC and TWUA helped the workers. Their presence caused southern owners to give more attention to improving wages and working conditions, as a means of warding off union penetration. Even the stretch out slowed down, or at least companies became more adept at explaining workload changes. Unlike the cycles of union failure in 1929–31 and in 1933–34, the CIO cycle that began in 1937 never did end completely. TWOC's northern victories created a much stronger national union, and in the South TWOC was able to maintain at least a presence, if a feeble one. No matter how the final balance is calculated, however, no shining new day had come to the cotton textile workers of the South. Everything in the textile experience of the South in the 1930s — weak union bases, the structure of the industry, strong employer opposition, leadership problems, community hostility, and the heritage of past failures — conspired to keep the textile workers unorganized.

"We propose to go slowly, cautiously"

THE HOLLOW VICTORY OF THE FLSA, 1938–41

As the textile unionists struggled to make the New Deal collective bargaining policy work in their favor, they also placed much trust in another New Deal initiative, the movement to establish a minimum wage and a maximum hour standard. These had been the most popular provisions of the defunct NRA codes. By the Wagner Act, Congress had reestablished the right to collective bargaining, but only if union efforts could achieve it. The Fair Labor Standards Act of 1938 (FLSA) was a companion piece designed to give legal currency to the heart of the codes. The Democratic Party platform of 1936 endorsed such legislation and, after the New Deal victory over the Supreme Court's conservatives in 1937, its new constitutional feasibility led to legislative action. Unlike the case of the Wagner Act, the administration, led by Frances Perkins, was an early instigator and backer of this legislation.[1]

The bill was introduced into Congress 24 May 1937 by Sen. Hugo Black of Alabama and Rep. William F. Connery of Massachusetts. It quickly gathered the expected opposition from employer groups and conservatives, but it also drew outright opposition or only lukewarm support from a divided labor movement, particularly from the AFL trade unions. Nevertheless, through the long battle, Roosevelt remained a staunch supporter. Although the Senate passed the bill in 1937, it took a renewed effort by Roosevelt and the bill's backers to move the bill out of the House Rules Committee, where southern conservatives had blocked it, to a winning House vote in spring 1938. The final bill, much revised from its earlier simple version by a conference committee, was signed by the President on 25 June 1938.[2] Pleased, FDR took to the radio to categorize the FLSA as, with the exception of the Social Security Act, "the most far-reaching, far-sighted program for the benefit of the workers ever adopted here or in any other country."[3]

Some southern congressmen attacked the bill vigorously. They feared that higher labor standards would handicap the development of southern industry by removing the South's great advantage, cheap labor.[4] "The cries of anguish that were heard in the halls of Congress," said labor historian Sigmund Uminski, "came from the hearts of the southern congressmen. No-one needed to cross their palms with silver, they fought for what they believed in, and they believed the South must have factories."[5] "Cotton" Ed Smith roared to the Senate, "Everyone knows that the main object of this bill is, by human legislation, to overcome the splendid gifts of God to the South."[6] Southerners defended low southern wages as the key to eventually ending southern poverty by creating a broader industrial base. C.C. Gilbert of the Southern States Industrial Council wrote to Democratic Party chairman James A. Farley, grousing that nearly all the 17,000 manufacturers in the South opposed the bill because it could "cripple the industrial South beyond repair."[7] Southern congressmen even tried to incorporate into the law a differential in wages and hours favorable to the South, but they failed, in the face of FDR's strong opposition. The strongest southern protest came from the lumber and agricultural industries. Although the law exempted agricultural workers, southern agriculturalists feared a future extension of the law to include the farm. Southern opposition, however, was neither unanimous nor overpowering. In 1938, the Gallup Poll showed 56 percent of the southern public in support of the FLSA, and in congressional votes on the bill, the southern delegation often split.[8] The FLSA passed with comfortable margins, as the last major piece of New Deal legislation.

The southern cotton textile owners, who still enjoyed a favorable wage differential compared with remaining nonsouthern mills, had mixed feelings about the FLSA. Donald Comer of Alabama declared at the congressional hearings on the bill that he had long favored "federal legislation, fixing by enactment minimum wages, maximum hours, and a minimum age."[9] Most southern manufacturers, remembering the NRA cotton code, agreed with Comer that minimum wage and maximum hour standards were desirable. But the great majority, having long deserted the partnership table of the New Deal, opposed federal legislation that would establish such a standard. They hoped to achieve stability, insofar as wages and hours were concerned, by voluntary agreements within the industry, in a romantic return to the 1920s. Therefore, although they opposed the bill as federally mandated regulation, many cotton textile manufacturers were careful to admit the desirability of minimum labor standards agreed upon by the industry and voluntarily achieved. Only a few thundered against the bill as violently as William Anderson, who declared it an assault on personal property and the "worst piece of legislation that has been introduced since the New Deal became popular."[10]

Claudius Murchison, president of the CTI, reflected the more ambivalent attitude of most owners when he testified at the hearings. In his opinion, the FLSA was "a disillusionment for those whose hopes were high. It is a sheer fantasy for those who would be realistic." But Murchison said that "within its broad, monstrous, lugubrious form it holds the germ of economic sanity and progress. It is my hope and prayer that this germ may be segregated from its cancerous surroundings."[11] The cotton manufacturers did not fight the new government intrusion with a no-holds-barred attitude, and eventually the CTI, influenced by the New England mills which strongly wanted it, supported the bill.

TWOC supported the bill as warmly as it had the Wagner Act. Sidney Hillman, labor's most ferocious fighter for the bill, informed the joint hearings that he considered the bill a "companion measure" to the Wagner Act and claimed that "no more important labor legislation has ever been introduced into Congress."[12] A little remained of the old union fear that a legal minimum wage would interfere with collective bargaining over wages, but since the proposed minimum wage in the bill was to be considerably below the average textile wage, the fear was not strong enough to weaken textile labor enthusiasm for the measure. Speculation centered on the possibility that a significant percentage of textile workers would be affected by the law.

As passed, the FLSA established minimum wage and maximum hour requirements applicable to all employees engaged in interstate commerce, with certain specific exemptions. The act provided for the creation, within the Department of Labor, of a Wage and Hour Division to administer the law. The FLSA established a legal minimum wage of forty cents per hour, to be achieved through gradual steps: the legal minimum was to be twenty-five cents per hour on 24 October 1938, thirty on 24 October 1939, and forty by 23 October 1945. The hours provision of the act established a maximum work week, beyond which time-and-a-half was to be paid. A forty-four-hour work week was to be the legal standard on 24 October 1938, forty-two hours on 24 October 1939, and forty by 23 October 1940. It was made illegal to use children under sixteen to manufacture goods for interstate commerce.[13] The tentative, gradual nature of the legislation has often been overlooked, and the FLSA has become so widely accepted as to be considered almost a permanent fixture of the American experience by people have who forgotton the long struggle to achieve its fundamental goals.

The initial application of the FLSA provisions in October 1938 resulted in an increase of pay for approximately 300,000 workers who received less than 20 cents per hour and shorter hours for approximately 1.4 million workers who worked longer than forty-four hours a week.[14] Approximately 200,000 children were excluded from the labor market. Isador Lubin, commissioner of the Bureau of Labor Statistics, stated that nearly 35,000 cotton textile workers, most in the South and most in smaller, more rural mills, received pay increases on 24 October 1938.[15] The average textile wage at the time was 38.3 cents per hour in the South, while it was 44.6 cents in the North. Because of the shift system, the forty-hour week was already standard in most of the industry by 1938. Union support of the FLSA paid off handsomely for a small number of the least skilled workers, but only organization could bring higher wages for the rest. Nevertheless, for the first time a firm and lasting floor, protected by federal law, had been established.

Hard bargaining for the bottom wage, however, still lay ahead. The provision for a forty-cent-per-hour standard by 1945 represented the minimum statutory requirement. In an effort to achieve the forty-cent objective as soon as possible, the 1938 law directed the administrator of the Wage and Hour Division of the Department of Labor to appoint committees for specific industries, to determine the feasibility of a minimum wage above twenty-five cents. The committees, representing labor, management, and the public, could recommend a minimum higher than that specified in the FLSA, as long as it did not exceed forty cents per hour. The committees were to be appointed with due regard for the geographical regions in which an industry was located, and the wage and hour administrator was to give the committees any information gathered on wage problems in the industry, as well as legal and clerical help.

The industry committee system recalled the old code days in Washington in summer and fall 1933. The committees could hold hearings and perform other functions necessary to their work. After its investigation, a committee could issue a wage recommendation to the wage and hour administrator. Upon receiving wage recommendations from a committee, the administrator had to give due notice to the industry to allow interested parties an opportunity to object. If, after hearing any objections, the administrator approved the recommendation, the Wage and Hour Division was to take steps to put the wage increase into effect. If, following industry objections, the administrator disagreed with the recommendation of the industry committee, the wage proposal could be referred back to the same committee or passed on to a new committee. But the administrator could not issue a wage order that departed substantially from the recommendation of the industry committee or that was in excess of the forty-cent standard. The industry committee and the administrator were also charged with the responsibility of arriving at wage rates that would not curtail employment significantly or give a competitive advantage to any units in an industry. Both government and management were to have recourse to federal courts for grievances.[16] The procedures were much better thought out and clearer than those developed in the hectic days of the First New Deal.

Primarily concerned with minimum wages and maximum hours, the FLSA did not deal extensively with the problem of collective bargaining. The FLSA fell primarily into the category of protective labor legislation, but certain clauses in the act, as well as the general administrative procedure defined in the law, influenced labor-management relations. The act specifically mentioned collective bargaining and collective agreements in its references to exemptions from the forty-hour week and to fixing minimum wages above twenty-five cents per hour. Of even greater influence in labor relations was the establishment of the industry committees. Organized labor representatives on the committees would help to create and maintain the presence that labor unions had won with such difficulty in the 1930s. In the work of these committees, employer and employee representatives engaged in what amounted to collective bargaining on something approaching a national scale. It was collective bargaining carried on under government auspices (something not even contemplated in the Wagner Act deliberations), and with a definite, albeit limited, purpose. The process afforded a framework within which employer and employee representatives could meet and discuss their industrial problems together. Unfortunately for the textile union, the bargaining had only a limited goal, and although the result could affect thousands of workers, most of them were not in the union or even aware of the union's work. The union, despite its hopes, would not be able to create a larger base in the industry because of the new act.

In the bargaining to come, southern cotton textile manufacturers still grumbled over the law. As always, David Clark, the editor of the *Textile Bulletin*, voiced the extreme opposition: "The day the Wage-Hour law is held constitutional by a packed U.S. Supreme Court," he said in December 1938, "is the day that will mark the end of States Rights in the United States and will bring near the end of our form of government and the establishment of a Dictator."[17] The southern manufacturers saw the law as a punitive measure enacted by northern interests to halt the development of industries like southern cotton textiles and to place them at a competitive disadvantage. John Henry Cheatham, ACMA president in April 1939, spoke of the act as "sectional selfishness" and called it "a creation of the professional uplifters" which had been "seized upon by the politicians North of the Mason-Dixon Line and passed in an effort to hamstring Southern industry and draw the advantage back to their industries."[18] As the government implemented the FLSA in fall 1938, opposition from southern cotton mill manufacturers grew.

INDUSTRY COMMITTEE NUMBER ONE

By mid-August 1938 Frances Perkins had put together the new Wage and Hour Division in her department, and FDR appointed Elmer F. Andrews, a government bureaucrat thought to be a judicious man, to head the department. Andrews, trying to calm employer fears, stated his desire to enforce the act fairly and with as little coercion as possible. "We do not propose to surround it with panic psychology," he declared. "We propose to go slowly, cautiously, and as surely as we can."[19] As Andrews set to work, there was immediate speculation in Washington that the gigantic textile industry, with its labor-intensive mills, its sprawling structure, and its history of a strong NRA code, would be one of the first industries to be examined by the Wage and Hour Division. As early as 8 July 1938 the labor commissioners of the southeastern states had assembled at Columbia, South Carolina, to ask that the FLSA be applied quickly to the textile industry. In a belated reaction to the 1937–38 recession and with TWOC crippled, many southern mills had cut wages by as much as 12 percent. Although the wage cuts were soon abandoned in the fall, with the quick rebound from the recession, the commissioners argued that a minimum wage was needed to dampen "unrest among the textile workers of the Southeast, causing strikes and threats of strikes, and endangering the general welfare."[20]

On 17 August Andrews announced that the textile industry would, indeed, be the first industry for which a committee would be formed. This time the cotton textile industry was to be lumped with the silk and synthetic fiber industries. Andrews charged the committee to consider a wage minimum that might be more equitable than either the stated minimum of twenty-five cents per hour or the thirty cents due to become effective in October 1939. By 13 September 1938 Andrews had appointed a tripartite committee of twenty-one members, with jurisdiction over any firm spinning and weaving cotton, silk, flax, jute, synthetic fibers, and designated mixtures of these fibers with wool or animal fiber other than silk. Andrews appointed Donald M. Nelson, vice-president of Sears, Roebuck and Company, as chairperson. Besides Nelson, the public representatives were Fred Lazarus and E.L. Foshee, nontextile businessmen, George W. Taylor and P.O. Davis, academics, and George Fort Milton, a Chattanooga newspaper publisher. The southern manufacturers were represented by Robert R. West, John H. Cheatham, Robert Chapman, and Charles Cannon, while New England had three representatives. Andrews appointed seven labor representatives, five of them TWOC members led by Sidney Hillman. Two southern-born organizers, Roy Lawrence and Paul Christopher, were on the list.[21] Andrews had made sure that the union would at last have its chance to bargain collectively. The committee, quickly designated Industry Committee Number One, suggested in its first meeting that the woolen industry, because of its complexity and differences, be given a separate committee; Andrews agreed.

Despite their fears, industrialists greeted Industry Committee Number One with the decorum commensurate with its expected lack of importance. In the North, less than 1 percent of the workers was affected by the 25-cent-per-hour minimum. In the South, on the other hand, 11 percent of the workers earned less than 27.5 cents per hour, although the average wage was well above that figure. The Bureau of Labor Statistics estimated that the mere increase of the minimum to 30 cents per hour would involve an increase of no more than one-half cent in average hourly earnings for all workers.[22] In October 1938 William McLaurine, ACMA secretary-treasurer, declared that, as far as he knew, not a single mill would curtail its operations because of the FLSA.[23] Southern owners calmly watched and waited. But Francis Gorman, in fall 1938 still UTW president and still associated with TWOC, publicly demanded that the committee immediately grant a 40-cent-per-hour industry minimum. This goal he shared with Sidney Hillman, leader of the labor delegation on the committee.[24]

Industry Committee Number One held its first meeting on 11 October. The bargaining activity was really among the public members, the New England manufacturers, and the labor members. The southern manufacturers were committed to a maximum of 30 cents per hour. The union asked for 40 cents, expected 35, and would go no lower than 32.5 cents per hour.[25] By the time it made its wage recommendation to Andrews in March 1939, the committee or its subcommittees had held some twenty-two separate conferences. The committee staff gathered data on the textile industry from many sources, principally through hearings in which a variety of interested persons and organizations made their views known.

On 21 March 1939, after spending more than six months studying the testimony and facts submitted to it, the committee, by a close vote, recommended a 32.5 cent-per-hour minimum wage for the industry. At the time the minimum was 25 cents, mandated by the FLSA to rise to 30 cents on 24 October.[26] In its publications the union had played the meetings up as a great breakthrough in collective bargaining. "Indirectly," the union said, Industry Committee Number One "brought about a round-table conference between labor and management for the first time in the history of the textile industry, on a national scale. More of these national conferences may take place, with collective bargaining expected as a national consequence."[27] The union had claimed as a TWOC victory an interim decision by the committee to refuse the manufacturers' request that employees learning their jobs be exempted from the 25-cent minimum.[28] Although the union saw 32.5 cents as "far from ideal," it was called "an immediate gain for thousands of textile workers who are employed in the 20 cent level." But worker indifference to the victory soon had the union pushing hard for an immediate rise to 40 cents.[29] In July 1939 the new TWUA bitterly noted that the "textile magnates" would "not think of keeping their dogs or their horses in the low style and comfort that 32-½ cents can bring."[30]

On 22 May the committee formally submitted a majority report to Andrews, advocating the 32.5-cent-per-hour minimum. The committee majority estimated that the wage costs of the southern textile industry would be increased by 6 to 9 percent, but that was viewed as moderate enough to be absorbed by the industry or by its marketing agencies without unduly affecting competitive conditions within the industry. The committee majority also concluded that different minimum wage rates for different regions were undesirable and unjustified.[31]

The six southern business-minded members of the industry committee — P.O. Davis and E.L. Foshee, plus the four cotton manufacturers, Charles Cannon, Robert H. Chapman, John H. Cheatham, and Robert R. West — presented Andrews with a minority report asking for a 30-cent minimum. They claimed that southern industry was underrepresented on the committee and that the majority report failed to consider adequately the full economic consequences of its minimum wage recommendation, including closed plants, unemployment, and higher-priced goods for the public. Although the minority report did not ask directly for a regional differential in wages, its remarks left no doubt that it believed such a differential would be justified. In effect, the bargaining had come down to a choice between 30 cents and 32.5 cents per hour for the lowest-paid workers in the lowest-paid major industrial worker group in America.

Andrews opted for the majority report, and on 24 May 1939 he scheduled hearings for June and July on the recommendation.[32] Once again the snail's pace of government bureaucracy worked to the industry's advantage. William Anderson had written Committee member Robert R. West, president of Dan River Mills, on 24 September 1938, urging him to gather the southerners together in a caucus and delay. "Our only salvation," he said, "is to postpone all these things for awhile in the hope that this frenzy of legislation to tell everybody how to run their business will wear itself out before business is ruined by legislation." On 1 October 1938 he told West to do nothing the law did not compel.[33] The Anderson strategy, conscious or not, had unfolded. Throughout 1938–39, as the industry paid only a 25-cent minimum and the day approached when it would have to pay 30 cents, it was faced with only a 2.5-cent increase over that figure.

The ACMA board of governors met on 31 May and formally declared its opposition to the 32.5-cent proposal.[34] Secretary-treasurer William McLaurine now predicted that the increased cost of production resulting from the wage increase would cause some small southern mills to shut down, and he estimated that twenty-five to thirty thousand workers would lose their jobs if Andrews approved the recommended rate.[35] The southern manufacturers, however, were not uniformly intense in their opposition to the suggested rate. Many executives of large firms, which already paid averages well above the federal minimum, realized that the recommended minimum would affect them only slightly, if at all. Like McLaurine, however, they believed that many small mills would close, and they were still ideologically opposed to a federally-mandated minimum wage. Their opposition was not as strident as might have been expected, however, because they believed the minimum would lessen cut-throat competition to some degree.[36] Publicly, though, the southerners presented an unbroken front of protest. The few remaining northern cotton manufacturers urged Andrews to adopt the proposed minimum as a "step toward equalizing costs between the two sections and stabilizing the industry."[37]

Unlike the rushed code hearings of July 1933, the 1939 wage hearings proceeded at a leisurely pace. In late June and July Andrews heard testimony for five days in Washington and nine days in Atlanta, followed by two more days in Washington. The Washington hearings dealt with textile industries other than cotton and with the northern cotton textile industry. The hearings in Atlanta were devoted almost exclusively to examining the anticipated effect of the minimum wage on the southern cotton textile industry. A parade of witnesses in support and in opposition appeared before Andrews and Committee Number One. Many leading southern manufacturers, including Charles Cannon of Cannon Mills and Kemp P. Lewis, president of Erwin Mills and the current ACMA president, presented their negative opinions. New England interests supporting Andrews, led by Russel T. Fisher of the National Association of Cotton Manufacturers and Robert Amory of Nashua Mills, also testified in Atlanta. TWUA, which had replaced TWOC as the workers' representative, produced a number of pro-minimum wage witnesses, led by TWUA president Emil Rieve and his chief southern lieutenant, Roy Lawrence. Interested organizations also sent representatives to the hearings. For example, the liberal Southern Policy Committee, which supported the proposed 32.5-cent minimum, sent Herman C. Nixon, a political scientist, and Frank Graham, president of the University of North Carolina. The conservative Southern States Industrial Council presented testimony in opposition to the minimum wage recommendation, with the conservative economist from Vanderbilt University, Gustavus (Gus) Dyer, attacking the economic thought behind the very concept of minimum wage legislation.[38]

Andrews received constant pressure from southerners during and after the hearings urging him to reject the recommended minimum. The ACMA complained immediately after the exhaustive hearings that the industry committee had "failed to investigate thoroughly" the economic conditions in the industry.[39] On 1 August a congressional delegation from the southern cotton states even went to President Roosevelt to lobby him to intervene and ask Andrews to set aside the 32.5-cent minimum.[40] The President politely refused, and on 13 September 1939 Andrews announced that he had approved the minimum wage recommendation of Industry Committee Number One, to become effective on 24 October 1939, the same date the FSLA would have required a 30-cent minimum.[41] The next spring, in his report to the ACMA, Kemp Lewis complained that the "whole truth of the matter is that the law was such [as] to give the South little opportunity to secure an unbiased decision."[42]

TWUA treated the approval as a great victory. It contended that 125,000 to 175,000 cotton textile workers had their pay raised as a result of the order the union had bargained for (the figures were wildly inflated).[43] The union quickly called for a new push toward 40 cents, its original goal when it entered the year-long negotiations. During the year Andrews had formed a new textile committee, Industry Committee Number Twenty-five. In April 1941 the new committee unanimously recommended a further increase of the minimum wage to 37.5 cents per hour, which was approved on 8 June 1941 by Phillip Fleming, Andrews's replacement as administrator of the Wage and Hour Division. The new minimum became effective on 30 June.[44] The rate recommendation went unopposed, and no public hearings were held, although Fleming sent out investigators to interview mill executives. The booming prosperity of the industry apparently lessened the owners' drive to resist. By April

1942 the minimum wage in the southern cotton textile industry had been raised to 40 cents per hour, and before the end of 1942 the National War Labor Board had brought the minimum in a majority of textile plants to 47.5 cents, rendering almost comic in retrospect the 1939 struggle to get an extra 2.5 cents per hour.[45]

Appropriately enough, cotton textile manufacturers would lead the legal struggle against the FLSA.[46] In 1939, three mills—the Appenaugh and Sanders Mills of Jackson, Mississippi, and the better-known Opp Cotton Mills of Opp, Alabama—obtained state court injunctions against the enforcement of the 32.5-cent-per-hour minimum ordered by Elmer Andrews. The cases came together before the Supreme Court, and on 3 February 1941, in *Opp Cotton Mills, Inc. v. Administrator*, the Court upheld the constitutionality of the FLSA and administrator Andrews' order.[47] The permanent, inescapable impact of New Deal labor policy had been to put a floor under wages and a cap on the hours of the normal working day, the first objectives of the almost-forgotten cotton code.

The losing struggle over the federally-mandated minimum wage had stirred the southern cotton textile owners. They passionately believed that the minimum wage would drive smaller, inefficient mills out of business and create unemployment. They linked enactment of the minimum to northern envy of the tremendous advantage given southern mills by the regional differential in average wages. This differential had dropped during the minimum-wage NRA period to an all-time low of 18 percent, only to widen to 22 percent just before the passage of the FLSA.[48] The owners argued that southern workers were less productive than northern workers, that lower living costs justified lower wages, that freight-rate discrimination drove up competitive costs, and that the advantages of paternalistic services and the mill villages should be figured into worker compensation rates.[49] Just as passionately, the union lauded what it thought would be the great gains of the minimum wage, arguing that no mills would close, that the slight rise in labor costs easily could be absorbed by the mills' profit margins, that southern labor was just as productive and skilled as northern labor, and that nothing in the abhorrent paternalistic system justified lower southern wages. The real difference between North and South, said the union, was in the workers' standard of living.[50]

The employers really had little to fear and the union little to praise, given what had actually happened. Bargaining over the minimum set by federal law had not produced either the rationale or the climate for industrywide collective bargaining on any other issues. No southern mills closed because of the FLSA. Indeed, the industry expanded in the defense boom, and as late as 1945 the wage differential between North and South still stood at 14 percent.[51] The FLSA played a part in increasing the total wage outlay of the industry in the 1940s and 1950s, although the cost was quickly absorbed and passed on to consumers. Historian George Tindall found it difficult "to separate the effects of the Fair Labor Standards Act from other influences."[52] That was certainly true of the impact of the FLSA on the cotton textile industry and its workers.

From 1935 to 1941 the Wagner Act and the FLSA, linchpins of the Second New Deal, shaped labor-management relations. In the North, new industrial unions combined the Wagner Act with their own organizational power to increase their numbers and economic strength. Despite the best efforts of the textile union, however, the nature of the industry, the temper of the owners, the culture of the workers, and the different milieu of the South in which unions had to operate made the Wagner Act, with its impartial, drawn-out process less than a sturdy tool for achieving unionization and its rewards of higher wages, better working conditions, and higher individual status. The FLSA effectively put a floor under wages, but textile workers were not the worst-paid southern workers. The act did nothing to advance unionism. Its impact on southern cotton textile workers' lives and fortunes was slight.

"The union's slow. They're mighty slow"
EPILOGUE

Since the 1930s, the cotton textile industry has changed in many ways. Many of the mills, old even in the 1930s, still stand, and the looms and spindles still do their work, but most of the old core mills have new, modern buildings surrounding them. Family ownership, although still important, has often given way to that of corporations, widely held. Companies have also broken out of the trap of the old marketing system, and many do everything from the production of gray goods to finishing and converting under their own brand names. Some even manufacture apparel. It is even difficult to see anymore the clear demarcation of a southern cotton textile industry, once a matter of pride to owners such as Donald Comer. Companies manufacture sophisticated blends of cotton and synthetic fibers; single companies span the gamut of fiber production. Even though the textile industry, in comparison to other basic industries, is still the province of relatively small companies with very small segments of the market, three giants—the Burlington Mills, the largest textile company in the world; the J.P. Stevens Company, not even a southern company in the 1930s; and Dan River Mills—produce one-third of all the basic textile output in the country.

In the 1970s, the industry, facing the stiffest international competition in its history, benefited from a new technological explosion. Although the basic production stages of yarn and cloth remained the same, the mills became more fully automated, eliminating some of the steps in which workers tended machines or handled the product. In the process, machine speeds and productive capacities reached new highs. The result was greater efficiency with fewer workers, and greater profits. In short, the industry had become more capital intensive.[1] Whereas in the 1930s, breaking the bales of cotton and sending the fibers to the first straightening step, or picking, took hard, dirty work, the modern breaking room is often totally automated, with the cotton handled by big pincers, sophisticated blending machines, and efficient conveyers, and with one worker replacing ten. And, in the only step eliminated altogether since the 1930s, the fiber moves straight from the breaking room through a completely automatic picking system to the card machines, on its way to spinning.

Against great odds the industry has survived, and indeed, in some business cycles it has prospered, despite repeated predictions of its demise. The 1940s were exceptionally profitable years, followed by some lean years in the late 1950s before a rebound in the general prosperity of the 1960s. The 1970s were years of company consolidation and technological improvement, in which the survivors operated sound businesses and made reasonable, although lower, profits, More significantly, the industry stayed in the southern Piedmont, in the same towns, although some of the smaller cities like Charlotte, North Carolina, and Greenville, South Carolina, became metropolitan areas. Other textile industries joined cotton textiles and the apparel industry to create a vast new textile belt from North Carolina to Alabama.

There have been few modern studies of contemporary textile workers in the South, and the economic integration of the textile industry, the modernization and the mobility of the workers, and the interchangeability of workers from one kind of textile mill to another has destroyed the very concept of a southern cotton textile worker. The change was beginning in the 1930s; it is an absolute fact in the 1980s.

At the same time, there has been some remarkable continuity between the workers in the mills of the 1930s and those of the 1980s, despite the modernization and change in culture in the intervening years. That was the major point made by Glenn Gilman in his well-known 1956 work on the industry. The mill villages as such are gone, but the houses remain and children from the same families still enter the mills where their parents work, although Sun Belt industrialization has offered members of traditional textile families new industrial opportunities outside the mills. The last major study of cotton textile workers was John Kenneth Moreland's *Millways of Kent* (1958). To him worker culture still looked much like "the older patterns of mill life" described earlier in this book.[2] In 1964, in a study of several different groups of industrial workers in America, Robert Blauner focused a chapter on southern cotton textile workers. Subtitled "Integration Without Freedom in a Traditional Community," the chapter continued an older theme in descriptions of the workers.[3] Also in 1964, in a study of North and South Carolina workers in the twentieth century, Billy Ray Skelton concluded "that workers in these two states have rejected unionization more so than any other workers in the remainder of the country."[4] Little had changed in those states where the largest number of workers are textile workers. In 1980 North Carolina, at 6.5 percent, had the lowest percentage of union workers in its workforce of any state in the nation, while South Carolina followed at 6.7 percent.[5]

A recent study by Joseph McDonald of the tufted textile industry (the carpet and rug industry) in and around Dalton, Georgia, sketched a profile of workers in the 1970s that bore a remarkable resemblance to that of basic cotton textile workers in the 1930s. Workers in both periods were family centered, suspicious and distrustful of unions, relatively unskilled, poorly paid, minimally educated, low in self-esteem, and alienated, with a feeling of class only in the crudest sense of the market economy. In short, McDonald found "the formation of paternalistic-deferential class relations" that created a definite barrier to unionism.[6] On the whole, workers in the textile industry remained what they had been in the 1930s—machine tenders who were paid one of the lowest industrial wages in the country, and who found their identity and sense of purpose in self-made communities that were at best indifferent and at worst downright hostile to unionism.[7]

The only major change has been the entry of black workers into the mills, an effect of the civil rights era. In many mills black workers constitute 25 to 45 percent of the labor force. Although the blacks, with their unique history, have been far more receptive to unionism, they have not yet proven a revolutionary factor in labor relations. Certainly their presence in the textile industry represents a significant difference between the workforce of the 1980s and that of the 1930s.

Modern mill management consistently employs strategies to keep workers happy and enhance their attachment to the company. For example, in the January 1984 edition of the *Cannon News*, the Cannon Mills newspaper, a lead article reported a $200 million capital equipment program, stressing in photographs the importance of the *people* operating the company's massive new machines. The issue was filled with photos of workers, with only one page devoted to supervisory activities. The paper highlighted the company's role in creating a new $20 million mall in the town of Kannapolis, still company owned. According to David Murdock, chairman of the board, the project's goal was to "to build a city that people will drive hundreds of miles to see." The *Cannon News* emphasized teamwork and the company's appreciation of good, loyal workers. Rather than hiding behind barbed-wire fences and guard houses, the company has a popular tour for tourists which it advertises widely. Cannon Mills has never had a union local certified. The companies of the Piedmont no longer speak of paternalism and welfare services, but in the most modern ways, the companies contrive to maintain peace on the shop floor.

Union history since the 1930s is a study in bleak failure. TWUA reached its peak in the 1940s, when perhaps 20 percent of the total textile workers in the South worked under bargaining contracts. The union adroitly used the War Labor Board to force owners to conclude the previously interminable contracting process, and after the war TWUA enthusiastically participated in Operation Dixie, the CIO's broad organizing drive in the South from 1946 to 1952. But Operation Dixie failed to hold the wartime gains in cotton textiles. The old barriers worked to keep unionization to a bare minimum, and the companies were still able to defy the unions, despite the New Deal's labor revolution.[8]

In 1956 the Deering-Milliken Company closed a mill in Darlington, South

Carolina, a day after the workers had opted for an NLRB certification election and TWUA by a forty-vote margin. Although the case moved up through the NLRB's long bureaucratic process and eventually went to the Supreme Court, where Deering-Milliken was judged to have "chilled" unionism by closing the plant, the company kept the case alive for two decades without incurring serious penalty.[9] In addition to the humiliation of the Deering-Milliken case, TWUA also lost a widely-publicized strike at Henderson, North Carolina, in 1958–60, into which it had poured considerable prestige and money. By 1960 TWUA had lost half its northern strength and in 1964 had only approximately 13,000 southern members.[10] Earlier, in 1952, the union had suffered an internal struggle for power, similar to the Gorman-TWOC split in 1938. George Baldanzi, the vice-president for southern organizing, joined the UTW and took many southern locals with him. In 1973 TWUA reported a membership of 174,000, but that was mostly in northern textile plants. In 1976 TWUA and the Amalgamated Clothing Workers Union, recognizing the integrated nature of the industry, merged to form the Amalgamated Clothing and Textile Workers Union (ACTWU). The new union claimed to be the eleventh largest union in the country, with a membership of 500,000. The UTW had about 50,000 members. But even in the year of the merger, a southern ACTWU organizer, Bruce Reynor, emphasized the problems of southern organization rather than the possibilities of the future, arguing that the South had to be "broken" before the "dark yesterday" could be turned into a "brighter tomorrow."[11]

The most striking continuity has been the continuing inability of the union to use New Deal labor legislation as an effective tool to further its work. In 1979 the movie "Norma Rae" dramatized an NLRB election in a cotton textile mill. The setting was authentic—a functioning cotton mill in a small southern town. Sally Field, who received both the Oscar and the New York Film Critics' Best Actress Award for her role, starred as Norma Rae, a young southern textile worker, widowed, with two children, and living with her mother and father, who were also cotton textile workers. She lived a life without order or direction. The film's action centered on the efforts of a fast-talking young Jewish labor organizer from New York, Reuben Marshasky, to bring unionism to the cotton mill which dominated the town. Norma Rae became a devoted member of the union's drive to gain an NLRB election. In the process of unionization, Norma Rae developed self-reliance and a sense of her own worth and moved to put her personal life in order, even though her new husband Sonny remained skeptical of the union and her activities. The most dramatic scene in the movie occurred when, after the management detected her efforts to copy an antiunion company statement off the bulletin board, she was ordered out of the plant. She refused to go, and amid the deafening roar of the machines, she stood on a table displaying a crudely lettered sign that read "Union." Slowly, one by one, the workers stopped their machines to acknowledge her protest. Norma Rae was hustled out of the plant by the local police, but her protest and the sacrifice of her job were not in vain. The movie ended triumphantly with an election victory by the workers and the chants of unionism in the plant as Norma Rae listened outside, smiling.[12]

Reality can be more interesting than fiction. "Norma Rae," filmed in Opelika, Alabama, was based on the true story of Crystal Lee Jordan, a worker at a J.P. Stevens towel mill in Roanoke Rapids, North Carolina, a textile mill town that inhabitants like to boast is "ninety miles from nowhere." Jordan's life had many more twists and turns than Norma Rae's, though the movie and the reality have a rough similarity. Born Crystal Lee Pulley in 1940 in Roanoke Rapids, in a mill family (her father, mother, and siblings worked in the mills), Jordan graduated from high school and had a variety of jobs at one time or another. She actually worked only for short periods of time in mills, and her principal job in her last stint had been folding towels in packaging, rather than working in the spinning room as the film heroine did. But Jordan did indeed become a participant in TWUA's 1973 drive, led by the Industrial Union Department of the AFL-CIO, to organize the J.P. Stevens plant. Since 1963 the union had won only one election at a Stevens plant and had never won a contract. Working with organizer Eli Zivkovich, who headquartered at the Motel Dixie, Jordan, who had never liked to work in the mills, was caught up in unionism. "You know," she told her biographer, "cotton mill workers are known as trash by some, and I knew this union was the only way we could have our own voice, make ourselves better."[13]

On 30 May 1973 the famous scene of the union sign actually occurred. The company had posted a notice which implied that black workers wanted to support the union so they could take control of the jobs at the expense of the white workers. Jordan was seen copying it for Zivkovich and was ordered to stop. She refused and, in the ensuing argument, did stand on her folding table with the union sign. Some fellow workers, with no machines to stop, gave her the peace sign; and she left with the police, thinking they were taking her home, only to find herself charged with disorderly conduct. TWUA, although somewhat leery of her by then, hired Jordan as a fulltime organizer. Within months her already troubled marriage fell apart, as her husband, distraught over her activities, ordered her out of the house. "That union," he told her, "ain't done nothing for you, and it ain't done nothing for us, and I want you out of it starting now or you can get out of this house."[14] She moved to Burlington, North Carolina, to look for work in the mill there. After she left, the election drive continued at the mill, and the union, in a stunning victory, won 1,685 to 1,448.

Jordan's published biography ended there, but the election was certainly not the end of TWUA's push to bring a union to the plant she had worked in. The election settled nothing. J.P. Stevens, a textile firm founded in 1813 in New England to manufacture cotton, came South in 1946. As of 1978 it had eighty-three separate plants, sixty-three of them in the Carolinas, and ranked second only to Burlington Mills as the largest textile company in the country. TWUA's decision in 1963 to target the firm as the focus of a southern drive touched off a bitter struggle, as Stevens defied the nation's labor laws and, except for the Roanoke victory and one earlier, defeated the union consistently in mill after mill, ignoring or skirting adverse NLRB and court orders. Jordan's Roanoke victory turned out to be no more than a small skirmish in an infinitely larger contest. By 1975 the company had accumulated over fifteen major NLRB unfair labor practice cases, as well as five contempt-of-court citations.[15] The Roanoke election did not faze the corporation; it just refused to reach agreement even after four years of bargaining. In 1977 the Roanoke Rapids episode became just another NLRB unfair labor practice case for the company. Stevens had developed the tactics of delay to a fine art.

In its first major decision, in June 1976 the new ACTWU started a national boycott of the numerous J.P. Stevens products, a boycott quickly supported by the AFL-CIO and many liberal activist groups. The legal vise also began to close on the company as well. In March 1978, for the first time in its history, the NLRB requested a federal district court to issue a nationwide injunction against the company. Stevens got the NLRB to lift the injunction by agreeing to cooperate with the board. As of July 1978 Stevens was on trial before the NLRB for 275 separate labor law violations at twenty-nine of its more than eighty plants. In 1980, with the boycott hurting the company's corporate image if not its sales, the company agreed to work toward a settlement with the union at ten plants, and in return the union called off the boycott. But the union gained only three contracts.

In October 1983 the company, the union, and the NLRB settled all pending union complaints in a signed agreement. Although the company paid the union one million dollars, both sides "agreed that the union would try to organize its southern plants and the company would still resist."[16] The union claimed that 3,800 of Stevens' 28,000 workers were working under union contract. A twenty-year battle had ended, temporarily. The company had successfully fought the NLRB with blatantly unfair labor practices for two decades, and the union had been fatally "chilled" in the process.

Mimi Conway's *Rise Gonna Rise* was an account of workers caught up in the J.P. Stevens struggle. Conway's focus was on the courage, hope, and persistence of the workers. But among the many verbatim interviews she reported, one female worker, commenting on a friend's decision to join the union, said, "The union's slow. They're mighty slow."[17]

Irving Bernstein, in the epilogue to his *Turbulent Years*, asked himself how far organized labor had come in the New Deal years. He considered the rise of industrial unionism under the CIO as the most important development, one that literally remade American unionism. Wage increases, greater attention to seniority, and better grievance procedures were among the substantial improvements in working conditions that workers won. Bernstein saw that by the end of the 1930s American labor had become a major political force, but he argued that the most profound change came in labor law, particularly in the development of collective bargaining. The change was great enough, he said, "to constitute a revolution."[18] The government's commitment to, and regulation of, collective bargaining stimulated a growth in union membership, ameliorated antiunion activity by companies, diminished the need for strikes, undermined radicalism, strengthened the civil liberties of the rank-and-file workers, and created national labor law procedures. Furthermore, "the regulation of collective bargaining was to prove permanent."[19] With the New Deal labor policy in place, the turbulent years of labor relations had ended.

Undergirding Bernstein's arguments were the impressive percentage gains in union membership in America's basic industries.[20] In 1935–36, the AFL had regained and surpassed its membership peak of 4 million members in 1920, and both the CIO and the AFL had great spurts of growth between 1935 and 1941, when combined membership stood at around 9 million.[21] Two decades later the union membership in America was close to 19 million.[22] Nevertheless, Bernstein's impressive argument and his statistics showing union gains focused only on the good news. The bad news is that, in aggregate terms, by 1960 American unionism had stopped as if it had hit a brick wall. In 1980, twenty years later, only 20,095,000 workers, or only 23 percent of those employed, were unionized, and the recession of the early 1980s pushed that percentage down to approximately 18 percent.[23] In textiles the statistics are even more disheartening. Bernstein's percentages show that, nationally, textile unionism of all kinds comprised only 7.5 percent of all workers in unions in 1935 and only 14.3 percent in 1941.[24] During and after the New Deal, textile unionism, including that in cotton textiles, consistently failed. By 1980, nationwide, textile unionism had risen to only 14.9 percent.[25] In 1964 the southern membership of TWUA was only 11 percent of the union's total membership, and although it is very difficult to isolate cotton textile workers in the South, the most common estimate that union leaders make is that "less than 10 percent" of southern textile workers in the 1980s belong to a union.[26]

The South, however, had shared in Bernstein's revolution in some significant ways. The breakthroughs in industrial unionism did spread to the South in a limited fashion, particularly in the increasing numbers of unionized branch plants in the region in industries like automobiles, aerospace, and prime metals. Unionism in teaching and in government employment has been strong. In metropolitan areas and on large construction projects, AFL-CIO craft unions have had spectacular success. After the Civil Rights movement of the 1950s and 1960s biracial unionism has often been a key ingredient in successful union membership campaigns, particularly in textiles, and southern workers appear to have shared in the protection of civil liberties provided by the new shop rules and grievance prodecures that Bernstein described.[27] Even in textiles, employers have embraced a more open management style within the mills to keep workers happy and unions out.

But the New Deal failed to end the southern differential in wages, and union membership remained lower in the South than in the North. From

1935 to 1950, while southern unionism did increase in terms of raw figures, it grew only slightly in the vital percentage comparison. In nonagricultural employment, union membership grew from 21.5 percent of those employed in 1939 to 32.6 percent in 1953, but that growth, impressive as it was, meant that total southern union membership moved from 9.1 percent of the national total in 1939 to 10.5 percent in 1953.[28] In 1964, southern union membership comprised only 14.4 percent of the nation's total.[29] Clearly, in the years after the New Deal, and particularly in the crucial decades from 1945 to 1965, the South remained an under-unionized region.

Although unionism has not been the overwhelming success that most Americans think it was, organized labor has to be conceded as a major development profoundly affecting much of recent American history. In the late 1930s and in the 1940s, it became a solid component of the New Deal coalition, a coalition whose losses and victories governed the nation's political and economic life for decades after FDR. Furthermore, ahistorical, counterfactual speculation about a successful unionization of the cotton textile industry in the 1930s, or even the creation of a permanent union base, suggests that the South could have been a very different place than the one that really existed. Given the size of the workforce, cotton textile unionism could have been the vehicle for unionizing all the other textile and apparel industries now lumped together in the modern South. Such unionism would have created a southern base for unionizing many other southern industries in the years to come. Such unionization would also have created a political base for a New Deal coalition in the South comparable to the one that did develop in the heavily-unionized industrial states of the North. In fact, the spurt of wartime unionism in the 1940s actually threatened to create such a political realignment, until the emerging coalition was felled by racial politics and the Dixiecrat rebellion.

New Deal collective bargaining policy was too weakly conceived to crack the hard nut of the southern cotton textile industry. The New Deal labor policy was always impartial, regulatory, and stabilizing. The plight of organized labor in the 1980s indicates that the New Deal's labor policy, as progressive and welcome as it was, fell short of being the revolution Irving Bernstein claimed.[30] The New Deal did not provide a model for all seasons, and the failure of cotton textile unionism marked one of the important limits of reform that bounded the possibilities of change that could be achieved through the New Deal.

Key to Source Abbreviations

ACMA	American Cotton Manufacturers Association
Bruere Board Papers	"Records of the Cotton Textile National Industrial Relations Board," National Archives, Record Group 9
Christopher Papers	Paul Christopher Papers, Southern Labor History Archives, Georgia State University, Atlanta
Comer Papers	James McDonald Comer Papers, Birmingham (Ala.) Public Library
Erwin Mills Records	In Manuscript Division, William Perkins Library, Duke University, Durham, N.C.
FDR Papers	In Franklin D. Roosevelt Library, Hyde Park, N.Y.
Hopkins Papers	Harry Hopkins Papers, Franklin D. Roosevelt Library, Hyde Park, N.Y.
Mason Papers	Lucy Randolph Mason Papers, Manuscript Division, William Perkins Library, Duke University, Durham, N.C.
NA	National Archives, Washington D.C.
NLRB Records	National Labor Relations Board Records, Record Group 25, Federal Records Center, Suiteland, Md.
NRA Consolidated Files	"Consolidated Files on Industries Governed by Approved Codes," National Archives, Record Group 9
Piedmont Series	Interviews of the Southern Oral History Program, in Southern Historical Collection, University of North Carolina at Chapel Hill
RG	Record Group
Sloan Papers	George Sloan Papers, Wisconsin State Historical Society, Madison
TLRB Papers	NRA, "Records of the Textile Labor Relations Board," National Archives, Record Group 9

TWUA Papers   Textile Workers Union of America Papers, Wisconsin State Historical Society, Madison

UTW Papers   United Textile Workers Union of America Papers, Southern Labor History Archives, Georgia State University, Atlanta

Notes

CHAPTER ONE

1. Henry Steele Commager, "Introduction," in *The Journal of David E. Lilienthal: The TVA Years*, I (New York, 1964), xxix.
2. Allan Nevins, "The Place of Franklin D. Roosevelt in History," *American Heritage* 17 (Jan. 1966), 13, 103–4.
3. William E. Leuchtenburg, *Franklin D. Roosevelt and the New Deal, 1932–1940*, (New York, 1963), 326–48.
4. Paul K. Conkin, *The New Deal* (New York, 1967), 73.
5. Howard Zinn, "Introduction," in *New Deal Thought* (Indianapolis, 1966), xv–xxxvi.
6. Much of the New Left argument really was an extension of William Appleman Williams' view of the New Deal as sham reform. Williams, *The Contours of American History* (Chicago, 1966), 439–69.
7. A useful bibliography of key New Deal studies can be found in Alonzo L. Hamby, *The New Deal: Analysis and Interpretation* (New York, 1981), 249–57. See particularly his chapter on the development of orthodoxy and revisionism and the emerging synthesis, pp. 1–27. Two other recent bibliographical anthologies of the New Deal are Bernard Sternsher, ed., *The New Deal: Laissez Faire to Socialism* (St. Louis, 1979), and Lawrence Gelfand and Robert J. Neymeyer, eds., *The New Deal: Viewed From Fifty Years* (Iowa City, 1983).
8. Selig Perlman, *Labor in the New Deal Decade* (New York, 1945), 3.
9. Milton Derber and Edwin Young, eds., *Labor and the New Deal* (Madison, Wisc., 1957), v.
10. Walter Galenson, *The CIO Challenge to the AFL: A History of the American Labor Movement, 1935–1941* (Cambridge, Mass., 1960), xvii.
11. David Brody, *Workers in Industrial America: Essays in the 20th Century Struggle* (New York, 1980), 120.
12. Richard Hofstadter, *The Progressive Historians: Turner, Beard, Parrington* (New York, 1968), xv.

CHAPTER TWO

1. Arthur F. Hinrichs to Frances Perkins, Apr. 18, 1935, *Office Files of Madame Perkins*, NA, RG 174.
2. *Proceedings of ACMA*, Pinehurst, N.C., Apr. 28–29, 1933, p. 28.

3. Glenn Gilman, *Human Relations in the Industrial Southeast: A Study of the Textile Industry* (Chapel Hill, 1956), 207.

4. Interview with Franz Daniel, assistant director of organizing, AFL-CIO, 26 July 1960, Washington D.C. Daniel was active in organizing the South in the 1930s.

5. Boyce F. Martin, "Southern Industrial Development," *Harvard Business Review* 19 (Winter 1941), 162.

6. Textile Workers Union of America, *Half A Million Forgotten People* (New York, 1944), 1.

7. Herman E. Michl, *The Textile Industries* (Washington D.C., 1938), 80.

8. National Economic and Social Planning Association, *The Textile Industry in the United States* (Washington D.C., Apr. 1937), 12.

9. Martin, "Southern Industrial Development," 162.

10. *Textile Bulletin* (May 1936), 14.

11. David Carlton, *Mill and Town in South Carolina, 1880–1920* (Baton Rouge, 1982), 40. Gilman, *Human Relations in the Industrial Southeast*, cites the southern percentage (p. 67), but his discussion, like many discussions of the antebellum industry, relies on Broadus Mitchell, *The Rise of Cotton Mills in the South* (Baltimore, 1921), 9–76. See also Ernest McPherson Landers, *The Textile Industry in Antebellum South Carolina* (Baton Rouge, 1969), for a careful modern account of the early industry. Melton Alonzo McLaurin, *Paternalism and Protest: Southern Cotton Mill Workers and Organized Labor, 1875–1905* (Westport, Conn., 1971), 3–15, has an authoritative short account of the rise of the industry to 1880. See also Patrick J. Hearden, *Independence and Empire: The New Southern Cotton Mill Campaign, 1865–1901* (DeKalb, Ill., 1982), 3–19; Stephen J. Goldfarb, "A Note on the Limits to the Growth of the Cotton-Textile Industry in the Old South," *Journal of Southern History* 68 (Nov. 1982), 545–58.

12. W.J. Cash, *The Mind of the South* (New York, 1960), 181. The image of a cotton mill campaign, of course, came from Mitchell, *Rise of Cotton Mills in the South.*

13. Gerald W. Johnson, "Behind the Monster's Mask," *The Survey* 50 (Apr. 1, 1923), 21.

14. Glenn Gilman, *Human Relations in the Industrial Southeast*, 76.

15. Carlton, *Mill and Town*, 72.

16. Ibid., 60.

17. Ibid. Carlton's entire chapter on the cotton mill campaign, pp. 40–81, although concerned only with South Carolina, stands as a persuasive revision of Mitchell's view of the rash of new mills in the 1880s as a societal movement rather than primarily as a singular economic phenomenon.

18. McLaurin, *Paternalism and Protest*, 12.

19. William Walker Thompson, Jr., "A Managerial History of a Cotton Textile Firm: Spartan Mills, 1888–1958," (Ph.D. diss., Univ. of Alabama, 1960), 24.

20. Hearden, *Independence and Empire*, xiv.

21. William C. Kessler, "An Outline History of the Textile Industry," 9 in E.C. Bancroft, W.H. Crook, and William C. Kessler, "Textiles: A Dynamic Industry (mimeographed at Colgate University, 1951), located at U.S. Department of Labor Library.

22. Gilman, *Human Relations in the Industrial Southeast*, 89.

23. Jack Blicksilver, *Cotton Manufacturing in the Southeast: An Historical Analysis* (Atlanta, 1959), 5. See also Leonard A. Carlson, "Labor Supply, the Acquisition of Skills, and the Location of Southern Textile Mills, 1880–1900," *Journal of Economic History* 41 (Mar. 1981), 65–77.

24. Cathy Louise McHugh, "The Family Labor System in the Southern Cotton Textile Industry, 1880–1915" (Ph.D. diss., Stanford Univ., 1981), 56. See also Gavin Wright, "Cheap Labor and Southern Textiles Before 1880," *Journal of Economic History* 29 (Sept. 1979), 655–80.

25. Melvin Copeland, *The Cotton Manufacturing Industry in the United States* (Cambridge, Mass., 1923), 46.

26. Ben F. Lemert, *The Cotton Textile Industry of the Southern Appalachian Piedmont* (Chapel Hill, 1933), 161.

27. Carlton, *Mill and Town*, 43–59. See also Blicksilver, *Cotton Manufacturing in the Southeast*, 4–10; Andrew Warren Pierpont, "Development of the Textile Industry in Alamance County, North Carolina" (Ph.D. diss., Univ. of North Carolina, 1953), 275–76; Lemert, *Cotton Textile Industry of the Southern Appalachian Piedmont*, 155.

28. Gilman, *Human Relations in the Industrial Southeast*, 105. For New England's attempt to meet southern competition, see Hearden, *Independence and Empire*, 89–106.

29. Jules Backman and M.R. Gainsbrugh, *Economics of the Cotton Textile Industry* (New York, 1946), 173.

30. Ibid.; J. Herbert Burgy, *The New England Cotton Textile Industry: A Study In Industrial Geography* (Baltimore, 1932), 119.

31. Michl, *The Textile Industries*, 147.

32. Burgy, *New England Cotton Textile Industry*, 184.

33. Kessler, "An Outline History of the Textile Industry," 41.

34. Wilfrid H. Crook, "The North-South Differential in Labor Costs," in Bancroft, Crook, and Kessler, *"Textiles: A Dynamic Industry,"* 2.

35. Clarence Heer, *Income and Wages in the South* (Chapel Hill, 1930), 29; Backman and Gainsbrugh, *Economics of the Cotton Textile Industry*, 89. For a precise chart of the North-South differential between 1907–34, see National Economic and Social Planning Association, *The Textile Industry*, 39.

36. Charles A. Gulick, Jr., "Industrial Relations in Southern Textile Mills," *Quarterly Journal of Economics* 66 (Aug. 1932), 736. See also other arguments that the North-South differential was the key reason for southern growth. Burgy, *New England Cotton Textile Industry*, 145. U.S. Congress, House, Subcommittee of the Committee on Labor, *To Rehabilitate and Stabilize Labor Conditions in the Textile Industry of the United States*, Hearings, 74 Cong., 2 Sess. (Washington D.C., 1936), 617 (hereafter cited as *Ellenbogen Hearings, 1936*). Rep. Henry Ellenbogen of Pennsylvania, a Democrat, presented bills in 1936 and 1937 to reorganize the industry, and the hearings were commonly known as the Ellenbogen hearings. U.S. Congress, Senate, *Cotton Textile Industry: A Report on the Conditions and Problems of the Cotton Textile Industry*, 74 Cong., 1 Sess., Senate Document 26 (Washington D.C., 1935), 145 (hereafter cited as *Senate Document 26*). "Northern and Western Interests Give Reasons for Establishing Textile Plants in the South," *Manufacturers' Record* 60 (28 Oct. 1926), 95–98. See also *American Wool and Cotton Reporter* (27 Mar. 1934), 7, 9, 13, for New England's labor cost disadvantages.

37. Irwin Mack Stelzer, "The Cotton Textile Industry" (Ph.D. diss., Cornell Univ., 1954), 54.

38. Federal Trade Commission, *Textile Industries: Part I, Investment and Profit*, (Washington D.C., 1934) 11.

39. George Tindall, *The Emergence of the New South, 1913–1945* (Baton Rouge, 1967), 321.

40. Dewey W. Grantham, *Southern Progressivism: The Reconciliation of Progress and Tradition* (Knoxville, 1938), 199. See pp. 178–99 for a summary account of southern child labor in the progressive years; it concentrates on textile mills.

41. *American Wool and Cotton Reporter* (27 Mar. 1934), 9.

42. Stelzer, "The Cotton Textile Industry," 56.

43. American Federation of Labor, *Subsidized Industrial Migration: The Luring of New Plants to New Locations* (Washington D.C., 1935), 7.

44. Stephen J. Kennedy, *Profits and Losses in Textiles* (New York, 1936), 8.

45. E.B. Alderfer and H.E. Michl, *Economics of American Industry* (New York, 1942), 3.

46. Irwin Feller, "The Diffusion and Location of Technological Change in the American Cotton-Textile Industry, 1880–1970," *Technology and Culture* 15 (1974), 576, 581.

47. John L. Bell, Jr., *Hard Times: Beginnings of the Great Depression in North Carolina, 1929–1933* (Raleigh, N.C., 1982), 28.

48. For full accounts of the technology of cotton manufacturing in the 1930s, see Alderfer and Michl, *Economics of American Industry*, 294–310; and Elliot B. Grover and George H. Dunlap, *Fundamentals of Textiles* (Raleigh, N.C., 1952). I gratefully acknowledge the courtesy of the Dundee Mills, Griffin, Ga., who in January 1983 gave me a personal tour of a modern cotton textile plant and whose agent, Frank Stewart, made clear the many improvements in the machinery and plant conditions since the 1930s. Interestingly, modernization — although increasing production and decreasing the number of workers, particularly those who merely lift products from one stage to another — has only eliminated totally the picking machines as a stage of work. The mill in Griffin consists of several buildings, one of which dates back to the 1880s, but it had new high-speed machines from Czechoslovakia.

49. John Jewkes and Sylvia Jewkes, "A Hundred Years of Change in the Structure of the Cotton Industry," *Journal of Law and Economics* 9 (1966), 118, 130; Feller, "Diffusion and Location of Technological Change in the American Cotton-Textile Industry," 572. The available managerial histories of individual southern firms include Thompson, "A Managerial History of a Cotton Textile Firm"; Bobby Dean Jackson, "Textiles in the South Carolina Piedmont: A Case Study of the Inman Mills, 1900–1967" (M.A. thesis, Auburn Univ., 1968); and Robert Sidney Smith, *Mill on the Dan: A History of Dan River Mills, 1882–1950* (Durham, N.C., 1960). Although obviously chronicling successful ventures, these works indicate constant southern attention through the various decades to technological upgrading. So do the voluminous records of the Avondale Mills of Alabama, part of the Comer Papers.

50. U.S. Bureau of the Census, *Census of Manufacturers, 1935, Cotton Manufacturing* (Washington D.C., 1936), 34.

51. Michl, *The Textile Industries*, 85.

52. Jewkes, "A Hundred Years of Change in the Structure of the Cotton Industry," 118, 130.

53. Reavis Cox, *The Marketing of Textiles* (Washington D.C., 1938), 87.

54. Michl, *The Textile Industries*, 85.

55. *Textile Bulletin* (12 May 1938), 14.

56. Isadore Katz, *Taft-Hartleyism in Southern Textiles* (New York, 1950), 4.

57. Jonathan Daniels, *A Southerner Discovers the South* (New York, 1938), 23–33.

58. *Textile Notes* (Dec. 1934), 2.

59. "The Bolt in Cotton Textiles," *Fortune* 36 (July 1947), 62.

60. For an authoritative description in the 1930s, see Cox, *Marketing of Textiles*.

61. National Economic and Planning Association, *Report of the Committee on the Textile Industry*, 4.

62. "Textile Industry," *Encyclopedia of the Social Sciences,* (New York, 1934), xiv, 591–92; Blicksilver, *Cotton Manufacturing in the Southeast*, 98–145.

63. For a vivid description of the depression-ravaged New England mill towns, see Louis Adamic, *My America* (New York, 1938), 263–78.

64. Blicksilver, *Cotton Manufacturing in the Southeast*, 99.

65. Michl, *The Textile Industries*, 102; Blicksilver, *Cotton Manufacturing in the Southeast*, 99.

66. Backman and Gainsbrugh, *Economics of the Cotton Textile Industry*, 142.

67. Michl, *The Textile Industries*, 104.

68. *New York Times*, Jan. 3, 1933; Claudius T. Murchison, "Depression and the Future of Business," in W.T. Couch, ed., *Culture in the South* (Chapel Hill, 1935), 98.

69. Claudius T. Murchison, *King Cotton is Sick* (Chapel Hill, 1930), 34.

70. George R. Dickson, "History of the Code of Fair Competition for the Cotton Textile Industry, Code No. 1," NRA, "Division of Review," NA, RG 9, p. 105.

71. *Senate Document No. 26*, 101.

72. *Textile World* 96 (Jan. 1936), 62.

73. Blicksilver, *Cotton Manufacturing in the Southeast*, 103–4; Smith, *Mill on the Dan*, 539.

74. See Solomon Barkin, "The Regional Significance of the Integration Movement in the Southern Textile Industry," *Southern Economic Journal* 15 (Apr. 1949), 395–411.

75. Gustav T. Schwenning, ed., *Management Problems* (Chapel Hill, 1930), 43.

76. U.S. Congress, Senate, Committee on Education and Labor, *National Labor Relations Board*, Hearings on S. 1958, 74 Cong., 1 Sess. (Washington D.C., 1935), 695.

CHAPTER THREE

1. *Proceedings of ACMA*, May 1936, 47–48. In a letter to George Sloan, CTI president, 22 Nov. 1934, Comer Papers, Donald Comer argued the same thing.

2. Johnson, "Behind the Monster's Mask," 22.

3. Carlton, *Mill and Town*, 151–52.

4. Cash, *Mind of the South*, 213–14.

5. Dale Newman, "Textile Workers in a Tobacco County: A Comparison Between Yarn and Weave Mill Villagers," in Edward Magdal and Jon L. Wakeley, eds., *The Southern Common People: Studies in Nineteenth-Century Social History* (Westport, Conn., 1980), 348. Newman's article clearly points to the continuing interconnection of rural culture and mill culture. See also Valerie Quinney, "Farm to Mill: The First Generation," in *Working Lives: The Southern Exposure History of Labor in the South* (New York, 1980), 5–18; and Tom E. Terrill, "Eager Hands: Labor For Southern Textiles," *Journal of Economic History* 36 (Mar. 1976), 84–101.

6. Douglas DeNatale, "Traditional Culture and Community in a Piedmont Textile Mill Village" (M.S. thesis, Univ. of North Carolina, 1980), 17, 13–100.

7. Jennings J. Rhyne, *Some Southern Cotton Mill Workers and Their Villages* (Chapel Hill, 1930), 71–72.

8. Broadus Mitchell and George Sinclair Mitchell, *Industrial Revolution in the South*, (Baltimore, 1930), 134–35. John Kenneth Moreland, *Millways of Kent* (Chapel Hill, 1958), 22, discovered that even in the late 1940s, 52.1 percent of the workers in the cotton textile villages he studied still had parents who never left their farms.

9. Rhyne, *Some Southern Cotton Mill Workers*, 72.

10. Carlton, *Mill and Town*, 156, 271–72. See also Herbert Lahne, *The Cotton Mill Worker* (New York, 1944), 79; and Tindall, *Emergence of the New South*, 339–40.

11. Quoted in Oliver Carson, "Southern Labor Awakes," *Current History* 41 (Nov. 1934), 156.

12. *Proceedings of the ACMA*, Apr. 1931, p. 2. See also Mitchell and Mitchell, *Industrial Revolution in the South*, 134–35; and Tindall, *Emergence of the New South*, 319.

13. Gilman, *Human Relations in the Industrial Southeast*, 27–63. This view can be found in many places, but for a concise summary of its argument, see "Fundamental Difference Between Southern and Eastern Mill Help," *Manufacturers' Record* 40 (28 Oct. 1926), 125–28.

14. Cash, *Mind of the South*, 274.

15. Liston Pope, *Millhands and Preachers: A Study of Gastonia* (New Haven, 1942), 49–69, 50–51.

16. Dale Newman, "Work and Community Life in a Southern Textile Town," *Labor History* 19 (Spring 1978), 205; Newman, "Textile Workers in a Tobacco County," 346.

17. William T. Polk, *Southern Accent: From Uncle Remus to Oak Ridge* (New York, 1953), 227.

18. McLaurin, *Paternalism and Protest*, 57.

19. Newman, "Textile Workers in a Tobacco County," 348.

20. Clinton Edward Williams, "The Cotton Manufacturing Industry in Alabama" (M.A. thesis, Univ. of Alabama, 1927), 42.

21. For example, see Wade H. Harris, "Abundant American Labor South's Great Asset," *Manufacturers' Record* 90 (28 Oct. 1926), 125–28.

22. Interview with Jessie Lee Carter, Charlotte, N.C., 19 June 1979, Piedmont Series.

23. Interview with Mack Duncan, Greenville, S.C., 7 June and 30 August 1979, Piedmont Series.

24. Daniels, *A Southerner Discovers the South*, 29.

25. Harriet Herring, "The Industrial Worker," in Couch, ed., *Culture in the South*, 344, 352; Rhyne, *Some Southern Cotton Mill Workers*, 205; Paul J. Smith, "Labor Day in Dixie," *American Federationist* 38 (Sept. 1930), 1064.

26. No reliable census exists, but the generalization comes from Lahne, *Cotton Mill Worker*, 35.

27. Carlton, *Mill and Town*, 7.

28. "Transcript of Cotton Textile Code Hearings," K-5, NRA Transcripts of Hearings. NA, RG 9.

29. Sinclair Lewis, *Cheap and Contented Labor: The Picture of a Southern Mill Town in 1929* (New York, 1929); Paul Blanchard, *Labor in Southern Cotton Mills* (New York, 1927); Myra Page, *Southern Cotton Mills and Labor* (New York, 1929). See also Frank Tannenbaum, *Darker Phases of the South* (New York, 1949), 39–73; and Lois McDonald, *Southern Mill Hills: A Study of Social and Economic Forces in Certain Mill Villages* (New York, 1928).

30. "Textile Mill Village Development of South One of Greatest Contributions to Better Living Conditions of Industrial Workers," *Manufacturers' Record* 40 (28 Oct. 1926), 113. See also William Hayes Simpson, *Southern Textile Communities* (Charlotte, N.C., 1948), 7–8; William Hayes Simpson, *Life in Mill Communities* (Clinton, S.C., 1941); Harry Shumway, *I Go South* (New York, 1930); E.T.H. Shaffer, "A New South — the Textile Development," *Atlantic Monthly* 80 (Oct. 1922), 562–66; and Marjorie Potwin, "Cotton Mill People of the Piedmont: A Study in Social Change" (Ph.D. diss., Columbia Univ., 1927).

31. Rhyne, *Some Southern Cotton Mill Workers*, 37–64.

32. Tindall, *Emergence of the New South*, 325–27.

33. John Garrett Van Osdell, Jr., "Cotton Mills, Labor, and the Southern Mind, 1880–1920" (Ph.D. diss., Tulane Univ., 1966), 44. For the history of modernization in one village see Smith, *Mill on the Dan*, 393–402, 519–23. See also Jackson, "Textiles in the South Carolina Piedmont," 55–61.

34. Martha Gelhorn to Harry Hopkins, 11 Nov. 1934, Hopkins Papers. Lorena Hickock, on a southern trip, also reported that mill villages were much better than the living conditions she saw in the countryside. Lorena Hickock to Harry Hopkins, 16 Jan. 1934, Hopkins Papers.

35. Valerie Quinney, "Mill Village Memories," *Southern Exposure* 8 (Fall 1980), 99. See also Ida Moore, "A Day at Kate Brumbry's House," in W.T. Couch, ed., *These Are Our Lives* (New York, 1975), 129–64, for a sense of the daily rhythm of the village.

36. DeNatale, "Traditional Culture and Community in a Piedmont Textile Mill Village," 53.

37. John Bodnar, *Workers' World: Kinship, Community, and Protest in an Industrial Society, 1900–1940* (Baltimore, 1982), 66, 185.

38. Newman, "Work and Community Life in a Southern Textile Town," 216. The education statistics are from Rhyne, *Some Southern Cotton Mill Workers*, 144.

39. For concise accounts of mill village culture close to the New Deal period, see Van Osdell, Jr., "Cotton Mills, Labor, and the Southern Mind," 37–79; Newman, "Work and Community Life in a Southern Textile Town"; DeNatale, "Traditional Culture and Community Life in a Piedmont Textile Mill Village," 52–99. Although based on a year's field study in one cotton textile town of the Piedmont, in 1948–49 and thus somewhat removed from the New Deal years, Moreland, *Millways of Kent*, 52–203, reinforces the above view of mill culture. The interviews in the Piedmont Series also support this generalization. Since, except for a few outside workers, blacks were excluded from the mills in the 1930s, this study does not assess their relation to the industry. For a good history of the exclusion see Allan Stokes, "Black and White Labor and the Development of the Southern Textile Industry, 1880–1920" (Ph.D. diss., Univ. of South Carolina, 1977). See also Sister Mary Josephine Oates, "The Role of the Cotton Industry in the Economic Development of the American Southeast: 1900–1940" (Ph.D. diss., Yale Univ., 1969), 118–37; and Joel Williamson, *The Crucible of Race: Black-White Relations in the American South Since Emancipation* (New York, 1984), 429–44, for the exclusion of blacks and the development of white paternalism.

40. Cotton-Textile Institute, Mill Village Committee Report, NDC 1933, Comer Papers.

41. Rhyne, *Some Southern Cotton Mill Workers*, 9–12. See also Ida Moore, "A Day on Factory Hill," in Tom E. Terrill and Jerrold Hirsch, *Such as Us: Southern Voices of the Thirties* (Chapel Hill, 1978), 145.

42. Van Osdell, Jr., "Cotton Mills, Labor and the Southern Mind," 52–54. See also Abraham Berglund, George T. Starnes, and Frank T. DeVyver, *Labor in the Industrial South: A Survey of Wages and Living Conditions in Three Major Industries of the New Industrial South*, 84–85. For the early appearance of absenteeism and lax work discipline, see Smith, *Mill on the Dan*, 47–48, 100.

43. Interview with Harry Adams, Burlington, N.C., 11 May 1979, Piedmont Series.

44. Interview with Betty Davidson, Burlington, N.C., 2 Feb. 1979; interview with Vernon Cooper, Bynum, N.C., Nov. 1978; both in Piedmont Series.

45. William D. Anderson to Robert R. West, 24 Sept. 1938, copy in Comer Papers.

46. Gilman, *Human Relations in the Industrial Southeast*, 92.

47. Moreland, *Millways of Kent*, 34.

48. For an interesting discussion of public recognition of the incidence of brown lung disease since the New Deal years, see Bennett M. Judkins, "Occupational Health and the Developing Class Consciousness of Southern Textile Workers: The Case of the Brown Lung Association," *The Maryland Historian* 13 (Spring–Summer 1982), 55–71.

49. Generally, the minimum standard was 90 percent; that is, each worker was expected to produce at least 90 percent of what the machine should produce. The standard is still widely accepted today. Learners and sometimes older workers frequently failed to meet production standards and switched to less demanding jobs. Weavers would have minimum standards, and then would receive slightly extra pay for exceeding those standards; in other words, piece-work pay existed throughout the whole industry. The trick for the worker was neither to speed up or slow down after standards were met. Interview with Henry Adams, 11 May 1979, Piedmont Series.

50. Interview with Betty Donaldson, Burlington, N.C., 2 Feb. 1979; interview with

Zelma Montgomery Murray, Burlington, N.C., 4 March 1976; interview with Tessie Dyer, Charlotte N.C., 5 March 1980; interview with Mack Duncan, 6 July 1979. All, Piedmont Series.

51. DeNatale, "Traditional Culture and Community in a Piedmont Textile Mill Village," 100–32.

52. Interview with Edna Hargett, Charlotte N.C., 19 July 1979, Piedmont Series. DeNatale, "Traditional Culture and Community in a Piedmont Textile Mill Village," xiii, 139, discusses the family concept and argues that they *were* one big family. Interestingly, Tamara K. Hareven and Randolph Lagenbach, *Amoskeag: Life and Work in an American Factory City* (New York, 1978), 111–236, saw in their interviews with New England cotton textile workers the same themes of identity with work, enjoyment of the workplace, and the feeling of togetherness.

53. Francis Jones, "Personnel Policies in the Cotton-Textile Industry," *Monthly Labor Review* 42 (June 1936), 1479.

54. Chips Hughes, "A New Twist for Textiles," *Southern Exposure* 3 (1975–76), 66–72.

55. One modern study claims that only 1 percent of women workers in the modern industry are considered skilled, whereas 17 percent of their male counterparts are. Barry Elliot Truchil, "Capital-Labor Relationships in the United States Textile Industry: The Post–World War II Period" (Ph.D. diss., State Univ. of New York at Binghamton, 1982), 22.

56. Pierpont, "Development of the Textile Industry in Alamance County, North Carolina," 129; Smith, *Mill on the Dan*, 400. William H. Phillips, in "Wages, Earnings and Hours in a Southern Textile Mill" (unpublished paper used by permission of author), a study of one South Carolina mill's wage pattern in 1941, found that women were paid less and worked fewer hours, so their weekly earnings were 31.9 percent less than for male workers of similar attributes.

57. Harry Boyte, "The Textile Industry: Keel of Southern Industrialization," *Radical America* 6 (Mar.–Apr. 1972), 29–30. See also McDonald, *Southern Mill Hills*, 77, 144.

58. Lahne, *Cotton Mill Workers*, 290.

59. See Grantham, *Southern Progressivism*, 178–99, for the 1900–14 period; Elizabeth H. Davidson, *Child Labor Legislation in the Southern Textile States* (Chapel Hill, 1939); Lahne, *Cotton Mill Worker*, 102–28.

60. Tindall, *Emergence of the New South*, 323.

61. *Ellenbogen Hearings, 1936*, 617.

62. Paul H. Douglas, *Real Wages in the United States, 1880–1926* (Boston, 1930), 101, 246, 258.

63. U.S. Bureau of Labor Statistics, *Wages and Hours of Labor in Cotton-Goods Manufacturing, 1910 to 1930* (Washington D.C., 1931), 9.

64. Tindall, *Emergence of the New South*, 318. The annual income of a cotton textile mill worker in North Carolina in the mid-1920s was $662 a year. Pierpont, "Development of the Textile Industry in Alamance County, North Carolina," 128.

65. Paul Stroman Lofton, Jr., "A Social and Economic History of Columbia, South Carolina, During the Great Depression, 1929–1940," (Ph.D. diss., Univ. of Texas at Austin, 1977), 11–12.

66. *Ellenbogen Hearings, 1936*, 400.

67. *Textile Bulletin*, May 4, 1933, p. 7.

68. Donald Comer to William D. Anderson, 23 June 1933, Comer Papers.

69. *Textile Bulletin*, 16 Nov. 1933, p. 6.

70. Daniels, *A Southerner Discovers the South*, 294.

71. Lahne, *Cotton Mill Worker*, 137–39.

72. See over 400 interviews with southern workers in the Piedmont Series, a plurality of them with cotton textile workers. In addition, the Chapel Hill Historical Society's collection of interviews with cotton mill workers from Bynum, N.C., can be appreciated by reading DeNatale, "Traditional Culture and Community in a Piedmont Textile Mill Village," which uses them as a data base. The collection is located in the Southern Historical Collection, Univ. of North Carolina Library. Dale Newman, "Textile Workers in a Tobacco County" and "Work and Community Life in a Southern Textile Town," are based on over 200 extensive interviews conducted between fall 1971 and spring 1977 in one textile county in North Carolina. A few printed interviews can be found in Federal Writers' Project, *These Are Our Lives* (New York, 1975); Terrill and Hirsch, *Such As Us*; and John E. Robinson, *Living Hard: Southern Americans and the Great Depression* (Washington D.C., 1981).

73. Bodnar, *Workers' World.* See also the review of this book by Bruce Nelson, "Immigrant Enclaves Versus Class Consciousness: Miners and Steel Workers in Pennsylvania, 1900–1940," *Reviews in American History* 11 (Dec. 1983), 576–81. Nelson accepted Bodnar's arguments but found that they incompletely explained subsequent volatility in Pennsylvania's labor history. Hareven and Langenbach's interviews with New England cotton mill workers, in *Amoskeag*, discussed above, confirm that workers held fast to the familiar and accepted their lot, while still participating in a complex and thriving work culture.

74. Moreland, *Millways of Kent*, 251, 243–62.

75. Robert Blauner, *Alienation and Freedom: The Factory Worker and His Industry* (Chicago, 1964), 58–88.

76. Hamilton Basso, *In Their Image* (New York, 1935).

77. Ida Moore, "When a Man Believes," 170, and "No Union For Me," 188–89, both in Terrill and Hirsch, *Such As Us.*

78. McLaurin, *Paternalism and Protest*, 68–119; and Merle E. Reed, "The Augusta Textile Mills and the Strikes of 1886," *Labor History* 14 (Spring 1973), 228–46.

79. For the best account of the second cycle, see McLaurin, *Paternalism and Protest*, 120–95. For a concise account of textile unions' structure, see Gary Fink, ed., *Labor Unions* (Westport, Conn., 1977), 379–87.

80. Dennis R. Nolan and Donald E. James, "Textile Unionism in the Piedmont, 1901–1932," in Gary M. Fink and Merle E. Reed, eds., *Essays in Southern Labor History: Selected Papers, Southern Labor History Conference, 1976* (Westport, Conn., 1977), 53.

81. Fink, ed., *Labor Unions*, 381.

82. Van Osdell, Jr., "Cotton Mills, Labor and the Southern Mind," 102.

83. See ibid., 223–68, for the public response to this union challenge.

84. For the best published account of these strikes, see Irving Bernstein, *The Lean Years: A History of the American Worker* (Boston, 1960), 1–43. See also F. Ray Marshall, *Labor in the South* (Cambridge, Mass., 1967), 101–20; Tom Tippett, *When Southern Labor Stirs* (New York, 1931), 54–269; Samuel Yellen, *American Labor Struggles* (New York, 1956), 292–326; and Van Osdell, Jr., "Cotton Mills, Labor, and the Southern Mind," 106–222.

85. Marshall, *Labor in the South*, 121–33. Marshall argued that the unions had some limited success and that in 1932, for example, over 15,000 workers in the hosiery industry, the cotton textile industry, and the furniture industry in North Carolina struck against over 35 companies, 131–32.

86. Bernstein, *The Lean Years*, 40–41.

87. Van Osdell, Jr., "Cotton Mills, Labor and the Southern Mind," 216–17.

88. Marshall, *Labor in the South*, 132.

89. Tindall, *Emergence of the New South*, 340.

90. Schwenning, "Prospects of Southern Textile Unionism," *Journal of Political Economy* 39 (Dec. 1931), 786.

91. Benjamin U. Ratchford, "Economic Aspects of the Gastonia Situation," *Social Forces* 8 (Mar. 1930), 350–59.

92. Bell, *Hard Times*, 32.

93. For an interesting review of such literature, used in relation to current textile workers, see Judkins, "Occupational Health and the Developing Class Consciousness of Southern Textile Workers," 55–57.

94. Cash, *Mind of the South*, 221.

95. Schwenning, ed., *Management Problems*, 39–40.

96. *Ellenbogen Hearings, 1936*, p. 443.

97. "Transcript of Meeting by Officers and Employees of Bibb Manufacturing Company, Mill No. 1, in Community Club House, East Macon, Georgia, 7:40 PM, June 20, 1933," Comer Papers. William D. Anderson, president of Bibb, sent the transcript to Donald Comer.

98. Carson, "Southern Labor Awakes," 157.

99. Gustav T. Schwenning, "Prospects of Southern Textile Unionism," 806.

100. Interview by author with Solomon Barkin, research economist with TWUA, Washington D.C., 26 Aug. 1960.

101. U.S. Congress, House, *National Textile Bill*, Report 2590, 74 Cong., 2 Sess. (Washington D.C., 1936), 5–6.

102. Gilman, *Human Relations in the Industrial Southeast*, 235–36.

103. Textile Workers Union of America, *Proceedings of the First Constitutional Convention*, Philadelphia, May 15–19, 1939, p. 132. Hereafter cited as *TWUA Proceedings, 1939*.

104. "Cannon," *Fortune* 8 (Nov. 1933), 141.

105. *TWUA Proceedings, 1939*, p. 133.

106. For a perceptive analysis of the hostility of southern communities to unions, see Charles Martin, "Southern Labor in Transition: Gadsden, Alabama, 1930–1943," *Journal of Southern History* 47 (Nov. 1981), 545–65. What emerges is a complex mingling of events and beliefs, more than simple antiunionism.

107. For a discussion of this in one mill village and its churches, see Bernard M. Cannon, "Social Deterrents to the Unionization of Southern Cotton Textile Mill Workers," (Ph.D. diss., Harvard Univ., 1951), 483–532.

108. *Ellenbogen Hearings, 1936*, 281.

109. Pope, *Millhands and Preachers*, 20–48, 141–203. John Earle, Dean D. Knudsen, and Donald W. Shriver, Jr., *Spindles and Spires: A Restudy of Religion and Social Change in Gastonia* (Atlanta, 1976), studied Gastonia after 1940, where Pope left off. They argued for considerable modernization and more conflict within the church as opponent and proponent of change. But, on balance, Christian conservatism thrived, and Gastonia remained strongly an antiunion town.

110. Newman, "Textile Workers in a Tobacco County," 352.

111. Raleigh *News and Observer*, quoted in the *Textile Bulletin*, Oct. 12, 1933, p. 15.

112. William H. Nichols, *Southern Tradition and Regional Progress* (Chapel Hill, 1960), 66–67. See also McLaurin, *Paternalism and Protest*, for a full story of early paternalism in the industry; Frank T. DeVyver, "Paternalism — North and South," *American Federationist* 37 (Nov. 1930), 1353–58; Stewart D. Brandes, *American Welfare Capitalism, 1880–1940* (Chicago, 1976); and Tindall, *Emergence of the New South*, 329–31. See also the defense of southern cotton mill paternalism by M.L. Brittain, the president of Georgia Tech University, *Journal of Commerce*, 2 May 1938, clipping file in TWUA Papers.

113. Gerald W. Johnson, *The Making of a Southern Industrialist: A Biographical*

Study of Simpson Bobo Tanner (Chapel Hill, 1952), 49–55. Two recent studies of two different 19th-century North Carolina mill owner families disagreed as to whether paternalism was a rhetorical facade for profit or a genuine belief in Christian stewardship. Bess Beatty, "The Edwin Holt Family: Southern Capitalists," and Gary R. Freeze, "The John M. Odell Family: Master Mill Men and Protestant Stewards" (Papers delivered at the Annual Meeting of the Southern Historical Association, Charleston, S.C., 11 April 1983). The author listened to the papers and took notes.

114. *Textile World*, Jan. 1938, p. 57.

115. Arthur B. Edge, Jr., *Fuller E. Callaway (1870–1928): Founder of Callaway Mills* (New York, 1954), 27.

116. *Cotton*, May 1934, p. 47.

117. Recorded interview with Donald Comer at Harvard Business School, 18 May 1960, Comer Papers. Edward Akin, "Avondale's Welfare Program for Youth: The Programs and the People Who Made Them Work" (Paper delivered at the Annual Meeting of the Organization of American Historians, 11 April 1980); used by permission of the author. See also C. VanMeter, "Donald Comer and His 7,000 Partners," *The Rotarian*, Mar. 1951, reprint in Comer Papers.

118. Harriet Herring, *Welfare Work in Mill Villages: The Story of Extra-Mill Activities in North Carolina* (Chapel Hill, 1929).

119. Boyte, "The Textile Industry," 41–43.

120. Tindall, *Emergence of the New South*, 328.

121. DeNatale, "Traditional Culture and Community in a Piedmont Textile Mill Village," abstract on unnumbered page.

122. Virginius Dabney, *Liberalism in the South* (Chapel Hill, 1932), 331.

123. Charles A. Gulick, Jr., "Industrial Relations in Southern Textile Mills," 737.

124. Frank T. DeVyver, "Southern Textile Mills Revisited," *Southern Economic Journal* 4 (Apr. 1938), 472–73.

125. Solomon Barkin, "A Trade Unionist Appraises Management Personnel Philosophy," *Harvard Business Review* 28 (Sept. 1950), 60. For an entire book organized along this theme, see Gilman, *Human Relations in the Industrial Southeast*, particularly 233–48, 288–317.

CHAPTER FOUR

1. For an evaluation of the respective roles of the advisory groups, see Bernard Bellush, *The Failure of the NRA* (New York, 1975), 38–40.

2. *Textile World*, July 1933, 50.

3. *New York Times*, 28 June 1933.

4. Harold G. Moulton and Maurice Leven, *The Thirty Hour Week* (Washington D.C., 1935), 6–7.

5. U.S. Congress, Senate, Committee on the Judiciary, *Thirty Hour Week: Hearing*, 73 Cong., 2 Sess. (Washington D.C., 1933), 305.

6. Leuchtenburg, *FDR and the New Deal*, 56.

7. Bellush, *Failure of the NRA*, 13; see also pp. 1–29 for the original passage of the NIRA. Many people worked on the administration bill, but its final draft was prepared by Hugh Johnson; Senator Wagner; Donald Richberg, soon to be Johnson's deputy; Lewis Douglas, budget director; Frances Perkins, secretary of labor; and John Dickenson, under-secretary of commerce. For a discussion of the origins and drafting, see Arthur Schlesinger, Jr., *The Age of Roosevelt: The Coming of the New Deal* (Boston, 1959), 87–98; Irving Bernstein, *The New Deal Collective Bargaining Policy* (Berkeley, 1950), 18–33; Ellis Hawley, *The New Deal and the Problem of Monopoly*, 19–34;

Frank Freidel, *Franklin D. Roosevelt: Launching the New Deal* (Boston, 1973), 408–35; Peter H. Irons, *The New Deal Lawyers* (Princeton, 1982), 17–34; James E. Sargent, *Roosevelt and The Hundred Days: Struggle for the Early New Deal* (New York, 1981), 197–208. Personal accounts may be found in Raymond Moley, *After Seven Years* (New York, 1939), 184–91; Donald R. Richberg, *The Rainbow* (New York, 1936), 106–14; Hugh S. Johnson, *The Blue Eagle: From Egg to Earth* (New York, 1935), 189–206; and Frances Perkins, *The Roosevelt I Knew* (New York, 1946), 197–212. Rhonda Fay Levine, "Class Struggle and the Capitalist State: The National Industrial Recovery Act and the New Deal" (Ph.D. diss., State Univ. of New York at Binghamton, 1980), 151–229, reviewed the literature and argued that although "all" classes compromised, the NIRA was essentially a "capitalist" coup. The best account by far is Robert F. Himmelberg, *The Origin of the National Recovery Administration: Business, Government, and the Trade Association Issue, 1921–1933* (New York, 1976), 181–211. He argued persuasively that the NIRA was a triumph for the antitrusters of the 1920s.

8. *New York Times*, 17 June 1933.

9. *Textile World*, June 1933, p. 47.

10. For a concise commentary on the provisions of the act, see Charles L. Dearing et al., *The ABC of the NRA* (Washington D.C., 1934), 14–24.

11. This brief explanation simplifies the negotiations and bargaining at every stage. For comments on code-making in general, see Leverett S. Lyon et al., *The National Recovery Administration: An Analysis and Appraisal* (Washington D.C., 1935), 29, 88–140; Alfred L. Bernheim and Dorothy Van Doren, eds, *Labor and the Government: An Investigation of the Role of Government in Labor Relations* (New York, 1935), 261–77. Two modern accounts contain sharp views of the overall process of code-making during the NRA years. Hawley, *The New Deal and the Problem of Monopoly*, 53–71, and Bellush, *Failure of the NRA*, 30–54. Both argue that business overwhelmingly dominated code-making in all industries.

12. J. Joseph Huthmacher, *Senator Robert F. Wagner and the Rise of Urban Liberalism* (New York, 1968), 147; Frank Freidel, *FDR: Launching the New Deal*, 429–30; Leuchtenburg, *FDR and the New Deal*, 108.

13. The literature on collective bargaining policy and its development is broad and deep. When not indicated, this account relies on four older accounts: Bernstein, *New Deal Collective Bargaining Policy*; Harry A. Millis and Emily Clark Brown, *From the Wagner Act to the Taft-Hartley Act: A Study of National Labor Policy and Labor Relations* (Chicago, 1950); Derber and Young, eds., *Labor and the New Deal*; and Joseph Rosenfarb, *The National Labor Policy and How It Works* (New York, 1940). For a sprightly account, see Irving Bernstein, *The Turbulent Years: A History of the American Worker* (New York, 1969), 25–36, 172–216, 318–51, 635–81. For two interesting essays on the NRA and the development of collective bargaining, see Irons, *New Deal Lawyers*, 203–25, and Richard C. Cortner, *The Wagner Act Cases* (Knoxville, 1964), 44–71.

14. Bernstein, *The Turbulent Years*, 35.

15. Francis Biddle, *In Brief Authority* (New York, 1962), 35. NRA Press Release No. 34, NRA Consolidated Files.

16. Perkins, *The Roosevelt I Knew*, 200.

17. For some useful precise tables of capacity, production, prices, and profits, broken down by North and South, for the period 1927–32, see Louis Galambos, *Competition and Cooperation: The Emergence of a National Trade Association* (Baltimore, 1966), 135–37, 166–67

18. *Proceedings of ACMA*, Apr. 1931, pp. 30, 60.

19. Galambos, *Competition and Cooperation*, 3–112.

20. Ibid., 136–37.

21. George Sloan, The Cotton Textile Industry Under the NRA," in George B. Galloway, ed., *Industrial Planning Under Codes* (New York, 1935), 117.

22. *Thirty-Hour Week*, Senate Hearings, Jan. 1933, p. 299.

23. *Proceedings of ACMA*, Apr. 1933, p. 30.

24. Ibid., 24.

25. Galambos, *Competition and Cooperation*, 173–99.

26. Samuel S. Rosenman, ed., *The Public Papers and Addresses of Franklin D. Roosevelt*, vol. 2 (New York, 1950), 164–65.

27. Sloan, "The Cotton Textile Industry Under the NRA," 120.

28. George Sloan, "First Flight of the Blue Eagle: The Cotton Textile Code in Operation," *Atlantic Monthly* 153 (Mar. 1934), 322.

29. *New York Times*, 21 June 1933.

30. A full text of the proposed code can be found in *New York Times*, 20 June 1933.

31. Donald Comer to William D. Anderson, 23 June 1933, Comer Papers.

32. *Cotton*, June 1933, p. 39.

33. *Textile Bulletin*, 29 June 1933, p. 14

34. *New York Times*, 25 and 28 June 1933.

35. The *New York Times* extensively covered the first hearing of the NRA. In addition, a complete transcript of the hearings exists, "Transcript of the Cotton Textile Code Hearings," Transcript of Hearings, NA, RG 9. Galambos, *Competition and Cooperation*, 216–24, has a historical account of the hearings, concentrating on their business importance. The following account is based on these three sources.

36. *New York Times*, 29 June 1933.

37. Perkins, *The Roosevelt I Knew*, 224.

38. Most outside helpers in the South were blacks. On the third day of the hearings, John B. Davis, executive secretary of the Negro Industrial League, appeared at the hearings to protest the exclusion of blacks.

39. Bernstein, *The Turbulent Years*, 301; Galambos, *Competition and Cooperation*, 219. For a discussion of how a stronger union was able to bargain better at the code hearing, see James P. Johnson, "Drafting the NRA Code of Fair Competition for the Bituminous Coal Industry," *Journal of American History* 53 (Dec. 1966), 521–41. See also James P. Johnson, *The Politics of Soft Coal: The Bituminous Industry from World War I through the New Deal* (Urbana, 1979), 135–246, for an NRA experience where a large successful union with a brilliant leader did exist.

40. The term "Code Authority" later became the general term for industry groups that were to administer the NRA codes. Usually a handful of government representatives would be added, but only 51 Code Authorities ever had labor representatives. The Cotton Textile Code Authority had no labor representative until summer 1934.

41. For a full discussion of the code and overproduction, see Dickson, "History of the Code of Fair Competition for the Cotton Textile Industry, Code #1," NRA "Division of Review," NA, RG 9. Three government representatives were added to the twenty-person Code Authority—Hugh Johnson, Nelson Slater, and Leo Wolman. But they attended only a few meetings during the first year. "Memorandum on Attendance of Government Members of the Cotton Textile Code Authority, February 28, 1935," TLRB Papers.

42. Donald Comer to George Sloan, 12 June 1933, Comer Papers.

43. "Statement by George A. Sloan, President, Cotton-Textile Institute, Inc., on the Cotton Textile Code Becoming Effective," 17 July 1933, Sloan Papers.

44. *Daily News Record*, 29 June 1933.

45. *Cotton*, July 1933, p. 19.

46. *Daily News Record*, 11 July 1933.

47. Ibid., 17 July 1933.

48. *New York Times*, 16 July 1933.

49. *Daily News Record*, 12 July 1933.

50. *New York Times*, 1 July 1933.

51. *New York Times*, 11 July 1933, contains a full text of the code. See also "Code of Fair Competition for the Cotton-Textile Industry," *Monthly Labor Review* 37 (Aug. 1933), 267–72. The cotton textile industry, as is described in Chapter Two, took up a great deal of the NRA's time. For a chart of the other 24 textile industry codes, see *Textile World*, 8 Feb. 1934, pp. 85–88.

52. *Daily News Record*, 6 July 1933.

53. *New York Times*, 13 July 1933.

54. Sloan, "The Cotton Textile Industry under the NRA," 121.

55. *New York Times*, 5 Aug. 1933.

56. Ibid., 16 Sept. 1933.

57. Backman and Gainsbrugh, *Economics of the Cotton Textile Industry*, 112.

58. FTC, *Textile Industries: Part I, Investment and Profit*, 12.

59. *New York Times*, 19 Oct. 1933.

60. *Textile Bulletin*, 26 Oct. 1933, pp. 3–4.

61. Michl, *The Textile Industries*, 126.

62. Witt Bowden, "Employment, Hours, Earnings, and Production Under the NRA," *Monthly Labor Review* 38 (Oct. 1934), 1019.

63. A.F. Hinrichs, "Historical Review of Wage Rates and Wage Differentials in the Cotton-Textile Industry," *Monthly Labor Review* 40 (May 1935), 1174–76.

64. Galambos, *Competition and Cooperation*, 247–50.

65. Sloan, "First Flight of the Blue Eagle," 324.

66. Sloan, "The Cotton Textile Industry Under the NRA," 126–27.

67. *New York Times*, 17 Dec. 1933. For a reasoned statement of this view of machine curtailment, see Arthur Heltinger, Jr., to Leon Henderson, 9 May 1934, Records Relating to Labor Disturbances in the Textile Industry, Dec. 1933–Mar. 1937, NA, RG 9.

68. Galambos, *Competition and Cooperation*, 286.

69. *Textile World*, Feb. 1934, p. 102.

70. Sloan, "First Flight of the Blue Eagle," 325.

71. *Proceedings of ACMA*, Apr. 1934, p. 31.

72. Hawley, *The New Deal and the Problem of Monopoly*, 35–52.

CHAPTER FIVE

1. *Daily News Record*, 1 Nov. 1933.

2. Raleigh *News and Observer*, 6 Aug. 1934.

3. *Textile Worker*, 21 July 1933, p. 197.

4. Broadus Mitchell, *Depression Decade: From New Era Through New Deal, 1929–1941* (New York, 1947), 271–72.

5. Milton Derber, "Growth and Expansion," in Derber and Young, eds., *Labor and the New Deal*, 8.

6. Bernstein, *The Turbulent Years*, 37.

7. Joseph J. King, "The Durham Central Labor Union," *Southern Economic Journal* 5 (July 1938), 56.

8. *Daily News Record*, 1 Nov. 1933.

9. Robert R.R. Brooks, "The United Textile Workers of America" (Ph.D. diss., Yale Univ., 1935), 349–50.

10. Cannon, "Social Deterrents to the Unionization of Southern Cotton Textile Mill Workers," 293.

11. Brooks, "United Textile Workers of America," 350.

12. United Textile Workers, *Proceedings of the Sixth Biennial Convention*, New York, Aug. 13–18, 1934, pp. 3, 104.

13. Memorandum prepared for Robert Bruere, Bruere Board Papers.

14. U.S. Congress, Senate, Committee on Education and Labor, *To Create a National Labor Board*, Hearing, 73 Cong., 3 Sess. (Washington D.C., 1934), 274.

15. *Cotton*, Dec. 1933, p. 27.

16. *Textile World*, Oct. 1933, p. 56.

17. Bernstein, *The Turbulent Years*, 171; on the evolution of federal labor policy from the NRA to the Wagner Act, see pp. 172–323. For a particularly insightful contemporary view, see Sumner Schlicter, "Labor and the Government," *Yale Review* 25 (Dec. 1935), 258–74. See also Irons, *The New Deal Lawyers*, 203–25, and Cortner, *The Wagner Act Cases*, 44–71.

18. Lewis L. Lorwin and Arthur Wubnig, *Labor Relations Boards: The Regulation of Collective Bargaining Under the National Industrial Recovery Act* (Washington D.C., 1935), 268.

19. Huthmacher, *Sen. Robert F. Wagner*, 160–71.

20. NRA, "Division of Review," *Section 7(a): Its History, Interpretation and Administration*, Work Materials No. 45, NA, RG 9.

21. William Haskett, "Ideological Radicals, the American Federation of Labor, and Federal Labor Policy in the Strikes of 1934" (Ph.D. diss., Univ. of California at Los Angeles, 1958), 338–40. Haskett emphasized Johnson's commitment to recovery at all costs, and the NRA's willingness to let conformity to actual power determine the outlook toward any specific labor problem.

22. Feller, "Diffusion and Location of Technological Change in the American Cotton-Textile Industry," 572; Thompson, "A Managerial History of a Cotton Textile Firm," 122–32.

23. *The Industrial Leader*, 23 June 1939, clipping, TWUA Papers.

24. Cannon, "Social Deterrents to the Unionization of Southern Cotton Textile Mill Workers," 290–93.

25. Martha Gelhorn to Harry Hopkins, 11 Nov. 1934, Hopkins Papers.

26. Moore, "When A Man Believes," 181.

27. *New York Times*, 25 June 1933.

28. *Ellenbogen Hearings, 1936*, 53.

29. V.S. von Szelicki, "Cotton Textile Labor Productivity and the Stretch-out System" (unreleased report, c. 1934), NRA, Bruere Board Papers.

30. Donald Comer to George Sloan, 29 Aug. 1934, Comer Papers.

31. Joseph E. Sirrine, *The Truth About "Stretch-out,"* (New York, 1934).

32. *Cotton*, August 1933, p. 45.

33. Elliott Dunlap Smith, "Lessons of the Stretchout: A Preliminary Report of a Study of Some Human Problems in the Management of Technological Change" (Paper delivered at the 1933 Annual Meeting of the American Society of Mechanical Engineers); UTW Papers.

34. Daniels, *A Southerner Discovers the South*, 29.

35. UTW, "Official News Sheet," 24 Nov. 1934, located in Dept. of Labor Library, Washington, D.C.

36. Robert Bruere to Dr. Alexander Sacks, chief of NRA research and planning, 15 July 1933, NRA Consolidated Files.

37. Report to Hugh S. Johnson by Robert W. Bruere, Benjamin Geer, and George Berry, 21 July 1933, NRA Consolidated Files.

38. *New York Times*, 2 and 13 Aug. 1933.

39. Labor Advisory Board to Hugh Johnson, 29 July 1933, NRA Consolidated Files.

40. *New York Times*, 3 Aug. 1933.

41. Lorwin and Wubnig, *Labor Relations Boards*, 417.

42. John A. Fitch, "Labor Boards," *Survey Graphic* 23 (Nov. 1934), 567.

43. The procedures and operations of the board are set out in several memoranda, but the clearest explanation of the original theory of how the board should proceed was reported in a letter from Robert Bruere to John G. Winant, 8 Sept. 1934, Bruere Board Papers.

44. Theodore Johnson to Robert Bruere, 27 May 1934, ibid.

45. H.H. Willis, report to Robert Bruere, 21 May 1934, ibid.

46. Theodore Johnson, report to Robert Bruere, 1 June 1934, ibid.

47. For example, see copy of speech by Thomas Quigley, a professor at Georgia Tech University and chairperson of the Georgia State Committee of the CTNIRB, entitled "Industrial Relations Under the Cotton Textile Code," 24 May 1934; ibid. The boards were at best neutral toward unionism, but evidently there did not exist any overt antiworker feelings.

48. Bruere to Sloan, 13 Sept. 1933, ibid.

49. "Minutes of the Board, Nov. 25, 1933," ibid.

50. *New York Times*, 1 July 1934.

51. Ibid., 2 Aug. 1933. Nelson Slater, deputy administrator, and Leo Wolman of the Labor Advisory Board were the other two members of the phantom committee.

52. The raw material of the complaints lie either in long lists of complaints submitted by the UTW or buried in the large collection of NRA materials shelved by individual mills and now called "Records Relative to Labor Disturbances in the Cotton Textile Industry, December, 1933–March, 1937," NA, RG 9. Many original letters must have been destroyed. But copies of the one-page forms of excerpts that were forwarded to the Code Authority remain in the board's records. This discussion of the complaints is based on these records, "Excerpts From Complaints—Aug. 1933 to Sept. 1934," Bruere Board Papers. In *The Turbulent Years*, 302–03, Irving Bernstein accepts these complaints at face value.

53. *New York Times* 13 Aug. 1933.

54. Some copies of the reports for fall 1933 are in the Bruere Board Papers, though technically they did not have to be sent there. See P.L. Coonley's report of 1 Sept. 1934, covering the period 9 Dec. 1933–5 May 1934, Bruere Board Papers.

55. *New York Times*, 10 Oct. 1933.

56. Ibid., 12 Dec. 1933. The AFL did nothing, of course. It had its own problems in coping with the NRA and the new surge of industrial unionism.

57. *Daily News Record*, 5 Feb. 1934.

58. UTW, *Open Letter to Textile Workers by Thomas McMahon* (New York, Jan. 1934). Located in the Department of Labor Library, Washington D.C.

59. Ibid.

60. *Cotton*, Sept. 1934, p. 28.

61. *Proceedings of ACMA*, Charleston, S.C., Apr. 19–20, 1934, p. 40.

62. Marchant to Johnson, 23 March 1934, NRA Consolidated Files.

63. *Journal of Commerce*, 22 Dec. 1933.

64. Galambos, *Competition and Cooperation*, 246.

65. Comer to Anderson, 11 Oct. 1933, Comer Papers.

66. "Minutes of the Code Authority," Washington D.C., 1 Aug. 1933; ibid.

67. Sloan to Marchant, 22 Sept. 1933, copy in ibid.

68. Sloan to Hugh Johnson, 2 Oct. 1933, copy in ibid.

69. "Minutes of the Code Authority," New York, 17 Oct. 1933, copy in ibid.

70. Telegram, Robert Bruere to George Sloan, 15 Oct. 1933, Bruere Board Papers.

71. *New York Times*, 23 April 1934.

72. On the growing troubles in mid-1934 within the NRA, see Bellush, *The Failure of the NRA*, 136–57, and Hawley, *The New Deal and the Problem of Monopoly*, 91–110.

73. Sloan to Johnson, 1 Sept. 1933, copy in Comer Papers.

74. Transcript of telephone conversation between Sidney Munroe of the CTI and L.R. Gilbert of the Bruere Board's staff, in which Gilbert thinks stretch out complaints come only from substandard workers, 2 Mar. 1934, Bruere Board Papers.

75. Complaints from UTW, *Official News Sheet*, n.d. [spring 1934], Department of Labor Library.

76. Brooks, "The United Textile Workers of America," 365.

77. Jonathan Daniels, "Here Comes Gorman," *New Republic* 60 (3 Oct. 1934), 203–04.

78. *New York Times*, 2 March 1934.

79. *Proceedings of ACMA*, Apr. 1934, p. 32, 51.

80. "Report of the Conference Between Organizers of the UTW and the CTNIRB," NRA Consolidated Files.

CHAPTER SIX

1. *New York Times*, 25 Mar. and 5 May 1934.

2. Ibid., 8 and 23 May 1934.

3. Galambos, *Competition and Cooperation*, 57–58, 248–50.

4. McMahon to Johnson, 23 May 1934, NRA Consolidated Files.

5. *New York Times*, 29 May 1934.

6. *Textile Bulletin,* 31 May 1934, p. 14; *Textile World*, June 1934, p. 73–74; Charlotte *Observer*, 2 June 1934.

7. For a summary account of the famous 1934 strikes, see Bernstein, *The Turbulent Years*, 217–317. In 1934 there were 1,856 strikes involving over 1.4 million workers, the highest in many years. Four were of particular national importance—the May strike at the Electric Auto-Lite Company in Toledo, the truck drivers' strike in Minneapolis from May to late August, the general strike in San Francisco in July, and the textile strike in September.

8. *New York Times*, 1 June 1934.

9. Galambos, *Competition and Cooperation*, 274–78.

10. Anderson to Sloan, 19 and 25 May 1934, and Sloan to Anderson, 29 May 1934, copies in Comer Papers.

11. *New York Times*, 1 June 1934.

12. "Report of the Conference Between Organizers of the United Textile Workers of America and Cotton Textile National Industrial Relations Board, May 30, 1934," Bruere Board Papers.

13. "Final Terms of Settlement Between NRA Administrators and Officials of the United Textile Workers, June 2, 1934," NRA Consolidated Files. See also *New York Times*, 3 June 1934, and Brooks, "The United Textile Workers of America," 368–69. A copy of the agreement is also in the Sloan Papers.

14. *New York Times*, 3 June 1934.

15. Textile Workers Organizing Committee, *Building A Union of Textile Workers* (New York, 1939), 3.

16. Haskett, "Ideological Radicals, the American Federation of Labor, and Federal Policy in the Strikes of 1934," 309.

17. Galambos, *Competition and Cooperation*, 260. See Sloan's report on the negotiations to the Code Authority, 4 June 1934, Sloan Papers. Here Sloan argued that he had gone to Washington only because Johnson would have cut a deal anyway to avoid a blow to the image of the recovery program, and because even a small textile strike might have helped to pass the pending Wagner Labor Dispute Bill.

18. Anderson to Sloan, 4 June 1934, copy in Comer Papers; Comer to Stewart Cramer, another member of the Code Authority, 6 June 1934, ibid.

19. *New York Times*, 3 and 10 June 1934.

20. V.S. von Szelicki, "Machine Hour Requirements For Satisfying Normal Demand in the Cotton Textile Industry," Bruere Board Papers; *New York Times*, 16 June 1934.

21. V.S. von Szelicki, "What Wage Rise if Any is Possible in the Cotton Textile Industry," Bruere Board Papers; *New York Times*, 30 June and 15 Aug. 1934.

22. *New York Times*, 11 July 1934.

23. Francis Gorman to Hugh Johnson, 27 June 1934, Bruere Board Papers.

24. Oliver Carson, "Why Textiles Vote to Strike," *New Republic* 80 (5 Sept. 1934), 95.

25. Hamilton Basso, "Textile Trouble: Gastonia Before the Battle," *New Republic* 80 (19 Sept. 1934), 149.

26. *Textile World*, July 1934, p. 74.

27. Gorman to Johnson, 21 June 1934, Bruere Board Papers. Johnson had suggested 200,000 members as a necessity for proper standing.

28. Bruere to Johnson, 26 June 1934, ibid.

29. Transcript of telephone conversation between Sloan and Bruere, 3 July 1934, ibid.

30. A discussion of the summer grievances may be found in Gorman's fiery speech to the August UTW convention. UTW, *Proceedings of the 6th Biennial Convention*, 20–25.

31. Thomas I. Emerson to Robert Bruere, 20 March 1934, Bruere Board Papers.

32. Transcript of telephone conversation between Robert Bruere and Benjamin Geer, 27 June 1934, ibid.; Robert Bruere to F.B. Bradley, vice-president of Eagle and Phoenix Mills, Columbus, Ga., 22 July 1934, "Records Relating to Labor Disturbances," NA, RG 9.

33. Dickson, "History of the Code of Fair Competition for the Cotton Textile Industry, Code No. 1," NRA, "Division of Review," NA, RG 9.

34. "Statistical Report of Cotton Textile National Industrial Relations Board," Bruere Board Papers.

35. UTW, *Proceedings of the 6th Biennial Convention*, 24.

36. Sidney Munroe of CTI to L.R. Gilbert, secretary of the Bruere Board, 16 July 1934, Bruere Board Papers.

37. Frank Coffee to Lloyd Garrison, 9 Aug. 1934, copy in Bruere Board Papers; Paul Christopher to Robert Bruere, 6 Aug. 1934, Christopher Papers.

38. Atlanta *Journal*, 6 July 1934.

39. Raleigh *News and Observer*, 6 Aug. 1934.

40. *Proceedings of ACMA*, Apr. 1934, p. 40.

41. Sloan, "First Flight of the Blue Eagle," 325.

42. *New York Times*, 1 July 1934.

43. Ibid.

44. *Textile World*, Aug. 1934, p. 55.

45. Bureau of Labor Statistics, "Textile Report: Wages, Rates, and Weekly Earnings in the Cotton Goods Industry," 4 Feb. 1934, NRA Consolidated Files.

46. "Eagle and Phoenix Manufacturing Company," NRA, "Records Relating to Labor

Disturbances," NA, RG 9. The several folders in this collection give the clearest example of Bruere's mill committee–state board–national board system.

47. Alexander Kendrick, "Alabama Goes on Strike," *Nation* 139 (29 Aug. 1934), 233; Philip Taft, *Organizing Dixie: Alabama Workers in the Industrial Era* (Westport, Conn., 1981), 76–79. See also Birmingham *News* almost daily, 16 Aug.–30 Sept. 1934.

48. Hugh Johnson to Marvin McIntyre, 19 Aug. 1934, FDR Papers.

49. John Dean to Hugh Kerwin, 19 July 1934, Department of Labor, Records of the Federal Mediation and Conciliation Service, NA, RG 280.

50. Kendrick, "Alabama Goes On Strike,"

51. *Textile Bulletin*, July 1934, p. 15; see also *New York Times*, July 16, 17, 18, 19, 20, Aug. 2, 6, 1934.

52. Kerwin to Perkins, 18 July 1934, Department of Labor, Records of the Federal Mediation and Conciliation Service, NA, RG 280. See also Brooks, "The United Textile Workers of America," 371, and Taft, *Organizing Dixie*, 79–82, on the influence of the strikes on the UTW.

53. *New York Times*, 14 Aug. 1934. The *Times* covered the convention as a major news story. UTW, *Proceedings of the 6th Biennial Convention*, 5.

54. Ibid., 26.

55. Carson, "Why Textiles Vote to Strike," 95.

56. *New York Times*, 17 Aug. 1934.

57. Ibid., 18 Aug. 1934.

58. Bernstein, *The Turbulent Years*, 217–18; Jeremy Breecher, *Strike!* (San Francisco, 1972), 150–77.

59. *New York Times*, 18 Aug. 1934.

60. Ibid., 14 Aug. 1934; "Textile Strike Threat," *Business Week*, 25 Aug. 1934, p. 11.

61. Charlotte *Observer*, 16 Aug. 1934.

62. Columbia *State*, 1 Sept. 1934.

63. *Textile Bulletin*, 30 Aug. 1934, p. 15.

64. Frances Perkins to Marvin McIntyre, 17 Aug. 1934, Department of Labor, "Office Files of Frances Perkins," NA, RG 174.

65. Marshall, *Labor in the South*, 168.

66. Press Release from UTW Strike Committee, 28 Aug. 1934, TWUA Papers. This release made public a letter to Lloyd Garrison, NLRB chair. Gorman developed these demands in several public forums immediately after the convention. See also Federal Council of the Churches of Christ in America, *Information Service*, 8 Sept. 1934, TWUA Papers, for special fact sheet on the strike.

67. Geer to Sloan, 16 Aug. 1934, Bruere Board Papers.

68. Memorandum to files by Bruere concerning telephone conversation with Edwin Smith, NLRB member, 17 Aug. 1934, ibid. Sloan, just before the strike began, proposed a dual jurisdiction of Section 7(a) cases, with the complainant having the option where to file and with the investigation taken out of the Code Authority's hands; telegram, Sloan to Bruere, 29 Aug. 1934, ibid.

69. Minutes of the Bruere Board, 22 Aug. 1934, ibid.

70. *New York Times*, 23 Aug. 1934; Statement for Associated Press, 23 Aug. 1934, Sloan Papers.

71. *New York Times*, 25 Aug. 1934.

72. Minutes of the Bruere Board, 28 Aug. 1934, Bruere Board Papers.

73. *New York Times*, 28 and 29 Aug. 1934.

74. Ibid., 30 Aug. 1934.

75. Ibid., 1 Sept. 1934.

76. Garrison to FDR, 1 Sept. 1934, FDR Papers.

CHAPTER SEVEN

1. Copies of some of their talks can be found in TWUA Papers and Sloan Papers.

2. *New York Times*, 29 Aug. 1934.

3. Charlotte *Observer*, 3 Sept. 1934.

4. Daniels, "Here Comes Gorman," 204.

5. The "sealed orders" are located in TWUA Papers.

6. Daniels, *A Southerner Discovers The South*.

7. Columbia *State*, 5 and 6 Sept. 1934.

8. *Textile Bulletin*, Sept. 1934, p. 89.

9. *Cotton*, Sept. 1934, p. 40. Examples of similar editorial views are found in the Charlotte *Observer*, 7 Sept. 1934 and Birmingham *News*, 4 Sept. 1934.

10. Marshall, *Labor in the South*, 168. Gorman would later claim that he never authorized the flying squadrons, but this was days afterward, when the strike was failing; *New York Times*, 16 June 1934. He certainly had tacitly supported them by first failing to condemn them and then announcing their discontinuance; ibid., 10 Sept. 1934.

11. John Wesley Kennedy, "The General Strike in the Textile Industry, September, 1934" (M.A. thesis, Duke University, 1947), 63.

12. Bill Finger, "Textile Men: Looms, Loans and Lockouts," *Southern Exposure* 3 (1976), 58.

13. Interview with Ivy Norman, Burlington, N.C., 4 and 30 June 1979, Piedmont Series. See also Hamilton Basso, "Divided Southern Front," *New Republic* 78 (9 May 1934), 361.

14. Columbia *State*, 1 Sept. 1934.

15. Ibid., 5 Sept. 1934.

16. Ibid., 6 Sept. 1934.

17. Ibid., 7 Sept. 1934.

18. Interview with Mack Duncan, Greenville, S.C., 7 June and 30 Aug. 1979, Piedmont Series. See also UTW, "Killing of Textile Strikers and Sympathizers During General Textile Strike of 1934," 30 Oct. 1935, TWUA Papers.

19. Columbia *State*, 9, 10, and 11 Sept. 1934.

20. Ibid., 5, 6, and 7 Sept. 1934; *New York Times*, 14 Sept. 1934.

21. Columbia *State*, 14 Sept. 1934; *Textile Bulletin*, 20 Sept. 1934, pp. 6, 18.

22. Charlotte *Observer*, 4 Sept. 1934.

23. Ibid., 5 Sept. 1934.

24. Joseph Yates Garrison, "Paul Revere Christopher: Southern Labor Leader, 1910–1974" (Ph.D. diss., Georgia State Univ., 1977), 35.

25. Charlotte *Observer*, 8 Sept. 1934.

26. Ibid., 19 Sept. 1934. On 18 September two strikers on a picket line at Belmont, N.C., were bayoneted but not wounded seriously.

27. *Textile Labor Banner*, 2 Feb. 1935.

28. *Atlanta Constitution*, 5 Sept. 1934.

29. The *New York Times* gave front-page coverage to the strike almost daily, and the violence in the first week in the South and the later violence in New England received heavy play. The most accessible source for the strike may be the *Times*, although its coverage of the strike as a *national* event leads to the erroneous assumption that the strike events were a cohesive, planned effort by the UTW.

30. *Atlanta Constitution*, 6 Sept. 1934; John E. Allen, "Eugene Talmadge and the Great Textile Strike in Georgia, September 1934," in Fink and Reed, eds., *Essays in Southern Labor History*, 233–36.

31. *Atlanta Constitution*, 15 and 16 Sept. 1934.

32. Ibid., 18 Sept. 1934.

33. Ibid., 23 Sept. 1934.

34. Allen, "Eugene Talmadge and the Great Textile Strike in Georgia," 239; *Atlanta Constitution*, 18 Sept. 1934.

35. Birmingham *News*, 4 and 9 Sept. 1934. Instructive concerning the Alabama situation was Edward Akin, "'Mr. Donald's Help': Donald Comer's Birmingham Operatives and the United Textile Workers, 1933–34" (unpublished paper used by permission of author).

36. Roberts to Donald Comer, 4 Sept. 1934, Comer Papers; Taft, *Organizing Dixie*, 80.

37. James F. Findlay, "The Great Textile Strike of 1934: Illuminating Rhode Island History in the Thirties," *Rhode Island History* 42 (Feb. 1983), 17–29; *New York Times* 10, 11, 12, 13, and 14 Sept. 1934; Bernstein, *The Turbulent Years*, 312–13; Breecher, *Strike!*, 173–75.

38. *Cotton*, Oct. 1934, p. 59.

39. Jackson, "Textiles in the South Carolina Piedmont," 136.

40. Harry Hopkins to all state emergency relief administrators on relief to strikers, 5 Oct. 1934, Hopkins Papers; Bernstein, *The Turbulent Years*, 307–08, 312.

41. *New York Times*, 21 Sept. 1934.

42. Franklin D. Roosevelt, *Complete Presidential Press Conferences of Franklin D. Roosevelt*, vols. 3–4 (New York, 1972), Press Conf. No. 135.

43. Garrison to FDR, 1 Sept. 1934, FDR Papers.

44. Roosevelt, *Complete Presidential Press Conferences*, Press Conf. No. 141.

45. Bernard Bellush, *He Walked Alone: A Biography of John Gilbert Winant* (The Hague, 1968), 114–18, 155–221. The full text of the presidential order is in *New York Times*, 6 Sept. 1934.

46. Cited in Bernstein, *The Turbulent Years*, 310.

47. "Statement by George Sloan," 3 Sept. 1934, Sloan Papers. Some copies of Sloan's releases and talks are located here. See, e.g., CTI press release of 1 Sept. 1934.

48. *New York Times*, 5 Sept. 1934. Some of Gorman's radio talks are in the TWUA Papers.

49. *New York Times*, 9 Sept. 1934. The formal request for arbitration went to Winant from Gorman on 9 Sept. 1934, NRA. "Records of the Board of Inquiry," NA, RG 9.

50. *New York Times*, 10 Sept. 1934.

51. Galambos, *Competition and Cooperation*, 262–63.

52. Prince M. Carlisle, "Who Won the Textile Strike? Another Viewpoint," *Economic Forum* 2 (Winter 1935), 490.

53. Statement by Sloan, 5 Sept. 1934, Sloan Papers.

54. *New York Times*, 15 Sept. 1934.

55. A full text of the Winant Board Report is in *New York Times*, 21 Sept. 1934. A summary of the report is in "Report of the Board of Inquiry," *Monthly Labor Review* 39 (Nov. 1934), 1115–17.

56. *Newsweek*, 29 Sept. 1934, p. 10. See his letter of thanks to Winant expressing his pleasure in this "fair and reasonable proposal," 27 Sept. 1934, John G. Winant Papers, FDR Papers.

57. *New York Times*, 22 Sept. 1934.

58. Ibid., 23 Sept. 1934.

59. Francis Gorman to FDR, 3 Oct. 1934, FDR Papers.

60. "Summary of the Events of the Strike, the Demands of the Strike Leadership, Recommendations of the Winant Board and Recommendations of the Code Authority to the Industry with Respect to Same," 1 Oct. 1934, Sloan Papers.

61. Sloan to Squires, 13 Nov. 1934, TLRB Papers.

62. Galambos, *Competition and Cooperation*, 265–66; the Code Authority acquiesced in the necessary code amendments to establish the TLRB. See amended code of 16 Oct. 1934, Sloan Papers.

63. Conway, *Rise Gonna Rise: A Portrait of Southern Textile Workers* (New York, 1979), 166–67.

64. As quoted in Anne M. Ramsay, "Industrial Relations in the Southern Cotton Textile Industry, 1933–1935," *Vassar Journal of Undergraduate Studies* 9 (May 1935), 164.

65. *Textile Worker*, Dec. 1941; UTW, *The AFL Textile Worker: A History of the United Textile Workers of America* (Washington D.C., 1950), 21.

66. Conway, *Rise Gonna Rise*, 168.

67. *New York Times*, 9 Oct. 1940.

68. Charlotte *Observer*, 23 Sept. 1934.

69. Interview with Franz Daniel, 26 July 1960. Daniel, of course, was by then a CIO opponent of Gorman, who led a dissident AFL textile union.

70. Derber and Young, eds., *Labor and the New Deal*, 27.

71. Tindall, *The Emergence of the New South*, 515.

CHAPTER EIGHT

1. "Establishment of a Textile Labor Relations Board," *Monthly Labor Review* 39 (Oct. 1934), 870–72; *New York Times*, 27 Sept. 1934; Lorwin and Wubnig, *Labor Relations Boards*, 421–28.

2. "Work Assignment Boards in Textile Industries," *Monthly Labor Review* 39 (Dec. 1934), 1355–57; *New York Times*, 17 Oct. and 1 Dec., 1934.

3. Brent Dow Allison, "Who Won the Textile Strike?—One Viewpoint," *Economic Forum* 2 (Winter 1935), 481.

4. "Annual Report of Textile Labor Relations Board, September 30, 1934, to September 30, 1935," TLRB Papers.

5. Lloyd K. Garrison, "Section 7-a and the Future," *Survey Graphic* 24 (Feb. 1935), 54.

6. Harry A. Millis to Benjamin Squires, executive director of the TLRB, 1 Nov. 1934, TLRB Papers; Harry A. Millis to Walter P. Stacy, 13 Nov. 1934, Department of Labor, "Records of the NLRB," NA, RG 280.

7. Frank Douglass to Sloan, 21 Dec. 1934; Sloan to Douglass, 24 Dec. 1934; both in TLRB Papers.

8. "Memorandum by Telfair Knight, counsel for the TLRB in connection with the Textile Planning Committee," 28 Feb. 1935, ibid. The UTW leaders probably consented because in actuality the claims of wage and hour violations were often exaggerated, unlike claims of discrimination against union members and refusal to bargain. Also owners had a vested interest in seeing that fellow owners did not cheat in a way that gave them a competitive edge.

9. Ibid.

10. "Report to Frances Perkins from Frank P. Douglass on Procedures of TLRB," 28 Feb. 1935, ibid.

11. Squires to Cannon, 22 Oct. 1934, ibid.

12. Just as the NRA and TLRB disappeared, Frank Douglass notified Sloan on 20 March 1935 that the TLRB would take over all field investigations of wage and hour violations as soon as an ample staff could be hired. Sloan had assented, so long as copies of the complaints were sent to the Code Authority. Douglass to Sloan, 28 March 1935, ibid.

13. Report of Carl Gill, 14 Oct. 1934, on Bibb Manufacturing disputes, NRA. "Records Relating to Labor Disturbances," NA, RG 9.

14. *New York Times*, 30 Sept. 1934.

15. *Newsweek*, 29 Sept. 1934, p. 11.

16. Raleigh *News and Observer*, 25 Sept. 1934.

17. Benjamin Squires, executive director of TLRB to all mill managements, 17 Oct. 1934, TLRB Papers.

18. *New York Times*, 26 Oct. 1934.

19. *New York Times,* 18 Nov. 1934. See his formal note of complaint to Walter Stacy, chairperson of TLRB, 13 Nov. 1934, TLRB Papers.

20. Gelhorn to Hopkins, 11 Nov. 1934, Hopkins Papers.

21. William P. Mangold, "Who Won The Textile Strike?", *New Republic* 8 (17 Oct. 1934), 272.

22. Telegram of Benjamin Squires to all mills, 6 Nov. 1934, TLRB Papers; *New York Times*, 7 Nov. 1934.

23. Squires to Sloan, 16 Nov. 1934, TLRB Papers.

24. Sloan to Benjamin Squires, 13 Nov. 1934, ibid.

25. *Textile Bulletin*, 4 Oct. 1934, p. 14; 11 Oct. 1934, p. 18.

26. *The Bibb Recorder*, 28 Sept. 1934, copy in TLRB Papers.

27. Lorwin and Wubnig, *Labor Relations Boards*, 422–24.

28. Ibid., 425;

29. "First Quarterly Report of the TLRB, January 4, 1935," TLRB Papers.

30. Lorwin and Wubnig, *Labor Relations Boards*, 425.

31. Johnson, *The Politics of Soft Coal*, 177–80.

32. D. Williams to Samuel McClurd, 25 Feb. 1935, TLRB Papers.

33. Copy of Letter from Marchant to David Coker, 27 Oct. 1934, Department of Labor, Office Files of Frances Perkins, NA, RG 174.

34. Knight to John Peel of UTW, 3 May 1935, TLRB Papers. There is no record of a cotton textile mill in the South losing its Blue Eagle.

35. "Annual Report of Textile Labor Relations Board," 30 Sept. 1934–30 Sept. 1935, ibid.

36. *Textile Labor Banner,* 19 Jan. 1935.

37. Ibid., 2 Feb. 1935; Gorman to Samuel McClurd, 5 Feb. 1935, TLRB Papers.

38. *Ellenbogen Hearings, 1936*, p. 732. The union presented a list of 117 southern mills which it contended had ignored TLRB decisions, ibid., 761–67. In TLRB decisions, the UTW must have included on-the-spot judgments and attempts at mediation by field agents, as well as formal TLRB decisions. See also UTW, *Proceedings of the Seventh Biennial Convention*, New York, Sept. 14–19, 1936, pp. 26–27.

39. *Textile Labor Banner*, 13 Apr. 1935.

40. UTW, *Official News Sheet*, n.d. [ca. Oct. 1934].

41. *Textile Labor Banner*, 10 Dec. and 17 Dec. 1934.

42. Gorman to Christopher, 23 Oct. 1934, Christopher Papers.

43. *New York Times*, 18 Jan. 1935. Gorman obviously was in sympathy with the coming CIO, which the UTW would join.

44. *Textile Labor Banner*, 12 Jan. and 16 Feb. 1935.

45. Ibid., 9 Feb. 1935.

46. Ibid., 29 June 1935.

47. TLRB, "Summary of Activities in the Fiscal Year Ended June 30, 1936" and "Summary of Activities in the Fiscal Year Ended June 30, 1937," NRA, "Records Relating to Labor Disturbance," NA, RG 9.

48. UTW, *Proceedings of the 7th Biennial Convention*, 39–40.

49. *Textile Worker*, 19 Sept. 1936.

50. Ibid., 2 May 1936.

51. Ibid., 10 May 1936.

52. TWUA, *Proceedings of the First Constitutional Convention*, New York, May 15–19, 1934, p. 131.

53. Textile Workers Organizing Committee, *Building a Union of Textile Workers*, 3.

54. Interview with Mildred Shoemaker, Burlington, N.C., 23 March 1979, Piedmont Series.

55. Interview with Mareda Cobb, Bynum, N.C., 16 June 1979, ibid.

56. Christopher's weekly reports in 1935–37 have two-to four-sentence descriptions of his daily activity. See also his "Biennial Report to the Officers and Delegates of the 35th Annual Convention, 1936," Christopher Papers. See also Garrison, "Paul Revere Christopher," 42–65.

57. Christopher to James Starr, 19 Jan. 1936, and Christopher to Peel, 3 Mar. 1936; both in Christopher Papers.

58. Christopher to Peel, 22 April 1936, ibid.

59. Christopher to Gorman, 31 Dec. 1936, ibid.

60. Cannon, "Social Deterrents to the Unionization of Southern Cotton Textile Mill Workers," 296; Henry Cooper Ellenberg, "The Congress of Industrial Organization in South Carolina, 1938–1945," (M.A. thesis, Univ. of South Carolina, 1951), 48.

61. Cannon, "Social Deterrents to the Unionization of Southern Cotton Textile Mill Workers," 298.

62. "UTW Membership in April 1937," memorandum prepared by Solomon Barkin, Apr. 1937, TWUA Papers.

63. Columbia *State*, 18 Oct. 1934.

64. Ibid., 18 Oct. 1934.

65. *Cotton*, Dec. 1934, p. 44.

66. George Kamenow to TLRB, 4 Sept. 1935, NRA, "Records Relating to Labor Disturbances," NA, RG 9.

67. *Proceedings of ACMA*, Apr. 1935, pp. 53, 63.

68. Ramsay, "Industrial relations in the Southern Cotton Textile Industry, 1933–1935," 78.

69. FTC, *Textile Industries: Part I, Investment and Profit, Textile Industries: Part II, The Cotton Textile Industry, and Textile Industry in 1933 and 1934: Part I, The Cotton Textile Industry*.

70. *New York Times*, 20 Jan. 1935.

71. *Ellenbogen Hearings, 1936*, 524.

72. Arthur F. Hinrichs to Frances Perkins, 18 Apr. 1935, Department of Labor, Office Files of Frances Perkins, NA, RG 174.

73. "Report and Recommendations of the Cotton Textile Work Assignment Board to President Franklin D. Roosevelt for a Permanent Plan for Regulation of Work Assignments in the Cotton Textile Industry," TLRB Papers; *New York Times*, 13 May 1935.

74. Exhibit attached to copy of memorandum from William A. Mitchell to Frances Perkins, 4 June 1935, NRA, "Records Relating to Labor Disturbances," NA, RG 9.

75. Mitchell to Perkins, 4 June 1935, ibid.

76. Gorman to William Mitchell, 28 May 1935, TLRB Papers.

77. Peel to Mitchell, 23 May 1935, ibid.

78. *New York Times*, 28 Mar. and 2 Apr. 1935. See also "Temporary Reduction in Cotton-Textile Production," *Monthly Labor Review* 60 (May 1935), 1186–87.

79. *Textile Labor Banner*, 13 Apr. 1935.

80. Donald Comer to George Sloan, 8 Dec. 1934, Comer Papers.

81. *New York Times*, 23 Dec. 1934 and 1 Jan. 1935.

82. Ibid., 10 Mar. 1935.

83. *Proceedings of ACMA*, Apr., 1935, p. 27.

84. Ibid., p. 39.

85. *New York Times*, 25 and 26 Apr. 1935.

86. "Establishment of Textile Planning Committee," *Monthly Labor Review* 60 (Apr. 1935), 893; *New York Times*, 26 Feb. 1935.

87. Memorandum of TPC meetings by Telfair Knight, 27 Feb., 5 and 6 Mar., and 2 Apr. 1935, TLRB Papers.

88. "Current Information from the Cotton-Textile Institute, 14 March 1935," Sloan Papers.

89. Petition to FDR, dated 18 Apr. 1935, FDR Papers.

90. Roper to FDR, 19 Apr. 1935, ibid.

91. FDR to Roper, 26 Apr. 1935, ibid.

92. *New York Times*, 12, 19, 20, and 29 Apr. 1935.

93. The report was submitted to the Senate, then considering NRA replacement legislation, and has been cited earlier as *Senate Document 26*. A summary can be found in "Cabinet Committee's Recommendations for Cotton Textile Industry," *Monthly Labor Review* 61 (Oct. 1935), 944–45. See also *New York Times* 22 Aug. 1935.

94. Gorman to FDR, 20 May 1936, and FDR to Gorman, 2 June 1936, both in FDR Papers.

95. *New York Times*, 21 May 1937. See also Hawley, *The New Deal and the Problem of Monopoly*, 223–24.

96. "Southern Manufacturers Urge Change in NRA," *Manufacturers' Record* 104 (Jan. 1935), 123; "Revise NRA Codes," ibid., 104 (Mar. 1935), 22; *Cotton*, Apr. 1935, p. 116.

97. George Sloan to Donald Richberg, 3 Feb. 1935, Sloan Papers.

98. "Competition Under the Codes," speech in Washington D.C., 1 May 1935, ibid.

99. *Proceedings of ACMA*, Washington D.C., 13 May 1937, p. 23.

100. See this line of argument in *Textile World*, June 1935, p. 59.

101. Birmingham *News*, 28 May 1935; interview with Donald Comer at Harvard Business School, 18 May 1960, Comer Papers.

102. Charlotte *Observer*, 7 and 8, June 1935.

103. Ibid., 8 June 1935.

104. Anderson and Comer to all ACMA members, 24 July 1935, Comer Papers.

105. Columbia *State*, 24 May 1937.

106. McLaurine to ACMA members, 5 July and 10 Aug. 1935, Comer Papers.

107. *New York Times*, 18 Dec. 1935.

108. *Cotton*, June 1936, p. 41.

109. Cited in National Economic and Social Planning Association, *Report of the Committee on the Textile Industry of the United States of America*, (Washington D.C., 1937), 19.

110. *New York Times*, 25 Feb. 1936.

111. Calvin B. Hoover and B.U. Ratchford, *Economic Resources and Policies of the South* (New York, 1951), 55.

112. *New York Times*, 2 Jan. and 21 Nov. 1936. See also *Blue Book of Southern Progress* (Baltimore, 1936), 15.

113. *Cotton*, Apr. 1935, p. 116; *Textile Bulletin*, Jan. 1935, p. 14.

114. *New York Times*, 7 Dec. 1935.

115. Cotton-Textile Institute, *Current Information*, Nov. 1941.

116. Galambos, *Competition and Cooperation*, 285–86.

117. Backman and Gainsbrugh, *Economics of the Cotton Textile Industry*, 207.

118. Found in Bibb Manufacturing Company files, NRA, "Records Relating to Labor Disturbances," NA, RG 9.

CHAPTER NINE

1. Daniel Albert Sipe, "A Moment of State: The Enactment of the National Labor Relations Act, 1935," (Ph.D. diss., Univ. of Pennsylvania, 1981), 2. Although Sipe contends that the Wagner Act was a major element in a "welfare state liberalism" that sharply impeded labor power in a class sense—a thesis that would be unacceptable to some—his history of the act contains much useful analysis, particularly of support and opposition for the bill. For a documentary history of the bill, see National Labor Relations Board, *Legislative History of the National Labor Relations Act*, 2 vols. (Washington D.C., 1949). For some standard historical treatments, see Bernstein, *New Deal Collective Bargaining Policy*, 57–75, 84–128; Bernstein, *The Turbulent Years*, 318–351. See also Huthmacher's *Senator Robert F. Wagner*, 187–98. Huthmacher quotes a Wagner associate as saying the quick emergence and easy passage of the bill was a 200-to-1 shot, p. 196. See also Irons, *The New Deal Lawyers*, 226–53, and Cortner, *The Wagner Act Cases*, 72–88.

2. Richard C. Wilcock, "Industrial Management's Policies Toward Unionism," in Derber and Young, eds., *Labor and the New Deal*, 290–91.

3. National Labor Relations Board, *First Annual Report* (Washington D.C., 1936), 46, 48. See also Malcolm Ross, *Death of a Yale Man* (New York, 1939), 171–73.

4. *TWUA Proceedings, 1939*, 23.

5. U.S. Congress, Senate, Committee on Education and Labor, *NLRB and Proposed Amendments*, Hearings, 76 Cong., 1 Sess., (Washington D.C., 1939), 4113.

6. Cortner, *The Wagner Act Cases*, 90, 103, 179; Irons, *The New Deal Lawyers*, 254–71.

7. Ross, *Death of a Yale Man*, 342.

8. NLRB, *Second Annual Report* (Washington D.C., 1937), 1.

9. See its annual reports. See also Millis and Brown, *From the Wagner Act to Taft-Hartley*, 30–75. A short description of the NLRB's procedures in the 1930s can be found in James E. Pate, "The National Labor Relations Board," *Southern Economic Journal* 6 (July 1939), 56–76. For an exhaustive history, see James A. Gross, *The Making of the National Labor Relations Board, 1933–37*, (Albany, N.Y., 1974), and *The Reshaping of the National Labor Relations Board: National Labor Policy in Transition, 1937–1947* (Albany, N.Y., 1981). Christopher L. Tomlinson, *The State and the Union: Labor Relations, Law, and the Organized Labor Movement in America, 1935–1955* (New York, 1985), 103–243, portrays the limited nature of the New Deal's labor law revolution in the 1930s.

10. Wilcock, "Industrial Management's Policies Toward Unionism," 295–303.

11. "G-- D--- Labor Board," *Fortune* 18 (Oct. 1938), 52–53.

12. Charles W. Pipkin, "Social Legislation in the South," *Southern Policy Paper*, No. 3 (Chapel Hill, 1936); Virginius Dabney, "Southern Employers and Labor Reform," *Southern Review* 2 (1936–37), 279–88; "Independence," *Manufacturers' Record* 105 (July 1936), 24.

13. Thomas H. Webb, "Cotton Textile Industry Faces Better Prospects," *Manufacturers' Record*, 105 (Jan. 1936), 22, 26; *Cotton*, Feb. 1938, p. 84. Speeches in 1935, 1936, and 1937 before the ACMA constantly reiterated this view. See also "The New Deal viewed by Southern Papers," *Manufacturers' Record* 104 (Aug. 1935), 23, 52.

14. Anderson to Donald Comer, 28 Jan. 1936, Comer Papers.

15. Goldthwaite Dorr for the CTI to all the mills, 29 Aug. 1935, Sloan Papers.

16. *Textile Bulletin*, 21 Nov. 1935, p. 5.

17. *Cotton*, July 1935, p. 48.

18. *Ellenbogen Hearings, 1936*, p. 213–17.

19. *National Textile Bill*, 5–6.

20. *Textile Bulletin*, 1 Apr. 1937, p. 101, and 15 Oct. 1939, p. 98.

21. *New York Times*, 24 Nov. 1935.

22. Ibid., 23 Nov. 1935.

23. *Textile Labor Banner*, 27 Apr. 1935.

24. *New York Times*, 27 July 1935.

25. NLRB, "In the Matter of Mooreville Cotton Mills and Local No. 1221, United Textile Workers of America," *Decisions and Orders of the National Labor Relations Board* 2 (Washington D.C., 1937), 952–62; "In the Matter of Beower-Lois Mills and Local No. 1871, United Textile Workers of America," *Decisions and Orders* 1 (Washington D.C., 1936), 147–52. See other cotton mill cases in *Decisions and Orders* 1, pp. 57–67, 97–122, 147–58, and 2 pp. 20–38.

26. George W. Baker, "The Changing Structure of National and Industrial Labor, with Special Reference to the Southeast," (Ph.D. diss., Univ. of North Carolina,1951), 261–63.

27. Frank T. DeVyver, "The Present Status of Labor Unions in the South," 5 (April 1939), 394.

28. *Proceedings of ACMA*, Augusta, Ga., 1938, p. 27.

29. *Ellenbogen Hearings, 1937*, p. 94.

30. Virginius Dabney, *Below the Potomac: A Book About the New South* (New York, 1942), 101; Stetson Kennedy, *Southern Exposure* (New York, 1946), 300–01.

31. Lahne, *The Cotton Mill Worker*, 10.

32. *Textile Labor Banner*, 29 June 1935.

33. Ibid., 21 Dec. 1935.

34. *Textile Worker*, 18 Apr. 1936.

35. Garrison, "Paul Revere Christopher," 52.

36. See NLRB, *Governmental Protection of Labor's Right to Organize* (Washington D.C., 1936).

37. U.S. Congress, House, Subcommittee of the Committee on Labor, *To Regulate the Textile Industry*, 75 Cong., 1 Sess. (Washington, D.C., 1937), 184.

38. The standard work on the CIO during this period is Galenson, *CIO Challenge to the AFL*. See pp. 3–74.

39. *Textile Worker*, 15 Aug. 1936.

40. *Textile Worker*, 3 Oct. 1936; Galenson, *CIO Challenge to the AFL*, 44.

41. Typed memorandum, n.d. [1936], TWUA Papers.

42. Matthew Josephson, *Sidney Hillman: Statesman of American Labor* (New York, 1952), 424.

43. The *New York Times* covered the story of the negotiations, 5, 10, 11, and 19 March 1937. TWOC histories can be found in Lahne, *The Cotton Mill Worker*, 262–69; Bernstein, *The Turbulent Years*, 616–23; Galenson, *CIO Challenge to the AFL*, 326–48; John Wesley Kennedy, "A History of the Textile Workers Union of America, C.I.O.," (Ph.D. diss., Univ. of North Carolina, 1950), 57–96. Marshall, *Labor in the South*, 169–75; Paul David Richards, "The History of the Textile Workers Union of America, CIO, in the South, 1937 to 1945," (Ph.D. diss., Univ. of Wisconsin, 1978), 36–91. TWOC also printed a history of its activities, *Building A Union of Textile Workers*, and these accounts rely heavily on it.

44. *New York Times*, 19 Mar. 1937.

45. Lahne, *The Cotton Mill Worker*, 263; Bernstein, *The Turbulent Years*, 618.

46. Cited in Bernstein, *The Turbulent Years*, 617.

47. UTW, *Special Convention Proceedings* (Washington D.C., 1939), 21, 23.

48. Gorman to all UTW locals, 15 March 1937, copy in Mason Papers.

49. Len DeCaux, *Labor Radical: From the Wobblies to CIO* (New York, 1970), 284.

50. See Bernstein, *The Turbulent Years*, 619, for this view.

51. Josephson, *Sidney Hillman*, 416–25, devotes relatively little space to Hillman's efforts, reflecting the lack of day-to-day involvement.

52. Lucy Randolph Mason, *To Win These Rights: A Personal Story of the CIO in the South* (New York, 1952), 23. See also Herman Wolfe, "Cotton and the Unions," *Survey Graphic* 27 (Mar. 1938), 146.

53. Richards, "The History of the Textile Workers Union of America," 41–42.

54. *Union News Service*, 12 Apr. 1937.

55. Ellenberg, "The CIO in South Carolina," 25.

56. Josephson, *Sidney Hillman*, 420; Richards, "The History of the Textile Workers Union of America," 42.

57. Mary Heaton Vorse, "Bringing Unions to Textiles," *New Republic* 92 (Oct. 1937), 331.

58. TWOC, *Building a Union*, 13.

59. *Newsweek*, 10 Apr. 1937, p. 6.

60. Daniels, *A Southerner Discovers The South*, 296.

61. Christopher to Daniels, 20 Apr. 1937, Christopher Papers.

62. Solomon Barkin, "Report to Textile Organizing Committee on Activities, March 20, 1937," TWUA Papers; Kennedy, "A History of the Textile Workers Union of America," 67–73.

63. *TWOC Parade*, 1 July 1937.

64. Circular Memorandum to all organizers by A. Steve Nance, 6 July 1937, Christopher Papers.

65. Copies of different kinds of pledgecards exist in the TWUA Papers and TLRB Papers. They were simple statements authorizing the TWOC to bargain collectively.

66. Lahne, *The Cotton Mill Worker*, 264–66.

67. Raleigh *News and Observer* and *New York Times*, 30 Mar. 1937.

68. Anderson to Murchison, 3 Apr. 1937, copy in Comer Papers.

69. *New York Times*, 20 Mar. 1937; Ellenberg, "The CIO in South Carolina," 24–25; clipping from Richmond *Times Dispatch*, 31 Mar. 1937, in UTW Papers.

70. *Daily News Record*, 9 Mar. 1937.

71. Raleigh *News and Observer*, 11 Mar. 1937.

72. J.H. Marion, Jr., "Does the South Need John Lewis?", *Christian Century* 54 (19 May 1937), 645.

73. *Blue Book of Southern Progress* 25; "Best Textile Year Since 1929," *Manufacturers' Record* 105 (Jan. 1937), 24–26; "Cotton Manufacturing Near Peak," ibid. 106 (Apr. 1937), 40; *New York Times*, 15 Nov. and 20 Dec. 1936.

74. *Textile Bulletin*, 24 Dec. 1936, p. 1.

75. *Textile Bulletin*, 27 Jan. 1938, p. 1.

76. Ibid.

77. *New York Times*, 3 Jan. 1939.

78. Ibid., 19 Dec. 1938. The profit situation was different for North and South. The industry in 1935 and 1938 reported net deficits, but this was primarily because of the unprofitable operation of New England mills. For the cause of the slowly rising trend of profits in the industry between 1936 and 1941, see Bachman and Gainsbrugh, *Economics of the Textile Industry*, 143–65.

79. Christopher to Gorman, 18 Dec. 1937, Christopher Papers.

80. Christopher to John Peel, 10 Jan. 1938, and to Francis Gorman, 21 Apr. 1938, Christopher Papers.

81. James Starr to Christopher, 25 Jan. 1938, Christopher Papers.

82. *New York Times*, 3 Jan. 1938.

83. *Textile Bulletin*, 1 Feb. 1939, p. 1.

84. *Wall Street Journal*, 7 Aug. 1941. See also Paul Halstead, "Cotton Textile Outlook," *Manufacturers Record* 109 (Jan. 1940), 40, 60.

85. *Textile Bulletin*, 1 July 1941, p. 43.

86. For an example of this view, see Claudius Murchison's ACMA speech, in which he predicts the death of the New Deal and the return of "constructive conservatism." *Proceedings of ACMA*, White Sulphur Springs, W.Va., 1940, pp. 104–05.

CHAPTER TEN

1. Galenson, *CIO Challenge to the AFL*, 335. See also statistics on membership in Richards, "The History of the Textile Workers Union of America," 49–53.

2. Wolfe, "Cotton and the Unions," 146–48.

3. Adamic, *My America*, 416.

4. John Thomas Kneebone, "Race, Reform, and History: Southern Liberal Journalists, 1920–1940," (Ph.D. diss., Univ. of Virginia, 1981), 432–34.

5. Mason to Hillman, 11 Sept. 1937, Mason Papers.

6. *New York Times*, 25 Sept. 1937.

7. Ibid., 7 May 1937.

8. Ibid., 20 Sept. 1937.

9. *Textile Bulletin*, 18 Mar. 1937, p. 26.

10. *Daily News Record*, 24 Feb. 1939.

11. *New York Times*, 31 Oct. 1937.

12. *Textile Bulletin*, 3 Feb. 1939, p. 14.

13. Quoted in Ellenberg, "The CIO in South Carolina," 39.

14. Dabney, *Below The Potomac*, 13; see also Robert P. Ingalls, "Anti-Labor Vigilantes: The South During the 1930s," *Southern Exposure* 12 (Nov.–Dec. 1984), 72–78, and D. Witherspoon Dodge, *Southern Rebel in Reverse: The Autobiography of an Idol-Shaker* (New York, 1961), 70–129.

15. Mason, *To Win These Rights*, 39–59.

16. *Textile Labor*, June 1939.

17. *Atlanta Constitution*, 19 and 20 Sept. 1937; *New York Times* 30 Mar. and 14 May 1937.

18. TWUA, *Proceedings of the Second Biennial Convention*, 1941, p. 48.

19. *TWOC Parade*, 31 July 1937.

20. Wilcock, "Industrial Management's Policies Toward Unionism," 286.

21. DeVyver, "Southern Textile Mills Revisited," 468.

22. *Daily News Record*, 29 Apr. 1938.

23. Ibid., 30 Apr. 1937.

24. Quoted in *Cotton*, Feb. 1938, p. 111.

25. Barkin, "A Trade Unionist Appraises Management Personnel Philosophy," 59–60.

26. Samuel McClurd to Hugh Kerwin, director, Federal Mediation and Conciliation Service, 15 Mar. 1937, TLRB Papers.

27. John Connors to Samuel McClurd, 30 Mar. 1937, ibid.

28. Solomon Barkin, "Report to Textile Workers Organizing Committee on Activities, March 20, 1937," TWUA Papers.

29. Article by A. Steve Nance, as told to Carl Warren, New York *Daily News*, n.d., clipping in TWUA Papers.

30. Paul Christopher to P.L. Davis, 14 July 1937, Christopher Papers.

31. *Journal of Commerce*, 8 July 1937, clipping in TLRB Papers.

32. *New York Times*, 1 Apr. 1937.

33. *TWOC Parade*, 1 July 1937.

34. *Union News Service*, 12 July 1937.
35. TWOC 1937 pamphlet, in UTW Papers.
36. Ellenberg, "The CIO in South Carolina," 38.
37. TWOC report on pledgecards received through 7 August 1937, TWUA Papers.
38. File of this newsletter in UTW Papers.
39. Galenson, *CIO Challenge to the AFL*, 336.
40. Solomon Barkin, "Report on TWOC Progress," 8 Oct. 1937, TWUA Papers; *Daily News Record*, 7 Oct. 1937.
41. *Daily News Record*, ibid.
42. Garrison, "Paul Revere Christopher," 75–110.
43. Richards, "The History of the Textile Workers Union of America," 57–60.
44. *Journal of Commerce*, 16 July 1937; *Daily News Record*, 4 May 1937.
45. Mason to Sidney Hillman, 2 Oct. 1937, Mason Papers.
46. TWOC, *Building a Union of Textile Workers*, 72.
47. Ibid., 23.
48. Quoted in memorandum to NLRB from Charles Feidelson, director of 10th Region, NLRB, 21 Jan. 1938, "Limestone Mills, Case Number X-R-80," NLRB Records. The records of this case are confusing because the records begin separately at all three mills and then eventually are joined into a single case, "In the Matter of Alma Mills, Limestone Mills, and Hamrick Mills," in consecutive listings.
49. NLRB, "In the Matter of Alma Mills, Inc., and Textile Workers Organizing Committee," *Decisions and Orders of the National Labor Relations Board, May 29–June 30, 1940* 24 (Washington D.C., 1940), 9–10. This decision also lists in separate headings the Limestone Mills and the Hamrick Mills but is indexed in the volume as Alma Mills. An exceptionally long decision, it covers pp. 1–70. Hereafter cited as Alma Mills et al.
50. Feidelson to NLRB, 23 Aug. 1938, "Alma Mills, Case Number C-1243," NLRB Records. After the consolidation the case numbers became X-C-432, 444, and 436.
51. The testimony of all hearings before the NLRB, plus the 11 days of testimony in South Carolina in Dec. 1938, Jan. 1939, and Jan. 1940, are in "Transcripts and Hearings," NLRB Records. But the board's formal published summary of the testimony is sufficient for understanding the case.
52. Alma Mills et al., 10–16. For Dodge's vivid account of the conflict of the club and the union, see his testimony, transcript of NLRB regional hearings, Gaffney, S.C., 13 Dec. 1938, pp. 168–200 NLRB Papers. See also Dodge, *Southern Rebel in Reverse*, 105–11.
53. Alma Mills et al., 16–19.
54. TWOC Union Local No. 510T to NLRB, 12 Apr. 1939, "Alma Mills," NLRB Records.
55. Alma Mills et al., 55.
56. Ibid., 24–61; see transcripts of the Gaffney S.C., hearings of 15, 16, 19, 20, and 21 Dec. 1938 and 3, 4, 6, and 7 Jan. 1939, NLRB Records, for the testimony the NLRB used to come to its conclusion.
57. Mrs. M.E. Underwood to Charles Feidelson, n.d., "Alma Mills et al.," NLRB Papers.
58. Sumner Marcus to Mrs. Stern, 18 Feb. 1939, "Highland Park Manufacturing Co., Case Number V-C-359," NLRB Papers.
59. Richards, "The History of the Textile Workers Union of America," 91–122, summarizes some TWOC cases.
60. Mason to Hillman, 21 Jan. 1938, Mason Papers.
61. Interview by author with Franz Daniel, Washington D.C., 29 July 1960.
62. Christopher to Francis Gorman, 21 Mar. 1938, Christopher Papers.

63. Statistics computed by Richards, "The History of the Textile Workers Union of America," 65–68, 93–94, 96. See also "Interim Report of TWOC, 28 March 1938," TWUA Papers.

64. "Interim Report of TWOC, 28 March 1937," ibid. I have avoided listing the Upper South, since many of the locals there were in the synthetic fiber industry.

65. "Report for the Conference of the Committee on the experiences during the last year," n.d. [June 1938], TWUA Papers.

66. *CIO News*, 26 Mar. and 9 June 1938.

67. Solomon Barkin, "Report of TWOC Progress during the Last Several Months, 3 Nov. 1938," TWUA Papers. The report is notable for its restrained tone and sense of consolidation.

68. *New York Times*, 6 July 1938.

69. Charlotte *Observer*, 11 July 1938; *CIO News*, 16 July 1938.

70. *CIO News*, 3 Sept. 1938.

71. Richards, "The History of the Textile Workers Union of America," 99–101.

72. *Daily News Record*, 12 Nov. 1938.

73. "Minutes of the First Meeting of the TWOC Advisory Board, Nov. 3, 1938," TWUA Papers.

74. *Textile Bulletin*, 29 Apr. 1937.

75. *Daily News Record*, 12 Nov. 1938.

76. Mason, *To Win These Rights*, 21.

77. TWOC, *Building a Union of Textile Workers*, 47.

78. TWUA, *Executive Council Report, 1939–1941* (New York, 1941), 42.

79. Copies of the NLRB proceedings, Case Numbers R–552, 553, and 555, are contained in the Erwin Mills Records. TWOC formed a negotiating committee composed of two TWOC organizers and two representatives from each mill, although each plant could have been seen as a separate bargaining unit.

80. Memorandum by W.R. Ruffin, 28 June 1937, Erwin Mills Records.

81. Memorandum with the titles as explained, n.d. [1937], ibid. Internal evidence suggests preparation by Ruffin.

82. Kemp P. Lewis to W.R. Perkins, a company lawyer, 12 Nov. 1940, ibid. Several company memoranda imply this policy.

83. All the contracts are located together in a company file, though a fourth TWOC offer, either before or after Aug. 1938 and before 4 March 1939, is not there; ibid. An unsigned handwritten company diary of the 1939 negotiations with TWOC, consisting of only a few entries in an accounts ledger, record the company's near acceptance; hereafter cited as Diary, Erwin Mills Records.

84. 4, 5, and 18 Apr. 1939, ibid.

85. 8 June 1939, ibid.

86. 15, 16, 17, 18, and 19 June, ibid. This was the last entry of the diary. There is no evidence indicating who kept it.

87. Kemp Lewis to W.R. Perkins, 28 Mar. 1940, Erwin Mills Records.

88. Memorandum to Lewis of the meeting, 19 Aug. 1940, ibid.; memorandum of conference among TWUA officials, NLRB officials, and Lewis, 11 Nov. 1940, ibid.

89. The printed Cooleemee contract is in the Erwin Mills Records. The records of this set of negotiations and hearings are also in the company files, ibid. In 1945–46 the union, with its power consolidated, closed the Durham plant in a very long strike, from 8 Oct. 1945 until 3 Apr. 1946. The strike ended with the company agreeing to nonbinding arbitration of workloads and agreeing to continue to negotiate with the union. A large collection of newspaper clippings in the Frank T. DeVyver Papers, Perkins Library, Duke University, chronicle the strike. DeVyver was personnel director at the mill.

90. "Minutes of the Second Meeting of the TWOC Advisory Board, Jan. 4 and 5, 1939," TWUA Papers.

91. *Textile Labor*, Feb. and Mar. 1939.

92. *Daily News Record*, 13 Apr. 1939.

93. The Gorman-led flight from the TWOC is covered extensively by Kennedy, "A History of the Textile Workers Union of America," 86–93. The TWUA Papers also contain several key documents of the crisis. The union continues today as a separate union in the AFL–CIO. See its early history in United Textile Workers, *The AFL Textile Worker: A History of the United Textile Workers of America* (Washington D.C., 1950).

94. *Textile Labor*, Feb. 1939.

95. *Textile Labor*, May 1939; see also *TWUA Proceedings 1939*; Richards, "The History of the Textile Workers Union of America," 76–91; Kennedy, "A History of the Textile Workers Union of America," 97–117.

96. TWOC, *Building a Union of Textile Workers*, 44, 46, 48.

97. *TWUA Proceedings 1939*, 127, 166. TWOC press release, 15 May 1939, TWUA Papers.

98. *TWUA Proceedings 1939*, 26.

99. Ibid., 128.

100. Ibid., 8.

101. TWUA, *Executive Council Report, 1939–1941*, 68.

102. *CIO News*, 18 Dec. 1939.

103. *Textile Labor*, Jan. 1940.

104. TWUA, *Executive Council Report, 1941*, 44.

105. *Textile Labor*, 1 Apr. 1940.

106. Kennedy, "A History of the Textile Workers Union of America," 135–56; Lahne, *The Cotton Mill Worker*, 270. See also Paul Brinker, "The Enforcement of Collective Bargaining in the South," (Ph.D. diss., Pennsylvania State College, 1948).

107. *Daily News Record*, 13 Apr. 1939.

108. Barkin to Emil Rieve, 25 Oct. 1939, TWUA Papers.

CHAPTER ELEVEN

1. Perkins, *The Roosevelt I Knew*, 256.

2. For a detailed legislative history of the Fair Labor Standards Act, see Orme W. Phelps, *The Legislative Background of the Fair Labor Standards Act* (Chicago, 1939); Paul H. Douglas and Joseph Hackman, "The Fair Labor Standards Act," *Political Science Quarterly* 53 (1938), 491–515; and Elizabeth Brandeis, "Organized Labor and Protective Labor Legislation," in Derber and Young, eds., *Labor and the New Deal*, 217–30.

3. Rosenman, ed., *Public Papers of FDR*, 392.

4. "The 'Must' Wage and Hour Bill," *Manufacturers' Record* 105 (Nov. 1937), 29; "Views of Southern Employers on Wage and House Law," ibid. 106 (Nov. 1938), 30–31, 53. See also testimony of John Edgerton, president of the Southern States Industrial Council, before a congressional committee, in U.S. Congress, Senate, Committee on Education and Labor, and House, Committee on Labor, *Fair Labor Standards Act of 1937*, Joint Hearings, 75 Cong., 1 Sess. (Washington D.C., 1937), 760–807, hereafter cited as *FLSA Joint Hearings*.

5. Sigmund Uminski, *The Progress of Labor in the United States* (New York, 1939), 68.

6. Quoted in Leuchtenburg, *FDR and the New Deal*, 261.

7. Quoted in Paul E. Merz, *New Deal Policy and Southern Rural Poverty* (Baton Rouge, 1978), 228.

8. Tindall, *Emergence of the New South*, 533–34.

9. *FLSA Joint Hearings*, 435.

10. H.M. Douty, "Wage and Hour Legislation for the South," *Southern Policy Papers*, No. 19 (Chapel Hill, 1937), 9–10; "Textiles—New Deal Guinea Pig," *Business Week*, 10 Sept. 1938, p. 14; William Anderson to Rep. Frank Boykin of Alabama, 20 July 1937, copy in Comer Papers.

11. *FLSA Joint Hearings*, 814.

12. Ibid., 943. For Hillman's work on the bill, see Josephson, *Sidney Hillman*, 442–49.

13. For this first federal prohibition of child labor, see Jeremy P. Felt, "The Child Labor Provisions of the Fair Standards Act," *Labor History* 11 (Feb. 1970), 467–81.

14. U.S. Department of Labor, *First Annual Report of the Administrator of the Wage and Hour Division* (Washington D.C., 1939), 34, hereafter cited as *First Annual Report*.

15. *New York Times*, 21 Nov. 1938.

16. U.S. Department of Labor, *A Ceiling for Hours, a Floor for Wages, and a Break for Children: An Explanation of the Fair Labor Standards Act of 1938* (Washington D.C., 1938); Walter Boles, "The Fair Labor Standards Act, with Emphasis on Certain Regional Aspects" (Ph.D. diss., Vanderbilt Univ., 1939), 22–132; "Federal Wage and Hour Law of 1938," *Monthly Labor Review* 47 (July 1938), 107–12.

17. *Textile Bulletin*, 15 Dec. 1938, p. 27.

18. *Proceedings of ACMA*, Apr. 13–15, 1939, p. 61.

19. *New York Times*, 28 Aug. and 7 Oct. 1938.

20. "Statement of Labor Commissioners of the Southeastern States Assembled in Columbia, South Carolina, on July 8, 1938," Department of Labor, Records of the Federal Mediation and Conciliation Service, NA, RG 280.

21. *New York Times*, 18 Aug. 1938.

22. A.F. Hinrichs, "Wage Structure in Cotton Goods Manufacture," *Monthly Labor Review* 47 (Dec. 1938), 1248.

23. *New York Times*, 23 Oct. 1938.

24. Ibid., 3 Sept. 1938.

25. Paul Christopher to Sidney Hillman and Emil Rieve, 31 Dec. 1938, Christopher Papers.

26. *New York Times*, 22 Mar. 1939. For fuller details of the work of Industry Committee No. 1, see *First Annual Report*, 81, and Boles, "The Fair Labor Standards Act," 172–86.

27. *Textile Labor*, Feb. 1939.

28. Ibid.

29. Ibid., Apr. 1939.

30. Ibid., July 1939.

31. Department of Labor, "Report and Recommendation of Industry Committee No. 1 for the Textile Industry to the Administrator of the Wage and Hour Division of the United States Department of Labor," May 1939 (mimeographed), Department of Labor Library.

32. Department of Labor, "Statement of the Minority of Industrial Committee No. 1 for the Textile Industry to the Administrator of the Wage and Hour Division of the United States Department of Labor," May 1939 (mimeographed), ibid.; *New York Times*, 25 May 1939.

33. Anderson to West, 24 Sept. and 1 Oct. 1938, copies in Comer Papers.

34. *New York Times*, 1 June 1939.

35. Ibid., 8 June 1939.

36. *Daily News Record*, 14 Aug. 1939.

37. *New York Times*, 19 June 1939.

38. Department of Labor, "Testimony of Public Hearings on the Recommendation of the Industry Committee No. 1, Concerning Minimum Wage Rates for Textile Industry" (mimeographed), June-July 1939, Department of Labor Library. The transcript of the hearings, which covers over 3,000 pages, hereafter cited as *Public Hearings.*

39. *New York Times*, 23 Aug. 1939.

40. Ibid., 2 Aug. 1939.

41. Ibid., 14 Sept. 1939; "Minimum Wages for Cotton Textile Industry Under Wage and Hour Act," *Monthly Labor Review* 49 (Dec. 1939), 1446–48.

42. *Proceedings of ACMA*, Apr. 1940, p. 34.

43. *Textile Labor*, Oct. and Nov. 1939.

44. *New York Times*, 11 Apr. and 9 June 1941. The complete membership of the Industry Committee No. 25 is listed in the Department of Labor, *Third Annual Report of the Administrator of the Wage and Hour Division* (Washington D.C., 1941), 159.

45. U.S. Bureau of Labor Statistics, *Union Agreements in the Cotton Textile Industry*, Bulletin No. 85 (Washington D.C., 1946), 8.

46. *New York Times*, 23 Oct. 1939.

47. *Opp Cotton Mills, Inc. v. Administrator*, 312 U.S. 126; *New York Times*, 4 Feb. 1941; Kennedy, "A History of the Textile Workers Union of America," 159–68.

48. Lahne, *The Cotton Mill Worker*, 166.

49. For a clear statement of these arguments and fears, see testimony by Kemp Lewis, ACMA president, at the minimum wage hearings held in Atlanta, Ga., *Public Hearings*, 1422–43. Every pro-employer witness to some degree reiterated Lewis' testimony.

50. For an example of this oft-repeated line of refutation of the owners, see the testimony of Emil Rieve, TWUA president, at the Atlanta hearings, *Public Hearings*, 1187–1231.

51. Backman and Gainsbrugh, *Economics of the Cotton Textile Industry*, 89.

52. Tindall, *Emergence of the New South*, 537.

CHAPTER TWELVE

1. For insight into these changes in the textile industry, see Truchil, "Capital-Labor Relations in the United States Textile Industry."

2. Moreland, *Millways of Kent*, x.

3. Blauner, *Alienation and Freedom*, 58.

4. Billy Ray Skelton, "Industrialization and Unionization in North Carolina and South Carolina: An Economic Comparison" (Ph.D. diss., Duke Univ., 1964), v.

5. Andrew Hacker, *US: A Statistical Portrait of the American People*, (New York, 1983), 139.

6. Joseph A. McDonald, "Textile Workers and Unionization: A Community Study" (Ph.D. diss., Univ. of Tennessee, 1981), 239.

7. For a description of the often confusing and ambiguous attitudes toward unionism in Gastonia County, N.C., since the 1930s, see Earle et al., *Spindles and Spires*, 171–237.

8. Helen M. Gould, "Union Resistance, Southern Style," *Labor and Nation*, 4 (Jan. 1948), 6–9; William S. Fairchild, "The Southern Textile Industry: A Union Man's Nightmare," *Reporter* 7 (22 July 1952), 33–36; Kennedy, "A History of the Textile Worker's

Union in America," 124–33; Skelton, "Industrialization and Unionization in North Carolina and South Carolina," 85–110.

9. Bill Arthur, "The Darlington Mills Case: Or 17 Years Before the Courts," *New South* 28 (Summer 1973), 40–47.

10. Marshall, *Labor in The South*, 302.

11. Bruce Reynor, "Unionism in the Southern Textile Industry: An Overview," in Fink and Reed, eds., *Essays in Southern Labor History*, 80–96.

12. See Review by Vincent Canby, *New York Times*, 2 Mar. 1979; but the author's summary is based on viewing the film twice.

13. Harry P. Leiferman, *Crystal Lee: A Woman of Inheritance* (New York, 1975), 111.

14. Ibid., 180.

15. Bill Finger and Mike Krinosh, "Stevens vs. Justice," *Southern Exposure* 4 (1976), 42. For one of the better of many articles on the TWUA-Stevens dispute, see George Tucker, "The Struggle to Organize J.P. Stevens," *Political Affairs* 57 (May 1978), 2–9, as well as Conway, *Rise Gonna Rise*.

16. Chicago *Tribune*, 21 Oct. 1983.

17. Conway, *Rise Gonna Rise*, 24.

18. Bernstein, *The Turbulent Years*, 786.

19. Ibid., 786–90.

20. Ibid., 769–71.

21. Harry A. Millis and Royal E. Montgomery, *Organized Labor* (New York, 1945), 196.

22. Irving Bernstein, "The Growth of American Unions, 1945–1960," *Labor History* 2 (Spring 1961), 135.

23. Hacker, *US*, 137.

24. Bernstein, *The Turbulent Years*, 770.

25. Hacker, *US*, 138.

26. Marshall, *Labor in the South*, 303.

27. See Wayne Flynt, "The New Deal and Southern Labor," in James C. Cobb and Michael V. Namorato, eds., *The New Deal and the South* (Jackson, Miss., 1984), 63–95, for an argument for limited success of labor in the 1930s in the South.

28. Leo Troy, "The Growth of Union Membership in the South," *Southern Economic Journal* 24 (Apr. 1959), 412–13. See also DeVyver, "The Present Status of Labor Unions in the South."

29. Marshall, *Labor in the South*, 298.

30. For two perceptive analyses in this vein, see Tomlinson, *The State and the Unions*, and James B. Atleson, *Values and Assumptions in American Labor Law*, (Amherst, Mass., 1983). See also David Montgomery, "American Workers and the New Deal Formula," *Workers' Control in America: Studies in the History of Work, Technology, and Labor Struggles* (New York, 1980), 153–80.

Bibliographical Essay

S everal general works had sharp importance for me as I undertook this book. Still the best narrative generalization studies for labor in the 1930s are Irving Bernstein, *The Turbulent Years: A History of the American Worker* (Boston, 1969), and Walter Galenson, *The CIO Challenge to the AFL: A History of American Labor* (Cambridge, Mass., 1960). The essays in Milton Derber and Edwin Young, eds., *Labor and the New Deal* (Madison, 1957), still answer some fundamental questions about New Deal labor policy and its evolution. David Brody's thoughtful interpretive comments on the labor history of the 1930s, most collected in *Workers in Industrial America: Essays on the Twentieth-Century Struggle* (New York, 1980), assist any scholar in making sense of what happened. Anyone studying New Deal labor policy still has to start with Irving Bernstein, *The New Deal Collective Bargaining Policy* (Berkeley, 1950). Also valuable are Harry A. Millis and Emily Clark Brown, *From the Wagner Act to the Taft-Hartley Act: A Study of National Labor Policy and Labor Relations* (Chicago, 1950); Joseph Rosenfarb, *The National Labor Policy and How It Works* (New York, 1940); James A. Gross, *The Making of the National Labor Relations Board: National Labor Policy in Transition, 1933–1947* (Albany, N.Y., 1974); and James A. Gross, *The Reshaping of the National Labor Relations Board: National Labor Policy in Transition, 1937–1947* (Albany, N.Y., 1981).

More reflective historical accounts about the development of labor law in the 1930s can be found in Richard C. Cortner, *The Wagner Act Cases* (Knoxville, 1964) and Peter H. Irons, *The New Deal Lawyers* (Princeton, 1982). Two recent dissertations embody provocative new revisionist attitudes about the nature of the liberal change in New Deal labor law: Daniel Albert Sipes, "A Moment of State: The Enactment of the National Labor Relations Act, 1935" (Ph.D. diss., Univ. of Pennsylvania, 1981) and Christopher L. Tomlinson, "The State and the Union: Federal Labor Relations and the Organized Labor Movement in America, 1935–1955" (Ph.D. diss., John Hopkins Univ., 1980), forthcoming as *The State and the Unions: Labor Relations, Law, and the Organized Labor Movement in America, 1935–1955* (New York, 1985).

In writing the book, I faced the tactical problem of how much to write about the better-known New Deal labor policy before plunging into the labor relations of the southern cotton textile industry itself. I decided that the briefest of introductions to that policy and to labor relations generally in the 1930s would suffice. But I suggest that readers interested in the more general labor history of the 1930s turn to the two excellent bibliographical essays on this literature by Robert H. Zieger in his books, *Madison Battery Workers, 1934–35: A History of Federal Labor Union 19587* (Ithaca, N.Y., 1977), 111–23; and *Rebuilding the Pulp and Paper Workers Union, 1933–1941* (Knoxville, 1984), 223–32.

As are all scholars of recent southern labor history, I am in the debt of F. Ray Marshall, *Labor in the South* (Cambridge, Mass., 1967). His book provides a singular sketch of southern labor; I hope this book yields a deeper understanding of what he had to touch so lightly. George Tindall, in his indispensable *The Emergence of the New South, 1913–1945* (Baton Rouge, 1967), cited the dissertation out of which this book grew; I have often gratefully used his sharply-turned sentences in this work. The recent collection of essays by James C. Cobb and Michael V. Namorato, *The New Deal and the South* (Jackson, 1984), illuminates the ambiguity of change and progress in the South of the 1930s and provides an alternative to the pessimistic view of cotton textiles. The collection invites comparison with the older, heftier work, W.T. Couch, ed., *Culture in the South* (Chapel Hill, 1935).

THE INDUSTRY

Jack Blicksilver, *Cotton Manufacturing in the Southeast: An Historical Analysis* (Bulletin 5, Bureau of Business and Economic Research, Georgia State University, 1959), is the best source for the industry's history as a whole, followed by the ever-useful Jules Backman and M.R. Gainsbrugh, *Economics of the Textile Industry* (New York, 1946). Third in the trilogy of "must" reading is Herman E. Michl, *The Textile Industries* (Washington D.C., 1938), followed closely by Irwin Mack Stelzer, "The Cotton Textile Industry" (Ph.D. diss., Cornell Univ., 1954). Sister Mary J. Oates, "The Role of the Cotton Textile Industry in the Economic Development of the American Southeast, 1900–1940" (Ph.D. diss., Yale Univ., 1969) has an uneven narrative but contains valuable statistics, as does Stephen Kennedy, *Profits and Losses in Textiles* (New York, 1936). The clearest explanation of the complex marketing structure of the 1930s is in Reavis Cox, *The Marketing of Textiles* (Washington D.C., 1936). For its clarity and conciseness, I also recommend the 1951 mimeographed manuscript of E.C. Bancroft, W.H. Crook, and William Kessler, "*Textiles: A Dynamic Industry*," which I found at the Department of Labor Library. The article "Textile Industry," *Encyclopedia of the Social Sciences*, vol. 14 (New York, 1938), 580–95, is well worth reading. Claudius Murchison,

King Cotton is Sick (Chapel Hill, 1930), is a lively account of the textile depression of the 1920s. Elliot B. Grover and George H. Dunlap, *Fundamentals of Textiles* (Raleigh, 1952), most clearly outlines the technical aspects of the manufacturing process.

Government studies done in the 1930s, even if weighted toward immediate economic problems, also give a clear picture of the industry. The most valuable one is U.S. Senate, *Cotton Textile Industry: A Report on the Conditions and Problems of the Cotton Textile Industry*, Document 26, 74 Cong., 1 Sess. (Washington D.C., 1936). The Federal Trade Commission's three studies present important facts about the industry: *Textile Industries: Part I, Investment and Profit* (Washington D.C., 1934); *Textile Industries in 1933 and 1934: Part I* (Washington D.C., 1935); and *Textile Industries: Part II, The Cotton Textile Industry* (Washington D.C., 1935). The House of Representatives' hearings on the textile industry have testimony that also bears on the economic structure and problems of the industry, as well as on labor relations; see Subcommittee of the Committee on Labor, *To Rehabilitate and Stabilize Labor Conditions in the Textile Industry of the United States*, 74 Cong., 2 Sess. (Washington D.C., 1936), and *To Regulate the Textile Industry*, 75 Cong., 1 Sess. (Washington D.C., 1937).

I used four major trade journals and read every issue between 1933 and 1941 — *The American Wool and Cotton Reporter, Cotton, The Textile Bulletin,* and *Textile World.* All had editorials that reflected the industry's opinions, as well as relevant articles on business conditions. I found myself using *Textile Bulletin* editorials more because its editor, David Clark, was a radical and pungent observer, and because it was preeminently a southern cotton textile magazine. I also read through *Manufacturers' Record* and *Monthly Labor Review* and found many relevant articles.

As for historical accounts of the industry, Glenn Gilman, *Human Relations in the Industrial Southeast: A Study of the Textile Industry* (Chapel Hill, 1956), and Broadus Mitchell, *Rise of the Cotton Mills in the South* (Baltimore, 1921), remain controversial, Gilman for his pro-owner bias and Mitchell for his romantic view of the cotton mill campaign. Most helpful in understanding the early origins is Patrick J. Hearden, *Independence and Empire: The New South's Cotton Mill Campaign, 1865–1901* (DeKalb, Ill., 1982). Melton Alonzo McLaurin, *Paternalism and Protest: Southern Cotton Mill Workers and Organized Labor, 1875–1905* (Westport, Conn., 1971), deserves the widespread respect that it enjoys. David Carlton, *Mill and Town in South Carolina, 1880–1920* (Baton Rouge, 1982), is the story of the industry, its owners and workers, and their politics in one state. Both McLaurin and Carlton were important to me, and I carried part of the story forward in time. Andrew Warren Pierpont, "Development of the Textile Industry in Alamance County, North Carolina" (Ph.D. diss., Univ. of North Carolina, 1953), and Ben F. Lemert, *The Cotton Textile Industry of the Southern Appalachian Piedmont* (Chapel Hill, 1933), also helped. Cathy Louise McHugh, "The Family Labor System in the Southern Cotton Textile Industry, 1880–1915," has much useful information. Among the several articles that aided me in understanding the history of the industry, see particularly Stephen J. Goldfarb, "A Note on the Limits to the Growth of the Cotton-Textile Industry in the Old South," *Journal of Southern History* 68 (Nov. 1982), 545–58; Gavin Wright, "Cheap Labor and Southern Textiles Before 1880," *Journal of Economic History* 29 (Sept. 1979), 655–80; Leonard Carlson, "Labor Supply, the Acquisition of Skills, and the Location of Southern Textile Mills, 1880–1900," *Journal of Economic History* 41 (Mar. 1981), 65–77; Irwin Feller, "The Diffussion and Location of Technological Change in the American Cotton-Textile Industry, 1880–1970," *Technology and Culture* 15 (1970), 569–93; and John Jewkes and Sylvia Jewkes, "A Hundred Years of Change in the Structure of the Cotton Textile Industry," *Journal of Law and Economics* 9 (1966), 115–34. Two unpublished studies gave sharp detail to individual mills: William Walker Thompson, Jr., "A Managerial History of a Cotton Textile Firm: Spartan Mills, 1880–1958" (Ph.D. diss. Univ. of Alabama, 1960), and Bobby Dean Jackson, "Textiles in the South Carolina Piedmont: A Case Study of the Inman Mills, 1900–1967" (M.A. thesis, Auburn Univ., 1968). Robert Sidney Smith, *Mill on the Dan: A History of Dan River Mills, 1882–1950* (Durham, 1960), is a good managerial history, but disappointingly brief on the workers and labor relations.

WORKER CULTURE

In this area, the major work one has to contend with is Gilman's influential *Human Relations in the Industrial Southeast*. Gilman argues that from the very beginning the industry created a distinctive workforce, more attuned to southern "folkways" and "benevolent" paternalism and modern industrial management than to worker-owner conflict and unionization. I believe that my discussion of worker culture, while accepting some of Gilman's views, gives a different explanation of worker conservatism, built not around inherent "southernness" and native "antiunionism," but around rational decisions based on workers' knowledge of past labor history, their culture, and their understanding of economic vulnerability. Jennings J. Rhyne, *Some Southern Cotton Mill Workers and Their Villages* (Chapel Hill, 1930), is an early scientific sociological work that I consider the best objective account of some aspects of worker culture as the New Deal was about to begin. John Kenneth Moreland, *Millways of Kent* (Chapel Hill, 1958), does the same for the period after the 1930s. Both are more useful than the better-known Herbert Lahne, *The Cotton Mill Worker* (New York, 1944), which is highly derivative. I read with profit and admiration the well-written and interesting work of John Garrett Van Osdell, Jr., "Cotton Mills, Labor, and the Southern Mind, 1880–1930" (Ph.D. diss., Tulane Univ., 1966). Sympathetic to the workers, it is an account of labor relations in the years just before this study begins. Much remained the same. See also an article by Tom E. Terrill, "Eager Hands: Labor for South-ern Textiles," *Journal of Economic History* 36 (Mar. 1976), 84–101.

The period of the late 1920s and early 1930s produced a glut of studies of mill villages and their inhabitants. My notes and discussion in the text briefly summarize this often contradictory literature. The best arguments for a culture of the oppressed and desperate are Myra Page, *Southern Cotton Mills and Labor* (New York, 1929), and Lois McDonald, *Southern Mill Hills: A Study of Social and Economic Forces in Certain Mill Villages* (New York, 1928). For sunnier and more optimistic observations, see William Hayes Simpson, *Life in the Mill Communities* (Clinton, S.C., 1941), and Harry Shumway, *I Go South* (New York, 1930).

The direct words of workers of the 1930s, collected by the Southern Oral History Program, University of North Carolina at Chapel Hill, in its Pied-mont Series, contributed vitality and understanding to this book. Dale Newman, "Textile Workers in a Tobacco County: A Comparison Between Yarn and Weave Mill Villages," in Edward Magdal and Jon C. Wakley, eds., *The Southern Common People: Studies in Nineteenth Social History* (Westport, Conn., 1980), 345–68, and Dale Newman, "Work and Community Life in a Southern Textile Town," *Labor History* 19 (Spring 1978), 204–25, are both based on extensive oral history in one textile town in North Carolina. Doug-las DeNatale, "Traditional Culture and Community in a Piedmont Textile Mill Village" (M.A. thesis, Univ. of North Carolina at Chapel Hill, 1980), is a valuable work relying on oral history from Bynum, N.C. Tom E. Terrill and Jerrold E. Hirsch, eds., *Such As Us: Southern Voices in the Thirties*, and W.T. Couch, ed., *These Are Our Lives* (New York, 1975), provided some vivid oral history, as did several articles in the journal *Southern Exposure*. Liston Pope, *Millhands and Preachers: A Study of Gastonia* (New Haven, Conn., 1942), and its sequel, carrying the story of Gastonia County from the 1930s to the 1970s, by John Earle, Dean Knudsen, and Donald W. Shriver, *Spindles and Spires: A Study of Religion and Social Change in Gastonia*, relies in part on oral history and survey work. Finally, I was much influenced by John Bodnar, *Workers' World: Kinship, Community, and Protest in an Industrial Society, 1900–1941* (Baltimore, 1982). Bodnar's explanation of worker conservatism makes great sense to me, and despite the cultural differences between the ethnic workers of Pennsylvania and the Piedmont workers, I was struck by the same worker response to unionism, change, industrial work, and modernization. The stunningly good book by Tamara Hareven and Randolph Langenbach, *Amoskeag: Life and Work in an American Factory City* (New York, 1978), powerfully brings home the power of oral history, as well as the fact that in-dustrial workers have to be understood on their own terms.

My understanding of paternalism was formed by McLaurin, *Paternalism and Protest*, and Carlton, *Mill and Town in South Carolina, 1880–1920*, much more than by Mitchell, *Rise of the Cotton Mills in the South*. Instructive was Ber-nard M. Cannon, "Social Deterrents to the Unionization of Southern Cotton

Textile Mill Workers" (Ph.D. diss., Harvard Univ., 1951). The paternalistic ideology of the owners appears throughout the speeches printed in the *Proceedings of the American Cotton Manufacturers Association*, which I found in the Library of Congress. Arthur B. Edge, Jr., *Fuller E. Callaway (1870–1928): Founder of Callaway Mills,* (New York, 1954) reports the views of a first-generation owner who deeply believed in paternalism. The testimony of William D. Anderson, president of the Bibb Manufacturing Company, at the Cotton Code hearings in June 1933 ("Transcripts of the Cotton Code Hearings," NRA, NA, RG 9), is a colorful if overblown statement of what owners meant when they talked of paternalism. For a more sophisticated view, see Frank T. DeVyver, "Paternalism—North and South," *American Federationist* 37 (Nov. 1930), 1353–58 and DeVyver, "Southern Textile Mills Revisited," *Southern Economic Journal* 4 (Apr. 1938), 466–73. Harriet Herring, *Welfare Work in Mill Villages: The Story of Extra-Mill Activities in North Carolina* (Chapel Hill, 1929), takes a cleareyed look at the limited reality of paternalism. Gilman, in *Human Relations in the Industrial Southeast*, more than anyone illuminates how successful paternalism was and traces how, in the 1930s and beyond, the owners resuscitated its outworn principles and moved into modern management techniques. On this point I was greatly affected by Solomon Barkin, "A Trade Unionist Appraises Management Philosophy," *Harvard Business Review* 28 (Sept. 1950), 59–64.

THE NRA ERA

Louis Galambos, *Competition and Cooperation: The Emergence of a National Trade Association* (Baltimore, 1966), in the latter part of his book concentrates on the business story of the Cotton Code, the Code Authority, and the Cotton-Textile Institute. I gratefully acknowledge my debt to this book for enhancing my understanding of the code and its business supporters. Central also to this understanding is the material I drew from the James McDonald Comer Papers at the Birmingham (Ala.) Public Library; Comer was a southern industry leader and a member of the Code Authority. The papers of George Sloan at the State Historical Society of Wisconsin in Madison consist mostly of speeches and press releases, but to that extent they gave valuable information about owners' views and strategies.

Two standard historical accounts of the NRA era help to place this book in perspective: Bernard Bellush, *The Failure of the NRA* (Washington D.C., 1934), and Ellis Hawley, *The New Deal and the Problem of Monopoly* (Princeton, 1966). Three studies of other industries are interesting for comparative purposes: James P. Johnson, *The Politics of Soft Coal: The Bituminous Industry from World War I through the New Deal* (Urbana, 1979); Robert W. Connery, *The Administration of an NRA Code: A Case Study of the Men's*

Clothing Industry (Chicago, 1939); and the much-lauded Sidney Fine, *The Automobile Under the Blue Eagle: Labor Movements and the Automobile Manufacturing Code* (Ann Arbor, 1963). Robert F. Himmelberg, *The Origins of the National Recovery Administration: Business, Government, and the Trade Association Issue, 1921–1933* (New York, 1976), best explains how the NRA bill came about. The two articles by George Sloan, "The Cotton-Textile Industry Under the NRA," in George Galloway, ed., *Industrial Planning Under Codes* (New York, 1935), and "First Flight of the Blue Eagle: The Cotton Code in Operation," *Atlantic Monthly* 153 (Mar. 1934), 321–25, are intelligent defenses of the NRA and the Cotton Code. I relied on the *New York Times* for a chronological development of the industry from 1933 to 1941. The *Daily News Record*, a textile industry newspaper on file at the Library of Congress, often carried essential information about the southern cotton textile industry and its labor relations.

The central information about the NRA experience came from the NRA papers at the National Archives. They are still in metal boxes, just as they came from the Division of Review, and are getting yellow and brittle as they await a delayed transfer to acid-free boxes. Judicious use of the guide can bring up the relevant files: "Consolidated Files on Industries Governed by Approved Codes," "Records of the Cotton Textile National Industrial Relations Board," "Records of the Board of Inquiry for the Cotton Textile Industry," "Records of the Textile Labor Relations Board," "Transcripts of Hearings, 1933–35," and "Records Relating to Labor Disturbances in the Textile Industry." The last is a large collection, being an alphabetical collection by company name of correspondence with the several NRA offices. Much of that material, while heavily particularized, is rewarding for understanding the general pattern of the Cotton Code's labor relations. The Franklin D. Roosevelt Papers at Hyde Park, N.Y., are disappointingly slim, except for a few scattered files on the 1934 strike. The same can be said for the Harry Hopkins Papers and John G. Winant Papers there. The records of the Federal Mediation and Conciliation Service at the National Archives were too locally focused to be of service.

Unfortunately, the UTW's central office files for the 1930s cannot be located and are believed to have been destroyed. I, however, used the complete run of the union's monthly magazine in the Department of Labor Library (also in the State Historical Society of Wisconsin). The UTW published *Textile Worker* from 1933 to 1935, briefly changed its name to *Textile Labor Banner* in 1935–36, and then went back to *Textile Worker*. When the Gorman faction rejoined the AFL, they took the title *Textile Worker* with them, and in 1939 the new TWUA published under the name *Textile Labor.* The UTW records in the Southern Labor History Archives are those of the AFL's UTW since 1939, and there are only a few scattered files for the 1930s that Gorman probably brought with him. Although I read the *New York Times* and *Daily News Record* extensively, I used southern newspapers sparingly and only for key dates. For a more local study they would be essential.

Lewis L. Lorwin and Arthur Wubnig, *Labor Relations Boards: The Regulation of Collective Bargaining Under the National Industrial Recovery Act* (Washington D.C., 1935) is helpful, but more central is Robert R.R. Brooks, "The United Textile Workers of America," (Ph.D. diss., Yale Univ., 1935), even though it is based on secondary and printed materials rather than archival materials. Essential for the entire NRA period are William Haskett, "Ideological Radicals: The American Federation of Labor and Federal Labor Policy in the Strikes of 1934" (Ph.D. diss., Univ. of California at Los Angeles, 1958), and John Wesley Kennedy, "The General Strike in the Textile Industry, September, 1934" (M.A. thesis, Duke Univ., 1947). Lahne, *The Cotton Mill Worker*, is still good, though brief. Bernstein, *The Turbulent Years*, also touches cotton textile unionism here and there. Dennis R. Nolan and Donald E. James, "Textile Unionism in the Piedmont, 1910–1932," in Gary M. Fink and Merle E. Reed, eds., *Essays in Southern Labor History: Selected Papers, Southern Labor History Conference, 1976* (Westport, Conn., 1977), 48–79, is the best summary account of unionism before the New Deal.

THE TWOC ERA

Two dissertations are suggested beginning points. The older one, John Wesley Kennedy, "A History of the Textile Workers Union of America, CIO" (Ph.D. diss., Univ. of California at Berkeley, 1950), is based only on printed sources, while Paul David Richards, "The History of the Textile Workers Union of America, CIO, in the South, 1937–1945" (Ph.D. diss., Univ. of Wisconsin, 1978), uses the TWUA Papers, which have a slim collection of TWOC records. I mined the latter extensively for careful statistics and for my understanding of the union's holding operation during World War II. The Paul Christopher Papers at the Southern Labor History Archives, Georgia State University, had some very rich files on his UTW experiences and the TWOC years. These papers and Joseph Yates Garrison, "Paul Revere Christopher: Southern Labor Leader, 1910–1974" (Ph.D. diss., Georgia State Univ., 1977), gave me the best inside look at union activities and problems. The Lucy Randolph Mason Papers at Duke University also contain ample TWOC material that supplements Lucy Randolph Mason, *To Win Their Rights: A Personal Story of the CIO in the South* (New York, 1952). D. Witherspoon Dodge, *Southern Rebel in Reverse* (New York, 1961), is interesting on the TWOC, but particularized. The TWOC publication, *Building a Union of Textile Workers*, is a standard source for many accounts, but by itself it often misleads. The *Proceedings* of the UTW in 1934 and 1936 and of two special TWUA conventions in 1939 and 1941, located in the Department of Labor Library, contribute important looks at the union.

For New Deal labor policy in action, I researched through some of the ma-

The New Deal and Southern Cotton Textiles

jor NLRB cases at the Federal Records Center, Suiteland, Md., RG 25. These records contain the all-important transcripts of hearings, as well as frank field reports and summaries of cases as they progressed. It is essential to use these alongside the NLRB's formal reports, *Decisions and Orders of the National Labor Relations Board*. All labor historians of the 1930s should consult these extensive records, even if by necessity they are always particularized evidence. At the William Perkins Library, Duke University, the Erwin Mills Papers yielded a rich description of how one company deliberately, by a policy of delay and non-negotiation, obstructed NLRB policy. Two dissertations should also be used by labor history students interested in the South of the 1930s and 1940s: Paul Brinker, "The Enforcement of Collective Bargaining in the South" (Ph.D. diss., Pennsylvania State College, 1948), and Billy Ray Skelton, "Industrialization and Unionization in North Carolina and South Carolina: An Economic Comparison," (Ph.D. diss., Duke Univ., 1964).

The notes for the FLSA chapter fully reflect my research. The transcripts of the public hearings held by the administrators of the Wage and Hour Divisions are often full compendiums of an industry's economic and labor relations problems. Over three thousand pages of testimony on the cotton textile industry give great insight into the entire range of questions about the industry in the 1930s.

I have not systematically researched the history of the industry and its workers for the period since the 1930s. My comments in the epilogue are only suggestive. For beginning reading and bibliographical suggestions, see Barry Elliot Truchil, "Capital-Labor Relationships in the United States Textile Industry: The Post-World War II Period," (Ph.D. diss., State Univ. of New York at Binghamton, 1982). Bruce Reyner, "Unionism in the Southern Textile Industry: An Overview," in Fink and Reed, eds., *Essays in Southern Labor History,* 80–96, sums up the problems of the ACTWUA to the late 1970s. There is a wealth of periodical and newspaper coverage of the conflict between the union and the J.P. Stevens Company. Mimi Conway, *Rise Gonna Rise: A Portrait of Southern Textile Workers* (New York, 1979), is an undigested oral history of the conflict, but its grassroots approach makes it a unique primary source. I am also indebted to one of my undergraduate students who wrote an honors senior independent study thesis on the union–J.P. Stevens conflict: Irene Korsak, "The Amalgamated Clothing and Textile Workers Union Versus J.P. Stevens and Company, Inc.: A Case Study of an Effort to Unionize Southern Textile Workers" (unpublished senior thesis, The College of Wooster, 1979). Joseph A. McDonald, "Textile Workers and Unionization: A Community Study" (Ph.D. diss., Univ. of Tennessee, 1981), is a sociological study of worker culture in the 1970s in the carpet industry of Dalton, Ga. Despite the difference in time, his finding bears a haunting similarity to that of Moreland, *Millways of Kent*, and Rhyne, *Some Southern Cotton Mill Workers and Their Villages.*

Index

New Deal Labor Policy and the Southern Cotton Textile Industry, 1933–1941 was composed on a Compugraphic digital phototypesetter in ten point Garamond with two points of spacing between the lines. Garamond was also selected for display. The book was designed by Jim Billingsley, composed by Metricomp, Inc., printed offset by Thomson-Shore, Inc., and bound by John H. Dekker & Sons. The paper on which the book is printed is designed for an effective life of at least three hundred years.

THE UNIVERSITY OF TENNESSEE PRESS : KNOXVILLE

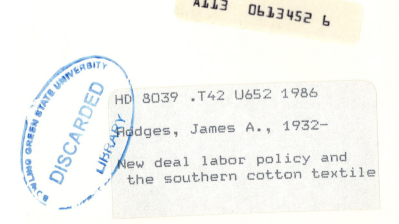